Steven Jirsa

Baltimore, MD
May 1, 2002

IMPERIALISM AND JEWISH SOCIETY,

200 B.C.E. TO 640 C.E.

JEWS, CHRISTIANS, AND MUSLIMS

FROM THE ANCIENT TO THE MODERN WORLD

SERIES EDITORS

R. Stephen Humphreys, William Chester Jordan, and Peter Schaefer

Imperialism and Jewish Society, 200 B.C.E. to 640 C.E.
by Seth Schwartz

IMPERIALISM AND JEWISH SOCIETY, 200 B.C.E. TO 640 C.E.

Seth Schwartz

PRINCETON UNIVERSITY PRESS

PRINCETON AND OXFORD

LIBRARY OF CONGRESS CATALOGING-IN-PUBLICATION DATA

SCHWARTZ, SETH.

IMPERIALSIM AND JEWISH SOCIETY, 200 B.C.E. TO 640 C.E. / SETH SCHWARTZ

P. CM.—(JEWS, CHRISTIANS, AND MUSLIMS FROM THE

ANCIENT TO THE MODERN WORLD)

INCLUDES BIBLIOGRAPHICAL REFERENCES (P.) AND INDEX.

ISBN 0-691-08850-0 (ALK. PAPER)

1. JEWS—HISTORY—168 B.C.–135 A.D. 2. JEWS—HISTORY—70–638.

3. JUDAISM—HISTORY—POSTEXILIC PERIOD, 586 B.C.–210 A.D.

4. JEWS—CIVILIZATION—GREEK INFLUENCES. 5. PALESTINE—HISTORY—TO

70 A.D. I. TITLE. II. SERIES.

DS121.7 .S39 2001

933—dc21   2001021486

CONTENTS

ACKNOWLEDGMENTS

I WOULD LIKE to thank the following people for having read and commented on parts of this manuscript: Roger Bagnall, Benjamin Gampel, Catherine Hezser (who read parts of the book in early versions, and the entire manuscript for the Press), Martha Himmelfarb, Richard Kalmin, Natalie Kampen, Hayim Lapin, Lee Levine, Ivan Marcus, Bruce Nielsen, and Jeffrey Rubenstein. Leslie Kurke read and made crucial suggestions about the introduction, as did Juliet Fleming, who has furthermore been a source of inspiration throughout the overlong gestation of this book. Martin Goodman not only endured my stumbling presentations of primitive versions of segments of this book at his seminar in Wolfson College, Oxford, but also read it in its entirety for the Press and made many important comments. Keith Hopkins read nearly the entire manuscript, talked me through its writing and rewriting, and has been infinitely encouraging and provocative. Without Keith I could never have written this book.

I have been fortunate to have lived and taught in environments—King's College, Cambridge, and the Jewish Theological Seminary—richly endowed with colleagues and students who made it fun to work out the argument of the book. I will not attempt to provide a full list, since it would contain hundreds of names if it could be compiled. However, I should thank especially the conveners of the King's College Research Centre, Martin Hyland and Alan Macfarlane, for enabling me to begin the book; Simon Goldhill for his friendship, generosity, and stimulation during the period of its composition; and the chancellor and provost of the seminary, Ismar Schorsch and Jack Wertheimer, for enabling me to complete it, by granting me a premature sabbatical leave. The generosity of the John Simon Guggenheim Memorial Foundation allowed me to extend the leave to a full year.

Components have been presented at conferences and seminars in (from east to west) Jerusalem, Berlin, Heidelberg, Cambridge, London, Oxford, New Haven, New York, and Princeton; I am indebted to the organizers and participants for invitations and comments. Finally, I thank Mark Cohen and Shalom Sabar for timely advice.

ABBREVIATIONS

Aq Ap	*Against Apion* (in *Josephus*, ed. H. St. J. Thakeray et al., 9 vols. Loeb Classical Library (Cambridge, 1926–1965)
AJP	*American Journal of Philology*
ANRW	*Aufstieg und Niedergang der Römischen Welt*, ed. W. Haase and H. Temporini (Berlin, 1974–)
Ant	*Jewish Antiquities*
B	Bavli (Babylonian Talmud)
BA	*Biblical Archaeologist*
BAR	*British Archaeological Reports*
BASOR	*Bulletin of the American Schools of Oriental Research*
Beth Shearim	B. Mazar et al., *Beth Shearim*, 3 vols. (New Brunswick, 1973)
BJPES	*Bulletin of the Jewish Palestine Exploration Society*
BullEp	J. and L. Robert, *Bulletin Epigraphique* (Paris, 1938-)
CBQ	*Catholic Biblical Quarterly*
CERP	A.H.M. Jones *The Cities of the Eastern Roman Provinces* (Oxford, 1971)
CIJ	J.-B. Frey, *Corpus Inscriptionum Judaicarum*, 2 vols. (Paris, 1936–1952)
CIL	*Corpus Inscriptionum Latinarum*
CJ	Codex Justinianus
CPJ	*Corpus Papyrorum Judaicarum*, ed. V. Tcherikover, A.Fuks, and M. Stern, 3 vols. (Cambridge, 1957–1964)
CRINT	*Compendia Rerum Iudaicarum ad Novum Testamentum*
CSEL	*Corpus Scriptorum Ecclesiasticorum Latinorum*
CTh	Codex Theodosianus
Donateurs	B. Lifshitz, *Donateurs et fondateurs dans les synagogues juives* (Paris, 1967)
EI	*Eretz Israel*
EJ	*Encyclopedia Judaica*, 16 vols. (Jerusalem, 1971)
GCS	Griechische Christliche Schriftsteller
GLAJJ	M. Stern, *Greek and Latin Authors on Jews and Judaism*, 3 vols. (Jerusalem, 1976–1984)
HA	*Hadashot Arkheologiyot*
HTR	*Harvard Theological Review*
HUCA	*Hebrew Union College Annual*
IEJ	*Israel Exploration Journal*

IGLS	*Inscriptions grecques et latines de la Syrie*
IGRRP	R. Cagnat, *Inscriptiones Graecae ad Res Romanas Pertinentes* (Paris, 1906)
INJ	*Israel Numismatic Journal*
JBL	*Journal of Biblical Literature*
JECS	*Journal of Early Christian Studies*
JJS	*Journal of Jewish Studies*
JNES	*Journal of Near Eastern Studies*
JQR	*Jewish Quarterly Review*
JRA	*Journal of Roman Archaeology*
JRS	*Journal of Roman Studies*
JSJ	*Journal for the Study of Judaism*
JSOT	*Journal for the Study of the Old Testament*
JSP	*Journal for the Study of the Pseudepigrapha*
JSQ	*Jewish Studies Quarterly*
JThS	*Journal of Theological Studies*
LCL	Loeb Classical Library
Life	Josephus, Autobiography
Linder	A. Linder, *The Jews in Roman Imperial Legislation* (Detroit, 1987)
LRE	A. H. M. Jones, *The Later Roman Empire*, 2 vols. (Oxford, 1964)
LSJ	H. G. Liddell, R. Scott, and H. S. Jones, *A Greek-English Lexicon*, 9th ed. (Oxford, 1968)
M	Mishnah
MGWJ	*Monatsschrift für Geschichte und Wissenschaft des Judenthums*
NEAEHL	*New Encyclopaedia of Archaeological Excavations in the Holy Land*, ed. M. Avi-Yonah and E. Stern (Jerusalem, 1993)
PAAJR	*Proceedings of the American Academy for Jewish Research*
PCPS	*Proceedings of the Cambridge Philological Society*
PEQ	*Palestine Exploration Quarterly*
PG	*Patrologia Graeca*, ed. J. P. Migne (Paris, 1857–1866)
R.	Rabbi
RB	*Revue Biblique*
REJ	*Revue des études Juives*
RIDA	*Revue Internationale de Droit de l'Antiquité*
RQ	*Revue de Qumran*
Schürer-Vermes	E. Schürer, *The History of the Jewish People in the Age of Jesus Christ*, rev. and ed. G. Vermes et al., 4 vols. (Edinburgh, 1973–1987)
SCI	*Scripta Classica Israelica*

SEG	*Supplementum Epigraphicum Graecum*
SH	*Scripta Hierosolymitana*
T	Tosefta
TDNT	*Theological Dictionary of the New Testament*
War	Josephus, Jewish War
Y	Yerushalmi (Palestinian Talmud)
YCS	*Yale Classical Studies*
ZPE	*Zeitschrift für Papyrologie und Epigraphik*

IMPERIALISM AND JEWISH SOCIETY,

200 B.C.E. TO 640 C.E.

INTRODUCTION

*I*MPERIALISM AND JEWISH SOCIETY traces the impact of different types of foreign domination on the inner structure of ancient Jewish society, primarily in Palestine.[1] It argues that a loosely centralized, ideologically complex society came into existence by the second century B.C.E., collapsed in the wake of the Destruction and the imposition of direct Roman rule after 70 C.E., and reformed starting in the fourth century, centered now on the synagogue and the local religious community, in part as a response to the christianization of the Roman Empire.

This book thus covers a longer period and has a broader scope than is conventional for books on ancient Judaism, aside from the not uncommon handbooks, which are characterized by varying degrees of comprehensiveness but the absence of an explicit argument. One reason I chose to treat a broad topic is the character of the evidentiary basis of ancient Jewish history. In brief, it is slender. This fact has paradoxically contributed to, though it is certainly not the only cause of, the common tendency to produce monographic studies of extremely limited issues, on the assumption that only minute study of small selections of material can yield reliable results. Clearly such work has its place, but, as I will argue in more detail below, hypotheses about the society that produced the artifacts must necessarily accompany their interpretation, and the evidence as a whole must be used to construct these hypotheses. Thus it seems worthwhile to get a sense of the entire system before, or while, examining its parts.

Swallowing the evidence whole is necessary but not sufficient for this task. It is intuitively obvious that the ancient Jews (assuming that they behaved like a recognizably human group) were profoundly affected by the imperial powers under which they were constrained to live.[2] It is equally obvious that the effects of imperialism were not limited to reaction—to the impulse to "circle the wagons" that has so often been attributed to the Jews by historians and others. Nor can the effects of domination by Hellenistic kingdoms and the Roman Empire all usefully be crowded under the rubric of "hellenization." The effects of domination were complex, pervasive, and varied, and we cannot begin to apprehend the structure of the system without paying careful attention to them. This consideration explains the importance of power and its

---

[1] Though the Greco-Roman Diaspora is frequently mentioned, I have omitted all discussion of the Jews in the Parthian and Sassanian empires, due to the nearly complete absence of information outside the Babylonian Talmud.

[2] See T. Endelman, "Introduction: Comparing Jewish Societies," in *Comparing Jewish Societies* (Ann Arbor: University of Michigan Press, 1997), pp. 1–21, especially 10–13.

influence on social and cultural integration in the historical scheme that I propose in this book. For example, the rulers of the Jews in the later Second Temple period were empowered by their overlords to use the "ancestral laws" of the Jews—the Torah—as their constitution. I argue that this fact had profound but complex effects and cannot be ignored in a description of Palestinian Judaism before 70 C.E. Conversely, that the descendants of the Jewish leaders for several centuries after 70 had no such authorization helps to explain the importance of Greco-Roman urban culture in northern Palestine demonstrated by archaeological remains. The political marginality of "rabbinic Judaism" matters profoundly for our understanding of it and for our interpretation of rabbinic texts, not to mention for our understanding of the history of the Jews in the period of its consolidation.

Method

This book has four main methodological characteristics: First, it is moderately positivistic. I believe that it is possible to know something about the distant past. I do not think, however, that this knowledge can ever really claim to be more than a sort of hermeneutical model that can help us make sense of the paltry scraps of information that have come down to us.

Second, it combines induction and deduction in its interpretation of evidence. Historical remains, both literary and physical, are in reality opaque. Pure induction can never work because it assumes that the artifacts are meaningful in themselves and that the interpreter's job is merely to uncover this meaning and then reconstruct the relationship between the discrete artifacts. But this assumption seems to me false; even the most determined empiricist never *actually* works this way, whatever he or she may claim. It is best to be aware of what we are doing and, while not eschewing detailed examination of the evidence, at least admit our need for certain kinds of models.

Third, one of the components of its deductive structure is concern about how societies work. Every artifact is the product of social interaction; some theory of society, appropriately complex and nonreified, must therefore be involved in the act of interpretation. I am suggesting that a theory of society is just as essential an element of method as a theory about how to "read" the evidence.

Fourth, it tends to interpret evidence minimalistically. The realization that the evidence is socially specific leads to self-consciousness about the act of generalization. Thus, a positive statement in an ancient Jewish literary text cannot be taken without further argumentation as evidence for what "the Jews" thought or did. Rather, it is a nugget of ideology, telling us what some limited (perhaps more or less elite) group of Jews considered worth committing to writing at a specific time, which is in itself nothing to sneeze at. We may then ask, Did its authors have the means to impose their view on others? Are others likely to have agreed with them for other reasons? Thus, it may indeed correspond to what other classes of Jews, or Jews living at other times, thought or did, but this needs to be demonstrated. Material remains are no less socially and chronologically specific, and similar considerations constrain our interpretation of them, too. This does not mean that generalizing is always illegitimate, only that it must always be done with cautious skepticism.

Social Theories

One of the purposes of this book is to apply a type of analysis to ancient Jewish history that had been long established among Roman and to a lesser extent Greek historians. Like its models, this book is informed mainly by structural functionalism—a tendency in Anglo-American social thought which assumes that there are such things as societies and regards societies as usually complex, organism-like systems that can be understood by analyzing the relations of their component parts. Of particular importance for this analysis, at least in my version of it, is the distribution of power in a society and its effect on the society's integration.[3]

Several qualifications are in order. My adherence to this system is neither complete nor exclusive. I believe that it is neither the true nor the only way to understand human social interaction, only that it has proved an intermittently helpful way of thinking about my topic. I am also aware of, and have tried to incorporate, some of the fundamental criticisms of structural functionalism— most seriously that it depends on a long series of metaphors that treat human social behavior reductively and misleadingly ignore agency, the complex ways in which people constantly negotiate with each other and with normative ideologies, which themselves are constituted through agency. Furthermore, in imagining societies as working, more or less stable systems, structural functionalism has trouble accounting for change.[4] (On the other hand, theorists who emphasize agency to the exclusion of structure have trouble accounting for continuity.)

I have attempted to compensate for the second criticism by building change into my account—by producing what might be thought of as three time-lapse photographs of ancient Jewish society and also, I admit, by deferring the problem. The Jews were a small subculture in a larger Mediterranean world, and one of my points in this book is precisely that the crucial changes sometimes

---

[3] I am anticipated in this project by Albert Baumgarten's excellent book on ancient Jewish sectarianism, *The Flourishing of Jewish Sects in the Maccabean Era: An Interpretation* (Leiden: Brill, 1997).

[4] For a concise statement of this critique, see A. Giddens, *Central Problems in Social Theory: Action, Structure, and Contradiction in Social Analysis* (Berkeley: University of California Press, 1979), pp. 235–59.

occurred in that larger world: why the Roman Empire rose, why it was more centralizing than its predecessors, and why, finally, it eventually became Christian—three developments of central importance in this account—are questions I happily leave to others.

As to the more substantial criticisms of structural functionalism, associated especially with such skeptical social theorists as Anthony Giddens and Pierre Bourdieu, I agree with them up to a point.[5] Structural functionalism certainly is reductive but should be seen only as a set of heuristic schematizations. Indeed, analytic schemes are necessarily reductive, though there is some point in reducing the reduction as far as possible. The only way to avoid reductive schematization is through complete skepticism, a totally reflexive and critical sociology, which neither Giddens nor Bourdieu advocated.

Furthermore, it must be recalled that the semiskeptical sociologies of Giddens and Bourdieu, like structural functionalism, are social theories of modernity, and as such rarely have to confront the crucial problem of premodernity, the absence of information. In fact, social theory functions differently for ancient historians than for modernists. For the latter, it is purely an analytic tool, whereas for the former it is also an aid to reconstruction, a way of filling in or otherwise compensating for gaps in information. So, it is precisely the schematic character of structural functionism, the fact that it tends to view its subject from a great distance, through a telescope rather than a microscope, that makes it especially useful for my purposes.

Criticism of Conventional Analytical Categories and Assumptions

In a field that depends more on reinterpretation of familiar material than on exposition of new, it is inevitable that books aspiring to innovation will be characterized by a critical attitude toward their predecessors. There is some justification for the skeptical view that this dynamic owes more to the boredom and restlessness of each generation of scholars with the work of their elders than to the inexorability of intellectual progress. In either case, we should be sobered by the expectation that our successors will reject our work when the time comes. Still, perhaps this position is just a bit too skeptical. Innovations sometimes do enter the *koiné* of scholarly consensus, and stay there. For example, it is difficult to imagine any serious scholar ever again describing the Judaism of the later Second Temple period as a rigorous, monolithic ortho-

---

[5] For a helpful introduction, with bibliography, see Bourdieu and L. J. D. Wacquant, *An Invitation to Reflexive Sociology* (Chicago: University of Chicago Press, 1992); despite (or rather because of) the obvious similarities between them, Bourdieu strives to distance himself from Giddens. I have found little engagement with Bourdieu in what I have read of Giddens's work.

doxy, as was still common only a generation ago. Criticism of old categories, and construction of new ones, may contribute to a slow accretion of under-standing.

All this is to apologize not only for publishing a large-scale synthetic revision in a field that has already been studied so intensively but also for the polemics that follow. In fact, I have tried to avoid polemics in the body of the work, except where absolutely necessary, mainly as a way of keeping the book's length manageable. The introduction seems an appropriate place for critical discussion of some of the previous scholarship.

Nationhood

This book is, among other things, a sustained examination of the question of whether the Jews constituted a group in antiquity and, if they did, of the character of that group. Admittedly, this question cannot really be answered satisfactorily. An essential component of groupness is the subjectivity of the agents—a point generally associated with Benedict Anderson but actually al-ready made by Max Weber.[6] Indeed, even this point is something of a sche-matic oversimplification, since it does not consider the fact that not all subjec-tivity is the same: do the agents need to be strongly self-conscious of belonging to a group? Must it be a central element of their self-construction? Or can a group consist of or contain people who are only peripherally or occasionally aware of belonging? While we must be conscious of all these questions when considering the case of the ancient Jews, we cannot answer them because we simply do not have enough information. But this does not entitle us to ignore the problem in interpreting the information we do have. It must be said though that most ancient Jewish historians have not been concerned with such issues at all: the groupness, and even the nationhood—a very specific type of groupness—of the Jews has usually been assumed.

One reason for this is that many Jewish historians are writing from deep inside some sort of romantic nationalist ideology, nowadays usually Zionism.[7] The Zionist historians of the first generation, most importantly for our pur-poses Gedalyahu Alon (1901–1950), argued that the Jews had always consti-tuted what amounted to a nation, even in periods when they lacked political self-determination, mainly because Judaism always had a national component

[6] *Economy and Society: An Outline of Interpretive Sociology* (Berkeley: University of California Press, 1978), p. 4, the first paragraph of the book.

[7] For some discussion, see D. N. Myers, *Re-Inventing the Jewish Past: European Jewish Intellec-tuals and the Zionist Return to History* (New York: Oxford University Press, 1995), pp. 109–28. It should be noted at once that the embrace of history, as opposed to historicizing philology, is something I share with, and probably owe to, Zionist and Israeli scholarship (the only courses in ancient Jewish history I ever took were at the Hebrew University, and I found them inspiring). The historical study of Jewish antiquity is rare outside Israel.

at its center.[8] And conversely, the Jews were always devoted to Judaism because of their overwhelmingly powerful national sensibility. Alon expressed this view in a ringing passage in the introduction to his Hebrew University lectures published posthumously as *The Jews in Their Land in the Talmudic Age*:

> we shall begin our study by regarding the [Talmudic] age as a continuation of the Second Commonwealth, expecting to find the Jews with all the attributes of a people dug in on its native soil; undergoing changes in its national, social, and economic life; struggling to regain its freedom; trying with might and main to hold together its scattered limbs, to unite its far-flung diasporas around the central homeland, to strengthen them, and to fan their hopes for final reunification and liberation—a consummation that still appeared to be a practical possibility, perhaps just around the corner.

This view, which I will argue against in detail in the second section of this book, has several interesting consequences. For Alon and his followers the "spiritual" (i.e., religious) character of the Jews' nationhood, which is only implicit in the passage quoted here but is a basic assumption of Alon's work, meant that there was an unusually close connection between the prescriptions of the rabbis, the ancient Jews' presumed spiritual leadership, and the Jews' behavior. Indeed, it is difficult to find in Zionist and Israeli scholarship even a hint that the rabbis were anything other than the distillation of the Jewish national will. This has important implications for how such historians read rabbinic literature: in short, they used what we might call a hermeneutics of goodwill, as opposed to the hermeneutics of suspicion now widespread among non-Israeli scholars. According to this model, rabbinic prescriptions could be used to *describe* Jewish life, rabbinic disagreements were thought to reflect deeper social and political conflicts among the Jews, and so on.[9] In fact, Alon was more careful about the deployment of this model than his followers have been. Thus, although his historiography remains resolutely rabbinocentric, Alon was at least aware, because the Palestinian Talmud told him as much, that the authority of the rabbis in Palestine in the third and fourth centuries was neither absolute nor unchallenged.

[8] Alon (sometimes spelled Allon) was the founder of the field of Jewish history in the "Talmud period" in Israel. As far as I am aware all the current practicioners there with the exception of Lee Levine (in addition to several Roman historians who sometimes work on Jewish topics, for example, Hannah Cotton, Joseph Geiger, and Menahem Mor) are students of his students. Michael Avi-Yonah was also influential, though primarily for archaeologists and art historians (see below). This field has been unusually conservative, with no counterparts to Moshe Idel, who has revolutionized the study of Kabbalah.

[9] It should be noted that although nowadays it is almost only Israeli scholars who work this way, these assumptions were standard among scholars of *Jüdische Wissenschaft* and their successors down to the middle of the twentieth century, who were of course no less romantic than their Zionist epigones. For general discussion, see I. Schorsch, *From Text to Context: The Turn to History in Modern Judaism* (Hanover: Brandeis University Press, 1994).

The Israeli view of the "Talmud period" is not typical of Zionist historiography. The Talmud period had a special status in that it functioned for many of the historians and their audience as a kind of utopia, when, as Alon put it, the Jews "still lived as a nation on their land" and still lived lives characterized by untrammeled commitment to the Torah as expounded by the rabbis, in opposition to an oppressive foreign empire.[10] The unrealistic harmony attributed to the Jews of this period by such historians contrasts sharply with the realistic complexity of Jewish social and political life described by Zionist historians of other periods. One fundamental cause of this difference was information. The documents discovered in the Cairo Geniza, for instance, allowed Alon's contemporary Shelomo Dov Goitein, no less a Zionist than Alon, to produce a rich, detailed, and tension-filled account of Jewish life in high medieval North Africa.[11] But Alon and his followers had no comparable sources for their period, or so they thought, and so were free to impose their ideological readings on the past without encountering the corrective of historical evidence.

In fact, there *was* other information, which they did not ignore but felt they could explain away. While almost all Jewish literature written between the second and sixth centuries was produced by rabbinic circles and is characterized by a much more pronounced uniformity of genre, discourse, and ideology than Jewish literature earlier and later, archaeological remains render its status problematic. Erwin R. Goodenough's, monumental collection of material remains, *Jewish Symbols in the Greco-Roman Period* (1953–1968), argued that the rabbis did not control Jewish life to the extent imagined by earlier scholars. On the contrary, most Jews of the rabbinic period practiced a profoundly hellenized, mystical, platonic version of Judaism that received its classic literary formulation in the works of Philo of Alexandria. The second half of

---

[10] For some suggestive observations, concerning Alon's colleague and friend Yitzhak Baer, see I. Yuval, "Yitzhak Baer and the Search for Authentic Judaism," in D. Myers and D. Ruderman, eds., *The Jewish Past Revisited: Reflections on Modern Jewish Historians* (New Haven: Yale University Press, 1998), pp. 77–87. But Baer's work on ancient (as opposed to medieval) Jews was not influential, a neglect that needs to be partly reevaluated. Alon awaits his Boswell. In the meantime, see the foreword by G. Levi to the 1980 edition of *The Jews in their Land*, vii–x; Baer's eulogy of Alon, printed as the preface to *Toldot Hayehudim Be'eretz Yisrael Bitequfat Hamishnah Vehatalmud* (Jerusalem: Hakibbutz Hame'uhad, 1959), z'–y', which captures the tension between *engagement* and science (as well as that between traditional Torah study and academic scholarship), which *mutatis mutandis* was characteristic also of Baer's own work.

It should be added that though *The Jews in their Land*, which was patched together from Alon's lecture notes, is in every way a problematic book, many of the articles collected in *Mehqarim* (most of which are translated in *Jews and Judaism in the Classical World* (Jerusalem: Magnes, 1977)) retain their importance.

[11] The Cairo Geniza refers to the contents of the attic of the "Palestinian rite" synagogue in Fustat (old Cairo), where, starting in the tenth century, the local Jews deposited not only discarded religious texts but also documents, personal letters, receipts, and so on. At the end of the nineteenth century, most of the material was brought to the Cambridge University Library.

Goodenough's argument, based as it was on a highly problematic method of "reading" ancient Jewish art, was immediately and universally rejected. The first half of the argument, though, laid the foundations for the revolution in the study of ancient Judaism produced by the early work of Jacob Neusner, a revolution that I embrace in this book. It was Neusner who first argued consistently that rabbinic documents were not simply repositories of tradition but careful selections of material, shaped by the interests, including the self-interest, of tradents and redactors. In his view the documents did not simply reflect reality but constituted attempts to construct it, that is, they are statements of ideology. Finally, they are the writings of a collectivity of would-be leaders, scholars who aspired to but never in antiquity attained widespread authority over the Jews. In sum, Neusner's work *historicized* rabbinic literature and reduced it to an artifact of a society in which it was in fact marginal.

Unity and Diversity: Judaisms

Especially since the early 1980s, positions that Neusner first embraced out of interpretive caution have rigidified into orthodoxies. To insist on questioning the accuracy of "attributions" in rabbinic literature (i.e., the common sort of statement that begins, "Rabbi X said . . . " or ends, " . . . so said Rabbi Y") on the grounds that later rabbis and/or the editors of the documents had some motivation to falsify them, and may in any case simply have misremembered, is salutary. But to conclude that we must assume the falsity of attributions, that therefore (?) the documents are essentially pseudepigraphic and can be assumed to provide evidence only for the interests of their redactors, is in fact no longer a skeptical but a positivist position and is less plausible than the one it replaced.

Similarly, Neusner began with the view that rabbinic documents should be read separately, on their own terms, before the relationships between them can be worked out.[12] This view is actually less reasonable than it seems at first glance, since, given the obvious fact that the documents overlap, presuppose, and comment upon one another, and so on, some theory of the documents' relationships should logically precede the description of the discrete texts (and in real life, as opposed to programmatic pronouncements, internalist and comparative reading proceed hand in hand). In any case, Neusner once again pushed this ostensibly cautious view too far by insisting that the documents

---

[12] In his preface to *Judaisms and Their Messiahs at the Turn of the Christian Era*, ed. W. S. Green and E. Frerichs (Cambridge: Cambridge University Press, 1987), p. xiii, for example, Neusner writes, in a passage that seems to me typical: "All we propose is to describe things item by item, and to postpone the work of searching for connections and even continuities until all the components have had their say, one by one." In the meantime, Neusner asserts, we should continue to speak of "Judaisms"; cf. more persuasively *The Systemic Analysis of Judaism* (Atlanta: Scholars, 1988), pp. 9–15.

are *in fact* self-contained (and not simply that for heuristic purposes they should be read as if they were), that each one is as it were a summary statement of the ideology of a discrete social organization. The result is not only bad history but also tautologous reading: if texts must be read in a rigorous way on their own terms, the only thing to say about them is to recapitulate their contents.

Here Neusner, along with many other scholars of ancient Judaism, was influenced by an important tendency in New Testament scholarship, though he applied its methods in an uncompromising way. It is not uncommon among New Testament scholars to posit a discrete social context to serve as a hermeneutical framework in which to set each Gospel. This method has an element of circularity to it, since the hypothetical context is inferred mainly from the Gospel itself, but is not unilluminating. However, scholars are frequently seduced by their own creations: the hermeneutical models are reified into real communities, which are supposed to have existed more or less in isolation from each other, so that each literary work is approached as if it were the hypostasis of a single monadic community. When the same technique is applied to Jewish literature of the Second Temple and rabbinic periods, the result is "Judaisms," a term introduced by Neusner and widely adopted. Once again, what started as interpretive restraint ended in implausible positivism: because it is advisable to read the literary works on their own, even though they obviously have close relatives (and because their social context is on the whole poorly known), each work begins to seem utterly different from its congeners and so must be the product of an impermeably discrete social organization.

In this book I assume that ancient Judaism was complex, capacious, and rather frayed at the edges, and I devote a chapter to a description of these qualities. In doing so, I reject the characterization of Judaism as multiple, as well as the atomistic reading of the sources that justifies it. This is an appropriate place to consider some of the problems with the latter characterization, which I think is the enlightened consensus in America and Europe, influential even among those who refrain from using the term "Judaisms."

In the first place, the hypothesis of radical diversity seems to me inadequate. The notion that each piece of evidence reflects a discrete social organization is obviously wrong. Communities do not write books, individuals do, and several individuals in even a very small community might write very different sorts of books (as the library discovered at Qumran demonstrates) and few of these books are likely to be ideological manifestos.[13]

---

[13] In any case, it is probable that for most Jewish sectarian groups, including Christians, the most important books, those that the groups themselves considered central to their self-definition, were precisely not the sectarian books but the Hebrew Bible.

In addition, the search for differences neglects ancient political, demographic, and social realities. As far as politics is concerned, the empowerment of certain Jewish elites in the later Second Temple period imposed limits on acceptable variety. There was necessarily a normative core of Judaism before 70 C.E., though as we will see in the first section of this book, this core is by no means easy to describe, and it certainly had no special connection with the pharisaic/rabbinic Judaism regarded as normative by pre-Neusner and most Israeli scholars.

Furthermore, and here we move on to a discussion of demography, the authors of all ancient Jewish literature—little of which, outside Qumran, is in any obvious way sectarian—necessarily belonged to a tiny elite, a basic and undeniable fact that to my knowledge has never been mentioned in considerations of the issue. It may be worth briefly speculating about the number of these elites at various periods. There can be no claim of precision here, only of a rough heuristic plausibility.

In the third and early second centuries B.C.E., when, according to the generally accepted view, 1 Enoch, Kohelet, and the Wisdom of Ben Sira were composed, there are unlikely to have been more (and probably there were many fewer) than 150,000 Jews living in Palestine, if we assume that the maximum possible population of the country in premodern conditions was one million and that before about 130 B.C.E., almost all Palestinian Jews lived in the district of Judaea.[14] It is highly unlikely that as much as 10 percent of

---

[14] On the geographical distribution of the Jews, see below. On the size of the population, see M. Broshi, "The Population of Western Palestine in the Roman-Byzantine Period," BASOR 236 (1979): 1–10, supported by G. Hamel, Poverty and Charity in Roman Palestine, First Three Centuries C.E. (Berkeley: University of California Press, 1990), pp. 137–40. Their figures, adopted here, are based on the carrying capacity of the land and on estimates of population density in built-up areas. Though these are imperfect criteria, they yield a far more realistic figure than that produced by taking Josephus' numbers seriously, as earlier scholars did; see I. Finkelstein, "A Few Notes on Demographic Data from Recent Generations and Ethnoarchaeology," PEQ 122 (1990): 45–52. By contrast, the calculations offered by Z. Safrai, "Godel Ha-ukhlusiya Be-eretz Yisrael Bi-tequfah Ha-Romit-Bizantit," in Y. Friedman, Z. Safrai, and J. Schwartz, eds., Hikrei Eretz: Studies in the History of the Land of Israel Dedicated to Prof. Yehuda Feliks (Ramat Gan: Bar Ilan University Press, 1997), pp. 277–305, are impossible, based as they are on estimated average wheat yields of about 35 to 1, and population density in built-up areas of 150 people per dunam—as opposed to the approximately 20 per dunam suggested by Finkelstein! For a systematic criticism of the use of population numbers provided by ancient writers, on the grounds that they are regularly demographically impossible, see T. Parkin, Demography and Roman Society (Baltimore: Johns Hopkins University Press, 1992), pp. 58–66. Another hint about population size is provided by the recent survey of "the Land of Ephraim," whose southern half corresponds with the northern part of Hasmonean and Herodian Judaea. On the basis of ancient settlement patterns and Ottoman and British Mandatory population and crop production figures, Finkelstein estimated its peak population, attained in "Iron II" (roughly 800–600 B.C.E.), the first century C.E., and the "Byzantine" period (I assume this means the fifth and sixth centuries), as 26,000–30,000. This suggests that my estimate for Judaea as a whole may be rather high, though "Ephraim" is on the whole less fertile than the district of Jerusalem immediately to its south.

been the province of a Jewish elite, came, in the course of the Second Temple period or the rabbinic period, or both, to be shared by the Jews generally. So, the spread outside priestly circles (but never very far outside them) of a rigorous attitude toward ritual purity, the privileging of Torah study over priestly descent, and the rise of the synagogue, an institution in which Jews worshiped God through study and prayer rather than sacrifice, are all regarded as aspects of a general "democratization."[18]

Democratization is, first of all, an apologetic term: it makes sense as a description of the above processes only as an attempt to make ancient Judaism attractive in a liberal Western environment. If democracy is characterized by elections and by representative government, then there was no tendency toward democracy among the ancient Jews, except in the trivial sense that some Diaspora communities located in Greek cities may conceivably have borrowed the practice of voting from their environment (though this is in fact unknown); even here we should recall that in such cities in the Hellenistic and Roman imperial periods, voting was mainly a ceremonial supplement to a political system that was essentially oligarchic. We should also not ignore the fact that at least half the Jewish population, that is, women, were (in most places? everywhere?) excluded from the process.

Most significantly, though, I do not believe that Judaism experienced any such process. It is true of course that Judaism has an unusually highly developed sense of its (male) constituency as a notionally egalitarian citizen body, "Israel," but at the same time the sense that certain Israelites are naturally privileged. We may speak of a tension between egalitarianism and hierarchy. But this tension is already strongly present in the Pentateuch, and it has never been absent. The privileging of Torah study (which is, again, already understood to be a key to power in the Pentateuch itself) of course in theory broke the monopoly of the priesthood, but (1) in the Second Temple period expertise at Torah seems to have been mainly a priestly prerogative and (2) even later, when it became partly detached from priestly descent, it certainly did not make the system more democratic, since access to the acquisition of expertise at Torah was and has always been highly restricted. The privileging of Torah study slightly changed the character of the Jews' religious leadership without making it in any way more democratic. In any case, as we will see, it is far from certain that the post-Destruction Torah scholars par excellence—the rabbis—actually enjoyed much authority before the Middle Ages.

This brings us to the synagogue because in late antiquity, though the rabbis were not totally insignificant, the real religious leaders probably were the heads of the synagogues, that is, of the local Jewish communities (see part III). It would be perfectly legitimate to think of the diffusion of the synagogue,

---

[18] For a criticism of "democratization" similar to the one proposed here, see D. Boyarin, "A Tale of Two Synods: Nicaea, Yavneh, and Rabbinic Ecclesiology," *Exemplaria* 12 (2000): 33–34.

mainly in the fourth through sixth centuries, as a diffusion also of access to the sacred. Synagogues seem to have been generally regarded as holy places, and the local religious communities that built and maintained them as holy fellowships, perhaps even miniature "Israels." But the local community was characterized by precisely the same tension between egalitarianism and hierarchy as the fictive biblical community of Israel. And what this meant in practice, as most scholars acknowledge, is that local communities were oligarchic, precisely like the notionally democratic Greco-Roman cities, which were the other main model of the late antique local religious community. The rulers of the community were the well-to-do; they may also have been relatively learned and may have regarded some knowledge of Torah as an obligation especially incumbent on their class.

Summary

The first part of *Imperialism and Jewish Society* concerns the Second Temple period (539 B.C.E.–70 C.E.) but focuses on the that period between roughly 200 B.C.E. and 70 C.E., for which relatively abundant information is available. The Jews were then ruled by a series of empires that shared the tendency to govern autonomous provinces through local intermediaries (the period of truly independent rule by the Hasmonean dynasty was very brief and, even then, the Jewish rulers never fully ceased being vassals of their stronger neighbors).

I argue that imperial support for the central national institutions of the Jews, the Jerusalem temple and the Pentateuch, helps explain why these eventually became the chief symbols of Jewish corporate identity. The history of the Second Temple period is one of integration, in which more and more Jews came to define themselves around these symbols. The implications of this development are complex, and we cannot produce an account of Jewish life in the Second Temple period solely on the basis of Pentateuchal legislation. We can say, though, that the institutional power and symbolic importance of the Torah and temple empowered their human representatives to engage in a constant *negotiation* with Palestinian Jews, whereby their behavior was interpreted in light of and reconciled with the laws of the Torah.

Another symptom of the integration of Jewish society is the rise of apocalyptic mythology, starting in the third century B.C.E. Though this mythology is suffused with a worldview that is at odds with that of the Hebrew Bible in that it regards Creation as a failure and the world as an evil mess, in its extant form it has been thoroughly judaized: its heroes are taken from Bible stories, which usually can serve as the main "intertexts" for the apocalyptic books; its angels may be extremely powerful but are still Jewish angels, their names and functions derived exegetically from the Bible; finally, Yahweh always wins in the end. This mythology was pervasively influential in the literature of the later

Second Temple period (in only a few books are traces of it absent), and it is always juxtaposed with temple- and Torah-centered material. It is thus the product of the same scribal and priestly elites and subelites who produced Jewish literature in general, and presumably it reflects their attempt to neutralize, judaize (i.e., interpret in Jewish terms), and assert control over problematic, perhaps in part magical, elements of Judaean religion, while also providing a way of explaining, and perhaps controlling, the presence of evil in the world, as the Deuteronomic theology of most of the Bible fails adequately to do.

The second part of the book concerns the period from 135 C.E. to 350, the period when the Jews of Palestine were under the direct rule of the relatively centralizing pagan Roman state (I select 350, rather than 312 or 324—when Constantine conquered the East—in recognition of the fact that christianization was a gradual process that only began with Constantine; the date is to some extent arbitrary). The striking characteristic of this period is the disjointed nature of the evidence: on the one hand, the literature, which is entirely rabbinic, demonstrates the preservation of Judaism by a segment of the Palestinian Jewish population; on the other, the archaeological remains, and some literary hints, suggest that at least in the cities and large villages Judaism had disintegrated and was replaced, as other local identities elsewhere in the Roman Empire were, by the religious, cultural, and social norms of the Greco-Roman city.

I suggest that under the combined impact of the Destruction and the failure of the two revolts, the deconstitution of the Jewish "nation," and the annexation of Palestine by an empire at the height of its power and prosperity, Judaism shattered. Its shards were preserved in altered but recognizable form by the rabbis, who certainly had some residual prestige and thus small numbers of close adherents and probably larger numbers of occasional supporters. But for most Jews, Judaism may have been little more than a vestigial identity, bits and pieces of which they were happy to incorporate into a religious and cultural system that was essentially Greco-Roman and pagan. Most Jews may have been Jews in much the same (tenuous) way as people like, for example, Lucian of Samosata, the satirical writer of the second century who, despite his mastery of the classical tradition and of Greek style, and his possession of Roman citizenship, nevertheless regarded himself as irreducibly "other", were Syrian.[19]

The third part of the book concerns the Christian empire, still a centralizing (though weaker) state, but one in which the Jews had for theological reasons a special status. The law codes demonstrate that the Christian state had an interest, which the pagan Roman state had lacked, in regarding the

---

[19] See S. Swain, *Hellenism and Empire: Language, Classicism, and Power in the Greek World, AD 50–250* (Oxford: Clarendon, 1995), pp. 298–329.

Jews as constituting a separate and discrete religious community. This is one reason, though not the only one, for the revival of Judaism in late antiquity to which archaeology and an explosion of literary production testify.

This revived Judaism was Torah and synagogue centered. One of its chief manifestations was the widespread conviction, absent or rare as far as we can tell in the Second Temple period, that the village was a religiously meaningful entity. In this part I trace the spread of the synagogue and the ideology of the religious community, attending to the ways in which they are characteristically late antique—not only a consequence of state policies but also ways in which the Jews shared general (i.e., Christian) cultural norms but appropriated them and marked them as distinctively Jewish. I do not see the late antique revival of Judaism as in any way a product of rabbinic influence, though the revival may in the long run have contributed to the rabbis' medieval rise.

PART I

THE JEWS OF PALESTINE TO 70 C.E.

ONE

POLITICS AND SOCIETY

I N THIS CHAPTER I provide some of the political and social background for the discussion in chapter 2 of the functioning of a loosely integrated Palestinian Jewish society in the later first millennium B.C.E. I focus here on some of the crucial episodes in the prehistory of Jews' political and social integration: the activities of Ezra and Nehemiah (about which little can really be known), the Maccabean revolt, the fundamentally important but little studied or understood Hasmonean expansion, and, perhaps rather surprisingly, the activities of Herod. I also offer an account of "hellenization," a process—or rather a complex of processes—that might have been expected to hinder the Jews' internal integration by introducing or sharpening social divisions between Jews and by allowing some or many among the elites to cease regarding themselves as Jewish at all. But hellenization is a rather misleading concept that requires critical attention.

Persian Sponsorship of the Jerusalem Temple and the Torah of Moses[1]

I assume that the Israelite religion, as practiced before the destruction of the kingdom of Judah by the Babylonians in 586 B.C.E., was distinct from the religion practiced by the Israelites' putative descendants, the Jews, in the Second Temple period.[2] The Israelites, to be sure, worshiped Yahweh, whose cult was then, as later, centered in Jerusalem, and they seem to have shared many

---

[1] A bibliographical note: this chapter covers well-trodden ground; it would be counterproductive even to aspire to provide comprehensive annotation for relatively uncontentious points (there are no absolutely uncontentious points). It will suffice here to refer to the standard handbooks, especially E. Schürer, *A History of the Jewish People in the Age of Jesus Christ (175 B.C.–A.D. 135)*, ed. and rev. by G. Vermes, F. Millar et al., 4 vols. (Edinburgh: T & T Clark, 1973–1987); L. Grabbe, *Judaism from Cyrus to Hadrian* (Minneapolis: Fortress Press, 1992), containing much recent bibliography. P. Schäfer, *The History of the Jews in Antiquity* (Luxembourg: Harwood Academic Publishers, 1995), provides an especially accessible and reliable account of political history.

[2] I am following a tendency in scholarship that starts with Wellhausen and was much later taken up by Morton Smith, *Palestinian Parties and Politics That Shaped the Old Testament* (New York: Columbia University Press, 1971), and has now gained widespread acceptance, especially in circles not influenced by Yehezkel Kaufmann; see, for example, N. P. Lemche, *Ancient Israel: A New History of Israelite Society* (Sheffield, U.K.: JSOT Press, 1988).

other practices with the Jews. For example, males seem to have been circumcised, pigs were rarely consumed, and mourning rituals seem to have included fasting, sackcloth, and ashes. But on the whole, except for brief periods of pietistic reform, most Israelites were not henotheists, and they may not have known of many characteristic biblical observances, such as the festivals of Passover and Sukkot, allegedly instituted either by the reformist king Josiah (reigned 639–609 B.C.E.) shortly before the Babylonian conquest or by Ezra or Nehemiah, in the fifth century. And their rituals seem often to have included practices forbidden by the Pentateuch, such as skin cutting, a mourning custom. Most importantly, perhaps, there is no evidence that the Israelites possessed a single authoritative "Torah" that bore any resemblance to the Pentateuch. The implications of the shift from the Israelite religion to Judaism will be discussed in detail in the next chapter. Here we will briefly consider some aspects of its history.

This history is controversial and poorly understood. According to the biblical books of Ezra-Nehemiah, Haggai, and Zechariah, the Persian emperors permitted several groups of Judahite exiles to return from their exile to Judah and build a temple in Jerusalem. The temple, devoted to the worship of Yahweh alone, was completed in 515 B.C.E. Two generations later, Artaxerxes I permitted first Ezra and then the courtier Nehemiah (or perhaps the order was reversed) to return to Judah and establish the "Torah of Moses," apparently a book, as the official law of the Judahites. To judge from the biblical accounts, this book closely resembled the Pentateuch but may not have been identical with it. The account of Ezra's career is incomplete, but Nehemiah is said to have been successful in his mission, mainly because of his political skill.

In the absence of external confirmation, it is difficult to know what to make of these stories. Most scholars, impressed by their meaningful translatability into rational historical narrative (i.e., their verisimilitude), have been inclined to take them seriously, notwithstanding some problematic details. Others, perhaps a growing number, reject the stories on the grounds that they are after all stories, whose biases are quite conspicuous.[3] We need not solve this problem, since it is nearly certain that the Jerusalem Temple was built under the aegis of the Achaemenids, and likely too that some version of the Torah became the authorized law of the Jews in the same general period, if not in the circumstances the biblical books describe. We may wonder why the Persian emperors should have been interested in imposing Judaism on the Jews.

---

[3] For discussion, see S. Japhet, "In Search of Ancient Israel: Revisionism at All Costs," D. Myers and D. Ruderman, eds., *The Jewish Past Revisited: Reflections on Modern Jewish Historians* (New Haven: Yale University Press, 1998), pp. 212–34, which cites the most important "revisionist" works. I agree with Japhet that the extreme skeptics are wrong. Indeed, they can actually be seen as naive positivists, since they tend to regard the stories as pure ideology (as opposed to complicated mixtures of history, tradition, invention, and folklore combined into ideologically

In comparison to the Assyrians and Babylonians, who were mainly interested in collecting tribute from their subjects, and punished brutally those
who failed to pay, the Persians were mild but interventionist. Cyrus posed as
a liberator, a restorer of gods and peoples following the depredations and
deportations of the Babylonians, and this pose became a fixture of Persian
imperial rhetoric. In practice, the Persians tended to patronize native oligarchies, preferably those with strong connections to temples, and encouraged
them to try to regulate the legal and economic activities of their provinces.
This last consideration may help explain the imperial patronage of the Torah.
Though probably the work mostly of reformists and radicals, the Torah
claimed to be the traditional law of the Israelites and was the only Jewish law
code available. An Egyptian text informs us that the emperor Darius I had
created a committee of Egyptian priests to compile an authoritative code of
Egyptian law, and Artaxerxes or another Persian emperor, in authorizing the
Torah, may have been doing the same sort of thing for the Jews.[4] The desired
and sometimes attained result of the Persians' interventionism was a smoothly
running, peaceful, and consistently profitable empire, which depended on the
loyalty of the hand-picked oligarchs, a royal provincial administration more
elaborate than anything the Babylonians had had, and mild intimidation produced by the presence everywhere of small numbers of Persian-commanded
garrison troops.[5] Persian policy thus contrasted with Babylonian, with its alter-
nating periods of complete laissez-faire and brutal terror. In some cases, then,
Persian interventionism practically created the nations the Persians ruled. It
is in the light of these practices that the events reported in the biblical books
of Ezra, Nehemiah, Haggai, and Zechariah should be seen.

The regime initiated in Judaea by the Persian emperors and their Jewish
vassals lasted, with a few interruptions, until the middle of the second century
B.C.E. Though the history of Yehud/Judaea (the province acquired its Greek
name after Alexander the Great conquered it in 332 B.C.E.) in much of this
period is very obscure, the apparent institutional stability of Judaea suggests

driven, usually analysis-resistant narratives), written to serve the purposes of Jewish leaders in the
third or second centuries B.C.E., as if they were more reliably attested than Nehemiah.

[4] See W. Spiegelberg, *Die sogennante demotische Chronik des Pap. 215 der Bibliothèque Natio-
nale zu Paris* (Leipzig: J. C. Hinrichs, 1915), pp. 30–32; M. Dandamaev and V. Lukonin, *The
Culture and Social Institutions of Iran* (Cambridge: Cambridge University Press, 1989), p. 125;
J. Blenkinsopp, *The Pentateuch* (New York: Doubleday, 1992), pp. 239–42; E. Bickerman, *The
Jews in the Greek Age* (Cambridge: Harvard University Press, 1988), pp. 29–32.

[5] On the Assyrian and Babylonian empires, see A. L. Oppenheim, *Ancient Mesopotamia: Portrait of a Dead Civilization* (Chicago: University of Chicago Press, 1977), pp. 165–68; for a
general characterization of the Achaemenid empire, see Dandamaev and Lukonin, *The Culture
and Social Institutions of Iran*; for a discussion of and literature on the Achaemenids' restorative
radicalism, see P. Briant, "The Seleucid Kingdom and the Achaemenid Empire," in P. Bilde et
al., eds., *Religion and Religious Practice in the Seleucid Kingdom* (Aarhus: Aarhus University
Press, 1990), pp. 53–60.

that the impression of calm created by the silence of the sources, preceding the well-attested dynamism and disorder of the two and a half centuries beginning in 170 B.C.E., is no mirage.

Hellenization: A Constraint on Group Integration?

According to 1 Maccabees (1:11), some Jews in the early second century B.C.E. believed that their people's separation from the surrounding nations was the source of all their woes. The implication, that the Jews were less integrated into their eastern Mediterranean social environment than many of their neighbors, is probably correct. But enduring integrative pressures forced them to find ways to circumvent the separatist requirements of Jewish law; this may explain, for example, how the Tobiad family, regarded as Ammonite in the book of Nehemiah, despite their marriage alliance with an important Jerusalemite priestly family (Nehemiah 13:1–8), were considered Jewish by sometime in the third century B.C.E.[6] The same pressures also encouraged the Jews to embrace aspects of the common culture of the eastern Mediterranean, which Jewish law did not unambiguously prohibit.

The most significant cultural development in the eastern Mediterranean in the fifth century B.C.E. and following was the process modern historians call "hellenization" (there is no precise ancient equivalent for the word). This term is used to denote a confusing variety of phenomena, ranging from non-Greek's use of imported Greek tableware to development of a taste for Greek and imitation Greek painted vases and sculptures to worship of Greek gods to adoption of the Greek language and reading of Greek literature to, finally, the acquisition of citizenship in Greek cities, that is, becoming "Greek" (citizenship, at least as much as descent, was an essential requirement for Greekness). To confuse matters still further, Jewish and Christian scholars, especially, use the term with a marked lack of chronological specificity—this at a time when ancient historians and classicists are increasingly recognizing the distinctions between the still rather exclusivistic Hellenism of the Hellenistic period, the characteristic urban culture of the high imperial Roman east,

---

[6] The Tobiad family is discussed in more detail below. On the social, economic, and political importance of elite interethnic marriages in the pre-Roman eastern Mediterranean, see G. Herman, *Ritualised Friendship and the Greek City* (Cambridge: Cambridge University Press, 1987). S. Cohen, *The Beginnings of Jewishness: Boundaries, Varieties, Uncertainties* (Berkeley: University of California Press, 1999), has repeatedly argued that conversion to Judaism did not exist before the early second century B.C.E., an argument that I accept from a legal and institutional perspective. But I would suggest that the development of a ritual of conversion is just one episode in the long history in what was at least in antiquity the fixed systemic tension between separatism, enjoined by the Torah, and integration, required by the realities of life in the eastern Mediterranean. So, the Tobiads may not have converted, but they may have done something very like it.

which simultaneously served to integrate the upper classes of the empire and was a site of subtle resistance to Roman rule, and the Greek *paideia* of the late empire, which first united and then divided pagans and Christians.[7]

In recent decades, interest in the hellenization of the Jews in the high and later Roman Empire has waned, in part because some of the main issues seem relatively uncontroversial—the material culture of Roman Palestine appears quite unambiguously hellenized—but also because the opposing viewpoints about the extent to which the rabbis participated in the common culture of the Roman east are frozen in place and no longer in dialogue. In reality, these issues are far more complex and interesting than they have come to seem, and I will discuss them in detail in the relevant sections of this book.

By contrast, the question of the hellenization of the Jews in the Second Temple period is enduringly controversial. Scholars still disagree as to whether "the Jews" were hellenized or not, as if the answer to such a question could ever be meaningful. Even those who admit that the real cultural situation was complex often regard Hellenism as a defining issue in Jewish society after 332 B.C.E. Differing attitudes to Hellenism are thought to have generated social fissures and even conflict. In what follows, I will briefly explain how and why I disagree.[8]

The process of hellenization in Jewish Palestine in the Second Temple period seems on the whole to have been relatively unproblematic. As elsewhere in the Greek east, the practice of adopting the trappings of Greek culture functioned to sharpen the divisions between rich and poor and city and country, which existed in any case. But hellenization rarely *produced* divisions or catalyzed conflicts. Furthermore, it is misleading to crowd all the effects of Macedonian rule under the rubric of hellenization. The latter may have been an important consequence of Alexander's conquests and their aftermath, but scholars have too often tended to think that all Jewish cultural production of the Hellenistic period is best viewed as a set of artifacts either of hellenization or of opposition to it. In what follows, therefore, I will first of all introduce some terminological precision, by distinguishing several types of hellenization, and then pay special attention to those novel aspects of Jewish culture in the Hellenistic period that would be unilluminating to understand in relation to Greek culture.

Let us begin by separating hellenization in the sense of "acting Greek" while maintaining one's own cultural identity from hellenization in the sense of "becoming Greek" and so necessarily abandoning one's previous cultural

---

[7] Such distinctions are taken for granted in the work of an ancient historian who has recently begun to write about Judaism: E. Gruen, *Heritage and Hellenism: The Reinvention of Jewish Tradition* (Berkeley: University of California Press, 1998), p. xvii.

[8] Cf. L. Levine, *Judaism and Hellenism in Antiquity: Conflict or Confluence?* (Seattle: University of Washington Press, 1998), pp. 3–32.

identity.[9] (One of the differences between Greekness in the Hellenistic and Roman imperial periods was that in the former it was not compatible with open retention of other ethnic or cultural identities).[10] Hellenization in the first sense might culminate in hellenization in the second sense, but need not do so. In fact, it may even function to preserve a native non-Greek culture. And hellenization in the second sense need not presuppose, rather surprisingly, prior hellenization in the first sense.[11] For the time being it is the first type of hellenization that concerns us.

Until 332 B.C.E. the Judaeans and their neighbors were subject to Persia, far in the east, but they remained part of the cultural and economic world of the eastern Mediterranean, which included not only the cities and nations of the Syro-Palestinian coast and Egypt but also the old Greek cities of western Asia Minor and, at its western fringe, Greece itself. There had been trade and other contacts between Greece and the east coast of the Mediterranean, including Israel, for as long as there had been boats. The Philistines, who infiltrated the coastal cities of Palestine around 1200 B.C.E., probably came from the Aegean and had close ties to the Mycenaean Greeks. Greeks served as mercenaries in the armies of the kings of Judah and Israel, and Greek traders were not unknown in the region in the same period.[12] Presumably, though, there was nothing noteworthy about these people—they were just part of the general eastern Mediterranean ethnic stew, along with Egyptians, Phoenicians, and various groups of Asians.

The Greek victory over Persia in 478 B.C.E., the subsequent rise of the Athenian empire, the consolidation of classical Greek culture (which was among other things an important item for export), and of Athenian economic dominance, which survived the decline of their empire, changed matters. By the fifth century, Greek goods predominated over all other imports in the cities of the Syro-Palestinian coast.[13] The well-to-do there had always liked nicely decorated imported goods, but the trickle of Greek imports now turned

[9] This is rather different from the distinction posited by U. Rappaport, "The Hellenization of the Hasmoneans," in M. Mor, ed., *Jewish Assimilation, Acculturation, and Accommodation* (Lanham, Md.: University Press of America, 1992), pp. 1–13.

[10] See S. Schwartz, "The Hellenization of Jerusalem and Shechem," in M. Goodman, ed., *Jews in a Graeco-Roman World* (Oxford: Clarendon, 1998), pp. 37–45.

[11] Cf. S. Sherwin-White and A. Kuhrt, *From Samarkhand to Sardis: A New Approach to the Seleucid Empire* (London: Duckworth, 1993), pp. 141–49; F. Millar, "The Phoenician Cities: A Case Study in Hellenisation," *PCPS* 209 (1983): 55–71; E. Will, "Poleis hellénistiques: Deux notes," *échos du monde classique/ Classical Views* 15 (1988): 329–51.

[12] See M. Hengel, *Judaism and Hellenism: Studies in Their Encounter in Palestine during the Early Hellenistic Period* (Philadelphia: Fortress, 1974), 1:32–35; on the Philistines, T. Dothan, *The Philistines and Their Material Culture* (New Haven: Yale University Press, 1982).

[13] For a survey, see E. Stern, *Material Culture of the Land of the Bible in the Persian Period 538–332 B.C.* (Warminster, U.K.: Aris & Phillips, 1982).

into a flood—a development of profound cultural significance that is frustratingly difficult to interpret. Why, apart from the commercial strength of Athens, should Greek products and the Greek style have acquired such prestige in coastal Syria, Phoenicia, and Palestine in the fifth century B.C.E.? What are the implications of this development? In the absence of written sources, it is almost impossible to say.[14]

By the fourth century, the flood of Greek goods reached the Palestinian interior, including Judaea. The coins of Persian Judaea, for example, are all modeled on Greek, especially Athenian, coins. Indeed, the practice of stamping pieces of preweighed silver (probably originating in the seventh century B.C.E. in the kingdom of Lydia in western Turkey) spread in the eastern Mediterranean in the sixth and fifth centuries primarily due to Greek influence;[15] the minting of coins itself was thus in some measure an aspect of hellenization. The coinage of Judaea's northern neighbor, Samaria, is similar to that of Judaea, but remarkably enough some of these tiny coins bear Greek inscriptions. These coins were almost all of very small denomination and so intended for local use, not interstate trade.[16] They reflect the tastes and interests of Judaeans and Samarians, not their foreign commercial partners. When Alexander the Great conquered the east coast of the Mediterranean in 332 B.C.E., he found a world that was not completely foreign to him, in which certain aspects, at least, of Greek culture already enjoyed widespread acceptance.

The Macedonian Conquest and Its Impact

Josephus recounts that when Alexander marched down the Palestinian coast, he detoured to Jerusalem to meet the high priest, Jaddus (Yaddu'a). When he saw that venerable figure, he at once realized that it was Jaddus who had appeared in his dreams, foretelling his victory over the Persians; so the great conqueror prostrated himself at the old man's feet. (*Ant* 11.321–39) This is surely a folktale. In reality, Alexander never left the coastal road but entrusted

---

[14] The most serious attempt at interpretation is J. Elayi, *Pénétration grecque en Phénicie sous l'empire perse* (Nancy: Presses Universitaires de Nancy, 1988).

[15] On the origins and early history of coinage, see L. Kurke, *Coins, Bodies, Games, and Gold: The Politics of Meaning in Archaic Greece* (Princeton: Princeton University Press, 1999), pp. 6–23; C. Howgego, *Ancient History from Coins* (London: Routledge, 1995), pp. 1–11.

[16] On the Judaean coins, see L. Mildenberg, "Yehud: A Preliminary Study of the Provincial Coinage of Judaea," O. in Mørkholm and N. Waggoner, eds., *Greek Numismatics and Archaeology: Essays in Honor of Margaret Thompson* (Wetteren: Cultura, 1979), pp. 183–96, with corrections of D. Barag, "A Silver Coin of Yohanan the High Priest and the Coinage of Judaea in the Fourth Century B.C.E.," *INJ* 9 (1986–1987) 4–21. On the Samarian coinage, Y. Meshorer and S. Qedar, *The Coinage of Samaria in the Fourth Century B.C.E.* (Jerusalem: Numismatic Fine Arts International, 1991). See also my discussion: S. Schwartz, "On the Autonomy of Judaea in the Fourth and Third Centuries B.C.E.", *JJS* 45 (1994): 159–61.

the reduction of the Palestinian interior to a subordinate.[17] The following decades, down to 301, were chaotic. Alexander died in 323, and his immense empire, stretching from Greece to India, fell into several pieces, each ruled by one of Alexander's generals initially eager to seize the whole. Palestine was especially controversial, since it was claimed by Ptolemy son of Lagos, whose base was Egypt; Seleucus, the ruler of Mesopotamia and Syria; and Antigonus the One-Eyed, the greatest of all of Alexander's generals. In the event, Ptolemy's conquest of the region in 301 B.C.E. was decisive, and Palestine remained part of Ptolemy's kingdom until 200 B.C.E., when Seleucus's descendant Antiochus III wrested it from Ptolemy V. Although coastal Palestine and Phoenicia in this century witnessed nearly constant warfare between the two dynasties, Judaea, which was a poor hill country district off the main roads and of little strategic interest, remained at peace.[18]

Alexander and his successors retained much of the administrative structure set in place by the Persians. Like the Persians, they tended to grant subject nations, such as the Jews, limited autonomy. And like the Persians, they nowhere actively forced their own language or culture on their subjects. However, the rulers themselves were adamantly Greek (despite, or because of, not actually being Greek at all, but Macedonian), instinctively assumed the superiority of Greek culture, and seem to have preferred Greeks as administrators, friends, and courtiers.[19] These preferences induced wealthier, politically ambitious natives to adopt elements of Greek culture. But Alexander also introduced an unprecedented practice that had profound though probably unintended consequences in all the lands he conquered. To secure his empire throughout the Near East, he founded cities to be settled by his mainly Greek or Greco-Macedonian veterans and other Greek immigrants. These cities were "Greek," that is, they had constitutions and a public life loosely modeled on those of Athens, were legally autonomous (because "freedom" was an essential characteristic of Greekness; in reality, of course, as opposed to self-aggrandizing rhetoric, the cities were subjected to the kings), and had a rural

[17] See V. Tcherikover, *Hellenistic Civilization and the Jews* (Philadelphia: Jewish Publication Society, 1959), pp. 41–50; S. Cohen, "Alexander the Great and Jaddus the High Priest According to Josephus," *AJS Review* 7–8 (1982–1983) 41–68; Josephus's story has had some defenders, such as A. Momigliano, "Flavius Josephus and Alexander's Visit to Jerusalem," *Athenaeum* 57 (1979): 442–48; and A. Kasher, "Some Suggestions and Comments Concerning Alexander Macedon's [*sic*] Campaign in Palestine," *Beth Mikra* 20 (1975): 187–208 (in Hebrew).

[18] The standard studies of Ptolemaic Palestine remain Tcherikover, "Palestine under the Ptolemies," *Mizraim* 4–5 (1937): 9–90; and R. Bagnall, *The Administration of the Ptolemaic Possessions outside Egypt* (Leiden: Brill, 1976), pp. 11–24. For a general political and military history of the period, see E. Will, *Histoire politique du monde hellénistique* (Nancy: Presses Universitaires de Nancy, 1979).

[19] See Sherwin-White and Kuhrt, *From Samarkhand to Sardis*, pp. 141–87; on the potentially profound cultural consequences for subjects of imperial *preferences*, see K. Hopkins, "Conquest by Book," in John Humphrey, ed., *Literacy in the Roman World*, JRA suppl. 3 (1991) 133–58.

territory assigned to them. These territories were farmed not like those of the cities of Old Greece, by citizen farmers, but, by native peasants who were subjected to the citizens, and enjoyed very few civil rights.

Thereafter, founding new Greek cities became a normal activity for all of the so-called Hellenistic kings who succeeded Alexander, and, even more so, for the Romans who succeeded them, so that the entire eastern Mediterranean and Near East was eventually linked by a web of Greek cities. These cities enjoyed no more legal rights than autonomous non-Greek nations did, but they were unquestionably prestigious and prosperous, their self-confidence enhanced by royal patronage and friendship. They were thus soon joined by ancient non-Greek cities, like Sardis in Asia Minor, or Tyre and Sidon in Phoenicia, which in the third century succeeded in transforming themselves into Greek cities, though few of their citizens were of Greek descent.[20]

Given the omnipresence of Greek cities in the Fertile Crescent and the pressures on better-off natives to adopt Greek culture wholesale and even to become Greek (pressures, it bears emphasizing, not consciously imposed by the rulers but rather built in to their system of rule), the stakes in hellenization changed dramatically after Alexander the Great. It was now not unthinkable that nations long in existence or established by the Persians might simply be willed out of existence by their upper classes' desire to be Greek, to reconstitute themselves as the citizen body of a Greek city. Indeed, such a process, indirectly attested for many cities of Asia Minor and Phoenicia in the third century, may be precisely what occurred in Jerusalem and Shechem in the second century, precipitating the Maccabean revolt.

The Tobiads

We can get some sense of the complex effects of Macedonian rule on Jewish society, and the limits of the utility of hellenization in explaining them, by briefly considering two bodies of information. The first of these is Josephus's "Tobiad romance," a historical fiction embedded in book 12 of the *Antiquities* (154–236). Josephus misdated the story to the early years of Seleucid rule, though its content makes it clear that the story is set in the last generation of Ptolemaic rule.[21] The second body of information consists of several pieces of writing from the third and early second centuries, which allow us to see how Macedonian rule affected the concerns of Judaean priests and scribes, but in ways that have no obvious connection to hellenization.

In Josephus's account, Joseph son of Tobias, a member of the Tobiad family mentioned previously and nephew of the Judaean high priest Onias II, suc-

---

[20] See S. Schwartz, "Hellenization of Jerusalem and Shechem."

[21] On the story, see most recently D. Gera, *Judaea and Mediterranean Politics, 219 to 161 BCE* (Leiden: Brill, 1997), pp. 36–58.

ceeded in wresting the tax-farming contract for Judaea from his ineffectual uncle. (The Ptolemies collected taxes by auctioning tax-farming contracts district by district, often to wealthy natives; the tax farmers were then left to raise what they could. They had to pay for shortfalls out of their own pockets but could keep profits.) Josephus embroidered Joseph's exploits and those of his son and heir, Hyrcanus, with so many swashbuckling details that it is tempting to dismiss the entire tale as a fabrication produced by an adventure writer. Nevertheless, the story is not wholly devoid of interest. It suggests that Ptolemaic policies created important opportunities for men with capital, even if they were not exactly members of the traditional ruling classes. The story also portrays the Tobiads as Jewish heroes who take a kind of accountants' revenge on the Judaeans' traditional enemies in the Greek cities of Palestine by exacting taxes from them with special rigor. The Tobiads' assertive Judaism is striking in light of their non-Judaean ancestry; but their Judaism is of a peculiarly modern-seeming secular-nationalist kind. The story portrays Joseph and Hyrcanus as persistent and unself-conscious violators of Jewish law. And for all their alleged hostility to the Greek cities, they are entirely comfortable in the Hellenic environment of the Ptolemaic royal court in Alexandria, Egypt. The family's ease around high government officials, at least, is confirmed by some papyri written in the 250s B.C.E. concerning the business and political arrangements of one Toubias, possibly Joseph's father, a large landowner whose private army had been integrated into the Ptolemaic forces, and the royal agent Zenon.[22] Thus, despite the dubious details of Josephus's story, it introduces us to an element of the Judaean elite in the process of transformation, in the form of a wealthy, marginally Jewish but Jewishly well-connected family. This family had greatly benefited both economically and politically from the Ptolemies' preference for capital-rich subjects and participated in the common Greek culture of eastern Mediterranean elite society. Yet it resisted actually becoming Greek and, successfully walking this tightrope, came to play an important role in Judaean society.

The New Wisdom

There are several pieces of Judaean literature that most scholars agree were composed in the third century B.C.E. These works introduce us to a different segment of Judaean society from that which is the subject of Josephus's stories. The priestly and/or scribal circles who produced the literature were no less affected by the new conditions created by Macedonian rule than Josephus's Tobiads were, but they changed at first in more subtle ways. For despite the ascendancy of people like the Tobiads, the Temple and the Torah remained the centrally important institutions in Judaea. Scribes now presumably

---

[22] See *CPJ* 1: 115–30; S. Schwartz, "A Note on the Social Type and Political Ideology of the Hasmonean Family," *JBL* 112 (1993): 305–7.

needed to be literate in Greek, but acquisition of this skill can have posed little challenge to a class whose main characteristic had always been linguistic talent.[23]

I have argued elsewhere that the Ptolemies may not have recognized the traditional autonomy of the Jews. This would help explain the rise of the Tobiads and perhaps others like them and might also help explain the spotty evidence for tensions between the high priests and the Ptolemies, as well as the apparent fact that the high priest, Simon, openly supported the Seleucids (which may in turn explain why Antiochus III recognized Simon's authority over the Jews).[24] Nevertheless, for all their interventionist aspirations, the Ptolemies still ruled mainly through local elites, especially in their non-Egyptian holdings. Thus, the priests and scribes remained empowered, if not as extensively or as exclusively as under the Achaemenids.[25]

Despite the essential stability of the scribal and priestly classes in the third century, things were changing for them. We can see this clearly if we look at the way they transformed the classical Israelite/Jewish wisdom tradition, the recording of which was one of this class's chief literary activities.[26] In the earliest complete example, the biblical book of Proverbs (seventh-sixth centuries B.CE.?), wisdom is an adjunct of official Jewish piety. Here fear of God is identified with wisdom, the righteous with the wise. Like the Deuteronomic history and some of the Psalms, Proverbs supposes that wisdom/righteousness is the key to prosperity. Though Proverbs has an undeniable worldliness, its central themes are specifically and conventionally Israelite.

This bureaucratic piety was subjected to criticism.[27] The book of Job (fifth century B.C.E.?) had already drawn on Second Isaiah's transcendental monotheism to reject, in a rhetorical tour de force, the traditional Deuteronomic piety, which supposed that a powerful but immanent God could be counted on to reward the righteous and punish the wicked. Jewish writers of the third century produced even more radical revisions of the wisdom tradition. The author of Ecclesiastes, who came closer than any other ancient writer in Hebrew to producing a Greek-style philosophical treatise, as opposed to the loose collection of sayings typical of Israelite-Jewish wisdom, went well beyond Job in taking for granted God's total withdrawal from the world, the unchanging

---

[23] See Dandamaev and Lukonin, *Culture and Social Institutions of Iran*, 113–16; Naveh and Greenfield, "Hebrew and Aramaic in the Persian Period"; W. D. Davies and L. Finkelstein, eds., *Cambridge History of Judaism* (Cambridge: Cambridge University Press, 1984), 1:115–16.

[24] See Tcherikover, *Hellenistic Civilization and the Jews*, 73–89.

[25] This paragraph summarizes my argument in "On the Autonomy of Judaea."

[26] For an account of the wisdom books emphasizing their "scribal" character (how many ancient books were not scribal?), see L. Grabbe, *Priests, Prophets, Diviners, Sages: A Socio-Historical Study of Religious Specialists in Ancient Israel* (Valley Forge, Pa.: Trinity Press International, 1995), pp. 154–62. For criticism of the "scribal" category, see C. Schams, *Jewish Scribes in the Second Temple Period* (Sheffield, U.K.: Sheffield Academic Press, 1998).

[27] On the bureaucratic character of Proverbs, see J. Blenkinsopp, *Sage, Priest, Prophet* (Louisville: Westminster John Knox, 1995), pp. 28–41.

character of nature, and the futility of all human endeavor, including righteous behavior and the seeking of wisdom.[28] If Ecclesiastes recommended pious behavior at all, it was only for pragmatic reasons: conformity with the laws of the Torah was likely to be less painful than nonconformity.

Another Jewish book written in the third century B.C.E., known as 1 Enoch, is preserved not in the Hebrew Bible but only in translation into Ge'ez (see the next chapter for more discussion). Fragmentary manuscripts of the work in the original Aramaic have been found among the Dead Sea Scrolls.[29] This book, like Ecclesiastes and Job, is much concerned with the presence of evil in the world, but its explanation may be the most radical of all. 1 Enoch 1–36 is based on the brief and enigmatic biblical story, which immediately precedes the story of Noah's flood, of the sons of God who descended to earth and took for themselves the daughters of man (Genesis 6:1–4). 1 Enoch follows Job in imagining that God's ways are mysterious, though in contrast to Job, Enoch seems to think that some humans actually have access to God's mysteries. Chief among these mysteries is that God, having created the universe, quickly relinquished control over it, allowing humanity to fall into the hands of wicked deities (the sons of God of Genesis). These deities were God's servant angels, who had successfully rebelled against their master. God responded by withdrawing to the remotest part of heaven but promised that one day he and the angels who had remained loyal to him, together with a selected part of humanity, would overthrow the forces of evil and restore God's sole rule over the universe.

1 Enoch thus responds to the claim of traditional Israelite wisdom that the one God is both good and powerful (a claim made problematic by the presence of evil in the world) not by reducing the reader to awed and uncomprehending silence, like Job, or by dismissing the claim with a resigned and world-weary shrug, like Ecclesiastes. 1 Enoch solves the problem of evil by infusing the biblical cosmology with myth, by restoring to his rewriting of Genesis 1–11 the divine drama and tension that the biblical author was so careful to omit. The result is a worldview that is closer to dualism than monotheism and certainly supposes that many divine beings aside from God can act independently and are extremely powerful. 1 Enoch is also deterministic: its human characters are more or less pawns to be manipulated by the divine protagonists.

The Wisdom of Ben Sira, composed in Hebrew soon after the Seleucid conquest of Palestine in 200 B.C.E., is unique among ancient Hebrew books

---

[28] For recent discussion, positing an Achaemenid dating, and a rather too specific social context, see C. L. Seow, *Ecclesiastes*, Anchor Bible 18C (New York: Doubleday, 1997), especially pp. 11–36; cf. E. J. Bickerman, *Four Strange Books of the Bible* (New York: Schocken, 1967), pp. 141–67.

[29] See J. T. Milik, *The Books of Enoch: Aramaic Fragments of Qumran Cave 4* (Oxford: Clarendon, 1976).

written after the biblical books of the Prophets in that the author reveals his identity and tells something of himself—a characteristic the book shares with Greek literature.[30] Ben Sira had been a government official and had taught wisdom to the well-to-do youth of Jerusalem. He was a great admirer of the high priest Simon and was perhaps a priest himself. His book constitutes a ringing reassertion of the views of the author of Proverbs and of the Deuteronomic historian. In what is very likely to be an intentional rejection of the radicalism of Job and Ecclesiastes, Ben Sira repeatedly emphasizes the traditional identification of wisdom and fear of the Lord. Like all wisdom writers, Ben Sira contemplated the meaning of nature. Although for Job nature proved God's inscrutability, and for Ecclesiastes it proved the fundamental amorality of the world, for Ben Sira, as for the Psalmist, nature demonstrates only God's majesty. Ben Sira doubts not for a moment that the righteous prosper and, in an apparent rejection of the views of 1 Enoch, eschews the pursuit of hidden wisdom. Ben Sira did not react against inner-Jewish developments alone. Though his own wisdom, like that of Proverbs, is heavily borrowed from Egyptian and perhaps even some Archaic Greek sources, his insistent identification of righteousness, or Torah, as the font of all wisdom has been understood as a reaction against a growing vogue for Greek literature among the wealthy youth of Jerusalem.[31]

For all the radicalism of these books, there is little in them that is demonstrably Greek. The Israelite wisdom tradition *is* transformed in these works but remains recognizably itself—the books are motivated by traditional Israelite-Jewish concerns and in every line betray their authors' familiarity with earlier Israelite literature. Apparently, Palestinian Jews were not yet composing books in the Greek language and in Greek genres (at least no such works have been preserved), as their coreligionists in Egypt had already begun to do (though in content such works were often far more conservative than the more formally traditional Palestinian books). Although it is overwhelmingly likely that there is some connection between the intellectual crisis of the priestly and scribal classes and the new conditions created by Macedonian rule, it is very difficult to say precisely what this connection may have been. Indeed, the new literature, except perhaps for Ben Sira, demonstrates that the search in Jewish sources for Greek influence and native resistance in the form of opposition to Hellenism is largely misguided. We should be conducting instead a more subtle search for cultural reorientation.[32]

---

[30] For an excellent account of Ben Sira, see J. J. Collins, *Jewish Wisdom in the Hellenistic Age* (Louisville: Westminster John Knox, 1997), pp. 42–111. P. McKechnie, "The Career of Joshua Ben Sira," *JThS* 51 (2000): 3–26, has now argued that the book was composed in Egypt.

[31] Hengel, *Judaism and Hellenism*, 1:138–53.

[32] This is an approach Martha Himmelfarb attributes (I think correctly) to Elias Bickerman; it has now been adopted by many Hellenistic historians. See M. Himmelfarb, "Elias Bickerman on Judaism and Hellenism," in *Jewish Past Revisited*, pp. 199–211.

The Maccabean Revolt (175–134 B.C.E.)

If Judaean society in the Second Temple period was characterized by a constant tension between internal and external integration—between separatism and assimilation—then the reformist high priests of the 170s and 160s tried to resolve that tension by downgrading the Jews' separatism, if not eliminating it. Thus, Jason may have tried to transform Judaea into a Greek city-plus-territory, following the example of the rulers of Tyre, Sidon, and Sardis, among others.[33] Like them, Jason may have intended to preserve elements of his native tradition and in fact seems not to have attempted to alter the traditional cult of the Jerusalem temple, or to have prevented the Jews from observing Jewish law. This limited retention of Judaism may explain why there was no discernible armed opposition to Jason's reforms. But it also made the reforms inherently unstable, since Judaism, unlike the traditional religions of the Phoenician cities, was exclusivistic: the God of Israel, unlike Melqart, tolerated the worship of no other gods.[34]

Elias Bickerman famously speculated that this fact (among others) underlay the more drastic reforms imposed by Antiochus IV in 168–167 B.C.E., in which observance of the laws of the Torah was prohibited and the Jerusalem temple was rededicated to Zeus Olympios-Baal Shamim—reforms inspired by Jewish leaders more radical than Jason. This hypothesis, like Tcherikover's suggestion, that the royal persecution was a reaction to a revolt centering on the temple that had broken out the previous year, rests on the failure of the sources to provide a satisfactory account of the events of about 169–167. Aporia seems the only solution to this disagreement, barring new discoveries.

[33] See Tcherikover, *Hellenistic Civilization*, pp. 152–74; E. Bickerman, *God of the Maccabees* (Leiden: Brill, 1979), pp. 38–42, arguing that Jason established not a Greek city but a Greek corporation within the still Jewish city of Jerusalem. (The sharply divergent accounts of Tcherikover and Bickerman remain fundamental, and my debt to them in the paragraphs that follow should be taken for granted). See also G. Le Rider, *Suse sous les Séleucides: Les trouvailles monétaires et l'histoire de la ville*, Mémoires de la mission archéologiques en Iran 38 (Paris: Paul Geuthner, 1965), pp. 410–11, supporting Tcherikover's argument on the basis of such common Seleucid coin legends as *Antiocheon ton en Ptolemaidi*, in which the reference is clearly to a Greek city, not a Greek corporation in a native city; F. Millar, "The Background to the Maccabean Revolution: Reflections on Martin Hengel's 'Judaism and Hellenism,' " *JJS* 29 (1978): 10; C. Habicht, 2. *Makkabäerbuch: Historische und legendarische Erzählungen*, JSHRZ 1.3 (Gütersloh: G. Mohn, 1976), pp. 216–17. Verse 19: "Jason . . . sent as *theoroi* (envoys to a religious festival) men who were Antiochenes from Jerusalem [or, as *theoroi* from Jerusalem men who were Antiochenes], carrying three hundred silver drachmas." This is, on the face of it, difficult to reconcile with Tcherikover's view. Perhaps the author of 2 Maccabees himself misunderstood what his source, Jason of Cyrene, had written. For the comparison with Sardis, Tyre, and Sidon, see S. Schwartz, "Hellenization of Jerusalem and Shechem."

[34] Some have argued that Jason's reforms were less extreme: I. Heinemann, "Wer veranlasste den Glaubenszwang der Makkabäerzeit?"*MGWJ* 82 (1938): 145–72—also a comprehensive critique of Bickerman; Gruen, *Heritage and Hellenism*, 28–31.

POLITICS AND SOCIETY 33

The debate about the character of the revolt, which gradually coalesced under the leadership of the Hasmonean family after the imposition of the royal reforms, may be more easily resolved. A close reading of the sources does not sustain Tcherikover's view of the Maccabean revolt as a mass popular uprising. 1–2 Maccabees consistently describe the rebel forces as being small, enjoying only fluctuating popular support, and having enemies even apart from the relatively small numbers of radical reformists. Indeed, the Hasmoneans' initial military opposition to the Seleucids ended in failure with the death of Judah and the routing of his army in 161; Jonathan emerged as a leading figure in Judaea only in 152, under circumstances that cannot be reconstructed due to the failure of 1 Maccabees to say anything at all about the previous eight years. The dynasty was established only after having risen through the ranks as Seleucid courtiers, and, once established, had to deal not only with royal treachery but with unceasing domestic opposition. In sum, Bickerman was surely right to argue that the revolt was the work of a committed minority, not the Jewish masses. Furthermore, it is reasonable to suppose, following Joseph Sievers, that it succeeded, ultimately, by patching together an inherently unstable coalition of different and competing interest groups.[35] It is, finally, clear that the eruption in 164 of a century-long war of succession in Antioch was essential for Hasmonean success—a point made already by Tacitus (*Histories* 5.8.3) and obvious from even a cursory reading of 1 Maccabees: the constant warfare in Syria generated for the pretenders an enduring need for vassals who disposed of manpower, apart from making them ever less competent to press their proprietary claims over their subjects. Hasmonean independence was always contingent on Seleucid weakness and came to an end when the Seleucid empire expired in 63 B.C.E.[36]

Why the Hasmoneans Fought

Scholars have occasionally doubted the Hasmoneans' claim to have been priests of the order of Yehoyarib—another unresolvable debate.[37] It seems certain, though, that the family resisted neither Jason's reforms nor Antiochus's, at first. In fact, whatever their ancestry, their ties to Jerusalem seem initially to have been weak; they were influential mainly in their native town, Modein, in the western part of the border zone between Judaea and Samaria.[38] They thus constituted another case of a peripheral but aggressive family exploiting local disorder to seize power at the center, like the Tobiads earlier and the

[35] *The Hasmoneans and Their Supporters from Mattathias to the Death of John Hyrcanus I* (Atlanta: Scholars, 1990).
[36] See Gruen, *Heritage and Hellenism*, 18–22.
[37] See M. Smith, *Studies in the Cult of Yahweh* (Leiden: Brill, 1996), 1:320–26.
[38] See J. Schwartz and J. Spanier, "On Mattathias and the Desert of Samaria," *RB* 98 (1991): 252–71.

Herodian family later.[39] This observation may help explain the Hasmoneans' rise *structurally*, but we must still wonder about the mechanisms of their rise, especially their shifting and varied self-presentation. In other words, we must wonder why the Hasmoneans claimed to be fighting.

Until the end of the persecution and the restoration of the traditional cult in the late autumn of 164, there seems little doubt that the Hasmoneans presented themselves primarily as champions of the Torah and the temple, that is, of Judaism. This claim must have lost some of its utility subsequently. Simon's public celebration of his reduction of several Seleucid fortresses, and his claim that a set of standard royal concessions amounted to Judaean independence, probably indicate that he posed not only as preserver of the Torah but as liberator of the Jews, though whether Judah and Jonathan had done the same is unknown.

In fact, the Hasmoneans' precise religious inclinations are difficult to recover. They certainly behaved in untraditional ways and introduced innovations in law and temple procedure. Their very assumption of the high priesthood and secular authority, without possession of either Zadokite (legitimate high priestly) or Davidic descent, was at the very least problematic. Their constant exposure to corpse impurity was a more or less blatant violation of biblical law. There were surely other changes, too, about which less is known. (One especially striking case, their decision to regard vast numbers of non-Judaean Palestinians as Jews, will be discussed presently.) Many Judaean traditionalists quickly developed reservations about the Hasmoneans, and some openly opposed the dynasty, while others, less willing to incur the dangers of open opposition, unhappily reached a modus vivendi. Nevertheless, there can be no doubt that the Hasmoneans were in general terms traditionalists. They may have engaged in a creative interpretation of the Torah that differed from what their Zadokite predecessors had done, but still they upheld the Torah's validity as the constitution of Judaea.[40] This may have been enough to satisfy most Judaeans.

Despite the Hasmoneans' essential traditionalism, in some respects they stood for integration as surely as Jason did, though on different terms. Every Judaean leader living under Persian, Macedonian, or Roman rule had to mediate between the integrative pressures of the eastern Mediterranean environment and the separatist pressure exerted by the Jews' gradually deepening devotion to the Torah. The Hasmoneans demonstrated that it was possible, at least under certain political conditions, for Judaea to participate politically and economically in an increasingly tightly knit eastern Mediterranean world

---

[39] This summarizes my argument in "A Note on the Social Type."

[40] Note Tacitus's comment, *Hist.* 5.8.3, that the Hasmoneans "*superstitionem* [i.e., *Iudaicam*] *fovebant*."

without surrendering that which made it distinctively Judaean. Embracing elements of Greek culture facilitated the Hasmoneans' integration with their neighbors.[41]

Although the author of 2 Maccabees believed Judah Maccabee was engaged in a battle against Hellenism,[42] he was surely wrong, if by Hellenism we mean the adoption of elements of Greek culture by non-Greeks. The evidence is unambiguous. Even Judah had counted the most culturally hellenized Judaeans among his partisans. One of these was an aristocratic priest named Eupolemus, whose father, John, had led the Judaean embassy to Antiochus III in 200 B.C.E. securing the king's benefactions to the temple and nation of the Judaeans. John could not have addressed the king if he did not have some grasp of Greek rhetoric, a skill necessarily shared by his son Eupolemus, who in 161 B.C.E. led Judah's embassy to the Roman senate, which permitted easterners to address it in Greek. Furthermore, in 159 B.C.E., Eupolemus published a *History of the Judaean Kings*, of which only brief excerpts survive. This book was composed in the Greek language according to the canons of Greek historiography. The excerpts concern David and Solomon, and one wonders whether the point of the book might not have been to argue that Judah and his brothers were worthy heirs of the ancients, notwithstanding their deficient ancestry. It is in any case surely significant that the earliest Palestinian Jewish book to have been written in Greek was published by a partisan of Judah Maccabee at the height of the Maccabean revolt and may well have been addressed to a mainly local Jewish audience.[43]

The Maccabean brothers necessarily acquired facility in the Greek language, if they did not have it from childhood, and must have learned, like the Tobiads before them, how to behave in the presence of royal officials (a point Gruen missed). In their political behavior in Judaea, too, they depended heavily on Greek norms, demonstrating that hellenizing pressures came not only from the eastern Mediterranean environment but from Judaea itself. The engraving of the resolution of the assembly convened by Simon in 140 B.C.E. on tablets, and their display in the temple, conform with practices that originated in the Greek cities of the later sixth and fifth centuries B.C.E. In the same period in Judaea, the public assemblies convened by Ezra and Nehemiah produced not inscribed resolutions but oral oaths. When Simon's son John Hyrcanus I wished to give material expression to Judaea's independence,

[41] This is not a novel point, but it has now been argued with novel force, and in exhaustive detail, by Gruen, *Heritage and Hellenism*, 1–40, with extensive bibliography.

[42] See S. Schwartz, "Israel and the Nations Roundabout," *JJS* 42 (1991): 23; Gruen's rejection of this point (*Heritage and Hellenism*, p. 5 n. 8) is based on a reductive reading of the book: cf. M. Himmelfarb, "Judaism and Hellenism in 2 Maccabees," *Poetics Today* 19 (1998): 19–40.

[43] On Eupolemus, see C. R. Holladay, *Fragments from Hellenistic Jewish Authors, vol. 1, Historians* (Chico, Calif.; Scholars, 1983), pp. 93–156.

he minted coins—another practice derived from the cities of Old Greece.[44] Like the much earlier coins of Persian Yehud, these coins were almost all of very small denomination and so intended only for local use. In the case both of Simon's resolution and of John's coinage, it is apparent that it was the Jews themselves, or some section of them, whose expectations about the behavior of their rulers were under strong Greek influence.

The Hasmoneans exemplified the proposition that adopting Greek culture could function in the Hellenistic world to preserve a native culture. They also resolved, for the time being, the tension between exclusivity and integration fairly strongly in favor of the former and were surely helped in doing so by the progressive decrepitude of their Seleucid overlords.[45]

Expansion

Hasmonean policies and actions changed the character of Palestinian Jewish society in more blatant ways, too. The most consequential set of events under Hasmonean rule was their territorial expansion, begun toward the end of the reign of John Hyrcanus I, and extended by his sons Aristobulus I and Alexander Yannai. In 130 B.C.E. the boundaries of Jewish Palestine contained only the district of Judaea, but by 100, the Hasmoneans ruled the entirety of the Palestinian hinterland, from the high hills of Upper Galilee in the north to the edge of the Negev Desert in the south, and from the Jordan River, or even slightly beyond it, in the east to the edge of the coastal plain in the west. The people who dwelled within these boundaries, who had apart from the Judaeans previously been a mixed multitude of Edomites, Samarian Israelites, and in Galilee probably a mixture or patchwork of Arabs, Greeks, and Syrian pagans (some of remotely Israelite descent) now became in some sense Jewish.[46]

Josephus, the main source for the expansion, provides only sketchy information about the causes and the progress of this momentous set of events. Ac-

---

[44] That John was the first Hasmonean to mint coins has been proved by the recent excavations on Mount Gerizim: see D. Barag, "Jewish Coins in Hellenistic and Roman Time," in T. Hackens et al., eds., A Survey of Numismatic Research, 1985–1990 1 (Brussels: International Society of Professional Numismatists, 1991), 1:106; this replaces the view of Y. Meshorer, Ancient Jewish Coinage (New York: Amphora, 1982), 1:35–47, that the Hasmonean coinage began with Alexander Yannai. Meshorer's collection of material, though, remains standard.

[45] For a different, though complementary, account of the Maccabean revolt as a pivotal event in the history of Jewish self-definition, see Cohen, Beginnings of Jewishness, 109–39.

[46] The recent excavations at Yodfat, Josephus's Jotapata, in Lower Galilee, suggest a shift from pagan to Jewish habitation at the end of the second century B.C.E. and also suggest that the shift was not peaceful: M. Aviam, "Yodfat: Uncovering a Jewish City in the Galilee from the Second Temple Period and the Time of the Great Revolt," Qadmoniot 118 (1999): 92–101.

cording to Josephus, when John was freed of Seleucid domination by the death of Antiochus VII in Parthia, in 129 B.C.E., he undertook a series of campaigns. Recent excavations suggest, however, that Josephus's chronology of these campaigns is incorrect. They all seem to have come toward the end of his reign.[47] John first conquered territory across the Jordan River that he apparently failed to retain, probably because the east bank of the Jordan was claimed also by the increasingly powerful Nabataean kingdom. He then marched against the Judaeans' northern neighbors, the Samaritans, conquered their main city, Shechem, and destroyed their temple on Mount Gerizim, just outside of Shechem. Evidently, the Samaritans, who were Israelites, were expected to switch their religious loyalties to the Jerusalem temple, and in return were regarded by the Judaean authorities as Jews.[48]

Also perhaps later than Josephus dates it was John's conquest of the Judaeans' southern neighbors, the Idumaeans, and their main cities, Marisa and Adora. These people were descendants of the biblical Edomites, who had settled in southern Judaea (from Beth-Zur just south of Bethlehem and south to the Negev Desert) when their traditional homeland south of the Dead Sea was infiltrated by Arab tribes starting in the sixth century B.C.E.[49] Like the Samaritans, the Edomites/Idumaeans had a centuries-long history of close relations with the Judaeans, the earliest stages of which are reflected in the biblical stories about the ambivalent relationship between Jacob, ancestor of the Israelites, and his twin brother Esau, ancestor of the Edomites. As the biblical stories suggest, the Idumaeans were not Israelites but shared many customs with them, including male circumcision (cf. Jeremiah 9:24ff.; Ezekiel 32:29).[50] John is said to have demanded that the Idumaeans adopt the customs and laws of the Judaeans or leave their country. Many of the Idumaeans acceded to John's demand and from that time on began to regard themselves and to be regarded as Jews. Since circumcision was evidently an inescapable requirement for entry of males into the community of Israel, the fact that the Idumaeans perhaps already practiced it obviously facilitated their

[47] See D. Barag, "New Evidence on the Foreign Policy of John Hyrcanus I," *INJ* 12 (1992–1993): 1–12.

[48] See S. Schwartz, "John Hyrcanus I's Destruction of the Gerizim Temple and Judaean-Samaritan Relations," *Jewish History* 7 (1993): 9–25.

[49] For a survey of the little known about the Idumaeans before their conversion, see A. Kasher, *Edom, Arabia, and Israel* (Jerusalem: Yad Ben Zvi, 1988), pp. 9–13; Kasher's extensive discussion of the conversion (48–76) is highly problematic.

[50] See M. Smith in S. Cohen, ed., *Studies in the Cult of Yahweh* (Leiden: Brill, 1996), 1:274–76. But R. Steiner, "Incomplete Circumcision in Egypt and Edom: Jeremiah 9.24–25 in the Light of Josephus and Jonckheere," *JBL* 118 (1999): 497–505, has suggested that the Edomites did not practice circumcision in quite the same way as the Jews and so may have required "recircumcision." On the Hasmonean conversions, see also S. Cohen, *The Beginnings of Jewishness*, 13–24, 104–39.

conversion. Nevertheless, some Idumaeans fled to Egypt, and some of those who stayed behind remained secretly devoted to their ancestral religion.[51]

John's final conquests, apparently in the last years of his reign, were of the Greek cities Samaria and Scythopolis–Beth Shean. These cities John treated differently from the territories of the Samaritans and Idumaeans. He "destroyed" them, which almost certainly means that he threw down their walls, deconstituted them, enslaved part of their inhabitants, reduced the remainder to subjection, and perhaps installed Jewish colonies. John's treatment of the Greek cities thus forms a sharp contrast to his treatment of the non-Greek ethnic territories, which he apparently recognized as partly autonomous components of his state, provided the inhabitants became Jewish.

John's son Aristobulus (reigned 104–103) seems to have conquered all or part of the district of Galilee, hitherto a pagan area with a small Jewish minority partly (?) ruled by an Arab tribe called the Ituraeans. Like the other non-Greek inhabitants of Palestine, the Galileans were forced/encouraged to convert to Judaism. The Ituraeans among them may, like many Arab tribes, have practiced circumcision in any case, but this is uncertain.

Alexander Yannai (reigned 103–76) greatly extended the Hasmonean conquests, concentrating on the Greek cities of coastal Palestine and the mainly Greek cities east of the Jordan River. It is likely that his normal treatment of these cities was to "destroy" them in much the same way that his father had destroyed Samaria and Scythopolis, but it is not impossible that he judaized some of the cities and simply reduced others to subjection and tribute; Josephus is remarkably vague. He was not invariably successful in his campaigns, especially in Transjordan, where he came up against the Nabataeans.[52]

Character, Causes, and Consequences of the Expansion

Several factors have suggested to many scholars that the conquests were not quite what they seem from Josephus's sketchy accounts, including the speed and ease with which the conquests of the Palestinian interior (but not the Greek cities) occurred, the fact that the newly conquered districts never rebelled, and the shakiness of the Hasmonean kingdom at the time of the conquests, under John Hyrcanus I and Aristobulus I. Some have argued that the conquests may be more profitably viewed as a series of alliances formed by the Hasmoneans with the leaders of the non-Greek districts surrounding Judaea aimed primarily against the local Greek cities. In return for adopting

---

[51] On the Idumaean refugees, see D. Thompson [Crawford], "The Idumaeans of Memphis and Ptolemaic Politeumata," *Atti del XVII congresso internazionale di papirologia* (Naples, 1984), pp. 1069–75; U. Rappaport, "Les Iduméens en Egypte," *Revue de Philologie* 43 (1969): 73–82.

[52] On the reigns of Aristobulus and Alexander, see Schürer-Vermes 1.216–28.

Judaism, probably more gradually and incompletely than Josephus implies, the Idumaeans and the rest received not only Hasmonean protection but also a chance to share in the spoils of further conquests.[53]

This is an attractive hypothesis that likely contains some truth, but it fails to explain why Josephus speaks so unambiguously of conquest. In all likelihood the expansion depended on a combination of coercion and persuasion, and gave the annexed nations a status that combined subjection and alliance—but was in any case distinct from the fate of the conquered Greek cities. The annexed districts seem to have retained a sort of limited autonomy under the rule of native governors who may have enjoyed the status of "friendship" with the Judaean king (cf. *Ant* 14.10). In a Hellenistic context, "friendship" is a semiformal state of reciprocal obligation, not necessarily between equals.[54] Thus, the Idumaeans became Jewish but remained simultaneously Idumaeans. The Judaism of the annexed districts must indeed have been gradually adopted and was perhaps not at first very deep. Surely it involved loyalty to the Jerusalem Temple and submission to the legal authority of the high priest. Its main initial effect, though, must have been to change the character of the public life in the annexed districts. John Hyrcanus I shut down not only the Israelite temple on Mount Gerizim but also the pagan temples of Idumaea. Perhaps town markets were closed on the Sabbath. But otherwise, life, even religious life, in the annexed districts at first went on pretty much as before. Even if the Hasmoneans had wished to eradicate all traces of the pre-Jewish religions of the districts, they could not have done so; the state simply had no way to police the day-to-day activities of hundreds of thousands of people. Probably the judaization of the districts—which was in the long term successful in that Idumaea and Galilee remained Jewish even after the end of Hasmonean rule and were thoroughly incorporated in the Jewish nation—was helped by the profound cultural and religious ties that existed in any case among the non-Greek peoples of Palestine. Still, there was resistance. The Idumaeans who fled to Egypt in the late second century B.C.E. zealously cultivated there, over the course of centuries, the worship of their ancestral god Qos; and in the late first century B.C.E. an Idumaean associate of King Herod tried to restore the worship of Qos in his native district (*Ant* 15.253–66). It may, furthermore, be no coincidence that Christianity, which was from the start ambivalent about the central institutions of Judaism, originated in Galilee, another of the annexed districts.

---

[53] See M. Smith, *Studies in the Cult of Yahweh*, 1:269–83, emphasizing the military alliance; Kasher, *Edom, Arabia, and Israel*, pp. 48–76, follows the old hypothesis of U. Rappaport in regarding the conversions as entirely voluntary; Cohen, *Beginnings of Jewishness*, pp. 109–39, presents a more complex and convincing account.

[54] See G. Herman, note 6, above.

Causes

It is unclear why the Hasmoneans undertook their expansion. An obvious answer should not be overlooked—they expanded because they could. Historically most states have viewed acquisition of territory and people with favor, and there is no reason for the Hasmoneans not to have done the same. Though they were weak, they may still have been stronger than poorly centralized districts like Idumaea and Galilee and surely had a more experienced army. Conquest tended to generate conquest because it was sensible to pacify conquered peoples by giving them a share in future plunder—one of the chief sources of new wealth in the premodern state.[55] As to the Hasmoneans' policy of judaizing the conquered nations, we have already seen that the notion that outsiders could join the Jewish nation was several centuries old by the time John Hyrcanus pushed it to its logical limits. The first description we have of a more or less formal ritual of conversion to Judaism appears in a work of fiction, the apocryphal book of Judith, probably written around the time of the Maccabean revolt; the second appears in 2 Maccabees, where, in one of the book's more absurd scenes, Antiochus IV, on his deathbed, promises to convert to Judaism, having recognized the error of his ways! Although there was no precedent for mass conversion, it was at least based on firmly established conceptual ground, and the idea of conversion seems to have exerted special fascination in circles close to the Hasmoneans.[56] When they imposed Judaism on their subjects, the Hasmoneans may have been motivated by the biblical idea that the Land of Israel should be "unpolluted" by idolatry. Or they may have been inspired by the example of their allies and friends the Romans, who had for centuries been successfully expanding their territory by combining exceptionally violent military activity with judicious grants of Roman citizenship to some of the people they conquered.[57]

Consequences

Obviously, the Hasmonean expansion exerted a profound effect on every aspect of Jewish and eastern Mediterranean history. The finances of the Jerusalem temple and the Judaean priesthood felt the impact of the vast expansion of their tax base, and the entire Judaean economy was unsettled by the influx

[55] In other words, I am suggesting that Hasmonean imperialism was a small-scale version of Roman imperialism: see W. V. Harris, *War and Imperialism in Republican Rome, 327–70 B.C.* (Oxford: Clarendon, 1979).

[56] See S. Cohen, *Beginnings of Jewishness*, 109–74

[57] So M. Smith, "Rome and the Maccabean Conversions," in E. Bammel et al., eds., *Donum Gentilicium: New Testament Studies in Honour of David Daube* (Oxford: Clarendon, 1978), pp. 1–7.

of so much new wealth into the district.[58] It is therefore especially frustrating that our main ancient source, Josephus, has so little to say about the expansion and its consequences. In part this was because Josephus, who lived in the wake of the expansion, was blind to its effect on Palestinian Jewish life and was hostile to and contemptuous of the non-Judaean Jews. It is nevertheless clear that as a result of the conquests Palestinian Jewish society became exponentially more complex, much richer, and much more turbulent than it had ever been. Otherwise, the effects of the expansion may be summarized in terms of four categories: demography, economy, politics, and religion.

Demography. The size of the population of ancient Palestine cannot be determined, but 500,000 is a plausible figure for the population of the Palestinian interior.[59] This would imply a population of 100,000–200,000 for the district of Judaea, and so approximately a two- to fivefold increase in the Jewish population of Palestine in the wake of the expansion, bearing in mind, though, that an unknown proportion of the inhabitants of the annexed districts fled.

Economy. The Hasmonean state was enriched by its constant warfare and plunder, especially of the wealthy Greek cities of the coast and the desert fringe, under Alexander Yannai. Much of this wealth went, first, into the pockets of the kings, second, into the temple treasury, and, third, to the priests, who were entitled to receive taxes in kind from all Israelites living in the land of Israel. But the general population profited, too, for it was they, especially perhaps the residents of the annexed districts, who formed the rank and file of the Hasmonean armies and kept part of what they plundered. Although we would like to have numbers, the ancient sources, as always, provide none. Perhaps of some limited heuristic value is Josephus's statement that when the Roman general Crassus plundered the Temple in 54 B.C.E., only nine years after Pompey and at the height of the Judaean civil war, he found 2,000 talents of silver, a gold bar weighing 300 mnai (a mna is equivalent to at least one Roman pound), and 8,000 talents of gold plate—which should be worth the astonishing sum of 96,000 silver talents (*Ant* 14.105–6). But these figures may be unsalvageable. By contrast, Herod's annual tax income was probably around 1,000 silver talents.[60]

Politics. Little is known for certain about how the Hasmoneans administered their state, but it does seem likely that they ruled Judaea through the established national institutions, and the annexed districts through "friendly"

---

[58] See the final section of the next chapter.

[59] On the size of the population, see introduction, note 13.

[60] The commentators try to salvage Josephus's figures by supposing that the gold plate was worth 8,000 silver talents. This is more plausible, but it is not what Josephus says. On Herod's tax revenues, see E. Gabba, "The Finances of King Herod," in A. Kasher, U. Rappaport, and G. Fuks, eds. *Greece and Rome in Eretz Israel: Collected Essays* (Jerusalem: Yad Ben Zvi, 1990), pp. 160–68, especially 161.

native governors.[61] The expansion strengthened the representatives of the Ju-daean institutions—the priests and scholars of the Torah—in some respects, for they now had at least some limited sort of jurisdiction over a vastly in-creased population. But the expansion weakened them in other ways, for they now had to compete for royal favor with non-Judaean generals and friends of the kings. This process was confirmed and accelerated by the lengthy Hasmo-nean civil war (67–37 B.C.E.), which tended to favor the advancement of the non-Judaean generals and friends and to marginalize the Judaean priests and Torah experts.

Religion. The mass conversions ought to have been controversial among Judaeans, yet there is surprisingly little evidence that they were. We know that some Judaeans were contemptuous of the annexed nations, but there is no indication that they were not regarded as Jews. What their Judaism consisted of is a different question, which has already been briefly discussed, and they may have introduced some of their own practices into standard Judaism. For example, archaeologists have traced the practice of burial in *kokhim*–niches hewn out of the walls of caves—from Marisa, the main city of Idumaea, in the third and second centuries B.C.E., to Judaea, in the first century B.C.E., to all of Jewish Palestine, in the first century C.E. and following.[62]

The Civil War (67–37 B.C.E.)

Hyrcanus II, the elder son of Alexander Yannai and Salome Alexandra (reigned 76–67), had served as high priest during his mother's reign and was named heir to the kingdom. When she died, however, he was immediately attacked and defeated by his brother Aristobulus II. Aristobulus assumed the high priesthood and royal throne and allowed his brother to live in retirement. However, Hyrcanus had a friend, an Idumaean called Antipater, whose father had been a friend of Alexander Yannai and had governed Idumaea on the king's behalf. He had also prudently maintained ties of friendship or marriage in the Nabataean royal court.[63] Antipater convinced Hyrcanus to go to war against Aristobulus and promised him the help of the Nabataean king Aretas. For his part, Aristobulus seems to have enjoyed the support of some Ituraean dynasts who ruled the land just north of the Hasmonean kingdom in what is

[61] See S. Schwartz, "King Herod, Friend of the Jews," in J. Schwartz, Z. Amar and I. Ziffer, eds, Jerusalem and Eretz Israel: Arie Kindler Volume (Tel Aviv: Rennert Center and Eretz Israel Museum, 2000) pp. 67–76.

[62] See E. Oren and U. Rappaport, "The Necropolis of Maresha-Beth Guvrin," *IEJ* 34 (1984): 149–51.

[63] On the importance of friendship in late Hasmonean and Herodian politics, see S. Schwartz, "King Herod, Friend of the Jews," B. Shaw, "Tyrants, Bandits, and Kings: Personal Power in Josephus," *JJS* 44 (1993): 184–89.

now Lebanon, and also a group of otherwise unidentified generals. One would have expected Hyrcanus to have inherited his mother's patronage of the Pharisees, and Aristobulus therefore to have taken up his father's Sadducees, yet these religious groups play next to no role in Josephus's accounts of the civil war. The princes needed the support of generals and of others who could deliver military manpower, not of Torah scholars.

In 66 B.C.E., the Roman general Gnaeus Pompeius Magnus (Pompey) invaded Asia Minor, defeated Mithridates VI, the Asian king who had expelled the Romans from the district, and accepted the surrender of his son-in-law, the Armenian king Tigranes. In 65, a Roman detachment arrived in Syria, and the warring brothers at once began to compete for the favor of the new regional superpower. (Meanwhile, a contingent of Judaean aristocrats tried to convince the Romans to remove the Hasmoneans altogether.) Pompey eventually backed Hyrcanus and in 63 B.C.E. marched into Jerusalem and captured Aristobulus. He then named Hyrcanus high priest (but not king), removed the Greek cities conquered by Alexander Yannai from Jewish rule, and restored their Greek constitutions.

Scholars often treat the arrival of the Romans in Palestine in 63 B.C.E. as a watershed in Jewish history. But little changed for the first 140 years of Roman rule. The Romans were more interventionist than their Hellenistic predecessors but initially preferred to rule through local agents. The Romans made many changes small and large in the administrative organization of Jewish Palestine and meddled tirelessly in the affairs of the Jewish ruling classes, but they allowed the Jews to remain a more or less autonomous nation centered on the Jerusalem temple and governed by the laws of the Torah. This changed only in the later first century C.E.

In any case, the short-term effect of the Roman conquest was to intensify the Jewish civil war. The Roman Republic itself collapsed into factional warfare, which among other things allowed each of the Jewish parties to have the support of one of the competing Roman senatorial factions. On the whole, the Hyrcanian party enjoyed the upper hand, largely because of the talent of Hyrcanus's leading partisan, Antipater, at the all-important skill of making friends with whichever Roman senatorial warlord was more powerful at the moment. However, in 40, the Parthians took advantage of the chaos in the Roman world by attacking and conquering Syria and Palestine. Antipater's sons Herod and Phasael tried but failed to win the Parthians' favor. The Parthians named Antigonus, son of Aristobulus, king and dragged Hyrcanus off to Mesopotamia, after his nephew had sliced off his ear, thereby rendering him unfit to serve as high priest ever again. Phasael meanwhile committed suicide in the course of battle and Herod escaped to Rome.

There, the senate declared Herod king, without specifying a constituency or a territory, and assigned him the task of reconquering Palestine from the Parthians. Herod gradually conquered the Palestinian hinterland—the Jewish districts of Galilee, Samaria, Judaea, and his native Idumaea—with the help of a detachment of Roman troops and Jewish troops that he succeeded in raising himself. By unspoken agreement with his overlords, he left the Greek cities of the coast and the Transjordan in peace. Jerusalem was the last place to fall to Herod, and when it did, in 37 B.C.E., Herod's Jewish troops committed a great slaughter of their coreligionists besieged in the city, which Herod restrained only with difficulty. This event, at first glance surprising, is not difficult to understand if we assume that the troops were non-Judaean Jews, like Herod himself. Among such people, resentment against the Judaeans may never have been far from the surface. King Antigonus was captured and sent off to Antony for execution, and Herod now reigned as king of the Jews.

Herod (reigned, 37–4 B.C.E.)

Herod was a product of the age of the civil wars, both Hasmonean and Roman, an age that offered great opportunities to the ruthlessly ambitious. From his grandfather and father he inherited a complex of friendships with Hasmoneans, Nabataean kings and courtiers, and important Roman personages. He exploited this inheritance brilliantly and extended it when, as a young commander and an administrator in Galilee, he earned the friendship of various local Jewish and pagan grandees. He deepened and broadened his relations with leading Romans, most importantly in the later 40s with Marc Antony, leader of the Caesarian faction for a time after the dictator's assassination in 44 B.C.E. Thanks to his friendship with Antony, when the Parthians conquered Palestine in 40 B.C.E., the Roman senate granted Herod, and not a Hasmonean, the royal title and the job of providing local military support to the Roman legions in their attempt to reconquer southern Syria.[64]

Herod himself helped conquer Jewish Palestine and was later given extensive gifts of non-Jewish territory—the coastal Greek cities, the Golan Heights, and other rural territories in southern Syria—by Antony and subsequently the emperor Augustus. But he was considered and considered himself primarily king of the Jews; he seems to have administered the pagan territories on behalf of the emperor and senate and to have received a portion of the revenues from them.[65] But Herod was not of priestly descent, and so he could not serve

[64] On the importance of "friendship" in Herod's early career, see S. Schwartz, "King Herod, Friend of the Jews," and Shaw, "Tyrants, Bandits, and Kings," 184–89.

[65] See Josephus, Ant 14.9, 15.373, 15.409, 16.291, 16.311; Nicolaus of Damascus apud Ant 14.9; Cassius Dio 49.22.6; Macrobius, Saturnalia 2.4.11; Persius, Saturae 5.180; Tacitus, Historiae 5.9.1–2; Strabo, Geographica 16.2.46; Eusebius, Historia Ecclesiastica 1.7.11–12; Aelian, De Natura Animalium 6.17; H. Cotton and J. Geiger, Masada II: The Yigael Yadin Excavations 1963–5, Final Reports: The Greek and Latin Documents (Jerusalem: IES, 1989), nos. 804–16, with the comments on pp. 147–48. In these documents, Herod is called rex Herodes iudaicus.

simultaneously as king and high priest. He was furthermore not a Judaean but a judaized Idumaean, and many of his domestic policies reflected the concerns of the non-Judaean Jews and their sometimes ambivalent relations to the central Judaean institutions as they had been administered by the Hasmoneans.[66] One of the main tendencies of his reforms seems to have been, in fact, to turn *Judaean* institutions into *Jewish* ones by enhancing their attractiveness to non-Judaean Palestinian Jews and Jews of the Diaspora.

Herod's Reforms

Given his inability to serve as high priest, Herod had to reform the high priesthood. His reforms had several interesting characteristics. Under Herod, and after his time until the destruction of the temple in 70 C.E., the high priesthood was no longer held for life and passed from father to son. Rather, the incumbents held the position for brief terms of irregular length, and the king retained exclusive right of appointment. Clearly Herod was interested in keeping tight control over a position that could easily turn into a focus of political opposition.[67] After Herod's death the high priesthood became again de facto dynastic, since Herod's descendants and Roman successors preferred to appoint to the post descendants of Herod's high priests. But the only distinctive characteristic that Herod's appointees shared, as far as we can tell, is that five of the seven who served in the course of the thirty-three years of Herod's reign were not Judaean: one was brought from Babylonia, one resided in Galilee, and several came from Egypt. Of the Judaeans, one was Herod's young brother-in-law, the Hasmonean prince Aristobulus (sometimes assigned the dynastic number "III"), of whom the king was profoundly jealous. He drowned under suspicious circumstances, to say the least, after a very brief term of office (*Ant* 15.50–56).

Herod failed to assign an important role to the old religious organizations of the Pharisees and Sadducees. We have already seen that after the death of Salome Alexandra in 67 B.C.E., the Pharisees and Sedducees, which had played an important administrative role previously, were pushed to the margins by the conditions prevailing in the civil wars. Herod ended the civil war but did not restore the sects. The fact that they had been elite *Judaean* organizations may explain Herod's interest in depriving them of any significant role in his state. From now on they would be small organizations competing for

---

[66] See S. Cohen, *Beginnings of Jewishness*, 13–24.

[67] See Schürer-Vermes, 2.227–36; P. Richardson, *Herod: King of the Jews and Friend of the Romans* (Columbia: University of South Carolina Press, 1996), pp. 240–47; M. Stern, "The Politics of Herod and Jewish Society towards the End of the Second Commonwealth," *Tarbiz* 35 (1966): 235–53.

the patronage of the royal women and high priests and vying with each other for a voice in temple affairs.[68]

Herod exploited his connections at Rome on behalf of the Jews of the Diaspora. These Jewish communities were permitted by Roman law and convention to conduct their lives according to Jewish law, even when it came into conflict with the laws of the cities in which the Jews resided, for example, Jews could not be forced to come to court on the Sabbath. However, local authorities did not always recognize the Jews' rights, and Herod made a practice of intervening with imperial officials on behalf of these Jewish communities. His generous gifts to Greek cities and institutions such as the Olympic games may have been intended primarily to secure Greek cities' goodwill from their Jewish residents.[69] Herod's recruitment of high priests from the Diaspora also indicates his desire to cultivate the support of the Diaspora communities.

Josephus was perhaps right to think that Herod undertook his public construction projects for self-aggrandizement, but this was surely not his only motivation. Herod built and refurbished fortresses across the country, restored and fortified cities, and built a massive shrine at the cave of the Machpelah in the old Idumaean town of Hebron. The Jews regarded this site as the tomb of the biblical patriarchs and matriarchs, and the Idumaeans, also descendants of Abraham and Sarah and Isaac and Rebecca, may have done the same, even before they became Jewish. But Herod's building projects had twin, closely related, centerpieces. He completely rebuilt a tiny, declining old Greco-Phoenician city called Strato's Tower as a grand port city and named it Caesarea in commemoration of Herod's friendship with Augustus Caesar. Archaeologists discovered in the 1980s and 1990s that Caesarea's harbor, one of the largest in the eastern Mediterranean, was built according to the most up-to-date principles of Roman engineering. The city at once became the leading port of the southern part of the east coast of the Mediterranean, easily crowding out such competitors as Gaza, Ascalon, and Joppa, as well as the main point of entry for the burgeoning Jewish pilgrim traffic from the Diaspora.[70]

The other twin star of Herod's construction was Jerusalem, which was rebuilt from top to bottom. Although the amount of money flowing into the temple treasury had increased tremendously under the Hasmoneans, they

---

[68] For a full discussion of this issue, see L. Levine, "On the Political Involvement of the Pharisees under Herod and the Procurators," *Cathedra* 8 (1978): 12–28; also A. Saldarini, *Pharisees, Scribes, and Sadducees in Palestinian Jewish Society: A Sociological Approach* (Wilmington, Del.: Michael Glazier, 1988), pp. 95–106. For a denial of the significance of the phenomenon, see G. Stemberger, *Jewish Contemporaries of Jesus: Pharisees, Sadducees, and Essenes* (Minneapolis: Fortress, 1995), pp. 117–19.

[69] On Herod's benefactions, see Richardson, *Herod*, 174–96.

[70] See Richardson, ibid., and in general, A. Raban and K. Holum, *Caesarea Maritima: A Retrospective after Two Millennia* (Leiden: Brill, 1996).

undertook almost no public construction in the city. The residential quarters grew, and so the city walls were extended and a palace was built. But the temple remained the tiny structure built by Zerubbabel in the late sixth century, incapable of containing a vastly increased Jewish population. Herod rebuilt all the public areas of the city on a much grander scale than ever before, but the main feature of his construction was the new temple, now one of the largest structures in the Roman Empire, with a courtyard that could accommodate vast numbers of pilgrims. It was Herod's Jerusalem that the Roman writer Pliny the Elder could describe as "by far the most famous city of the East," and that a Talmudic storyteller could call the recipient of nine of the ten measures of beauty that God allotted to the world.[71]

Herod's construction had several important effects. It created many thousands of jobs and would continue to do so for several decades after Herod's death. The temple was not completed until 64 C.E., only six years before its destruction, and its completion is said by Josephus to have put 18,000 laborers out of work (*Ant* 20.219–22). Herod's construction projects may thus be seen as the functional equivalent of the Hasmoneans' conquests, now ruled out by the Roman peace, which had also provided incomes for thousands of Jews.

The construction also changed the character of Jerusalem and of Jewish Palestine as a whole. Jerusalem was no longer a remote hill country town, of interest mainly to Judaean peasants and to the occasional foreign general looking to steal some silver from the treasury of its temple. It was now the metropolis of all the world's Jews, whether they were Judaean or hailed from the annexed districts of Palestine or the Roman or Parthian Diaspora. Jerusalem had perhaps long been the symbolic or sentimental Jewish center, but now it was so in reality, as well. It is only in Herod's reign and later that we hear of throngs of Jews from all over the world gathered in the city for the pilgrimage festivals of Passover, Shavuot (the Feast of Weeks), or Sukkot (the Feast of Booths), and of the disturbances that sometimes broke out as a result.[72]

In sum, Herod's policies built on those of the Hasmoneans and turned Jewish Palestine into a single state, a state furthermore that was closely tied to the Jewish communities of the Diaspora. This achievement, which was of enduring significance, by no means contradicts the probable baseness of his motivations or the brutality of his character, but surely it is as deserving of attention as his sordid family life, which is the main concern of the ancient sources but will not detain us here.

[71] See N. Avigad et al. "Jerusalem," *NEAEHL*, 2.717–57; Richardson, *Herod*, 174–215; M. Goodman, *The Ruling Class of Judaea: The Origins of the Jewish Revolt against Rome* (Cambridge: Cambridge University Press, 1987), pp. 51–75.

[72] See L. Levine, "Josephus' Description of the Jerusalem Temple: War, Antiquities, and Other Sources," in F. Parente and J. Sievers, eds., *Josephus and the History of the Greco-Roman Period: Essays in Memory of Morton Smith* (Leiden: Brill, 1994), pp. 242–44; S. Weitzman, "From Feasts into Mourning: The Violence of Early Jewish Festivals," *Journal of Religion* 79 (1999): 545–65.

Herod died in 4 B.C.E., and a series of small-scale uprisings at once broke out. Augustus decided to divide Herod's Jewish state into several pieces and distribute them among Herod's lesser sons, the only ones who survived. Archelaus was assigned Samaria, Judaea, and Idumaea, and Herod Antipas, Galilee. The pagan territories of southern Syria were assigned to Herod Philip. Archelaus was vicious and incompetent. In 6 C.E., the leading Jews and Samaritans asked Augustus to remove him, and he did so. Antipas ruled peacefully for forty-two years, a successful and competent ruler, notwithstanding his reputation among the early Christians, and Philip ruled until 34 C.E. Though Herod's Jewish state did not survive his death as a political unit, as a religious, cultural, and social entity it fell only in 70 C.E.

TWO

RELIGION AND SOCIETY BEFORE 70 c.e.

I BEGIN MY ACCOUNT of Palestinian Jewish society and the impact of foreign rule on its integration by observing how the three pillars of ancient Judaism—the one God, the one Torah, and the one Temple—cohere in a single neat, ideological system. I will then disturb this coherence, first, by observing the messiness, diversity, and unpredictability of the *effects* of this system in Jewish Palestinian society in the first century and, second, by noting the existence of a subsidiary ideological system—basically, a mildly dualistic mythological narrative—that implicitly contradicted the main one. I will then try to determine what its social effects might have been. Finally, I will briefly discuss one of the outstanding characteristics of first-century Judaism, sectarianism, and argue that the main sects were in fact an integral part of the Torah-centered Judaean mainstream elite. Here I am taking issue with the common characterization of ancient Judaism as radically diverse, a characterization for which the Pharisees, Sadducees, and Essenes are the main evidence.[1] Though we know of more radical Jewish organizations in the first century—the Christians are the best-known example—the three main sects are evidence not simply of Judaism's diversity but also of the power of its ideological mainstream. For their part, the Christians illustrate the proposition that there were limits to acceptable diversity in ancient Judaism, for those who remained Jewish did so by affirming their adherence to the Torah and at least the idea of a temple, while the rest in short order ceased to regard themselves as Jews.

God, Temple, and Torah in First-Century Palestine

The ideological complex I mentioned above, God-Temple-Torah, was symbolically central in the Palestinian Judaism of the first century.[2] If many or most Palestinian Jews had been asked what it was that made them what they were (and it is worth remembering that few of them were ever asked such a

---

[1] For an account that makes some points similar to mine, see J. D. G. Dunn, "Judaism in the Land of Israel in the First Century," in J. Neusner, ed., *Judaism in Late Antiquity, Part 2: Historical Syntheses* (Leiden: Brill, 1995), pp. 229–61.

[2] On ideology and symbol, see C. Geertz, "Religion as a Cultural System," and "Ideology as a Cultural System," *The Interpretation of Cultures* (New York: Basic, 1973), pp. 87–125, 193–233.

question), they would likely have answered that it was the worship of their one God, in the one Temple of Jerusalem, in accordance with the laws of his Torah; at any rate, they would have mentioned some part of this ideological complex in their answers. ("We Jews don't worship the pagan gods . . . we rest every seventh day . . . we abstain from certain foods," etc.) In ritual, and in public assemblies, images associated with the Temple or Torah, or rhetorical evocations of them, or the actual Torah scroll, might function synecdochically to evoke Judaism as a whole, hence, for example, the (Temple-associated) menorah so often carved on ancient (especially post-70) C.E. Jewish tombstones, the ceremonial display of a Torah scroll before battle ascribed to Judah Maccabee, and so on.[3]

Some readers may find it odd that this point requires argumentation, while others may be inclined to dismiss my claim out of hand: how can the centrality of God-Temple-Torah in Jewish self-definition be proved? What about the Judaean settlements at Elephantine or, more chronologically relevant, at Leontopolis in Egypt?[4] Or the worshipers of the Most High God settled in the Cimmerian Bosporus? Did these Jews, too, if that is what they were, live in symbolic worlds whose central components were the Temple and the Torah?

In response to the first set of objections, I contend that the centrality of Temple and Torah in ancient Jewish self-definition requires argumentation because it is not a priori an eternal truth of Jewish identity, uncontingent on changing social and political conditions. Rather, it was the result of a long

---

[3] See 1 Maccabean 3:46–48; this much is clear despite the obscurity of v. 48. The menorah became a commonplace iconographic marker of Judaism only in the third century C.E. and following; it was only then that Jews began to develop a widely used and distinctively Jewish pictorial language. This issue is discussed in detail in the following chapters; and see R. Hachlili, *Ancient Jewish Art and Archaeology* (Leiden: Brill, 1988). However, the menorah may have been used sporadically earlier to evoke the temple, as for example on the coins of Mattathias Antigonus (reigned 40–37), and on some clay lamps produced in Judaea soon after the Destruction; see most recently D. Barag, "A Coin of Mattathias Antigonos and the Shape of the Shewbread," *Qadmoniot* 105–106 (1994): 43–44 (Hebrew); and for a fuller treatment of the menorah as symbol, see Barag, "Hamenorah kesemel meshihi bitequfah haromit hame'uheret ubitequfah habizantit," *Proceedings of the Ninth World Congress of Jewish Studies*, B.I. (Jerusalem: World Union of Jewish Studies 1986) 59–62.

[4] In the case of Leontopolis, we think we know from literary sources that the Jewish colony there was centered on a temple modeled on that of Jerusalem and staffed by Zadokite (i.e., legitimate) priests, but the gravestones from Tell el Yahudieh are marked with no Jewish symbols, and the epitaphs contain no Jewish content whatever. Indeed, the religious content of the longer epitaphs is derived entirely from the commonplace language of the Hellenistic and Greco-Roman funerary epigram; only the names of the deceased and the location of the graves mark them as Jewish. On the temple, see Gideon Bohak, *Joseph and Aseneth and the Jewish Temple in Heliopolis* (Atlanta: Scholars, 1996); on the graves, W. Horbury and D. Noy, *Jewish Inscriptions of Graeco-Roman Egypt* (Cambridge: Cambridge University Press, 1992), nos. 29–105. The explanation of this disjunction may be that before the third or fourth centuries C.E., it rarely seems to have crossed anyone's mind that graves need to be marked as Jewish; see below.

and obscure series of historical processes, which probably reached a peak in Judaea only after the Maccabean revolt.[5]

Another reason the ideological centrality of God-Temple-Torah cannot be taken for granted is that by the turn of the era Jewish Palestine consisted of much more than the little district of Judaea. As we have seen, in the late second century B.C.E., the Hasmonean rulers of Judaea annexed the non-Judaean districts of Palestine—Idumaea, Samaria, Galilee, and Peraea. Some inhabitants of Samaria had long seen themselves as Israelites, but the inhabitants of the other districts were by and large pagan. Having passed under Judaean rule, all now became in some sense Jewish (see above). Can we assume that the Judaism of Idumaea, Galilee, and Peraea (Samaria presents a special set of problems) was roughly the same as that of Judaea?[6]

That the judaization of the outlying parts of Palestine took place after the Maccabean revolt implies that the Judaism introduced in these districts was unambiguously Temple and Torah centered. But, as I have suggested, there was necessarily an element of duress, since we must suppose that some inhabitants of the annexed districts were unwilling to become Jewish or to leave their homes—the two alternatives reportedly offered them by the Hasmoneans. Thus there must have persisted alongside public Judaism a subterranean pre-Jewish religious tradition. This would explain the famous case of Herod's kinsman Costobar (Ant 15.253–58) who preserved, three generations after the judaization of Idumaea, devotion to the ancestral god, Qos. It may also explain an Aramaic incantation text, possibly of the early first century B.C.E., found near Beer Sheva, in Idumaea, which invokes such deities as Ta', Tinshar, Hargol, and Shebatbata, daughters of El, and A'asas son of Shamash.[7] In the Idumaean case, the persistence of elements of the traditional religion in the neighboring district of Nabataea and in the Idumaean diaspora in Egypt must have facilitated the preservation of native traditions in Idumaea proper.[8] In the course of time, though, these traditions themselves are likely to have lost

---

[5] See S. J. D. Cohen, "Religion, Ethnicity, and 'Hellenism' in the Emergence of Jewish Identity in Maccabean Palestine," in P. Bilde et al., Religion and Religious Practice in the Seleucid Kingdom (Aarhus: Aarhus University Press, 1990), pp. 204–23, who argues that the Antiochan persecution and the Maccabean revolt greatly enhanced the status of the Torah as a component of Jewish self-definition.

[6] See S. Schwartz, "John Hyrcanus I's Destruction."

[7] See J. Naveh, "A Nabatean Incantation Text," IEJ 29 (1979): 111–19. Naveh calls it Nabatean because of some features of the script, while acknowledging that it is likely to have been written by an Idumaean (112). The interpretation and dating of the text are, however, tentative.

[8] For the worship of Qos in Nabataea, see most recently R. Wenning, Die Nabatäer—Denkmäler und Geschichte (Göttingen: Vandenhoeck-Ruprecht, 1987), pp. 77–81 (with some updating in D. Graf's helpful review, Critical Review of Books in Religion 3 [1990]: 98–101), and in most detail, J. Bartlett, "From Edomites to Nabataeans: A Study in Continuity," PEQ 111 (1979): 53–66. On the Edomite diaspora in Egypt, see especially U. Rappaport, "Les Iduméens en Egypte"; and Thompson [Crawford], "Idumaeans of Memphis."

their subversive character and become a naturalized part of the local version of Judaism—a body of practice roughly comparable to what in the Middle Ages would have been called *minhag*.[9] The situation in the other districts may have been similar: I have argued elsewhere, for instance, that in the first century the temple exerted a far weaker economic influence in Galilee than in Judaea.[10] This implies that Galileans were less willing than Judaeans to hand over their surplus production to the temple and its staff, which suggests that devotion to the temple was less widespread and deep there. But not nonexistent: Josephus reports that Jerusalem priests could apparently expect a priestly gift-gathering expedition to Galilee to yield a profit. And when the Roman legions invaded Palestine in 67 c.e., several thousand Galileans and Idumaeans marched on Jerusalem and endeavored to seize control of the temple.

Therefore, though we can be fairly certain that by the first century c.e. most inhabitants of the non-Judaean districts of the Palestinian hinterland had by and large internalized some version of the ideology that was centrally constitutive of Judaism, we must not assume that their Judaism was indistinguishable from that of the Judaeans.

Temple and Torah in Jewish Society

In arguing for the symbolic centrality of Temple and Torah, I begin with an account of their actual role in Judaean and, later, Palestinian Jewish society. Almost every imperial and native ruler of Palestine from Darius I in 515 b.c.e. (or, at any rate, from sometime in the Achaemenid period, if one is reluctant to believe Ezra-Nehemiah) to Nero, at the outbreak of the Jewish revolt against Rome in the summer of 66 c.e., supported the Temple of Jerusalem—and its priestly staff—to the exclusion of all other Yahwist (and a fortiori non-Yahwist) shrines in Judaea and later in the Palestinian hinterland (leaving aside as always the case of Samaria).[11] The character of imperial support for the temple

---

[9] Too little is known to provide many details. However, one case may be suggested: burial in *kokhim* is attested at Khirbet Za'aquqa in Idumaea as early as c.300 b.c.e. and was the standard mode of burial in third- and second-century Marisa. The practice not only persisted locally after the judaization but even spread to Judaea, where it predominated by the first century c.e., and then to the rest of Jewish Palestine. For Khirbet Za'aquqa, see A. Kloner, D. Regev, and U. Rappaport, "A Burial Cave from the Hellenistic Period," *Atiqot* 21 (1992): 27–50 (in Hebrew); for Marisa, Oren, and Rappaport, "Necropolis of Marisa." For some additional reflections on conversionist religious and cultural systems, see S. Schwartz, "Hellenization of Jerusalem."

[10] See S. Schwartz, "Josephus in Galilee: Rural Patronage and Social Breakdown," in eds., F. parente and J. Sievers, *Josephus and the History of the Greco-Roman Period: Essays in Memory of Morton Smith* (Leiden: Brill, 1994), pp. 290–306. L. Schiffman's discussion, "Was There a Galilean Halakhah?" in L. Levine, ed., *The Galilee in Late Antiquity* (New York: Jewish Theological Seminary, 1992), pp. 143–56, is problematic.

[11] The chief exception to this rule, the Seleucid emperor Antiochus IV, is well-known. There are also a number of questionable cases. Alexander the Great may have recognized the Temple and the priesthood, and the right of the Judaeans to use their own laws—as Judaean propaganda

and its staff is indicated by a series of letters, rescripts, and memoranda, quoted by Josephus in *Ant* 12, 14, and 16 and in 2 Maccabees 11. Most explicit is the letter sent by the Seleucid emperor Antiochus III to Ptolemy, governor of Coele-Syria-and-Phoenicia, a province that included Palestine, shortly after Antiochus's conquest of the province in 200 B.C.E. (*Ant* 12.137–44):

> King Antiochus to Ptolemy, greeting. Inasmuch as the Judaeans, from the moment we entered their territory, showed their enthusiasm for us, and received us splendidly when we visited their city, greeting us with their *gerousia* [council of elders], supplied our soldiers and elephants unstintingly, and helped us in expelling the Egyptian garrison in the citadel, we ourselves have seen fit to compensate them for these favors, to restore their city ruined by the accidents of war, and to resettle it by causing to return to it its scattered inhabitants. First, we have decided on account of their piety to provide for their sacrifices an allowance of sacrificial animals, wine, oil and incense, to the value of twenty thousand pieces of silver, and [. . . (number omitted)] sacred *artabae* of fine flour according to their native standard, and one thousand four hundred and sixty *medimnoi* of wheat and three hundred and seventy five *medimnoi* of salt. I [sic] wish that these things be done for them as I have commanded, and that the work on the temple be completed, the porticoes and anything else requiring construction. Let the timber be brought from Judaea itself and from the other ethnic districts [viz., of Palestine], and from the Lebanon, without the imposition of tolls—likewise for the other materials needed to make the restoration of the temple more splendid. Let all those from the nation conduct their lives according to their ancestral laws, and let the *gerousia* and the priests and scribes of the temple and the temple singers be released from the head-tax and the crown tribute and the remaining taxes [or, the salt tax]. In order that the city may be resettled more quickly, I [sic] grant both to the current inhabitants and to those who will return before the month of Hyperberetaios exemption from taxes for three years. And in future we release them from a third part of the tribute, so that the damage may be corrected. And all those taken from the city and enslaved, we set them and the children born to them free, and order that their property be returned to them.[12] (my translation, based on Thackeray, LCL)

---

claimed—but we cannot be certain. Nor is there any explicit information about Alexander's Successors, though the persistence of a Judaean silver coinage from about 380 B.C.E. through the reign of Ptolemy I (died 283–282 B.C.E.) suggests at least some form of autonomy. I have concluded from the subsequent suspension of coinage and the evidence of the Zenon papyri that Ptolemies II–IV did not recognize Judaea's autonomy, though there is disagreement on the matter. But from Antiochus III (conquered Palestine 200 B.C.E.) on, the evidence is unambiguous; see S. Schwartz, "On the Autonomy of Judaea."

[12] In the decree Josephus quotes immediately following (145–46), Antiochus also ratifies priestly regulations concerning admittance to the Temple and importation of forbidden animals into Jerusalem. This last clause has aroused interest because it is hard to imagine that donkeys and horses were excluded from the city; a similar law, furthermore, is found in the Temple Scroll, confirming the feeling that the law is utopian and the document in which it is found unhistorical. Perhaps. And it is indeed hard to imagine that standard beasts of burden were barred from the

There are always grounds for suspecting the reliability of official documents quoted by historiographers. In Josephus's case the grounds are especially abundant. Nevertheless, that the documents he quotes have been systematically and radically falsified—which would imply that the emperors never granted the temple, its staff, and its law any sort of public recognition—is at least as unlikely as the supposition (which no one has ever seriously entertained, as far as I am aware) that none of the documents was ever tampered with.[13]

It is important to remember the social and cultural context of *Antiquities* 12.137–44, assuming it is *basically* authentic. When Elias Bickerman called it, in medievalizing fashion, "the Seleucid charter of Jerusalem," he was to some extent being self-consciously paradoxical.[14] Antiochus's letter is not in fact a statement of imperial policy or law, but a prime example of the functioning of the common Hellenistic royal ideology of *euergesia*, of the great man expressing his gratitude to loyal inferiors by the bestowal of gifts. Many of the gifts listed—to the extent that they are not the product of editorial tampering—were short term and transparently motivated by the desire to restore Judaea to a productive and revenue-bearing condition. Furthermore, as Bickerman emphasized, the favors granted by such documents were valid only while the royal benefactor himself still lived. Antiochus's letter was not, strictly speaking, a *Seleucid* charter at all, and his son, Antiochus IV, failed in fact to recognize the validity of its terms.

Nevertheless, the document is of great importance for demonstrating the hierocratic character of Judaea. And the reaction, starting 167 B.C.E., to Anti-

---

city in the first century, when it was a big, bustling place. But it is worth remembering that pre-Maccabean Jerusalem was not a center of commerce but a tiny, inconsequential town within small and easily patrolled walls. How do we know that animals were not barred? Also important are the decrees of Julius Caesar and associates concerning the privileges of the high priest Hyrcanus II, quoted at *Ant* 14.192–212; remaining documents in *Ant* 14 (213–64) and 16 (162–73) grant permission to Jewish communities in Greek cities, mostly in Asia Minor, to observe their ancestral laws and send funds to Jerusalem. These documents are discussed in part 3.

[13] That the documents are to be supposed forgeries unless proven otherwise was argued by H. Moehring, "The Acta Pro Judaeis in the Antiquities of Flavius Josephus," in J. Neusner, ed., *Christianity, Judaism, and Other Greco-Roman Cults: Studies for Morton Smith at Sixty* (Leiden: Brill, 1975), 3:124–58, refining a long and not especially glorious tradition of German scholarship going back to H. Willrich; see also J.-D. Gauger, *Beiträge zur jüdischen Apologetik* (Cologne: P. Hanstein, 1977), who, however, examines only a few documents and is exemplarily careful to avoid any sort of generalization; the classic discussion is E. J. Bickerman, "Une question d'authenticité: Les privilèges juifs," *Studies in Jewish and Christian History* (Leiden: Brill, 1980), 2:24–43; for general discussion and bibliography, see Grabbe, *Judaism from Cyrus to Hadrian*, 1:259–63. Presumably, though some may be outright forgeries, the documents should be assumed to be worked over, abbreviated, "revised," slightly mistransmitted, etc., versions of genuine originals. See M. Pucci Ben-Zeev, "Caesar and Jewish Law," *RB* 102 (1995): 29 n. 2; for a full account with extensive commentary, Pucci Ben-Zeev, *Jewish Rights in the Roman World: The Greek and Roman Documents Quoted by Josephus Flavius* (Tübingen: Mohr Siebeck, 1998); for a still more optimistic view, see T. Rajak, "Was There a Roman Charter for the Jews?" *JRS* 74 (1984): 109.

[14] "La charte séleucide de Jérusalem," *Studies in Jewish and Christian History*, 2: 44–85.

ochus IV's denial of the Judaeans' right to live according to their own laws indicates that imperial recognition of Judaean self-rule (or perhaps in some cases total nonintervention in its practice) was normal. Indeed, the "royal favors granted the Judaeans" were sufficiently well known that the author of 2 Maccabees could accuse the hellenizing Jerusalem high priest Jason of having abrogated them by "destroying the life-style ordained by the Law and introducing unlawful customs" (4:11).[15] Furthermore, the successive Persian, Macedonian, and Roman rulers' support, in a general sense, for the temple and high priesthood is obvious from the course of events, and is in any case rendered unsurprising by a great many parallel cases that it is unnecessary to adduce.[16] In sum, there is no reason to doubt the unanimous claim of the ancient writers that the emperors patronized the temple, supported and were supported by the cult (in that sacrifices were offered on their behalf), favored the priests as a class (and at times other members of the temple staff), and recognized their right to rule the Jews of Palestine "according to their ancestral laws."[17]

Torah

The term "ancestral laws" implies that imperial support for the temple and the Torah were closely bound together, for it is overwhelmingly likely that concealed behind this standard Hellenistic administrative jargon are the laws of the Torah, as is implied in the passage from 2 Maccabees just quoted. Indeed, as suggested above, it is likely that the Pentateuch itself was, if not compiled, then at least adopted as the Judaean law code at the initiative of the Persian emperors.

The very same documents that demonstrate imperial support for the temple demonstrate their support for the "ancestral laws" of the Jews, though they also imply that local magistrates sometimes infringed on the rights of Jews outside Palestine to observe the laws of the Torah. The earliest piece of evidence for imperial support is the so-called Passover Papyrus (419 B.C.E.) from Elephantine, a military settlement in southern Egypt. This document seems to record the Persian emperor's authorization of the observance of the Feast of Unleavened Bread (not in fact Passover) more or less in accordance with the laws of some version of the Torah by a group of Judahite troops.[18] In

---

[15] See comments by J. Goldstein, *II Maccabees* (Garden City, N.Y.: Doubleday, 1984), pp. 228–29; E. Bi[c]kerman, *Institutions des Séleucides* (Paris: Paul Geuthner, 1938), pp. 135–40.

[16] See Bickerman, "La charte séleucide."

[17] And it matters little that such recognition may often have been reactive, as Rajak, "Roman Charter," argues. What matters is the knowledge that the emperor could be appealed to if necessary.

[18] A. E. Cowley, *Aramaic Papyri of the Fifth Century B.C.* (Oxford: Clarendon Press, 1923), no. 21; B. Porten, *Archives from Elephantine: The Life of an Ancient Military Colony* (Berkeley: University of California Press, 1968), pp. 130ff.; Porten, "Aramaic Parchments and Papyri: A New

addition to the documents, several reports of Josephus concerning the first century C.E. indicate that the Roman authorities could be expected to punish violators of the Torah.

Thus, it would not be an exaggeration to say that the Torah was the constitution of the Jews of Palestine. Its authority rested not simply, and initially perhaps not at all, on the consensus of the Jews, but on the might of the imperial and native rulers of Palestine. Furthermore, the final authorities over the interpretation of the Torah were the high priest and his entourage (cf. *Ant* 14.192–95); the high priest was himself technically an imperial appointee, even before the period when the Roman emperor's agent *actually* appointed him,[19] and the priesthood as a group had special interpretive authority granted it by the Torah itself and confirmed by the government. Therefore, the location, physical and metaphorical, of this authoritative interpretation was the temple of Jerusalem.[20]

Obviously, imperial sponsorship is not the full explanation for the significance—practical or symbolic—of the temple and the Torah. In the 500 or so years preceding its abrogation in 70 C.E., there was only one case in which Judaeans publicly challenged the constitutional status of the Torah—during the reforms instituted by the high priests Jason and Menelaus in the 170s B.C.E. The proconstitution reaction led by the Hasmonean family may not have been the mass national uprising imagined by Victor Tcherikover, among others. But its long- term success does indicate that even as early as the 160s and 150s B.C.E., some Judaeans enthusiastically supported the Torah and many others were at least willing to comply with its restoration. Thus, for reasons presumably lost in the obscurity of the Iron Age, or in the almost completely blank centuries of Achaemenid and Ptolemaic rule, the Judaeans themselves colluded in maintaining the constitutional status of the Torah. Nevertheless, I emphasize imperial sponsorship because its importance is indubitable and it is the only factor that is even partly recoverable. Furthermore, in the mildly sentimentalizing atmosphere that often pervades the study of

---

Look," *BA* 42 (1979): 91–92; P. Grelot, "Sur le papyrus pascal d'élephantine," in A. Caquot and M. Delcor, eds., *Melanges Bibliques et Orientaux en l'Honneur de M. Henri Cazelles* (Neukirchen-Vluyn: Neukirchener-Verlag, 1981), pp. 163–72; cf. Grabbe, *Judaism*, 1.54–55. Contra Grabbe, it is not clear whether the papyrus prescribes the introduction of the festival or merely authorizes its observance. In any case, the papyrus does not suggest that the emperor tried to impose the laws of the Torah consistently at Elephantine; or, if he did, he failed miserably, for the Judahites continued to worship many gods and intermarry with Egyptians and non-Judahite colonists, see Smith, *Palestinian Parties*, p., 209 n. 101.

[19] See Bickerman, *God of the Maccabees*, pp. 37–38; D. Goodblatt, *The Monarchic Principle: Studies in Jewish Self-Government in Antiquity* (Tübingen: Mohr, 1994), pp. 6–21.

[20] Note also the rabbinic texts which indicate that the authoritative recensions of the Pentateuch were housed in the Temple; see S. Lieberman, *Hellenism in Jewish Palestine* (New York: Jewish Theological Seminary, 1950), pp. 20–27.

ancient Judaism—admittedly, as an understandable and decent reaction to the hostility that used to prevail—it is a factor often ignored.

Imperial (and native royal) sponsorship meant in practice that radical dissent and public displays of extreme deviance were not tolerated, unless the authorities were too weak to control them or considered them harmless. Both were probably true of the Qumran community at different stages of its history; at any rate, the sect itself recalled an episode of persecution, obviously in the long term ineffective, apparently by an early Hasmonean ruler.[21] Clearly, later rulers could easily enough have eliminated the sect (which had settled, admittedly in rough terrain, only a few miles south of the Hasmonean-Herodian winter palace at Jericho) but probably considered it unthreatening.[22] Likewise, intolerance of radical dissent or deviance is probably the historical reality behind Josephus's tale of the flight from Judaea of the high priest Manasses and his associates, after the former had married the (non-Israelite?) daughter of Sanballat, Achaemenid governor of Samaria (*Ant* 11.306–12); whether it was the historical reality of the fourth century B.C.E., when the tale is set, or the first century C.E., when Josephus recorded it, is of little importance for my concerns. Intolerance of radical dissent also explains the nearly complete absence of any evidence for clear *public* violation of Jewish law—by Jews—in post-Maccabean and (pre-70) Roman Judaea and Jewish Palestine. Private violations have different implications and will be discussed below. We hear of no pagan shrines, and excavations have yielded little statuary and a remarkably small amount of representational decoration, given its importance for Palestinian Jews later on. The most prominent pre-Destruction example of such decoration is, significantly, from the walls of the Herodian palace in Tiberias, Galilee, and we know about it only from Josephus.[23] It is also significant that synagogues, whatever actually went on in them, were not called temples, but *proseuchai* (prayer houses) or *synagogai* (gatherings), indicating at least *nomi-*

---

[21] See 1QpHab (= Pesher Habakkuk), col. 11, on Habakkuk 2:15, "Woe to him who causes his neighbors to drink; who pours out his venom to make them drunk that he may gaze on their feasts." The sectarian commentator writes (trans. Vermes): "Interpreted, this concerns the Wicked Priest who pursued the Teacher of Righteousness to the house of his exile that he might confuse him with his venomous fury. And at the time appointed for rest, on the Day of Atonement, he appeared before them to confuse them, and to cause them to stumble on the Day of Fasting, their Sabbath of Repose."
That is, the high priest used force to compel the sect to abandon their peculiar calendar; see P. Callaway, *A History of the Qumran Community: An Interpretation* (Sheffield, U.K.: JSOT Press, 1988), pp. 160–1.

[22] This "official" attitude was perhaps adopted by Josephus, who viewed the Essenes as a harmless group of pious exotics rather than a threat to public order or a band of sinners.

[23] *Life* 65–67. And note also the pre-Hasmonean Tobiad palace (the "Qasr el-'Abd," according to the most recent excavators, probably not a temple, as used to be thought) at 'Araq el-'Amir, near Amman, with its animal friezes; see *NEAEHL*, sub s.v.

nal conformity with Deuteronomic prescription.[24] Josephus's incidental notice that the people of Lydda, in northwestern Judaea, carefully observed a pilgrimage festival indicates that sometimes such conformity was more than nominal (War 2.515). Archaeologists have noted the rarity of pig bones in excavations in Israel.[25]

The Temple and the Torah were thus not only the main mediators between Israel and its God, but also among the prime (though not the only)[26] repositories of power in Hellenistic and Roman Jewish Palestine, nodal points, like the temples of Egypt and the city oligarchies of Ionia and Caria, in imperial and native royal control of the native population of the country. There was thus, in broad terms, a coincidence of their positions in the cosmic and human political economies. As for imperial control, it was often loose. The central authorities had other concerns and tended to react rather than actively control, which would have constrained the rulers' local agents. And when native kings ruled, their fortunes too varied, and sometimes they had to tolerate opposition, as the Hasmoneans tolerated the Essenes, and Herod the Pharisees. Nevertheless, the power of the Temple and Torah was a real fact of life, indeed, one of central importance in ancient Palestinian Judaism; those who ignore it do so at their peril.

[24] Despite the rather odd insistence of, for example, H. C. Kee, "Early Christianity in the Galilee: Reassessing the Evidence from the Gospels," in L. Levine, ed., *The Galilee in Late Antiquity* (New York: Jewish Theological Seminary, 1992), pp. 3–14, it is indubitable that there were some synagogues in first-century Palestine (see, e.g., War 2.285), though it is equally indubitable that the monumental, purpose-built synagogue became an established feature in the Palestinian countryside only several centuries later; in the first century synagogues were located mainly in cities, including Jerusalem (as indicated by the famous "Theodotus inscription" which, once again pace Kee, was most likely made in the first century) and fortresses. For an account with less special pleading, see L. Levine, "The Second Temple Synagogue," in *The Synagogue in Late Antiquity*, (Philadelphia: Jewish Publication Society, 1987), pp. 7–31 (his account of what went on in the synagogue is based mostly on post-70 evidence). The evidence for sacrifice in diasporic synagogues should perhaps be taken seriously; see S. Cohen, "Pagan and Christian Evidence on the Ancient Synagogue," in the same collection, p. 166. For more detail, see part 3.

[25] For discussion see J. L. Reed, "Galileans, 'Israelite Village Communities,' and the Sayings Gospel Q," in E. Meyers, ed., *Galilee through the Centuries: Confluence of Cultures* (Winona Lake, Ind.: Eisenbrauns, 1999), pp. 98–102. The real issue, though, is not whether Jews occasionally ate pork; obviously those who could get hold of it sometimes did, just as some of them had sex with siblings, exposed unwanted infants, and lit fires on the Sabbath. What is at issue is *public* behavior: raising or importing pigs on a large scale, for instance, and thus the frequency of their bones in excavations. Of this there is no evidence.

[26] See below on manipulation of the demonic world. Furthermore, mediation between Jews and the Roman government outside the hierarchy of Temple and Torah was an important source of power at a time when Jewish Palestine was politically divided (so that the Temple staff probably had no legal jurisdiction over significant areas of Jewish settlement) and dominated by a non-priestly family, the Herodians. However, this sort of mediation was presumably not a significant element of Jewish self-definition. Subjection to Rome united the Jews with their neighbors; the mediating class thus cut across ethnic lines, as Josephus's accounts of the dynastic marriages of

The Symbolic Significance of Torah and Temple

By the first century C.E., the Temple and Torah had been transformed into central symbols of Palestinian Judaism. This transformation greatly enhanced their actual political importance and ultimately loosened their dependence on the brute realities of power and enabled them, or the memory of them, to survive political displacement (in the case of the Torah) and destruction.

I will not try to explain this internalization of the value of the Temple and Torah, beyond repeating that their political importance over half a millennium or so necessarily had some influence on the collective mentality of the Jews. But the effects of internalization *can* be isolated and described. The most striking and accessible examples concern, as I hinted above, the actual physical objects as displayed, in the case of the Torah, or represented, either pictorially or rhetorically. A full catalogue would be instructive but is unnecessary for my purposes. Rather, I will mention a few characteristic cases.

Given the importance of the Torah and Temple in Hasmonean ideology, it may not be accidental that it is 1 Maccabees, a strongly pro-Hasmonean book, that contains perhaps the earliest indications of the symbolic potency of the Torah scroll.[27] At the time of the Antiochan persecution, in 167 B.C.E., agents of the king are said not simply to have confiscated but to have ripped up and burned Torah scrolls; possession of a scroll was a capital crime (1:56–57). These claims may not be true. The parallel description of the persecution in 2 Maccabees 6:4–7 is interestingly different; for one thing, it fails to mention Torah scrolls. Which (if either) is a more accurate account of the events of 167 cannot be determined in this case. It seems preferable to treat both accounts as evidence for the ideological positions of their authors—a preference confirmed by another story in 1 Maccabees in which display of a Torah scroll is important (3:46–60, the assembly at Massepha) and again unparalleled in 2 Maccabees.[28] What we can learn from these passages about the ideological position of 2 Maccabees is not my concern here. The Law is unquestionably important in 2 Maccabees; why the physical object does not figure in the account is a complex issue. It is perhaps worth remembering

---

the Herodians, for example, makes clear. See S. Schwartz, *Josephus and Judaean Politics* (Leiden: Brill, 1990), pp. 110–69.

[27] The Letter of Aristeas has traces of the same theme; its date is uncertain, but if Bickerman was right to think that it was written around 130 B.C.E. ("Zur Datierung des Pseudo-Aristeas," *Studies in Jewish and Christian History*, 1: 123–36), then it is approximately contemporary with 1 Macc. This indicates that the fetishization of the Torah scroll occurred also outside the context of Hasmonean ideology; for some discussion see M. Goodman, "Texts, Scribes, and Power."

[28] Its parallel ought to be 2 Macc 8:12–20 where, instead of conducting an assembly dedicated to the reading and observance of the Torah, Judas gives the sort of prebattle pep talk standard in Greek historiography, in which the "ancestral constitution" (v. 17) is indeed invoked but is neither displayed nor consulted. The common temptation to find the 1 Macc account more credible should be resisted.

that 2 Maccabees, concerned as it is with the temple, warns against excessive reverence for its structure (5:19–20).[29] This may indicate that its author was anxious about attributing power to physical objects; but there is no way of telling how widespread such anxiety may have been. At any rate, 1 Maccabees, a book that reads as if it *ought* to be a straightforward presentation of the Hasmonean party line, does not share this anxiety about sacred objects, for it suggests that the Torah scroll itself somehow represents Jewishness. Its destruction is a synecdoche; it stands in for what Antiochus tried to do to the special lifestyle prescribed by the Torah, namely, to Judaism. And its display by Judas reminds "Israel" (that is, Judas's supporters) what they are fighting for.

Similar concerns are manifest at the other end of the period under discussion, in the works of Josephus. It is first of all interesting to find Josephus, in the introduction to *Antiquities* and in the account in *Antiquities* 12 of the translation of the Torah into Greek, appropriating pseudo-Aristeas's peculiar reverence for the actual words of the Torah, and his attribution to them of power best described as magical. Josephus hesitates about revealing the contents of the Torah to outsiders and is aware that God sometimes punished pagans like the historian Theopompus who looked into the Law; but he concludes, following his Alexandrian source, that the contents of the Torah may be revealed. Why? Perhaps he thought that God, in approving its publication in Greek, had implicitly approved its revelation to gentiles, too; or perhaps, as Josephus himself says, because it was customary among the Jews not to conceal their "beautiful things" (if so, then why the anxiety?).[30]

Such deliberations may admittedly tell us mainly about Josephus, though there is little reason to think that his attitude to the Torah was drastically different from that of other well-educated Jerusalem priests who survived the destruction of the temple — a class that may have been numerous and influential. But Josephus also reports stories that take for granted a more general attribution of symbolic force to the Torah scroll, though precisely how general it is impossible to tell. In the early 50s, a member of a unit of Roman troops searching some north Judaean villages for brigands found in one of them a Torah scroll (this may imply that not every Judaean village possessed one), which he cut up and, in one version of the story, burned. According to Josephus, masses of

---

[29] On the Temple in 2 Macc, see R. Doran, *Temple Propaganda: The Purpose and Character of 2 Maccabees* (Washington: Catholic Biblical Association 1981).

[30] See *Ant* 12.110–3, with Aristeas 312ff. Both report that Ptolemy "prostrated himself" (*proskunein*) to the book (pace Marcus's apologetic comment ad loc., the antecedent of the pronoun *autois*, the indirect object of *proskunein*, is unambiguous). They also report God's punishment of Theopompus and the poet Theodectes, who had looked into the Law. Why then did God not punish Ptolemy II, who had the Law translated? In Aristeas and *Ant* 12 the answer is clear enough: God himself approved of the translation. In *Ant* 1.9–11, though, Josephus implicitly rejects this view and argues that the high priest Elazar's decision to oversee the translation demonstrates that the Torah is a public document.

Jews, or Judaeans, marched to Caesarea and threatened the Roman governor with an uprising unless he punished the perpetrator of this outrage against God and the Law; the soldier was beheaded (War 2.228–31 = Ant 20.113–7). Similarly, Josephus says that during the revolt against Rome, his enemies in Tiberias were able to rouse opposition to him simply by displaying a Torah scroll, implying that it was this (i.e., the laws of the Jews, that which most made them what they were) that Josephus was planning to betray (Life 134).

These stories are not necessarily reported accurately. And even if accurate, they do not necessarily represent the views of all the Jews of Palestine. Yet the clear continuity of Josephus's stories with the ideology of 1 Maccabees and pseudo-Aristeas, with their striking (indeed, from the modern Western perspective, bizarre) fetishization of what was after all a book, demonstrates that the stories are not merely expressions of Josephus's own views. They necessarily reflect the significance of what the book was thought to represent for some part, at least, of ancient Jewish society.

For the symbolic significance of the Jerusalem Temple there is likewise a mass of evidence of which it is unnecessary to provide a detailed account. One of the most conspicuous traces I have already mentioned—the willingness of thousands of Galilean and Idumaean peasants and brigands at the time of the revolt against Rome to follow their leaders to Jerusalem, try to seize the Temple, and face what they must have known were the almost certain alternatives of death or enslavement. The importance of the temple in Jewish revolutionary ideology is demonstrated also by the prominence of imagery related to it on the silver sheqels of the Great Revolt; temple imagery is still more important on the coinage of the Bar Kokhba revolt.[31] Earlier, apparent Roman impiety toward the Temple aroused the same sort of mass opposition as (indeed, often more intense opposition than) the desecration of the Law just mentioned.[32] Similarly poignant anecdotes are obviously less readily available about peaceful times. The undeniable importance of discourse about the temple in surviving ancient Jewish literature may be thought to demonstrate the concerns of the literature's presumably limited audience, not those of the inhabitants of Jewish Palestine in general; even so, some of the writings betray a certain anxiety about the status of the Temple and its priests. The belligerency of their support probably hints at the intensity of others' opposition and may also reflect concerns about the legitimacy of a temple that even its builders regarded as a substitution for the Solomonic structure.[33] Furthermore, the

---

[31] See Meshorer, Ancient Jewish Coinage, 2: 96–165.

[32] This is clearest in the case of the reaction to the Emperor Gaius's command to place a statue of Zeus in the Temple: War 2.184–203/Ant 18.240–308.

[33] 2 Macc, for instance, often seems to be responding to claims that the temple was not entirely legitimate and its Hasmonean priesthood problematic: see Goldstein, II Maccabees, pp. 18–19. However, his suggestion that the work is anti-Hasmonean is baseless. Anxiety about the priesthood is discussed by M. Himmelfarb, "A Kingdom of Priests: The Democratization of the Priesthood

Temple (and the Torah, too) most probably was less important, actually if not symbolically, for non-Judaean than for Judaean Jews.

Yet it remains overwhelmingly likely that the Temple and its staff enjoyed tremendous prestige among the Jews. The very fact that Jewish groups whose activities in practice may have undermined the authority of the Temple and the priests nevertheless appropriated the priestly concern for purity, as the Pharisees may have done, or, like the Dead Sea sect, felt constrained to view their holy community (or in the case of some Christians, their messiah) as a replacement for the Temple, indicates as much.[34] For nonsectarian Jews, the symbolic power of the Temple is best demonstrated by the fact that the Temple treasury was overflowing with silver. Relatively little of this silver could have been extracted from areas where priests had recognized legal jurisdiction, which for most of the first century was probably restricted to Judaea, and perhaps also Idumaea and the western part of Lower Galilee—assuming that priests had some sort of jurisdiction in areas under the rule of the Roman prefect/procurator. Much of it was given voluntarily, in some cases by Jews who had to petition the Roman government for permission to do so, as we know from the documents quoted by Josephus, discussed above. It is worth emphasizing that these voluntary gifts were made to an institution that could offer nothing tangible in return, in a society whose economy was probably functioning not far above subsistence level, and in which there was intense competition for what little surplus was produced.[35]

God, Temple, and Torah as an Ideological System

It is much easier to establish the likelihood that many or most Palestinian Jews in the first century considered God, the Temple, and the Torah important factors in making them what they were than to determine what exactly they

---

in the Literature of Second Temple Judaism," *Journal of Jewish Thought and Philosophy* 6 (1997): 89–104.

[34] This point is well made by Himmelfarb, "Kingdom." That the Pharisees believed that laypeople should observe the laws of purity the Pentateuch imposed only on the priests is commonly accepted but has been challenged by E. P. Sanders, *Jewish Law from Jesus to the Mishnah* (Philadelphia: Trinity Press International, 1990), pp. 131–254. There is no reason to think the Pharisees were opposed to the Temple or priesthood (many of them were in fact priests). Himmelfarb pointed out that Jubilees provided strikingly cultic interpretations of the generally applicable biblical laws forbidding consumption of blood and certain sexual relations.

[35] As far as the fact of widespread voluntary contribution is concerned, there was nothing unique about the Jerusalem Temple—Egyptian peasants in the Hellenistic and Roman periods made voluntary contributions to their temples, too. On the economy of the Jerusalem Temple, the best and most wide-ranging treatment is Goodman, *Ruling Class*, pp. 51–75. See also M. Broshi, "The Role of the Temple in the Herodian Economy," *JJS* 38 (1987): 31–37; he attempts (35–37) a perhaps ill-advised computation of the value of annual income from the Temple tax and discusses (34) confiscations and Roman legislation forbidding them. E. P. Sanders, *Judaism: Practice and Belief*, provides a detailed but somewhat idealizing account of the Jews' devotion to the Temple and the priests.

thought about them. In attempting to do this, we must first of all fall back on the contents of the Torah itself and on what ancient Jews wrote about it and the Temple. Of course, this will not answer the question, for the literature is not simply evidence for what "the Jews" thought. In the first place, it is far from clear how much access most Palestinian Jews had to knowledge of the contents of the Torah. The synagogue, where Torah scrolls could probably be found and were probably read on a weekly basis, was not yet widespread. Nevertheless, there were some synagogues, and, if Josephus's story mentioned above may be believed, some villages possessed Torah scrolls, whether or not they had synagogues. It is also likely that whatever liturgical activity went on in the towns and villages of Jewish Palestine was informed by some knowledge of the Torah, and certain that some parts of the public liturgy of the temple — the firstfruits ceremony (Deuteronomy 26:1–11), the paschal sacrifice (Exodus 12) — were.

However, we *know* only what we can read in books written in the later Second Temple period, and the literate were ipso facto unrepresentative; furthermore, they were often priests or experts in the Torah — that is, mediators between the central institutions and the population at large, who shared, and had a professional interest in promoting, their institutions' ideologies. Though this fact is important in itself as a demonstration of the generative power of these ideologies (see below), it also implies that the literature throws up a sort of mirage. The coherent worldview that can be extracted from it cannot be assumed to be characteristic of "the Jews," for its coherence (which I am intentionally overstating here) is the creation of the ideologues who wrote the books. Nevertheless, a description of the components of this ideological complex (which I would not hesitate to describe as normative, i.e., politically authoritative) is necessary if we are to understand how it functioned in Palestinian Jewish society and how it interacted with ideological systems with which it coexisted.

God, Temple, and Torah constituted an ideological complex of remarkable simplicity. If its neatness and coherence gave it a certain force, its clear inadequacy as an explanation of the operation of the human world was its potential weakness. Everything in the system was unique: the one God chose the one people of Israel as his own, and the one Temple as the only place where they might worship him. He also gave them the one Torah, whose laws they are obliged to study and observe. The Torah was of course not only a law book (*nomos*), which was how its Greek translators represented it.[36] Nor was it only

[36] For a survey of the endless theological debate about the propriety of the Greek translation, a corollary of the central, even more theologically loaded debate about whether Judaism was "legalistic" (to which the correct answer is, Of course, and what of it?), see S. Westerholm, "Torah, Nomos and Law," in P. Richardson and S. Westerholm, eds. *Law in Religious Communities in the Roman Period: The Debate over Torah and Nomos in Post-Biblical Judaism and Early Christianity* (Waterloo: Canadian Corporation for Studies in Religion, 1991), pp. 45–56; cf. A. Segal, *The Other Judaisms of Late Antiquity* (Atlanta: Scholars, 1987), pp. 131–46.

a constitution (*politeia*), as Jewish apologists and Greek diplomats said, although it certainly functioned as one. Nor indeed was it merely the national epic of a recalcitrant people, as it seems if one reads only the narrative and skips the laws. It was primarily the record of an agreement—a contract between God and his people—obligating Israel to observe the laws specified in the contract, and God in return to protect Israel. There is nothing uniquely Jewish about the idea that the *pax Dei* (or *deorum*) is secured by following a set of (usually cultic) rules; and anyone familiar with the history of the rise of the Greek *polis* will recognize the conception of the fundamentally egalitarian national community underlying the contemporaneous biblical notion of "Israel." But the explicit framing of a national law code/constitution/epic as a written contract between a people and its patron deity has no precise parallel in antiquity, to the best of my knowledge.[37]

In any case, the ideological system embodied in the Torah implies a specific worldview (whose classic postbiblical formulations are in the *Wisdom of Jesus b. Sira*, also called *Ecclesiasticus*, and in the *Jewish Antiquities* and *Against Apion* of Josephus): its vision of society is characterized by a mild tension between hierarchical and egalitarian principles, of the human condition optimistic, and of the cosmos irenic and nonmythological.[38] That is, "Israelite society," in its ideal form, is egalitarian in that all adult males share the obligation to know and observe God's laws but hierarchical in that a hereditary priesthood is assigned a special role in maintaining God's favor toward Israel through proper conduct of the cult and interpretation of the laws. Many scholars have supposed that this tension between egalitarianism and hierarchy was a formative one in ancient Judaism, that, for example, it helps account for the rise of sectarianism and the beginnings of Christianity. It is indeed perfectly plausible to suppose that different groups emphasized different things—Pharisees, perhaps, the egalitarian aspect, priests and Sadducees, the hierarchical. Nevertheless, there is remarkably little evidence, between 200 B.C.E. and 70 C.E., that this ideological faultline produced clear-cut social rifts: Pharisees, some of whom were themselves priests, could not ignore the special authority the Torah gives to priests and the cult (at any rate, their rabbinic descendants certainly acknowledged their importance), and priests could not ignore the obligations that the Torah imposes on all Israel equally.[39] It is perhaps more

---

[37] Compare Millar, "Background to the Maccabean Revolution," 6–12.

[38] This is close to the characterization of ancient Judaism as a whole in the works of G. F. Moore and E. P. Sanders, both of whom drastically underestimated the importance of the irrational.

[39] There may be a growing tendency in scholarship to minimize the effects of this tension and its close relative, the supposed priest-scribe antinomy: see Himmelfarb, "Kingdom," and S. Fraade's forthcoming work on scribes mentioned by M. Himmelfarb, *Ascent to Heaven in Jewish and Christian Apocalypses* (Oxford: Oxford University Press, 1993), p. 24 n. 86, in which he argues that most scribes were in fact priests. See also Schwartz, *Josephus*, p. 69.

reasonable to suppose that the ideological disharmony was itself the product of a compromise between previously (viz., in the early Second Temple period or the late Monarchy) opposed groups. Alternatively, it may be that such tensions are in fact characteristic of all but the very simplest societies and generate rifts only rarely.

Contracts require volition. The Torah itself claims that Israel entered into its agreement with God of its own free will—that the Israelites placed their trust in God (*he'eminu*) and in his servant Moses when the latter saved them from the Egyptians at the Red Sea. The Exodus was in fact consistently seen in Israelite and Jewish literature as the legal foundation of the relationship of mutual obligation between the two parties, and the Pentateuchal narrative and subsequent histories, from Joshua through 2 Kings, are among other things the record of Israel's bad faith and God's patronal forbearance: Israel repeatedly violates the contract, and God, instead of declaring the contract (and Israel) void, repeatedly gives them another chance. This narrative presupposes that the terms of the agreement may be difficult but are certainly observable (as is stated explicitly in Deuteronomy 30:11–14), that Israel was able to keep to the agreement but often failed to do so. Some first-century Jews disputed this: the apostle Paul and the author of 4 Ezra at the end of the century both claimed that the Law was impossible to observe. For Paul the Law's unobservability abrogated the contract (though he was not consistent about this); for 4 Ezra it did not, but it meant that except for a few especially righteous men Israel is doomed. But these were necessarily exceptional positions among those who remained Jewish,[40] Paul's view having been generated by his Christian zeal and 4 Ezra's by his post-Destruction gloom. Anyone who accepted the Covenant ipso facto affirmed the ideal observability of its terms.[41]

Such a person also affirmed God's absolute dependability to reward and punish as appropriate, and so, by implication, that relations between God and

[40] And we should not exclude the likelihood of widespread attrition after the destruction of the temple in 70 C.E. (see next chapter).

[41] I follow Sanders in assuming the importance of the covenant as the foundation of Jewish observance. Neusner, by contrast, argues from the rarity of the mention of the covenant in the Mishnah for its unimportance in the Mishnaic system (and a fortiori in other "Judaisms"); see Neusner, "Comparing Judaisms," *History of Religions* 18 (1978): 177–91, and note the absence of the term, as far as I can make out, in the synthetic first chapters of *Judaism: The Evidence of the Mishnah* (Chicago: University of Chicago Press, 1981). This strikes me as empiricism reduced to the absurd, for in fact the Mishnah *never* explains why one should observe the Law; it prescribes, that is, neither covenantalism nor any alternative to it. This is because the Mishnah is a detailed and systematic *exposition* of the covenant's terms, not a book of legal theory. Thus, it takes either the covenant or some other legal theory for granted; since we know of no fully articulated theoretical basis of halakhic observance in antiquity apart from the covenant, and since the covenant is important in texts produced by groups closely connected to or descended from the framers of the Mishnah, it is overwhelmingly likely that the Mishnah's presumed basis for observance of the law is the covenant. For discussion, see Segal, *Other Judaisms*, pp. 147–65.

humanity are not subject to interference by other powers. The cosmos is thus a simple, well-ordered place—a cosmos in the literal sense. This does not exclude the possibility that God shares heaven with other divine beings (the Pentateuch itself mentions angels), but does require that these beings be non-volitional, mere executors of God's will, or hypostases of his attributes, in any case, absolutely his subordinates (the apparent exception is the highly enigmatic story of the descent of the sons of [the] god[s] in Genesis 6:1–4; see below). In this view, then, the cosmic world is not riven by conflict and shaken by instability; it is thus devoid of drama and cannot be described by means of mythological narrative. The Hebrew Bible, as is well known, is nearly devoid of cosmic mythology, though traces are detectable. In the main, its mythologizing is historical and concerns the vicissitudes of the behavior and fortunes of Israel and its neighbors, not those of the divine world.

Deviance?

What does this ideological system teach us about the beliefs and behavior of the Jews of first-century Palestine? Can we treat it as if it were simply an articulate, concentrated, and coherent expression of what for most Jews was embedded and diffuse? Can we follow Sanders in supposing that most Jews more or less believed in something like the "covenantal nomism" that I have just described? Can we, in sum, predict the behavior of the Jews from the prescriptions of the Torah, if we know they considered them a central component of their symbolic world?

The conventional answers to all these questions, at least among scholars not totally silenced by skepticism, is yes. Indeed, the "covenantal nomism" extractable from the Pentateuch and later texts presumably has some rough correspondence to what many Jews occasionally believed, though "belief" is such a mercurial category of experience that any statement about what a large number of people believe necessarily flirts with meaninglessness.[42] It is preferable to examine action, which at least sometimes leaves traces: when we do so, we find, as I observed above, that the texture of public life in the Jewish parts of Palestine—characterized as it was by the absence of pagan shrines, and so on—was indeed broadly influenced by the prescriptions of the Torah. Nevertheless, there are good reasons to be cautious. In the first place, I observed above that the very symbolic power of the central institutions could generate sectarian disregard for or opposition to them. A much more im-

---

[42] This much at least may be extracted from Paul Veyne, *Did the Greeks Believe Their Myths? An Essay in the Constitutive Imagination* (Chicago: University of Chicago Press, 1988). For a more positive account, emphasizing the difficulty and unprofitability, but not the impossibility and uselessness, of utilizing belief as a sociological category, see A. Eisen, *Rethinking Modern Judaism: Ritual, Commandment, Community* (Chicago: University of Chicago Press, 1998), pp. 8–19. Eisen, too, advocates attending primarily to behavior in the sociology of religion.

portant qualification (because it applies to all Jews, not only sectarians) is that the complex God-Temple-Torah—although it was politically and symbolically potent—does not imply that all Jews actually lived their lives according to the rules prescribed by the system; that is, it implies disappointingly little about the texture of daily, private life.[43]

One reason for this is that *no* set of prescriptions can be assumed to control completely the lives of those to whom they are addressed; even laws whose desirability has been to some extent internalized and theoretically are backed by the full force of a totalitarian, militarist government will necessarily be violated and evaded; standards of behavior and patterns of social relations in place when the prescriptive system is introduced cannot be totally eradicated (no government has ever been able to maintain complete control) and are likely to end by reshaping the very prescriptive system introduced to supplant them. There is absolutely no reason to think ancient Jewish society differed in this respect from any other. Indeed, this consideration, though it certainly applies to Judaea proper, is even more critical for the way we should think about the other districts of Jewish Palestine, where for many people the gulf between (recognizably Jewish) public and (still conspicuously Idumaean, Galilean, etc.) private life must, even in the first century, have been deep.

A complicating factor—one that is presumably characteristic, mutatis mutandis, of all written law codes—is the well-known opacity of Pentateuchal prescription. That it was often difficult, even for those intent on precise observance of the Law, to determine what the Law requires, created the need for a class of expert interpreters, and it had the effect of rendering the system fluid and, in principle, reconcilable with all sorts of local varieties of practice. Thus, for example, the Pentateuch instructs the man who comes to hate his wife to give her a *sefer keritut* ("bill of divorcement": Deuteronomy 24:1ff.) but nowhere says what this document should contain. In practice, the contents of the document, as well as the actual terms of the divorce, must have been determined by the scribe who wrote it, in accordance with local custom, which may have varied widely from place to place.[44] We should furthermore not exclude the possibility that men sometimes dismissed their wives without a written document or that wives divorced their husbands, as is attested in the Herodian family (*Ant* 15.259–60), perhaps in accordance with Idumaean law, and perhaps also in a recently published Judaean document. Additionally, it

---

[43] Here I disagree with Sanders, who has produced a detailed description of Palestinian Jewish life in the first century largely on the basis of biblical prescription in *Judaism, Practice, and Belief: 63 BCE–66 CE* (Philadelphia: Trinity Press International, 1992).

[44] In fact local variations are impossible to detect, since there is only one extant divorce document from pre-70 Jewish Palestine; see P. Benoit, J. T. Milik, and R. de Vaux, *Les grottes de Murabba'at*, Discoveries in the Judaean Desert II (Oxford: Clarendon, 1961). = P.Murab. 19, drawn up at Masada, perhaps in 111 C.E.

may be implied in a clause of P. Yadin 18.[45] Especially ingenious scribes and judges may have been able to reconcile even such apparently illegal practices with biblical requirements.[46]

It may be helpful at this point to introduce a more complex definition of Torah (which owes something to the work of Joseph Blenkinsopp). "Torah" does of course refer to the Pentateuch, but it had a rather broader meaning, too, referring to the entire body of traditional Jewish legal practice, which varied from place to place and time to time, and also in respect to the closeness of its relationship with the Pentateuch (which is not to deny that by the first century the Pentateuch was *the* normative canonical legal text). Local judges, teachers, scribes, and so on, who were as far as most Judaeans were concerned the representatives of Torah, whether or not they were learned men who had studied the Pentateuch and learned how to interpret it, necessarily had to confront all sorts of traditional local practices, which some of them may have sometimes tried to reconcile with the Pentateuch. To put it more formally, *the "Torah" was a series of negotiations between an authoritative but opaque text and various sets of traditional but not fully authorized practice*. It is this, and no more, but also no less, that the symbolic centrality and practical importance of the Torah in ancient Palestinian Jewish society implies. In what sorts of actual behavior this negotiation resulted, we are rarely in a position to know.[47]

The Torah in Judaea

Rarely, but not never: the one substantially extant legal document from pre-70 Judaea, P. Murab. 18, provides a remarkably explicit illustration of the complex relationship between prescription and practice: it is an acknowledgment of debt, written in Aramaic, in which the debtor agrees that in the event of his failure to repay his interest-free loan by a certain date, he will be subject to a 20 percent fine.[48] He furthermore agrees to repay the debt even if the

[45] See N. Lewis, *The Documents from the Bar Kokhba Period in the Cave of Letters: Greek Papyri* (Jerusalem: IES, 1989). (= Babatha Archive, or "officially" P. Yadin), no. 18, with comments of A. Wasserstein, "A Marriage Contract from the Province of Arabia Nova: Notes on Papyrus Yadin 18," *JQR* 80 (1989): 115; T. Ilan, "Notes and Observations on a Newly Published Divorce Bill from the Judaean Desert," *HTR* 89 (1996): 195–202, with the response of A. Schremer, "Divorce in Papyrus Se'elim Once Again: A Reply to Tal Ilan," with Ilan's response immediately following, *HTR* 91 (1998): 193–204.

[46] Despite Josephus's explicit statement that Salome's divorce of Costobar violated Jewish law.

[47] Let me just add parenthetically that I am not arguing for the antiquity of the Pharisaic *paradosis ton pateron* ("tradition of the fathers") or the rabbinic *Torah shebe'al peh* ("oral Torah") but for diverse patterns of behavior, all of which seemed to their practitioners to conform with the Torah and all of which were in some way by the first century more or less related to the Pentateuch—even if by no more than the naked claim that they were.

[48] . . .*la' dy zabinat* [in the slightly unusual sense of "pay" rather than the common "purchase"] *'ad zim[nah]/ denah, 'apra'unak behumash*. H. Eshel and E. Eshel, "Fragments of Two Aramaic Documents Which Were Brought to the Abior Cave during the Bar Kokhba Revolt," *EI* 23

sabbatical year intervenes. The Pentateuchal prohibition of interest is thus evaded in a way that would certainly have displeased the rabbis[49] but can at least be reconciled with the biblical prohibition. It is, however, remotely possible that the payment of fines on interest-free loans simply conformed with local custom, practiced also by pagans; a similar arrangement is stipulated in P. Yadin 17—a contract made between Jews, admittedly, but found in a corpus in which biblical law is never acknowledged.[50] Less ambiguous is the condition that follows, for here the biblical cancellation of debts in the sabbatical year is explicitly mentioned, but its force is equally explicitly repudiated. Though this repudiation has no connection with the rabbinic *prozbol* legislation, we must suppose that the parties or the scribe or the legal authorities behind the scribe had, like the sage who introduced the *prozbol*, some interpretive mechanism, not necessarily of great sophistication, for abrogating the rules of the sabbatical year.[51] Perhaps it presupposes that the pentateuchal cancellation of debts is a *favor* to the debtor and so may be renounced by him—a theory of the laws of *shemittah* subsequently rejected by the rabbis, but an entirely plausible approach to the biblical legislation.

The Babatha Archive

The implications of the Babatha archive, the most substantial ancient collection of legal documents produced by and/or for Jews, are very different. The documents so far published were written, in Greek, in the village of Maoza,

---

(1992): 276–85, argue on the basis of the phrase *meshalem lereba'in* in P. Murab. 19, a divorce document, that *'apra'unak behumash* here (as well as a similar phrase which appears in one of the extremely fragmentary Abior cave documents) means "I will pay in five installments"; how this is to be reconciled with the phrase's fairly certain function in P. Murab. 18 as the apodosis of a penalty clause they do not explain. J. Naveh, *On Sherd and Papyrus* (Jerusalem: Magnes, 1992), p. 84 n. 6, regards the reading *apra'unak behumash* as speculative.

[49] See M. Bava Metzi'ah 5:2: it is forbidden under the laws of *tarbit* (usury) to sell a field on the condition that a 20 percent fine (the Mishnah's figure is presumably *exempli gratia*, but interesting nonetheless) be added to the price if payment is delayed until after the harvest; the principle behind the case is identical to that of P. Murab. 18.

[50] Still, other documents in the archive make it clear that it was customary, at least among some people in Babatha's circle, to charge and pay interest. The failure to charge it is thus very likely, though not absolutely certain, to reflect a desire to conform with the requirements of Jewish law.

[51] See P. Murab. 18, 55–56 C.E., from Siwaya (?)—probably a Judaean village (Naveh, *On Sherd and Papyrus*, 84, reads "Suba," which he identifies as a village near Kesalon); the other party is from Kesalon, in the heart of Judaea, eighteen kilometers west of Jerusalem. The editors claim that the contract conforms with the *prozbol* decree described in the Mishnah (Shevi'it 10:3ff.) and attributed to Hillel the Elder (fl. c. 10 B.C.E.), but this is wishful thinking. The Mishnaic *prozbol* document is issued to the creditor, not the debtor, and only for loans secured by real estate. R. Yaron, "The Murabba'at Documents," *JJS* 11 (1960): 158, also claims P. Murab. 18 contains a *prozbol* clause, while (puzzlingly) acknowledging that it does not conform with the Mishnah's requirements and differs also from *prozbol* clauses attested in medieval documents.

at the southern tip of the Dead Sea, mostly in the 120s and early 130s. To judge from the names of witnesses and property owners listed in the documents, the population was mixed, Jewish and Nabataean, with the Jews perhaps slightly more numerous.[52] Babatha's family had close ties in Engeddi, Judaea, but Maoza itself was situated in the new Roman province of Arabia; before 106 it had been ruled by the Nabataeans. It was thus in an area that had not been under the jurisdiction of any Jewish authority since the days of Alexander Jannaeus (reigned 103–76 B.C.E.), if then (see *Ant* 13.397). We may speculate that Babatha's grandparents had come to Arabia from Judaea or Idumaea at the time of the Great Revolt, but perhaps there had "always" been Jews there.

The private law of the documents is of interest for the present purpose mainly because, unlike P. Murab. 18, though not devoid of Jewish influence, it betrays no *explicit* concern with Jewish law—this despite the fact that the two scribes who wrote the papyri, most of the parties, indeed probably most of the population of the town, were Jewish. Yet despite their neglect of Jewish civil law, the Jews of Maoza, at least the literate ones, were conscious of being different from their neighbors. Or perhaps a more rigorous formulation would be that there were among those of Jewish origin some who retained a sense of separateness, which they indicated by using Judaean (as well as some Arabic, Greek, and even Latin) names and writing in Judaean rather than Nabataean script (Jews who did not follow such practices would be invisible in the evidence). What are we to make of this contradiction? Wasserstein argued that these documents should be seen as mere formalities, that the Greek marriage contracts, for example, were made for the benefit of the government registry office; the Jews most likely had *ketubbot* written as well. Why then did Babatha save only the Greek contracts but not the *ketubbot*?[53] While A. Wasserstein's insistence on interpreting the documents in light of the law of the papyri of Hellenistic and Roman Egypt and not that of the rabbis is surely correct, we must conclude that it was the local version of Roman provincial civil law, with its mixture of Greek, Roman, and Near Eastern, including in this case Jewish, elements that actually governed the economic and in most respects familial lives of the Jews of Maoza.[54] The Jewish elements were em-

---

[52] Bowersock, *Roman Arabia* (Cambridge: Harvard University Press, 1983), pp. 76–89, thought he could infer from the documents a growth in the Jewish population of the town between the 90s and the 120s, and that a deed drawn up for Babatha's father in the 90s indicated that he had just arrived in the town from Judaea. But this is just guesswork. The documents *demonstrate* nothing about changing demographic patterns, only the trivial point that plots of land constantly changed hands.

[53] Cf. N. Lewis, "The Babatha Archive: A Response," *IEJ* 44 (1994): 245.

[54] Among the Jewish elements may be exaction of a penalty on an interest-free loan (see above); appointment of two guardians for an orphan, rather than the one guardian required by Roman law, though this is problematic, since one of the appointees was apparently pagan. A full

bedded in the system, and we cannot be sure that the legal practice, even of the local pagans, lacked them.

About the ritual practice of the Jews of Maoza we know nothing. Nowhere in the papyri so far published is there any mention of the Sabbath, festivals, food regulations, the sabbatical year, synagogues, or any other Jewish institutions. Several papyri report actions that violated Jewish law, though the violations are all surprisingly ambiguous, except perhaps the premarital cohabitation implied in P. Yadin 37; even Babatha's oath by the Tyche of the emperor (P. Yadin 16, a land registration document) is reported in the document itself to be a Greek translation of what Babatha supposedly said in Aramaic. There is no way of knowing whether she really swore by the *gada deKesar*. There are no ascertainable cases of intermarriage.[55] Nor, to judge from papyri on which Semitic dates are given, was business conducted on Jewish holidays, though the statistical sample is too small to be conclusive; in any case, it is not known whether the Jewish liturgical and Semitic civil calendars were in agreement.[56]

In Galilee

The legal lives of the Jews of pre-70 Judaea, to extrapolate with admitted recklessness from P. Murab. 18, were characterized by a high degree of explicit tension between Pentateuchal prescription and local practice (i.e., the Torah significantly influenced their legal activities), while those of the Jews of post-106 Roman Arabia were characterized by no such tension, as far as we know; the Torah, in other words, is invisible in the documents so far published. This is not to deny the probability that the Torah retained for these Jews its symbolic force and affected their behavior in some ways; this may explain why in 132

---

consideration will have to await publication of the second volume of the archive. In the meantime, Lewis's legal comments on the Greek papyri require supplementation and revision, for which, see Wasserstein, "A Marriage Contract"; M. Broshi, "Agriculture and Economy in Roman Palestine according to Babatha's Papyri," *Zion* 55 (1990): 269–81; M. Goodman, "Babatha's Story," *JRS* 81 (1991): 169–76; B. Isaac, "The Babatha Archive: A Review Article," *IEJ* 42 (1992): 62–75; T. Ilan, "Premarital Cohabitation in Ancient Judaea: The Evidence of the Babatha Archive and the Mishnah (Ketubbot 1.4)," *HTR* 86 (1993): 247–64; H. Cotton, "The Guardianship of Jesus Son of Babatha: Roman and Local Law in the Province of Arabia," *JRS* 83 (1993): 94–108.

[55] Goodman's suggestion ("Babatha's Story") that Babatha daughter of Simon herself was not Jewish is special pleading. Simon could be a Greek name, as Goodman argues, but in the Semitic documents it is invariably transcribed as ShM'WN—a name attested only among Jews, as far as I am aware.

[56] These same qualities characterize the more recently published "archive of Salome Komaise," also from Maoza in the 120s and 130s; see H. M. Cotton and A. Yardeni, *Aramaic, Hebrew, and Greek Documentary Texts from Nahal Hever and Other Sites*, Discoveries in the Judaean Desert 27 (Oxford: Clarendon, 1997), nos. 60–73, with introduction on pp. 158–65.

some of them joined a revolt intended in part to restore the temple and the authority of the Torah in Judaea—if that is how Babatha's papers reached the Judaean desert. The legal force of the Torah in pre-70 Galilee, Peraea, and Idumaea[57] probably occupied an intermediate position, for these districts differed from both Judaea and Roman Arabia in important ways. In Judaea, the temple staff exerted tight control, both formally and informally. It is likely that many of the large landowners in Judaea were the wealthier priests, like Josephus, or others who derived their fortunes from conditions created by the economic attractiveness of the temple and city of Jerusalem. They thus had an interest in supporting a bureaucracy of scribes and judges who would mediate between the temple and laws of the Torah, on the one hand, and the practice of the villagers on the other. There was a large class of such potential mediators available because the poorer part of the priesthood was vast and concentrated in Judaea, and its members often had some learning and had been assigned by the Torah itself a special role as legal authorities; they also enjoyed the prestige associated with Temple service.

In Arabia, on the other hand, priests and experts in the Torah had no official role of any sort; the great powers in the district were not wealthy Jewish priests, but members of the Roman administration and army. Local scribes, arbitrators, and so on, whether Jewish or pagan, had to master the language and norms of Roman and local Nabataean legal and administrative practice. The Torah, devoid of real power, was left only with its symbolic role, though in a district like Babatha's Zoarene, whose population was heavily Jewish, this may have been no small matter.

Galilee and Peraea were under less direct control of the temple and its staff than Judaea. Local bureaucrats were often appointees of the local Herodian rulers.[58] Josephus, in his account of his own experiences in Galilee, takes it for granted that the real power in the district was in the hands of the country landowners; but these men, unlike their Judaean counterparts, often lacked close ties to the central institutions, though from Josephus's account we know that some of them maintained alliances with prominent Jerusalemites. Their personal religious predispositions will thus have varied greatly. The future rebel leader, John of Gischala, for example, seems, if we discount Josephus's vituperation, to have been a pious Jew with a large clientele. Other great

---

[57] Idumaea was administratively associated with Judaea during the first century and so may have had a closer association with the Temple than Galilee; it is not impossible that P. Murab. 18 was drawn up in Idumaea; it is, by contrast, not unlikely that Babatha and company, whose practice of civil law owed little to biblical legislation, were of Idumaean origin.

[58] Local bureaucrats may have had very little power. Interestingly the Babatha archive shows that Babatha never took her many suits and complaints to local judges and arbitrators, but always to the Roman governor and his staff. Can we extrapolate from this to pre-70 Palestine? Probably not. Josephus considered the circuit riding of Herod Philip, who ruled a mostly pagan kingdom, especially noteworthy. See *Ant* 18.106–7; Goodman, "Babatha's Story," 171–72.

patrons may have been less interested in their clients' support for the Temple and Torah and thus apathetic toward local scribes and judges who attempted to negotiate between the Torah and local practice. With respect to civil law, their behavior may have been like that of Babatha's family, though perhaps biblical law was more important for the Galileans.[59] As for ritual law, there are scarcely grounds for speculation. We know that there were Galileans who objected to the paintings in Antipas's palace and the foreskins of Josephus's pagan friends, but this may mean only that a certain type of rigorous Jewish pietism was a cultural option in Galilee, as we could have inferred even in the absence of evidence. It is also interesting that the earliest post-destruction rabbis are said to have rendered legal decisions in Galilee—more frequently than in Peraea or Arabia, but less frequently than in Judaea.[60] We are, it may be suggested, more likely to encounter large-scale manifestations of aberrant behavior in Galilee and Peraea than in Judaea.

An example of radical aberrancy *may* be Jesus of Nazareth, whose followers claimed that he had an equivocal, or even hostile, attitude toward Jewish law. However, they also claimed that he was chased around Lower Galilee (then ruled by Herod Antipas) by a hostile Jerusalemite bureaucracy of Pharisees and scribes. Though the first claim is slightly more plausible than the second, both are perhaps best understood as reflecting the interests of later Christians.

In the Diaspora

The situation in the Diaspora differed in yet another way. There, membership in a community was optional, and the leaders of the communities rarely if ever had full legal jurisdiction over constituents (certainly, there was no *Personalitätsprinzip*—the common medieval and early modern principle that birth determined the legal system under which one was fated to live one's life and therefore that the executors of the legal system technically had full jurisdiction over their constituents).[61] Thus, no one was compelled to submit to the authority of the Jewish law and its local interpreters, so there was no legal way to enforce particular standards of behavior. Undoubtedly, though,

[59] It would be interesting to know what the legal background was, if any, of the Galilean practice of severing the hands of certain types of criminals, repeatedly reported by Josephus in his autobiography. It has no obvious connection with biblical law, though it can perhaps be reconciled with difficulty with the lex talionis of Exodus 21:24–25: one who sins with his hand (e.g., forgery—the crime of which Justus of Tiberias' brother was accused) has his hand severed. There is no evidence that the Galileans themselves engaged in such reasoning.

[60] See S. Cohen, "The Place of the Rabbi in Jewish Society of the Second Century," in *Galilee in Late Antiquity*, p. 160.

[61] Indeed, according to Rajak, "Was There a Roman Charter?" the right of the Jews in the cities to live according to their own laws was entirely informal and received government support only when challenged.

there were illegal ways, and in any case the force of social pressure should not be underestimated. Despite the fact that by the first century the Jews of at least the larger communities had, like those of Palestine, pretty well internalized the ideological centrality of the Torah and the Temple, it is in the Diaspora that one finds clearest evidence of radically anomalous types of Judaism, as well as a constant trickle of people both in and out of Judaism.[62]

To sum up, the *functioning* of the simple ideological scheme outlined earlier was complex, and its effects on social realities are not easy to predict. The official status and ideological centrality of the Torah had some readily discernible consequences in Jewish Palestine before 70, chiefly that public life had in many areas a special texture and that there had come to be a class of expert manipulators of the Torah. Furthermore, the ideological and practical importance of the Torah and Temple (but especially the Torah) provided a set of cultural options. Mastery of the Torah was a source of prestige and power, even to some extent, in the non-Judaean districts. The Torah thus generated around itself a class of expert manipulators and mediators, apart from the pious, who were dedicated to a life in full accordance with its precepts. This class, unlike the temple priesthood, was not restricted by descent or even necessarily by social class, though in practice the Torah itself gave priests and levites priority as its interpreters, and mainly the relatively well-to-do were able to educate their sons.[63] What our grasp of the normative ideological system of first-century Jewish Palestine does *not* allow us to do, however, is describe how most people actually lived their lives.

The Myth

The covenant constituted only one of the central ideological axes of Judaism in the first century; the other intersecting ideological axis was constituted by a mythological complex that received its classic literary formulation in some

[62] In addition, the papyri provide little (though not no) evidence that Jews in rural Egypt (as opposed to Alexandria)—even in the large villages and the nome capitals where they were numerous and certainly in some sense constituted communities—ever followed Jewish civil law; see part 3, chapter 8.

[63] But note that in Deuteronomy 16:18–20, 17:8–13, it is not said that the local *shofetim* and *shoterim* (types of magistrates) need to be priests—only those at the higher level; there is in fact no particular reason to think that local judges, scribes, and teachers in the later Second Temple period had to be priests or Levites, though many of them may have been, especially in Judaea, where priests were numerous. D. Schwartz's contention ("Scribes and Pharisees, Hypocrites: Who Are the Scribes in the New Testament," *Studies in the Jewish Background of Christianity* [Tübingen: Mohr, 1992], pp. 89–101) that scribes were generally Levites is possible but has not been demonstrated.

of the so-called apocalyptic books, especially 1 Enoch, and in related literature, like Jubilees, the Serekh HaYahad, and the War Scroll. This issue is complicated, controversial, and poorly understood.

I am not primarily interested in the apocalypse as a literary genre. I will not have anything to say about the still controverted definition of apocalyptic, nor, indeed, am I particularly concerned with some of the common features of the literary apocalypses (e.g., heavenly ascents or lists of revealed things), though such features may provide important hints about the milieus in which the books were composed.[64] What I am mainly interested in is the central myth of apocalypticism as an ideological system and its ethos as a worldview. (I will from now on refer to this as "the myth" or "mythology," using the term "apocalypticism" only to designate the rather confused but still common scholarly construct.) Evidence of this ideological system is, to repeat, not limited to apocalypses; indeed, one important type of apocalypse, the historical (e.g., Daniel 7–12), often features only traces of the main apocalyptic myth, while substantial accounts may appear in books like Jubilees and the Serekh HaYahad, which are not by any formal criteria apocalyptic.

I am also not interested in speculating about the origins of the narrative structure of the apocalyptic mythology, its relations to biblical prophecy, its debts to Persia, Egypt, Greece, Mesopotamia, or the royal propaganda of the long-departed kings of Canaan and Israel.[65] The genetic problem seems insoluble, but the very intensity of the search for origins tells us something about the strangeness of the phenomenon and implies that apocalypticism cannot be explained as a straightforward evolutionary development (from, e.g., classi-

---

[64] The main collection of material is J. H. Charlesworth, ed., *Old Testament Pseudepigrapha*, 2 vols. (Garden City: Doubleday, 1983–1985). Caution is in order, since the texts included in no sense constitute a canon. Many of the texts are Christian and medieval and have no more than a hypothetical connection to ancient Jewish apocalypticism; and all the texts were transmitted and revised, in ways that usually cannot be determined, by Christian copyists, so that it is often impossible to tell whether a particular text is "Jewish" or "Christian." Exceptions are those like Jubilees and parts of 1 Enoch, substantial fragments of which were found at Qumran. For a brief discussion of the character of the apocalyptic genre, see J. J. Collins, "Genre, Ideology, and Social Movements in Jewish Apocalypticism," in J. J. Collins and J. Charlesworth, eds., *Mysteries and Revelations; Apocalyptic Studies since the Uppsala Colloquium* (Sheffield, U.K.: JSOT Press, 1991), pp. 13–23; and in much greater detail, in the same collection, D. Hellholm, "Methodological Reflections on the Problem of the Definition of Generic Texts," pp. 135–63. The lists are well discussed by M. Stone, "Lists of Revealed Things in the Apocalyptic Literature," *Selected Studies in Pseudepigrapha and Apocrypha* (Leiden: Brill, 1991), 379–418. They are especially important because they suggest that the books were written in a scribal-wisdom milieu. Heavenly ascents: M. Himmelfarb, *Ascent to Heaven*.

[65] The last is the subject of a series of books by Margaret Barker, starting with *The Older Testament: The Survival of Themes from the Ancient Royal Cult in Sectarian Judaism and Early Christianity* (London: SPCK, 1987). Despite its addiction to certain *idées fixes*, the book is worth reading for its account of the discontinuity of the Enochic myth with Deuteronomic ideology.

cal Israelite prophecy).[66] All we can say for certain, more or less, is that the narrative first appears in writing in the third century B.C.E. in the Enochic Book of Watchers (1 Enoch 1–36) and that accounts of or allusions to it are subsequently extremely common in Jewish literature and are of definitive importance for early Christians.

Not only is the genesis of apocalypticism obscure, but all attempts to connect its "emergence" with specific events have failed. It was once thought that Daniel, published around the time of the Maccabean revolt, was the earliest apocalypse and inferred from its date of composition that apocalypticism emerged because of the Antiochan persecution and became popular subsequently as a reaction to Roman oppression in Palestine. But the discovery at Qumran of manuscripts of the Enochic books, the earliest of them consensually dated to around 200 B.C.E.,[67] made this combination of logical fallacy (of the *post hoc ergo propter hoc* type), historical naïveté, and quasi-Marxian romanticism impossible, though elements of the mix survive.[68] Though the *historical* apocalypses *are* often reactions to foreign domination (and sometimes to inadequate native rule), the apocalyptic mythology as an ideological system has no unambiguous political content, nor is it reasonable to suppose that its "emergence" and spread were mainly reactions to specific events of political history. And there are no grounds for considering apocalypticism an artifact of popular reaction to social oppression either.[69] In its literary expression, at least, it is in fact an elite or subelite phenomenon, for the most part socially coextensive with wisdom literature.[70] As I will suggest in more detail below, the mythology is concerned with solving several related problems: How can the knowledge that the world was created by a just, powerful, and benevolent God be reconciled with the fact that the world is evil and chaotic; and how can the distance between the world and God that is implied by the existence of evil be bridged? The conception of apocalyptic mythology as a set of solutions to a complex of problems—reached, significantly, through mythopoiesis, not metaphysical speculation—has the inescapable consequence of loosening its connection to events of political and social history: awareness of

[66] Such an explanation was once common; its most recent and thorough proponent is P. D. Hanson, *The Dawn of Apocalyptic* (Philadelphia: Fortress, 1975); cf. Collins, "Genre, Ideology," 16–17. For detailed criticism of Hanson, see R. Carroll, "Twilight of Prophecy or Dawn of Apocalyptic?" *JSOT* 14 (1979): 3–35.

[67] See Milik, *Books of Enoch*, pp. 22–41; and M. Knibb, *The Ethiopic Book of Enoch* (Oxford: Clarendon, 1978), pp. 6–15.

[68] See G. Boccaccini, "Jewish Apocalyptic Tradition: The Contribution of Italian Scholarship," in *Mysteries and Revelations*, 34–35 (in general a summary of Sacchi).

[69] This point was well made by L. L. Grabbe, "The Social Setting of Early Jewish Apocalypticism," *JSP* 4 (1989): 27–47.

[70] See P. R. Davies, "The Social World of Apocalyptic Writings," in R. E. Clements, ed., *The World of Ancient Israel: Social, Anthropological, and Political Perspectives* (Cambridge: Cambridge University Press, 1989), p. 263.

the problem of evil was not generated (though it may admittedly have been intensified) by an event.[71] Jews were unhappy long before Antiochus IV or Pompey marched into Jerusalem.

This is not to suggest that the emergence and spread of apocalyptic mythology have no explanation—that they were generated entirely by the internal dynamics of Israelite and Jewish religious ideology and float free of material causation—or even that political developments had no influence on them. But we must be clear about what it is we are trying to explain. We can trace the emergence and spread of the myth at first in literature. What we need to account for, then, is the emergence of the ideology among the literate, especially in the very same scribal/wisdom circles that were responsible for transmitting and promulgating the covenantal ideology. Indeed, it seems likely that the historical process *mainly* responsible for generating apocalyptic mythology and causing its spread was the rise of the covenantal ideology, to which it seems both a reaction and a complement. We must also consider the character of the relationship between the quasi-official, literary version of apocalyptic mythology and the presumably more popular characteristics of ancient Judaism as the recognition of the power of demons, astrology, millenarianism, and so on—a relationship perhaps comparable to that between the Pentateuch and local legal praxis.

Content of the Myth

Although the various accounts of the myth differ significantly in detail, it is not especially difficult to detect the common narrative structure underlying them. As in the Genesis narrative, God created the universe. But in the myth, God was not alone but was surrounded by ranks of subsidiary deities that at some point gained full or partial control of creation. The earliest account, in 1 Enoch 1–36 (parts of which may have been composed as early as 300 B.C.E.—not long after the common dating of the Pentateuchal priestly document, which includes most of Genesis 1–11) connects this demonic revolu-

---

[71] I have been influenced on this point (indirectly) by Paolo Sacchi (*Jewish Apocalyptic and Its History* [Sheffield: Sheffield Academic Press, 1990], esp. pp. 32–87; Davies, "Social World," 268, also emphasizes the importance of the problem of evil in generating this myth; on the problem of God's distance, see M. Himmelfarb, "Revelation and Rapture: The Transformation of the Visionary in the Ascent Apocalypses," in *Mysteries and Revelations*, 79–90, especially 89–90, relying on Scholem), who also had the good idea of contrasting Enoch with two roughly contemporary works, Ecclesiastes and the slightly later Wisdom of Ben Sira. But Sacchi seems to take the problem of evil as directly generative of certain key apocalyptic texts, which seems to me unhelpfully reductionist; it also seems to constitute an attempt to define a literary genre by positing a shared theological concern, also a bad idea. I am merely arguing that the central myth of apocalypticism—variously transformed, chopped up, and even skipped altogether in the literary apocalypses—is concerned with the problem of evil and, more importantly, that it implies an ethos fundamentally at odds with that of the covenant.

tion with the enigmatically brief biblical story of the descent to earth of the
sons of the gods (Genesis 6:1–4). It is not impossible that Enoch reports here
a fuller version of the Israelite tale anxiously alluded to in Genesis. In any
case, the good God and his minions have been defeated by the forces of evil,
and the world is consequently a chaotic place, filled with wickedness, suffering, and disease. God and his throngs of supporters have retired in splendor
to the highest heaven, where they wait for the preordained drama to play itself
out and occasionally are paid court by human holy men. In the most dualistic
versions (e.g., in the Serekh HaYahad and the Pauline Epistles) the world is
actually considered the dominion of Satan and his attending demons, *tout
court*. In more moderate accounts, the world is more complicated, and Satan's
rule is less absolute, though he and his demons remain a powerful presence
in the world.[72] In all versions, though, there will one day come a struggle
between good and evil in which good will win. God will then rule the world
alone, his reign perhaps (but not in every version of the story) ushered in by
a messianic figure, and punish the wicked and reward the righteous.

Myth and Covenant

This story's stark contradiction of the covenantal ideology is remarkable. The
covenant imagines an orderly world governed justly by the one God. The
apocalyptic myth imagines a world in disarray, filled with evil; a world in
which people do *not* get what they deserve. God is not in control in any
obvious way; indeed, the cosmology of the myth is dualist or polytheist, depending on the version, though the rhetoric of the mythographers is usually
monotheist (which does not prevent the Dead Sea Scrolls from calling the
angels *elim*, gods).[73] The myth is also fatalistic: only the divine figures have
volition, while humans are basically their victims. Nor does the myth explicitly
promote observance of the commandments, although Daniel and some of the
Dead Sea Scrolls, for example, seem to imagine that it is those who observe
the commandments who will be rewarded at the "end of days."

And yet, most (if not all) of the literary works that allude to the mythological
narrative or are influenced by its ethos do in addition promote the covenant
or are otherwise concerned with the Torah and related literature. The visions
and "testaments" in which the myth is most fully recounted are all attributed
to or largely concern biblical figures. The Enochic tradition may owe some-

---

[72] Sectarians like Paul and the author of the Serekh HaYahad believed that their sects had
successfully liberated themselves from Satan's rule, though the importance of exorcisms in both
Qumran and Christian ritual indicates that this liberation was not achieved without a fight.

[73] For an interesting argument against the standard characterization of ancient (or indeed most
medieval) Judaism as monotheistic, see A. P. Hayman, "Monotheism: A Misused Word in Jewish
Studies?" *JJS* 42 (1991): 1–15. L. Hurtado, "What Do We Mean by 'First Century Jewish Monotheism'?" *SBL Seminar Papers*, 1993, pp. 348–67, provides a more nuanced discussion.

thing to Mesopotamian lore associated with the antediluvian hero Enmedura-nki,[74] but in its Jewish version this lore is associated with a biblical hero. It is furthermore possible to read the Book of Watchers as a dramatic expansion of the biblical Flood story, in which the entire mythological narrative is compressed into the few generations between the descent of the sons of the gods and Noah, with the Flood serving as the final act of the drama. It is only in the first and last chapters of 1 Enoch that the compiler of the collection made an explicit link between the book's expanded Enoch story and the "present." Jubilees is a rewriting of Genesis 1–Exodus 12, which argues that the Torah was studied and a particular version of halakhah was observed even by the pre-Mosaic patriarchs; yet it is also suffused with the mythological ethos, imagining a world filled with angels and demons. And it contains in chapter 23 an important account of the apocalyptic myth.

The juxtaposition of these incongruous systems seems to me to be present in its most poignant and self-conscious form in some of the Dead Sea Scrolls, for the Qumran sectarians had an especially stark dualistic cosmology (as sectarian groups often do), but also an extremely strong devotion to the study and strict observance of the Law (and plenty of time to contemplate the contradiction).[75] In the following passage, taken from the discourse that the master of the sect is commanded to deliver to novices, I have formatted the covenantal passages in bold type, and the mythological passages in italics:

From the God of knowledge comes all that is and shall be. Before ever they existed He established their whole design, and when, as ordained for them, they come into being, it is in accord with His glorious design that they accomplish their task without change. The laws of all things are in His hand and He provides them with all their needs.

He has created man to govern the world, and has appointed for him *two spirits in which to walk until the time of His visitation: the spirits of truth and falsehood. Those born of truth spring from a fountain of light, but those born of falsehood spring from a source of darkness. All the children of righteousness are ruled by the Prince of Light and walk in the ways of light, but all the children of falsehood are ruled by the Angel of Darkness and walk in the ways of darkness.*

[74] This is the main argument of both J. VanderKam, *Enoch and the Growth of an Apocalyptic Tradition* (Washington: Catholic Biblical Association, 1984), and H. Kvanvig, *The Roots of Apocalyptic: The Mesopotamian Background of the Enoch Figure and the Son of Man* (Neukirchen-Vluyn: Neukirchener-Verlag, 1988).

[75] See S. Fraade, "Interpretive Authority in the Studying Community at Qumran," *JJS* 54 (1993): 46–69; on Qumran dualism (with some perhaps excessively subtle conclusions), see J. Frey, "Different Patterns of Dualistic Thought in the Qumran Library: Reflections on Their Background and History"; M. Bernstein, F. García Martínez, and J. Kampen, eds., *Legal Texts and Legal Issues: Proceedings of the Second Meeting of the International Organization for Qumran Studies, Cambridge 1995, Published in Honour of Joseph M. Baumgarten* (Leiden: Brill, 1997), pp. 275–335.

The Angel of Darkness leads all the children of righteousness astray, and until his end, all their sin, iniquities, wickedness, and all their unlawful deeds are caused by his dominion in accordance with the mysteries of God. Every one of their chastisements, and every one of the seasons of their distress, shall be brought about by the rule of his persecution; for all his allotted spirits seek the overthrow of the sons of light.

But the God of Israel and His Angel of Truth will succour all the sons of light. **For it is He who created the spirits of Light and Darkness and founded every action upon them and established every deed [upon] their [ways]. And He loves the one everlastingly and delights in its works forever;** *but the counsel of the other He loathes and forever hates its ways. . . .* [this is sheer illogic, generated by the juxtaposition of opposites: if the all-powerful God, creator of all things, loathes the spirit of darkness, why did He create it?]

The nature of all the children of the men is ruled by these (two spirits), and during their life all the hosts of men have a portion of their divisions and walk in (both) their ways. And the whole reward for their deeds shall be, for everlasting ages, according to whether each man's portion in their two divisions is great or small. **For God has established the spirits in equal measure until the final age, and has set everlasting hatred between their divisions.** *Truth abhors the works of falsehood, and falsehood hates all the ways of truth. And their struggle is fierce in all their arguments for they do not walk together.*

But in the mysteries of His understanding, and in His glorious wisdom, God has ordained an end for falsehood, and at the time of the visitation, He will destroy it forever. Then truth, which has wallowed in the ways of wickedness during the dominion of falsehood until the appointed time of judgement, shall arise in the world forever. God will then purify every deed of man with His truth. (1QS, cols. iii-iv = Serekh Hayahad, or "Community Rule," trans. G. Vermes, with some revisions)

In this presentation of the ideology of the sect, distilled and simplified for catechetical use, the conflicting systems are not simply juxtaposed; each is slightly altered to produce a harmonized, though by no means entirely harmonious, whole. From the covenantal perspective, the central problem of the myth is God's defeat: how could God have allowed evil to prevail in the world? The sectarian ideology, taking up an idea found in the Enochic tradition and Jubilees, responded that God did so intentionally, in accordance with a plan whose meaning is a mystery, even if its course may be described. It has recently been suggested that the apocalyptists borrowed this notion, and the determinism it implies, together with the figure of Enoch from Mesopotamian soothsayers.[76] Perhaps. Yet there can be no question about the function of the claim that God withdrew intentionally as a tool for harmonizing the myth and the covenant. There is also no question about the importance of the claim that

---

[76] See Davies, "Social World," p. 261.

the rule of Evil accords with an inviolable but inscrutable divine plan in books like Jubilees, whose interest in chronology not only is scholastic but also reflects an attempt to discern a symmetry in God's plan, and so predict the time of its dénouement.[77] It is also important in the ideology of the Dead Sea sect. That is, for the sectarians and others, the harmonization of the systems, mechanical as it may seem to us, was not simply a matter of producing an orderly piece of metaphysical speculation. They meant it with utter seriousness.

The repeated juxtaposition of the covenant and the myth in ancient Jewish writing indicates that though the systems are logically incongruous, they did not for the most part generate social division. That is, the literary evidence provides no grounds for speaking of an "apocalyptic Judaism," or even "apocalyptic conventicles," constructs that were once popular among scholars.[78] Apocalyptic Judaism's opposite number, "covenantal Judaism," may have existed but is marginal in the literature. Only a few books written between 200 B.C.E. and 100 C.E., most notably Ben Sira, 1 Maccabees, and the works of Josephus (and the last not very rigorously), lack clear traces of the influence of the myth, either because their authors rejected it or because they had no taste for its esotericism or considered it unsuitable for their audience. The Sadducees are said to have denied resurrection and angels (Acts 23:8): if this report is accurate, it may imply rejection of the myth as a whole. However, if Jean Le Moyne's interpretation of this passage is correct and the Sadducees rejected not angels but only their role in resurrection, then even the Sadducees may have acknowledged some version of the myth.[79]

Thus, by the first century, if not earlier, the myth was a more or less fully naturalized part of the ideology of Judaism, although there remained, at least

---

[77] This concern is present in much apocalyptic literature: see J. Licht, "The Attitude to Past Events in the Bible and in Apocalyptic Literature," *Tarbiz* 60 (1990): 1–18, especially 5ff.

[78] Davies, "Social World," pp. 252–53; Collins, "Genre, Ideology," pp. 23–24. Michael Stone has argued that 4 Ezra, 2 Baruch, and the Ascension of Isaiah, all texts of the later first century C.E., show that apocalyptic visionaries, though they may sometimes have enjoyed wide popularity, often had small circles of followers to whom alone they revealed their esoteric knowledge. This is not quite the same thing in social terms as the conventicle, implying a small but institutionalized organization; see "On Reading an Apocalypse," in *Mysteries and Revelations*, 76–7. G. Boccaccini (*Beyond the Essene Hypothesis: The Parting of the Ways between Qumran and Enochic Judaism* [Grand Rapids, Mich.: Eerdmans, 1998]) has now revived the idea of an "Enochic Judaism," by which he apparently means a social organization; but Boccaccini has generally adopted bad habit shared by Neusner and some New Testament scholars of assuming that books correspond to groups, or "Judaisms": see his methodological reflections on pp. 8–11.

[79] See J. Le Moyne, *Les Sadducéens* (Paris: Gabalda, 1972), pp. 131–35; as Le Moyne observes, angels are mentioned in the Pentateuch, so it would have been difficult for the Sadducees to deny their existence. Some scholars think that Judaism in the first century basically was covenantal. Sanders, *Judaism: Practice and Belief*, p. 8, dismisses apocalypticism in a paragraph and, as far as I can tell, fails even to mention its more embarrassing, because less systematic, cousins magic and demonology.

in some circles, the consciousness that it was separate from the covenantal system, and some individuals or groups may have consciously rejected it. How did the myth function?

The Functions of the Myth

Wherever the myth and its components came from, our main information about them comes from literature. The classic formulations of the myth, with their interest in lists and systematization, and their scholasticism,[80] are evidently products of a scribal ethos.[81] There are indications in the books themselves that some of the scribes/wise men who formulated the myth considered it esoteric. Hence Ben Sira's advice not to concern oneself with hidden lore (perhaps apocalyptic speculation); the esoteric "heavenly tablets" often mentioned in the Book of Watchers and Jubilees;[82] the emphasis in the Dead Sea Scrolls on the "mysterious" character of the myth (and Josephus's statement that Essenes swore to keep the names of the angels secret—War 2.145); the suggestion in both the Dead Sea Scrolls and 4 Ezra that there exists an exoteric and an esoteric Torah, the latter probably to be identified with a corpus of mythological exegesis and/or apocalyptic books.[83] Thus some scribes/wise men supplemented the prestige and influence they enjoyed as priests, legal experts, and teachers by claiming access to divine mysteries even more obscure than those written down in the Torah. Other scribes may simply have had a taste for the abstruse. Though these developments are now often explained by adducing the influence of the convergence of scribalism and manticism in Babylonia, it is perhaps easier to suppose that such a convergence developed independently in Palestine in part as a result of the ever greater sanctity generally attributed to the Israelite books that the scribes interpreted, resulting in a "mantic" reading of the books—a reading motivated by the conviction that they conceal cosmic mysteries that can be revealed through exegesis.[84] This is not to deny the influence of Babylonian manticism on the

---

[80] On the derivation of the angels from exegesis, see S. Olyan, *A Thousand Thousands Served Him: Exegesis and the Naming of Angels in Ancient Judaism* (Tübingen: Mohr, 1993).

[81] In addition to Davies, "Social Setting," see J. Z. Smith, "Wisdom and Apocalyptic," *Map Is Not Territory* (Leiden: Brill, 1978), pp. 67–87; Stone, "Lists of Revealed Things."

[82] See now H. Najman, "Interpretation as Primordial Writing: Jubilees and Its Authority-Conferring Strategies," *JSJ* 30 (1999): 379–410.

[83] The scribal conception of the mythology as esoteric helps explain why none of this literature except Daniel, which is only half apocalyptic and which of all the apocalyptic books is most closely linked to classical prophecy, became canonical—this despite the fact that the Enoch books and Jubilees and a few others were widely read and were in fact considered holy at Qumran. "Our" (i.e., the rabbinic) canon is exoteric.

[84] On mantic, or "mantological" exegesis, see M. Fishbane, *Biblical Interpretation in Ancient Israel* (Oxford: Oxford University Press, 1984), pp. 443–505; also, Blenkinsopp, *Prophecy and*

substance of Jewish scribal esotericism; I wish only to suggest an internal social dynamic that might have made the influence productive.

The myth also had a function outside the scribal circles that formulated it. It was a way of compensating for the deficiencies of the covenantal system. Clearly, as a cosmology and an anthropology the covenant, for all its elegant simplicity (or rather because of it) was problematic. Life does not work the way the covenantal system says it should: God manifestly does not reward the righteous and punish the wicked, and Israel's observance of the covenant and performance of the cult does not guarantee its well-being. This problem was apparently recognized even by the classical formulators of the covenantal ideology in the sixth century B.C.E. Their main work, the Deuteronomic history (the name scholars give to Joshua, Judges, Samuel, and Kings) is after all a sustained attempt to *argue* that the history of Israel conformed with and so confirmed the covenantal worldview; that God let Israel prosper when it observed his commandments and punished it when it did not. To argue this they had to explain away such inconvenient but generally known facts as the prosperity of the "sinful" Northern Kingdom, the success of the wicked Judahite king Manasseh, and (most troubling of all because most recent) the failure of the pious Josiah and the destruction of his kingdom not long after the imposition of religious reforms undertaken in the spirit of the Deuteronomists themselves!

As we have already seen, Jewish writers of the third century B.C.E. were peculiarly concerned with the failure of the covenantal system to explain evil. To recapitulate, for Koheleth, as for many Greek thinkers (by whom he may not have been directly influenced), the response was to combine philosophical nihilism (God is not in control; the laws of nature are unchanging but blind; there is no point to anything, etc., etc.) with conformity with the requirements of the Law (since there is no point in not observing it).[85] Ben Sira, who wrote about 190 B.C.E., simply denied that there was a problem and stolidly affirmed the adequacy of Deuteronomic piety. And the author of the Book of Watchers responded with mythopoiesis.

It is an obvious inference from the fact that the books long continued to be copied and read that at various times various members of the Palestinian Jewish elites and subelites found all these responses attractive.[86] But the mytholog-

Canon: A Contribution to the Study of Jewish Origins (Notre Dame, Ind.: Notre Dame University Press, 1977), e.g., p. 71, referring to the "scribalization of prophecy."

[85] See Bickerman, *Four Strange Books*; see also N. Whybray, "The Social World of the Wisdom Writers," in R. E. Clements, ed., *The World of Ancient Israel: Sociological, Anthropological, and Political Perspectives* (Cambridge: Cambridge University Press, 1989), pp. 242–44.

[86] I am assuming that the very act of writing marked these authors as either elites (leading priests or landowners) or subelites (relatively well-to-do/respectable priests/scribes), classes that even when combined can scarcely have numbered more than a few hundred in Judaea around 200 B.C.E. Some have supposed that greater specificity is possible, especially in the case of Kohel-

ical response had the advantage of admitting cosmological schemes into the ideological center of Judaism—as well as associated behavior (see below)—that were at odds with the covenantal ideology but mitigated its deficiencies. Or, to put it differently, like the broad conception of Torah (which allowed for the legitimation of all sorts of non-Pentateuchal law), incorporating into the system a mythology that, a logician might say, contradicted the covenant but was nevertheless claimed as Jewish by the mediators of Temple and Torah, made possible the cooptation of the (threatening) elements of the mythology. And the same process gave these mediators the opportunity to claim control over the myth.

It may be helpful at this point to discuss in more detail what I have hitherto taken for granted. I am suggesting that a significant popular expression of the mythology—and an important source of its appeal, and probably of many of the details of its literary exposition—was the conviction that minor deities are responsible for suffering, illness, and other types of misfortune and mischief, and that these deities can be controlled and their power in some cases deflected.[87] Though this point is important for my argument, it must remain a suggestion. Evidence for Jewish magical practice before the fourth century C.E., when amulets, magical papyri, and so on start to be common, is too poor to enable us to be specific about its relationship to apocalyptic mythology: the apocalyptic books are entirely speculative and descriptive. For a full amalgamation of apocalyptic cosmology and magical prescription, we must wait for the late antique Hekhalot books and the *Sefer HaRazim*.

However, evidence about earlier times is not wholly nonexistent: Josephus reports that he witnessed a successful performance by a Jewish exorcist who depended on spells composed by King Solomon (*Ant* 8.45–49)—an important illustration of the convergence of scribal expertise in "ancient" writings, wisdom, and knowledge of/mastery over the demonic world, a mixture typical also of some of the apocalyptic books. The apostle Paul, a contemporary of Josephus's magician, displayed a similar combination of skills, in addition to

---

eth, whom Whybray and Bickerman (see last note) characterized as a disillusioned but detached aristocrat—probably because he pretended to be a king but probably also because detachment per se seems aristocratic, in contrast especially to the "bourgeois" dutifulness of Ben Sira. But both Bickerman and Whybray were thinking in terms derived from pre–World War I Europe. Perhaps a more productive approach would be to examine the writers' attitude to money and trade. Cf. Kurke, *Coins, Bodies, Games, and Gold*, for a sophisticated analysis of Herodotus, among others, in these terms. As usual, Jewish studies lags. In the meantime see J. Kugel, "Qohelet and Money," *CBQ* 51 (1989): 32–49, which is at least a start)

[87] There may be other ways in which the myth reflected, and influenced, popular religiosity, e.g., in its strong interest in astrology and its near worship of the sun, on which see M. Smith, "Helios in Palestine," *EI* 16 (1982): *199–*214. Smith argues that worship of the sun, traces of which he detects in the Enoch material (207), among the Dead Sea sect and the Essenes, and among the general Jewish population of Palestine in the first century (209) and later (210), was justified as adoration of a powerful angel.

a probably rudimentary and certainly eccentric familiarity with Greek rhetoric and popular philosophy. Paul may not have been alone among early Jewish Christian apostles in possessing these skills; he is just best known. The magical texts of the fourth through seventh centuries collected by Naveh and Shaked show no signs of direct knowledge of the old apocalypses.[88] However, their angelology and demonology is clearly in part indebted to a tradition initiated by the Book of Watchers, in that many of the divine characters invoked in the amulets are, like those of the Enochic tradition, clearly hypostases of divine attributes and the like, information about which was derived from biblical exegesis, endowed with personality and volition.[89] I suspect that the angels and demons in these amulets, as also in the Hekhalot books, are often identical with those of the apocalypses.[90] This suggests that the angelology of the scribes eventually became the angelology of the Palestinian countryside, or at very least hints at a tie between the subelite formulators of the myth and the magical practicioners in the villages. We can get some idea of what the new, Jewish angelology may have replaced from an incantation text, mentioned earlier, from pre-Jewish or recently judaized Idumaea.[91] Here the lesser deities invoked are the sons and daughters of El and Shamash (just as Enoch, perhaps following Job 1, identifies the angelic "watchers" with the sons of the gods of Genesis); similarly, an exorcistic psalm found at Qumran *may* mention Reshef, an old Canaanite god, here apparently demoted to demonic status.[92] We may infer from the late amulets and incantation bowls that magical activity, at least that of the most routine, day-to-day sort,[93] was largely in the hands of scribes—an inference based not only on the obvious fact that amulets are written but also on the fact that many of the texts contain evidence of learning: allusions to biblical verses, recherché puns, and the like. No doubt this "learn-

[88] *Amulets and Magic Bowls: Aramaic Incantations of Late Antiquity* (Jerusalem: Magnes, 1985); *Magic Spells and Formulae: Aramaic Incantations of Late Antiquity* (Jerusalem: Magnes, 1993).

[89] See Olyan, A *Thousand Thousands*.

[90] For continuities of rabbinic (which is closely related to that of the Hekhalot books) with apocalyptic angelology, see P. Schäfer, *Rivalität zwischen Engeln und Menschen*, Studia Judaica 8 (Berlin: De Gruyter, 1975), esp. pp. 41–72.

[91] See Naveh, "Nabatean Incantation Text."

[92] The text is 11QPsAp[a], published by J. van der Ploeg, *Tradition und Glaube* (Göttingen: Vandenhoeck & Ruprecht, 1971), p. 135. The reading is problematic; see J. Baumgarten, "On the Nature of the Seductress in 4Q 184," *RQ* 15 (1991): 134. The article (133–43) contains an instructive catalogue of demonological texts from Qumran. And see B. Nitzan, *Qumran Prayer and Religious Poetry* (Leiden: Brill, 1994), pp. 227–72.

[93] Indeed, the *content* of the amulets is unmistakably magical, closely akin to the Greek magical papyri and the spells recorded in Sefer HaRazim, and elsewhere. The *users* of the amulets may however often have been no more conscious of engaging in magical activity, or of subscribing to a particular cosmology, than a modern wearer of a "good luck charm." The routine use of apotropaic amulets, as opposed to hiring an exorcist or someone to write a love or curse spell, was just good sense.

ing" was often formulaic, copied from magical recipe books (though the Aramaic amulets themselves provide surprisingly little evidence of this).[94] If so, the traditional formulations were at any rate shaped by the learned. An additional hint that the mythic cosmology constitutes a scribal reshaping of a popular cosmology that had, we may suppose, implications for religious praxis is the prominence, especially in the ascent stories, of material derived from Canaanite mythology—a mythology thus apparently still extant, perhaps among the population of the Palestinian countryside.[95]

In sum, in social terms, the covenant and the myth formed a single complex. It was the mediators of the Torah and the Temple who gave the myth its classic formulations, pressed it into service to fill the gaps in the covenant, and worked out its relation to the Torah. The scribe and the holy man were thus often combined in one person, and the two roles spilled over into each other, the scribe searching his books for the mysteries he thought they concealed, and the holy man deriving his ability to prophesy, his knowledge of the divine and demonic worlds, in part from the scribe's Torah. Priests played a special role. Not only did the Torah itself give priests authority over its interpretation, but some priests believed that the temple provided them with a direct link to the divine world. If, as Josephus and Philo both said, the Temple symbolized the cosmos, then access to it gave one symbolic access to the upper world, and the conduct of the cult could maintain a semblance of order in the universe (some sectarians—Christians and Qumranians—rejected the legitimacy of the cult; they also believed the universe was in a state of complete disorder). Priests were therefore prominent not only as legal experts, teachers, and judges, but also as miracle workers and prophets (e.g., like John the Baptist and Josephus).

Thus, the incorporation of the mythology into the main ideology of Judaism—admittedly as a subsidiary element without a separate institutional base—was an aspect of centralization, of the rise in post-Maccabean Palestine of an integrated Judaism, controlled from Jerusalem by mediators of the Temple and Torah. It was an artifact of the transformation of the covenant from the ideology of the quasi-sectarian *benei hagolah* ("children of the exile") of the fifth century B.C.E. into that of Judaism as a whole. The expansion of the

---

[94] On the social position of magicians in late imperial Egypt, which is comparable to what I am suggesting for Palestine, see D. Frankfurter, *Religion in Roman Egypt: Assimilation and Resistance* (Princeton: Princeton University Press, 1998), pp. 198–237. On recipe books, see J. Naveh, "On Jewish Books of Magic Recipes in Antiquity," in I. Gafni, A. Oppenheimer, and D. Schwartz, eds., *The Jews in the Hellenistic-Roman World: Studies in Memory of Menahem Stern* (Jerusalem: Merkaz Shazar, 1996), pp. 453–65.

[95] Himmelfarb, *Ascent to Heaven*, pp. 16–18. There are also some Canaanite hints in Watchers: the sacred tree planted next to the heavenly temple, the theme of the battle between God and Nature; note also Jerome's comment that even in his time Jews were still observing the ancient (Canaanite/Israelite) mourning customs of head shaving and flesh cutting, prohibited by the Torah.

ideological system to include noncovenantal elements, some of them, like belief in the power of demons, astrology, bits of Canaanite mythology, almost certainly derived from popular Palestinian religion, was as much a corollary of the success of Judaism as the incorporation of elements of, say, Mithraism or neo-Platonism in Christianity indicated its success.

Yet the myth and the covenant remained separate, and the myth retained its *potential* to generate separate social organization, or, in Scholem's formulation, to subvert the Torah, even if such activity was normally confined to the social margins. It was not simply that the mediators themselves acknowledged, and in some cases institutionalized, the separateness of the myth by classifying it as esoteric, or, in the cases of Ben Sira, 1 Maccabees, and perhaps Josephus and the Mishnah, rejecting it altogether. The fact is, the covenant and the myth performed different social roles. The covenant told you whom to marry and how, what to eat, how to worship; the myth not only told you why things nevertheless went wrong but also could be used to improve them, to cure the sick, protect you from your enemies, discover, at the very least, when things are likely to change. If the correct adjudication of a property dispute, or proper preparation of food, were the day-to-day manifestations of the power of the covenant, the exorcism, cure, or oracle were the corresponding manifestations of the power of the myth.

Sophists, Holy Men, and Brigands

Thus, though these skills were often possessed by the same person, though both might involve consultation of holy books, and though people in fact needed access to both, they were undeniably different types of expertise and had the potential to empower different types of people. This potential was to some extent realized in the first century.

In periods of weak central control, social breakdown, economic decline, and the like, we should expect ideological systems to shatter, and their political and social effects to dissolve into their components. The period from the death of Herod, in 4 B.C.E., to the outbreak of the Great Revolt in 66 C.E. was thus one in which the ideological underpinnings of Palestinian Jewish society began to be especially conspicuous.

This is not to suggest that Palestine had already fallen apart at the seams. In fact, the old institutions retained their power, the high priests had their authority and prestige, the law of the Torah was still enforced, the land still yielded a reasonably dependable income for Herod's descendants and the Romans, there were long periods of calm, and many of the reported disturbances were minor. Josephus may report so many disturbances for the first century simply because they had occurred in his lifetime or in living memory, and/or because they seemed to him to provide an appropriate background to his main theme, the revolt of 66.

Nevertheless, it is overwhelmingly likely that the period before the revolt *was* one of growing economic and social distress.[96] Even if Josephus's focus on disorder is somewhat misleading, the detailed character of his account gives us the opportunity to see how individuals acquired followings in Jewish Palestine—to determine, in other words, what the keys to power were, apart from open collaboration with the Romans. For it is a noteworthy feature of Josephus's account that sixteen or seventeen of the twenty-odd disturbances he reports for the period between the death of Herod and the outbreak of the revolt were created by individuals who had gathered around themselves groups of followers. In a summary discussion in War 2 (254–65), Josephus divides the troublemakers into two classes, brigand chiefs and *goetes* (i.e., magicians or charmers). But the more detailed account in *Ant* 17–20 suggests a more complex classificatory scheme, although the individual reports are often long on vituperation and short on information, so that many cases are doubtful.

Sophists

On several occasions, prestigious legal scholars of a rigoristic tendency (whom Josephus normally designates *sophistai*) gathered crowds and preached against the legal transgressions of the Herodian family and the high priests appointed by them. In the first case, the sermon actually led to a raid on the Temple. The sophists' students hacked to bits the golden eagle Herod had erected over the Temple gate—which they, in apparent defiance of the legal authority of the high priests, who had evidently found a way of permitting the eagle, considered a violation of the Torah. Herod, though on his deathbed, enraged at what *he* considered an act of sacrilege, had the sophists and some of their followers executed. The survivors later led a protest against an insufficiently pious high priest which, again, ended in bloodshed.[97] A similar incident involving a rigoristic legal teacher and a Herodian's mischief in the Temple ended peacefully because the sophist was less threatening and the Herodian, Agrippa I, more conciliatory.[98] Possibly an additional entry in this category is the dynasty of Judas the Galilean (or Gaulanite). Josephus most often describes their activities as straightforward brigandage, yet in a celebrated passage he credits them with founding a so-called fourth philosophy (i.e., after Pharisaism, Sadduceism, and Essenism)—a schismatic form of Pharisaism that allegedly forbade submission to any human master.[99]

[96] For an account, see above, and Goodman, *Ruling Class*, especially pp. 50–75.

[97] *Ant* 17.149–64; 206–18. In *Ant* Josephus evinced sympathy for the sophists, but not for their hot-headed pupils.

[98] *Ant* 19.332–34.

[99] *Ant* 17.271–72; 18.4–10; 23–25; 20.102. In *Ant* 17 Josephus claims that Judas, in attacking a Herodian palace at Sepphoris, was aiming for royal rank. How can this be reconciled with their

Holy Men

More common among the troublemakers were the holy men. Josephus's hostility to this group was unqualified and his information often seems willfully misleading. Nevertheless, six individuals can be assigned to this group with some confidence: Jesus of Nazareth (*Ant* 18.63–64); the Samaritan who led his armed (!) followers onto Mount Gerizim, the site of the destroyed Samaritan temple (*Ant* 18.85–87); John the Baptist, who had committed no crime but aroused suspicion because of his ability to attract followers (18.116–19); Theudas, who said he was a prophet and led a group into the desert, promising to split the Jordan River (20.97–99; cf. Acts 5:36, which assigns him 400 followers); an Egyptian (Jew?) who led his many followers to the Mount of Olives, where he promised them he would make the walls of Jerusalem fall down and lead them in to take control (20.169–72; War 2.262);[100] James, the brother of Jesus, and some associates (Ant 20.200–203). In addition, Josephus mentions unnamed "magicians" and "deceivers," who flourished in the procuratorship of Felix (20.167–68).

Brigands

Men Josephus called brigands (*leistai*) are the most numerous group of troublemakers, and in some ways the most controversial in modern scholarship. One important tendency sees behind every brigand a revolutionary ideologue, motivated by "nationalism" or messianic ideology or legal zeal (i.e., it assimilates the brigands to other groups of troublemakers). Another tendency sees behind Josephus's greedy and tyrannical criminals social bandits in the Hobsbawmian sense—"primitive rebels," Robin Hood–like heroes of the downtrodden. I prefer to see the brigands as violent people who had fallen through the cracks of a rickety economy, though the case of Judas of Galilee reminds us that successful brigand groups might mutate into bands of armed messianists or legal rigorists.[101]

---

philosophy? How can their philosophy be reconciled with the Pentateuchal assumption that kingship is a legitimate form of government? Was it only foreign kingship they opposed?

[100] In War 2.262 he is said to have had 30,000 followers, which is patently absurd; in *Ant* Felix kills 400 and captures 200, figures that are no doubt equally false but at least may give a more realistic idea of the size of his following.

[101] See *Ant* 20.4–5; 113; 131; 160–66, passim for other mentions of brigand groups or unattributed acts of brigandage. The largest outbreak of brigandage occurred during the revolt. For brigands as ideologues the classic account is Hengel, *Die Zeloten*; for the social banditry approach, see R. Horsley, "Josephus and the Bandits," *JSJ* 10 (1979): 37–63; "Ancient Jewish Banditry and the Revolt against Rome," *CBQ* 43 (1981): 409–32. My view (see "Josephus in Galilee") draws on post-Hobsbawm discussions of ancient brigandage, especially by B. Shaw, "Bandits in the Roman Empire," *Past and Present* 105 (1984): 3–52, and some of the contributions to A. Wallace-Hadrill, *Patronage in Ancient Society* (London: Routledge, 1989); also B. Shaw, "Tyrants, Bandits,

These cases (except perhaps the brigands) were marginal, even in the relatively turbulent first century. In the main, power continued to be mediated in conventional ways by recognized authorities—at least until the period immediately preceding the outbreak of the revolt, when even the high priests began to gather bands of brigands, plunder the countryside, and vie with each other for control in Jerusalem. Josephus himself may serve as an example of the regular social functioning of Jewish ideology: he was a priest from a good but not leading family, well educated in the Torah,[102] "and so" also an inspired (*entheos*) foreteller of the future (War 3.351–54).[103] He was later disenchanted, but this seems to have been a reaction to the role of eschatological prophecy in promoting the failed revolt. In any case, this is precisely the sort of convergence of roles that I argue was normal for Palestinian Jewish elites and subelites. On the other hand, that the system was in some trouble is suggested by Josephus's apparent idleness before the revolt, an issue that I will discuss in more detail presently.

The marginal cases show, however, that the elements of the ideological complex that constituted Judaism could function as separate sources of power, especially when their institutional bases—the Temple, priesthood, official scribal class—were too weak to hold them together. The prestige and authority of the Torah could empower those who claimed expertise in its manipulation, and the prestige and authority of the myth could empower a different group of experts. And, because when all is said and done, Jewish Palestine was in many respects a normal part of the ancient Mediterranean world, expertise at violence and forcible redistribution of wealth, too, had its attractions, as it did throughout the region. But when brigand bands became successful, they often tried to tap into the ideological mainstream (e.g., Judas the Galilean, with his legal rigor).

I should add parenthetically that this conception of the separability of the two main ideological axes of ancient Judaism, with their potential to generate at the margins of society separate types of organization, crystalizing around individual experts, has the advantage of helping to explain the origins of Christianity. Jesus was the figure expected to usher in the end of the dominion of evil and the beginning of the rule of God; he and his followers were re-

---

and Kings: Personal Power in Josephus," *JJS* 44 (1993): 176–204.
Josephus mentions some troublemakers who seem to have attracted followings largely because they were tall and muscular, when most Palestinian men were not (*Ant* 17.273–84). This may not be the whole story.

[102] This is clearly so, though his account of his own precocity (Life 7–9) may stretch the point. My skepticism about his knowledge of the Torah (*Josephus*, pp. 24–35) has been correctly criticized.

[103] Josephus avoids calling anyone but the biblical authors "prophets"; the standard treatment of prophecy in Josephus is J. Blenkinsopp, "Prophecy and Priesthood in Josephus," *JJS* 25 (1974): 239–62.

nowned for their ability to manipulate demons and free people from their influence. It was a movement, or rather a loose collection of related groups, that took shape around a distinctive understanding of the myth complex, a movement in which the Torah was not ignored (it could not possibly have been) but was definitely of secondary importance. In this sense, at least, Josephus's classification of Jesus and James among the assorted troublemakers is entirely accurate.

The Sects

What place did the sects occupy in the system? Obviously, in my view, not a central one, for I have just presented an account of Palestinian Judaism in the first century in which the sects scarcely figure. Indeed, in my view, Sanders's attempt to leave the sects to one side in his account is one of the most interesting and significant characteristics of his work.[104] Nevertheless, it is probable that though the sects were not quite central, they were not quite marginal either. In the brief discussion that follows, I will concentrate on setting forth my own views, without explicit engagement in polemics.[105]

The following is, however, in dialogue with Albert Baumgarten's recent book, *The Flourishing of Jewish Sects in the Maccabean Era: An Interpretation* (1997), even where this is not explicitly stated. Though this book is not unproblematic, its insistence on viewing the sects as an essentially unitary, and essentially mainstream, phenomenon and, as a corollary, on trying to understand their relation to general Jewish society and its embrace of a comparative approach and adoption of a complex theory of causation, are all admirable and in general, if not always in the details of their exposition, correct.[106]

First, it is necessary to be specific about who "the sects" were. Though Josephus speaks of three (and in one polemical passage of four) sects, it seems certain that there were many more sectarian groups in first-century Palestine.[107] Christian heresiographers usually speak of seven sects, though sometimes, especially in later, derivative accounts of six, eight, or ten. The number seven is suspect and the components of the list differ in the different accounts;

---

[104] Sanders, *Judaism: Practice and Belief*.

[105] It may be worth pointing out that since the rescission of the monopoly on the publication of the Dead Sea Scrolls, and more specifically since the long-awaited publication of 4QMiqsat Maasei HaTorah (E. Qimron and J. Strugnell, *Qumran Cave 4, V: Miqsat Ma'ase ha-Torah*, Discoveries in the Judaean Desert 10 (Oxford: Clarendon, 1994)), many old questions of detail have now been reopened; see, e.g., J. Kampen and M. Bernstein, eds., *Reading 4QMMT: New Perspectives on Qumran Law and History* (Atlanta: Scholars, 1996).

[106] See also my review, *AJS Review* 24 (1999): 374–78.

[107] See Baumgarten, *Flourishing of Jewish Sects*, pp. 2–3.

nevertheless, some of the patristic information may be reliable.[108] At the very least, we know of an additional sect, the Christians, whom Josephus does not count. And such groups as Ophites and Hemerobaptists are mentioned often enough by later writers to make their existence a strong possibility. In any case, we would have to posit the existence of Jewish groups probably of sectarian character in order to explain the later emergence of, for example, the Elkesaites and the circles responsible for those gnostic texts of more or less definitely Jewish background.

But Josephus did not invent his list of Pharisees, Sadducees, and Essenes.[109] The polemical *pesharim* (biblical commentaries) from Qumran are plausibly supposed to refer to Pharisees and Sadducees, in addition to the sectarians themselves, perhaps an Essene splinter group (though consensus on this point has recently shown signs of dissipating).[110] The Gospels and Acts also refer to Pharisees and Sadducees; the Essenes, politically inactive and themselves sometimes mildly persecuted, were apparently not thought to have opposed Jesus. The rabbis, too, often speak of three sects. The third on the rabbinic list, the BYTSYN, apparently closely associated with the Sadducees (indeed, in some sources synonymous with them), are very obscure indeed, but the recently revealed similarities between Sadducean and Qumranian halakhah suggest, though admittedly not very strongly, that BYTSYN may represent not "Boethusians," as the word is usually transcribed,[111] but "the house of (BYT) the Essenes."[112]

The three sects, then, seem to have had almost an official status. Indeed, in his account of the alleged foundation of a fourth sect by Judas the Galilean, Josephus practically says as much, for his main accusation is that the very foundation of an additional sect constituted a dangerous and illegitimate inno-

---

[108] For a discussion, see M. Simon, "Les sectes juives chez les Pères," *Studia Patristica I*, ed. K. Aland and F. L. Cross, Texte und Untersuchungen zur Geschichte der Altchristlichen Literatur 63 (Berlin: Akademie Verlag 1957), 526–39. Simon argues that Hemerobaptists and Meristae really existed but were not sects (which, in Simon's view, did not exist in pre-70 Judaism, in the absence of an orthodoxy) but tendencies of thought or loose collections of conventicles characterized not by heretical but, on the contrary, ultraorthodox practices and beliefs (537). See also J. Lieu, "Epiphanius on the Scribes and Pharisees (*Pan.* 15.1–16.4)," *JTS* 39 (1988): 509–24.

[109] Contra S. Cohen, "Significance of Yavneh," 30–1, especially note 5. The oft cited claim of the Palestinian Talmud (Sanhedrin 10:6, 29c) that there were twenty-four sects of heretics in existence when the Temple was destroyed is of no independent value.

[110] See A. Baumgarten, "Crisis in the Scrollery: A Dying Consensus," *Judaism* 44 (1995): 399–413.

[111] Apparently reflecting the supposition that they are somehow connected to the Herodian high priestly family of Boethus—Ant 15.320–22, passim.

[112] See J. Sussmann, "The History of Halakhah and the Dead Sea Scrolls: Preliminary Observations on Miqsat Ma'ase HaTorah (4Q MMT)," *Tarbiz* 59 (1989): 40–58. The article (11–76) is a fundamental contribution to the study of the relationship between the sects; the interpretation of BYTSYN, however, is very uncertain.

vation (*Ant* 18.6–9).[113] We are thus confronted with a peculiar phenomenon—
a set of organizations that were to some extent exclusivist and conceived of
themselves as somehow set apart not only from each other but also from the
nonsectarian norm, which seem by the first century to have lost, *as groups*, the
authority they had once enjoyed—at any rate, they play no role in Josephus's
narrative after the Hasmonean period—[114] but which nevertheless enjoyed a
measure of recognition, respectability, and legitimacy.

Numbers

A good place to begin consideration of the sects' position in Palestinian Jewish
society in the first century is with the often neglected question of their size.
Josephus provides some numbers: 6,000 for the Pharisees toward the end of
Herod's reign (*Ant* 17.42) and 4,000 for the Essenes at an unspecified date,
presumably sometime in the early first century (*Ant* 18.21, in agreement with
Philo, *Quod Omnis Probus* 75). He provides no figures for the Sadducees but
indicates that they were a smaller group, though socially distinguished. The
general problems with figures provided by ancient historiographers are well-
known and need not be rehearsed. The questions raised by these particular
figures are no less serious. Josephus does not say where he found them, but
they are unlikely to come from anything as pretendedly accurate as a census
list. Their roundness suggests that they are guesses, and similarly round figures
provided by Josephus are sometimes dramatically wrong, for example, the
30,000 followers of the Egyptian *goes* mentioned above, or, still more absurdly,
the 100,000 troops Josephus claims he led in Lower Galilee—a figure that is
in all likelihood well over that of the adult male population of Galilee as a
whole. Sometimes, though, Josephus's guesses are plausible, and the fact that
in this case he gives, in two very different contexts, figures for two of the main
sects in the mid-thousands may argue (admittedly not very strongly) for their
utility as indicators of orders of magnitude.

Let us, then, take a wild leap of faith and suppose for the sake of argument
that the numbers are roughly correct. It is generally supposed that the sectarians
tended to live in Judaea. This can hardly be thought an absolute certainty: no
doubt sectarians sometimes emigrated. But it is true that Josephus, Mark, and
Matthew always treat the Pharisees as a Judaean organization, the presence
of some of whose members in Galilee was a noteworthy occasion.[115] Let us
furthermore assume for Judaea a population of 100,000–150,000, a figure consistent with Broshi's estimate of a maximum population of 500,000 for the

---

[113] See S. Schwartz, *Josephus*, p. 188.

[114] For discussion, see above, chapter 1, note 68.

[115] Cf. Baumgarten, *Flourishing of Jewish Sects*, pp. 45–46.

Jewish districts of Palestine.[116] This implies an adult male population of 30,000–60,000. The sectarians (who were presumably adult males) would have amounted to as much as 15–30 percent of the adult male population of Judaea.

Though most scholars have simply juxtaposed Josephus's figures with an estimate of the size of the Palestinian population (if they have considered the figures at all) and concluded that the sects were tiny,[117] a more nuanced consideration of the numbers shows that they are in fact remarkably high. They would, if correct, indicate among other things that almost no Judaean (of whatever social class) can have avoided contact, indeed, even family relationship, with a sectarian, and that no Judaean settlement apart from the smallest can have lacked a sectarian population (as Josephus in fact says of the Essenes: War 2.124). Perhaps this only proves that Josephus's or Broshi's figures were wrong.

But it is worth recalling here Martin Goodman's account of the social and economic history of Judaea in the first century, which in broad outline is completely convincing.[118] Goodman based his account on the undeniable fact that the Herodian Temple was a massive magnet for money: silver and gold poured into its treasuries from all over the Roman and Parthian worlds, as did pilgrims into its courtyards. This fueled an economy that was, though on a smaller scale, as abnormal as that of central Italy in the same period. Although much of the "investment" in the Temple was unproductive (except from the perspective of the Roman generals who occasionally plundered it), the rest funded a large establishment of priests, Levites, provisioners, construction and maintenance workers, clerks, and administrators. The masses of pilgrims may not often have invested in the city, but they certainly consumed a great deal of the production of the surrounding countryside, and spent money on lodging and locally manufactured goods. Thus, there came to be in Judaea an unusually large proportion of relatively well-to-do people, who, dependent as they were on the temple and the special status of Jerusalem for their well-being, are likely for the most part to have been pious.[119] Many of them were probably priests, for it seems clear that the priestly class had grown tremendously since the days of Ezra and Nehemiah, or of (pseudo-?) Hecataeus of Abdera, who

---

[116] "Population of Western Palestine"; this figure, and my guess for Judaea, may be slightly high. See Introduction, note 13.

[117] So Baumgarten, *Flourishing of Jewish Sects*, p. 42 n. 2; S. Cohen, *From the Maccabees to the Mishnah* (Philadelphia: Westminster, 1987), pp. 172–73, emphasizes the small size and marginal status of the sects without discussing Josephus's numbers. It is puzzling that Sanders, in his long (and, it must be said, rather odd) discussion of the social and political history of the Pharisees (*Judaism*, pp. 380–412), never discusses the size of the sect.

[118] *Ruling Class*, pp. 51–75.

[119] Goodman argues that the same development worked to the disadvantage of the Judaean peasantry, since the tendency of the wealthy to invest in land led to the alienation of smallholdings and the reduction of their owners to tenancy, and perhaps other types of dependency.

believed they numbered 1,500 (*AgAp* 1.88). Josephus claimed that in his day, presumably before the revolt, there were 20,000 priests. This number is obviously an approximation, arrived at by the impossible assumption that each of the four priestly "tribes" (whatever precisely these were) had precisely the same number of members.[120] It may also include only officiating priests, that is, adult males, which would raise the total number to around 60,000, which is flirting with absurdity. Nevertheless, Josephus's number at least suggests that in the first century the priests were very numerous, and it would be fair to assume that they lived disproportionately, though not exclusively, in the vicinity of Jerusalem. Both of these suppositions, in addition to Josephus's priestly chauvinism, would explain their disproportionate importance in Josephus's account of the history of Judaea in the first century, as well as their substantial overlap with the sectarians—including the Pharisees—for which Josephus's works again provide evidence, and their prominence among the early rabbis.[121] Priests or not, many of the well-to-do are also likely to have been idle, since the new conditions probably enriched many more people than the temple and city administrations, about which very little is known, could supply with honorable sinecures. Josephus, who by his own report had very little, except for some dabbling with the sects, to keep him busy before the outbreak of the revolt in 66, when he was twenty-nine years old, may not have been atypical of his class.

These conditions, combined with the unwillingness or inability of the Herodian rulers and Roman prefects and procurators to impose religious uniformity, favored the growth of the sects. Here I follow Baumgarten, who argued (to abbreviate drastically) that in ancient Judaea sectarianism was in part a response to sudden economic growth, as it was in England in the seventeenth century. However, Baumgarten was mistaken to date this economic spurt to the second century B.C.E., when there is no evidence for it and no reason in the absence of evidence to think it might have happened. Though Goodman did not say as much, the conditions he describes were peculiar to the last century of the Second Temple period, for reasons that are not difficult to reconstruct. Herod rebuilt Jerusalem in the wake of the Hasmonean expansion, which had greatly increased the size of the Jewish population of Palestine, and of the establishment of the Roman Principate, which had eased travel and enabled pilgrimage from the Diaspora on a large scale.[122] As a result of these developments, Judaea's economy and society became abnormal.

---

[120] Schürer-Vermes 2: 247 suggest that Josephus's "four tribes" is a scribal error for "twenty-four." This would explain the otherwise enigmatic tribes by identifying them with the *mishmarot* but would render the number nonsensical—which is not a compelling argument against the correction.

[121] *Josephus*, pp. 200–205; Hezser, *Social Structure*, pp. 70–71.

[122] For further discussion, see S. Schwartz, "King Herod: Friend of the Jews."

Mainstream or Marginal?

As scholars have long recognized and Baumgarten has recently confirmed, the three main sects shared a set of concerns. All of them, apparently at all periods of their existence, were mainly concerned with the interpretation of the Torah, a concern that includes the proper conduct of the Temple cult. Though the evidence is limited, Baumgarten has suggested that they shared to some extent a specialist language and many details of legal interpretation. This position probably requires some modification: they did share ways of talking and thinking about the Law, as well as ways of observing it, but there is also evidence that the sectarian groups all developed and carefully cultivated differences among themselves. Certainly the peculiarities of the language of the sectarian scrolls from Qumran are well-known. Given that the sects seem to have competed with each other and probably tried to appeal to the same segments of the Judaean population, it would be surprising if they did not emphasize the "small differences" (as Freud put it) among them.

This last point requires emphasis: though the Sadducees were known for the aristocratic character of their membership (one should not, however, suppose that the sect and the aristocracy were coterminous),[123] most sectarians were probably subelites, as Baumgarten compellingly argued, rather than elites—the rank-and-file priesthood, scribes, well-to-do landowners, officials, merchants, and Temple staff—groups that probably overlapped quite significantly. As Josephus implies in the introduction to his autobiography, which sect such people joined, if any, was mainly a matter of personal choice. The fact that, at least in Jerusalem and vicinity, most men of the appropriate class did choose to join a sect explains why Josephus could describe the sects as if they constituted the entirety of Judaism.

The concentration of the sectarians in and around Jerusalem and their connection with the temple demonstrates their essential cohesion but also sharpened the tensions among the groups.[124] Modern scholars have supposed that control of the ritual of the temple was vitally important. In this, they follow the lead of their sources: forty years after the fact, Josephus could still be outraged at Agrippa II's decision to allow the Levitical temple choristers to dress in white linen, like priests (*Ant* 20.218). Many centuries later, the Babylonian rabbis chose to imagine that the Sadducean high priests were

---

[123] As Sanders, *Judaism*, pp. 317–40, astonishingly does. Certainly, not all the high priests were Sadducees, and it would be very surprising if such other aristocrats as the descendants of Herod were. At most, such figures may occasionally have patronized the sects, as Agrippa I may have patronized the Pharisees.

[124] Cohen exaggerated the role of the Temple in generating sectarian differentiation: *From the Maccabees to the Mishnah*, pp. 131–32; "Significance of Yavneh."

compelled to follow Pharisaic rules in the Temple, rules they themselves secretly knew to be correct (B. Yoma 19b)!

In reality, though, apart from the rare episodes of royal interference reported by Josephus, we know nothing about how decisions regarding temple ritual were made. It is probably significant that Josephus never says that any sect controlled the ritual in the first century.[125] The sectarian arguments reported in the Mishnah and the Dead Sea Scrolls may have occurred in the Hasmonean Temple, or they may have been theoretical or imaginary. The Herodian high priests and high-ranking Temple staff may have had nonsectarian traditions of their own or may have patched together ad hoc compromises.[126] In any case, it seems very unlikely that the mass of the Jews had any interest in the issue.[127] Why should they have? They visited the Temple only infrequently, would have been wholly ignorant about how its affairs were generally run, and would have had little motivation to take sides even in any debates that might have existed about the pilgrimage festival sacrifices, which were actually witnessed by large groups of people.[128] Though the pilgrimage festivals in post-Herodian Jerusalem were often scenes of disorder and even violence, none of it is said to have been related to tensions about correct ritual.[129] The rabbis, it is true, imagined that "the people" rose against Alexander Yannai because he failed to perform the water libation in accordance with Pharisaic rules, but in what is presumably the original version of the story, in *Ant* 13.372–73, their objection to the king is the result not of his improper performance of the ritual but of his problematic descent. And both Josephus and the rabbis forgot that before Herod rebuilt the temple, the pilgrimage festivals were necessarily small-scale affairs. There was simply no room in the temple precinct for the sort of mass protest both described.

In sum, the sectarian divisions were important among priests, scribes, and other relatively well-off (and so presumably well-educated) Jews in the first century, especially in Judaea. Their importance demonstrates three things: the strength of the core ideology of Judaism; powerful devotion, which united

---

[125] *Ant* 18.15–7 refers quite explicitly only to rituals outside the Temple.

[126] Cf. Sanders, *Judaism*, pp. 458–90.

[127] Cf. the important discussion of D. Schwartz, "MMT, Josephus, and the Pharisees," in *Reading 4QMMT*, pp. 67–80.

[128] The alternative is to suppose that the legal disputes among the sects were the equivalents of the abstruse Christian theological debates of the fourth and fifth centuries, which produced divisions among masses of people who probably had little real interest in the details. But there is, once again, no evidence that Pharisees and Sadducees went through the countryside soliciting mass support for their halakhic views. There is little reason to doubt that Pharisaic scribes sometimes attempted to regulate the legal practice of their villages in accordance with their peculiar understanding of the laws of the Torah, but no evidence that sectarian divisions ever became rallying points for the peasantry. They never functioned as such during the revolt of 66.

[129] See Weitzman, "From Feasts into Mourning."

the sectarians even as disagreement over details of interpretation divided them; the weakness of central control over the religious life of the country—at a time when the high priests were a loosely constituted group rather than members of a single dynasty. They were relatively disempowered by the mild interventionism that distinguished the Romans, even before they openly annexed their eastern client kingdoms, from their Macedonian and Persian predecessors, and furthermore they had to cope with a society larger and massively more complex than it had been before the reign of Herod. Finally, the importance of sectarianism demonstrates the anomalous character of the economy and society of first-century Judaea, which had produced an unusually large class of well-to-do, pious, educated, and idle young men.[130]

But the sects had little discernible impact on Palestinian Jewish society as a whole. To the extent that local scribes, judges, and teachers belonged to one or another sect, they presumably tried to use their version of the laws of the Torah in arbitration, contracts, and so on, and may thereby have contributed to the local differences in practice discussed above. But there is no reason to believe that the villagers who patronized and were patronized by such officials were interested in their sectarian affiliations. Popular supporters of sectarian groups played no known role in Palestinian Jewish history in the first century, unless one joins Josephus in counting the "fourth philosophy" (probably somehow connected to the *sicarii*) as a sect.

Conclusion

In this chapter, I have been arguing that, as a result of the enduring tendency of the imperial rulers of the eastern Mediterranean to rule partly autonomous regions through local agents, a Jewish society gradually coalesced in Palestine. We may speak, for the later Second Temple period, of Judaism in the singular as the integrating ideology of the society. Judaism was complex and rather baggy, and the fact that most Jews professed adherence to it tells us surprisingly little about how they actually conducted their lives. The symbolic and practical importance of the Torah and Temple informs us mainly that their human representatives were engaged in constant acts of intermediation between the norms of Judaism and the behavior of the Jews. Furthermore, the chronic weakness of central control meant that the norms themselves were constantly disputed by the scribal and priestly elites and subelites. This dispute blossomed into the sectarianism that was so important in Josephus's narrative and in real life far from marginal in Judaea, at least in the first century. Neverthe-

---

[130] Which raises a question that will not detain us here: given that these same young men went on to form the backbone of the Judaean revolutionary movements, we may wonder why piety in the end failed to satisfy them.

less, there is ample evidence for Judaism's success in creating a Jewish society, loosely centralized and frayed at the edges though it was. One of the most important corpora of evidence for this process is the emergence of apocalypticism in literature starting in the third century, for this material seems to show that the scribal and priestly elites and subelites constantly engaged in the domestication, or judaization, of ideological systems apparently at odds with the Torah.

PART II

JEWS IN PALESTINE FROM 135 TO 350

THREE

RABBIS AND PATRIARCHS ON THE MARGINS

IN PART 2 I aim to provide a description of a society that disintegrated under the impact of an imperialism sharpened by the failure of the two Palestinian revolts. In this part I will give close attention to the interpretation of evidence because my view of the history of Palestine from 135 to c.350 is revisionist and requires argumentation. My thesis is that the core ideology of Judaism, as described in the previous section, ceased, after the two revolts, to function as an integrating force in Palestinian Jewish society. The intermediaries of the Torah lost not only their legal authority but also their status as cultural ideals. Indeed, if there was anything at all holding Palestinian Jewish society together, it may have been no more than an attenuated sense of a common past, a mild feeling of separation from their neighbors that the latter, who had shared memories of their own, may have conspired to maintain. Finally, some Jews, probably a very small number (among them were the rabbis) still insisted on the importance of the Torah, of Judaism, in their symbolic world, and these Jews, convinced of their elite status, tried to insinuate their way into general Palestinian society. Although marginal and to some extent turned in on themselves, the rabbis and their congeners nevertheless played a role, peripheral and weak though it was, in sustaining among some Jews some sense of separation.

But it would be misleading to focus attention only on the rabbis and implicitly suppose the rest of the Jewish population either to have been basically inert, quietly waiting to be convinced or, alternatively, under the temporary religious control of some nonrabbinic group of intermediaries of Torah (of whom there is scarcely a shred of evidence)—in short, to construct a history of the Jews between 70 and 350 (or even 640) around the story of the rise of the rabbis, whether they are thought to have risen ex nihilo or after a battle of exegetical wits with inferior Torah scholars.[1] In chapter 3, I try to explain why a rabbinocentric account is inadequate. I will argue that even though the rabbis established a foothold in urban and suburban Palestine in the course of the third century, and the grandee who led them, the patriarch (or *nasi*), by the middle of the fourth had become a very estimable figure indeed, the rabbis did not have any officially recognized legal authority until the end of the fourth century. Even then it was severely restricted and in any case not

---

[1] As even the most responsible and serious historians have trouble avoiding; see, e.g., S. Cohen, *From the Maccabees to the Mishnah*, pp. 214–31.

limited to rabbis. As for the patriarchs, they acquired much of their influence precisely by relaxing their ties to the rabbis and allying themselves instead with Palestinian city councillors, wealthy Diaspora Jews, and prominent gentiles.

Both rabbis and patriarchs were probably convinced that they had a right to exercise legal authority over the Jews by virtue of belonging to the class of scribes/Torah experts (furthermore, some of them were priests), a class empowered by the Torah itself. Yet in the wake of the Destruction and the Bar Kokhba revolt, and the imposition of direct Roman rule in Palestine, the Torah and its representatives lost their institutional position and much of their prestige, and they and their successors spent the rest of antiquity struggling to restore them. For the rabbis, the struggle did not finally succeed until the rise of Islam, at earliest. The patriarchate's meteoric rise in the fourth century predetermined its meteoritic fall in the early fifth. Indeed, even the restoration of the Torah to the center of Jewish life in late antiquity (to be discussed in part 3 of this book), though it may have set the stage for the official empowerment of the rabbis in the seventh century and following, occurred largely independently of rabbinic influence and in many places generated varieties of Judaism that were strikingly nonrabbinic. We need, therefore, to keep the rabbis to one side if we wish to understand the character of Jewish society between 70 and 640—a fortiori between 70 and 350.

If not the rabbis, then who? Rather surprisingly, no one, for there was not really any Jewish society to lead. In chapter 4, I will discuss *seriatim* various bodies of evidence—autonomous bronze city coinage, other archaeological finds, some rabbinic accounts of the public life of the Palestinian cities, funerary inscriptions from Tiberias, and inscriptions and art from the necropolis at Beth Shearim. All this material is mutually confirmatory in indicating that Jewish Palestine between c.100 and 350 scarcely differed from any other high imperial provincial society. All legal authority and political power were in the hands of the Roman state and its local representatives, and the cultural norms, even in the countryside, were overwhelmingly set by the elites of the Palestinian cities, including such "Jewish" cities as Tiberias, Sepphoris, and Lydda. These norms were pervaded by pagan religiosity and were basically shared by imperial Greek cities generally.

Part of the evidentiary foundation of my thesis is the pagan iconography that is so common in high imperial Palestinian art and decoration. Much of this material has long been familiar, though the recent excavations at Sepphoris have considerably added to the corpus. But it has also long been conventional to juxtapose it with the iconography of the necropolis at Beth Shearim and of the Palestinian synagogues, which mixes pagan and Jewish elements, and furthermore to see the whole complex of material through the prism of rabbinic prescriptions and presuppositions. Many scholars have sought to provide judaizing interpretations of the pagan material or, where that seemed implausible, to dismiss it either as trivial ornamentation or as non-Jewish. And yet the evidence, including, surprisingly, that from rabbinic literature, is quite uniform in regarding the Jewish cities of Palestine and their rural satellites as characterized by a predominantly pagan public life, though rabbinic and Christian literature nevertheless regard the cities as having simultaneously been in some sense Jewish. We perhaps need to assume that some Jews retained a sense of being Jewish if only to understand how northern Palestine could have become Jewish in a strong sense after 350. We can only speculate about the character of its Jewishness before that date; for now it may prove instructive to try to imagine Judaism, or rather the disintegrated shards of Judaism, surviving as a nonexclusive religious option in a religious system that was basically pagan.

Thus, the Jewish core (the most important component of which was the rabbis), as far as we know, was a part of the system. It was not very important sociopolitically (though probably increasingly influential with time) but functioned quite significantly in providing for the Jews a cultural option radically different from the Greco-Roman norm. How did the rabbis, who needed to take seriously the Pentateuch's horror of strange gods, cope with the basically pagan society in which they lived, even when they lived in Jewish cities like Tiberias and Sepphoris? In chapter 5, I will argue that the peculiar formalism of rabbinic legislation about paganism, whereby the rabbis defined, or rather misprised, a pervasive cultural norm as consisting exclusively of acts of worship directed at fetishes, was the rabbis' accommodative mechanism—an error that fortunately allowed them to live and function in the cities without whose resources they would have dwindled to sectarian insignificance.

Changes

With the outbreak of the Jewish revolt against Rome in 66 C.E., five centuries of imperial support for the Temple, the Torah, and their human representatives, the priests and scribes, came to an end. Though the hope of some Jews for their imminent revival ended only with the failure of the Bar Kokhba revolt in 135, the centralizing and integrating tendencies of the Roman Empire made such a revival unlikely from the start. Throughout the Near East in the late first and early second centuries the emperors were replacing quasi-autonomous local rulers, the "client kings," with Roman officials, establishing "colonies" (cities with more or less Greco-Roman constitutions and in some cases a citizen body that also enjoyed Roman citizenship and so favorable tax status),[2] imposing direct taxation, and introducing judges (primarily the

[2] On "colonies" in the imperial period, which often enjoyed little more than additional prestige, see P. Garnsey and R. Saller, *The Roman Empire: Economy, Society, and Culture* (Berkeley: University of California Press, 1987), pp. 26–28; 189–90; B. Isaac, *The Limits of Empire: The Roman Army in the East*, rev. ed. (Oxford: Clarendon, 1992), pp. 342–63.

governors and their staff) who ruled by complicated, largely ad hoc mixtures of Roman, Greco-oriental, and local law.[3]

Most of the little principalities the Romans annexed had no special ethnic self-consciousness that we are aware of, and their former rulers had usually come from elsewhere. No one apparently had ever identified himself as a "Chalcidian" or an "Agrippan" or a "Minor Armenian."[4] These principalities are probably best compared to the grand estates of early modern Ukraine or Ireland, before the rise of nationalism, ruled by foreign (Polish or English) lords. The lords simultaneously protected and exploited the peasants, with the help of intermediation by their relatives, wealthy natives, and outside administrators. Some autonomy may have been sometimes granted to such local institutions as churches, but pressure on them and their priests was constant and relations often tense or worse.

When the Romans annexed the ancient counterparts of such places, little in them, one might have thought, initially changed: the former rulers, Judaeo-Idumaean descendants of Herod, and various Ituraean, Nabataean, and sub-Seleucid grandees, disappeared or were absorbed into the Roman senatorial aristocracy, and the mediating class was altered by the introduction of Roman officials. But rich natives retained their importance, and the cities in these areas, as well as the temples and their priests, continued to enjoy a nervous and limited freedom (surely much more than the Catholic churches of Ireland and the Orthodox ones of the Ukraine).[5] Only rarely can we trace the cultural effects of direct Roman rule, in part for lack of evidence and in part because they were usually subtle, mostly by-products of the more immediate administrative, social, and economic changes. The local rulers had in any case been mediators of Hellenistic culture and had administered and judged in accordance with standard types of Greco-Oriental convention and law inherited from their Seleucid predecessors. In these respects, the Romans scarcely differed.

[3] For a recent discussion, see H. Galsterer, "Roman Law in the Provinces: Some Problems in Transmission," in M. Crawford, ed., *L'Impero romano e le strutture economiche e sociali delle province* (Como: New Press 1986), pp. 13–27. Galsterer offers a plausible compromise between those who suppose that Roman annexation involved a thorough going change in legal behavior (e.g., H. J. Wolff, "Römisches Provinzialrecht in der Provinz Arabia," in ANRW II.13 (Berlin: De Gruyter, 1978), pp. 788–804; and "Le droit provincial dans la province romaine d'Arabie," *RIDA* 23 (1976): 271–90), and the pure laissez-faireists, such as Millar.

[4] See, e.g., the discussion of Emesa in F. Millar, *The Roman Near East* (Cambridge: Harvard University Press, 1993), pp. 300–309. The distinction between the Jews (and perhaps the Phoenicians) and other inhabitants of the Roman Near East in this respect is implicit throughout Millar's book, and though he probably overstated his case, there seems to me to be a hard core of truth to it.

[5] See R. Gordon, "Religion in the Roman Empire: The Civic Compromise and its Limits," in *Pagan Priests: Religion and Power in the Ancient World* M. Beard and J. North, eds. (Ithaca: Cornell University Press, 1990), pp. 240–41.

But the two new provinces in which the effects of direct Roman rule can be traced more comprehensively—Judaea and Arabia—tell a slightly different story, of a more energetic imperialism. Admittedly, these provinces were unusual in other ways, too. Provincia Arabia had been the Nabataean kingdom, situated at the very fringes of the Hellenistic world, never fully part of it.[6] Its people, or some part of them, had come to have a distinctive identity. Their rulers were designated not simply as "kings" (no subjects required—like the Seleucids and their Herodian and Syrian epigones) nor as kings of a particular land, like the Ptolemies of Egypt. They were *malkei Nabatu*—kings of (the "nation" of) the Nabataeans—and *rahmei amhon*—lovers of their people. The Babatha archives, whose papyrus documents span roughly thirty-five years, twenty-five of them under the new regime (after 106), show how quickly and dramatically some things (e.g., legal and administrative rhetoric) changed with the arrival of the Romans.[7]

We are incomparably better informed about the new province of Judaea (renamed Syria Palaestina after the Bar Kokhba revolt), which included not just the old district of Judaea but all the inland districts and coastal cities of Palestine. Here the changes resulted from (1) the imperial policy of integrating the empire's eastern fringe and (2) the failure of the two Jewish revolts. The revolts account for the fact that from the early second century until the middle of the third, this very small province hosted two Roman legions.[8] The effects of their presence were complex. No doubt many loathed the arrogance and violence of the soldiers and resented the obligation to provide them with food and lodging on short notice: these at least are common complaints in rabbinic literature, and there is no reason to disbelieve them.[9] However, the

[6] For a general account, see Bowersock, *Roman Arabia*; Millar, *Roman Near East*, pp. 387–436.

[7] For some suggestive observations, see, in addition to his *Roman Arabia*, pp. 76–89, Bowersock, "Greek Culture at Petra and Bostra in the Third Century AD," in *Ho Hellenismos sten Anatole: Praktika a' Diethnous Arkhaiologikou Synedriou Delphoi 6–9 Noembriou 1986* (Athens: Evropaiko Politistiko Kentro Delphon, 1991), 15–22 (I thank Kostas Buraselis for bringing this to my attention); there is, however, a puzzling simplicity to Bowersock's insistence on viewing the adoption of Greco-Roman political institutions, iconography, etc., as aspects of "Arab self-expression," a formulation that needs to be rethought, though not necessarily wholly rejected, in the light of Millar's conclusions in *Roman Near East*. And see now the important discussion of H. Cotton, "The Languages of the Documents from the Judaean Desert," *ZPE* 125 (1999): 219–31, who notes the near disappearance of Nabataean from documents after 106 (there are two exceptions); oddly, the four Jewish Aramaic documents postdate 106, but all except for Babatha's *ketubbah* are in effect Roman documents (including a tax receipt!) written in a different language (I would add that these documents may be important evidence for the multilingualism of scribes in Mahoza).

[8] For detailed discussion, see B. Isaac and I. Roll, "Judaea in the Early Years of Hadrian's Reign," *Latomus* 38 (1979): 54–66; Isaac, *Limits of Empire*, pp. 106–7.

[9] See S. Lieberman, "Jewish Life in Eretz Yisrael as Reflected in the Palestinian Talmud," in *Texts and Studies* (New York: Ktav, 1974), pp. 180–89, for discussion of some relevant texts.

legions were surely responsible for the spurt in road construction after 69, which among other things eased exchange between city and country and between Palestine and its neighbors, and the effect on the local economy of the presence of approximately 10,000 cash-rich troops, though incalculable, was probably not negligible.[10] A complicating factor for the present purposes is that neither legion was stationed in Jewish territory, though the VI Ferrata, in Legio-Capercotna (Kefar 'Othnai), was only some twenty-five kilometers from Sepphoris by a new road. Until the mid-third century legionary detachments and auxiliary units were scattered around the country. The mounting prosperity of Palestine, including Jewish Palestine, in the second and third centuries, which may have culminated in a partly trade-fueled boom of the fourth through sixth, would have been impossible without direct Roman rule.

But Palestine's prosperity mounted only gradually, and as far as *some* Jews were concerned was insufficient compensation for Roman depredation. At first, the consequences of the failed revolts were the most pressing concern of these Jews. Many people had died or been enslaved; many others had fled. Ancient writers provide amazingly high numbers for casualties and prisoners, which are as always best ignored.[11] There is, however, no reason to doubt the extent of the depopulation and dislocation they imply, especially in Judaea proper, which had been the center of both revolts. Idumaea and Peraea were less affected, Galilee and Golan least.

Probably everywhere, though, the failure of the revolts had led to disaffection with and attrition from Judaism.[12] 4 Ezra, an apocalyptic book composed

[10] See in general Isaac, *Limits of Empire*, pp. 104–18. Z. Safrai, "The Roman Army in the Galilee," in *Galilee*, pp. 103–14 was right to insist on the economic and social importance of the army but went too far. On Roman roads, see the detailed discussion in B. Isaac, *The Near East under Roman Rule* (Leiden: Brill, 1998), pp. 48–75.

[11] For the Great Revolt, see Josephus, War 6.420: total number of prisoners, 97,000; total number of those killed in siege of Jerusalem, 1.1 million (the smaller number of prisoners is obviously the more plausible, and it could be argued that Josephus may even have had access to official figures; the number of dead cannot have been other than guesswork). For the Bar Kokhba revolt, Cassius Dio (apud Xiphilinus) 69.14.1: fifty Judaean fortresses and 985 villages destroyed; 580,000 Jews were killed in battle, and the casualties of famine and disease were innumerable. See comments of M. Stern, *GLAJJ* II, no. 440. For a general discussion of the statistics provided by ancient writers, see Parkin, *Demography*, pp. 58–66.

[12] The standard discussions of "responses to the destruction," e.g., B. Bokser, "Rabbinic Responses to Catastrophe: From Continuity to Discontinuity," *PAAJR* 50 (1983): 37–61; M. Stone, "Reactions to Destructions (*sic*) of the Second Temple," *JSJ* 12 (1981): 195–204, cf. also S. Cohen, "Significance of Yavneh," tend to concentrate on explicit post-70 discussions of the destruction—mainly 4 Ezra and similar works, and the heavily homiletic discussions in rabbinic literature, composed centuries after the event. Such accounts often describe the Destruction as a theological problem to which various intellectuals found generally acceptable solutions. Cohen observes that the earliest rabbinic literature manifests little direct concern with the Destruction. But when this literature was written, the Destruction *was* no more than a theological problem— a suitable topic for somber moralizing reflection. This is not to deny that rabbinic Judaism was

in the late first century, gives an idea of the gloom prevailing among some of the literate elites and subelites of Jewish Palestine after 70. What point is there, the author argues, in trying to observe an unobservable covenant when God rewards our efforts by destroying us? His response, according to one of the less implausible modern interpretations—a kind of submission to fate accompanied by a defiant assertion of the covenant's enduring validity—is likely to have consoled some people, or the book would not have been read and copied; and one can, with a little empathetic imagination (an imperfect tool but not therefore to be wholly neglected), grasp the appeal of surrender in the immediate aftermath of the destruction.[13] But it cannot have satisfied everyone, and those whom it failed to satisfy will have reacted with panic, despair, and finally abandonment of Judaism.

Other Jews greeted the end of the rule of the Temple and Torah as their emancipation and rushed openly into the waiting embrace of the paganism of the Greco-Roman cities of Palestine and elsewhere: Josephus may allude disapprovingly to such people, and they may be the real historical types behind Martial's stable of burlesque Jewish and crypto-Jewish actors, poets, and deracinated urban debauchees.[14] Furthermore, these may be among the people said by Suetonius to have been especially affected by Domitian's harsh exaction of the Jewish tax. This notice in the work of the imperial biographer and the coin of Nerva celebrating the easing of the collection procedure may indicate that such Jews were numerous.[15] Similarly, an enigmatic rabbinic passage (T. Shabbat 15[16]:9) says that many Jewish men who had submitted to epispasm,

---

shaped by the Destruction, a point emphasized by, for example, Bokser, in *The Origin of the Seder: The Passover Rite and Early Rabbinic Judaism* (Berkeley: University of California Press, 1986).

[13] See M. Stone, e.g., in *Jewish Writings of the Second Temple Period*, CRINT 2.2 (Assen: Van Gorcum, 1984), pp. 412–14; but one cannot help being impressed by the difficulty of adequately explaining the jarring transition halfway through the book from profound pessimism to standard piety. I adopt Stone's interpretation with diffidence. For a general discussion of the post-Destruction apocalypses, see C. Rowland, "The Parting of the Ways: The Evidence of Jewish and Christian Apocalyptic and Mystical Material," in J. D. G. Dunn, ed., *Jews and Christians: Parting of the Ways, AD 70 to 134*, WUNT 66 (Tübingen: Mohr, 1991), pp. 213–37, esp. 219–22. Rowland is especially good on why 4 Ezra's surrender (for he too adopts Stone's interpretation) may have been attractive after 70.

[14] See S. Schwartz, *Josephus*, pp. 176–77 and, for Martial, the relevant passages in *GLAJJ* I. (For a different approach to Martial, see M. Williams, "Domitian, the Jews and the 'Judaizers'—A Simple Matter of Cupiditas and Maiestas?" *Historia* 39 [1990]: 196–211.) Josephus, *Ant* 4.145–49 seems, for example, to reflect arguments against legal observance used by Jews in Josephus's time—arguments that, interestingly enough, depend for their appeal on a critique of submission to authority and of the Law's empowerment of its mediators, exemplified by Moses. The account as a whole (126–155) is a warning to such scoffers. Cf. also Syriac Baruch 41.3, "those who forsake the covenant."

[15] See M. Goodman, *Mission and Conversion: Proselytizing in the Religious History of the Roman Empire* (Oxford: Clarendon, 1994), pp. 121–24.

the surgical restoration of the foreskin, were recircumcised in the days of Bar Kokhba; the most plausible explanation is that their epispasm was to enable full and unembarrassing participation in pagan municipal life, and that their subsequent recircumcision was forcible.[16] For still others, the mere fact of dislocation—the destruction of native villages, the violent deaths of family members, resettlement in coastal Greek cities or Galilean or Golanite towns and villages—must have eroded adherence to a way of life that no longer seemed validated by common sense.[17] Were these among the ancestors of the pagan and Christian villagers of Palestine mentioned by writers of the fourth century and later, and so prominent in the archaeological record? Or perhaps rather (or also) of the Jewish villagers of the Palestinian Talmud and the distinctively Jewish part of late antique Palestinian archaeology?

For many, or even most, Palestinian Jews, especially those outside Judaea proper, the revolts had caused less drastic disruptions.[18] Here the main changes, aside from an influx of Judaeans of unknown extent, were produced by the collapse of the central institutions—no more pilgrimages, no enforced deference to representatives of the Temple and Torah, no obligatory gifts to the priests. Whatever formal constitutional authority the Torah and its interpreters had had was now abrogated; authority resided almost exclusively in the Roman government and its representatives.

Rabbis and Patriarchs after 135

There is serious disagreement among Jewish historians concerning the effects of the Destruction and the Bar Kokhba revolt on the Jewish leadership. For some, there was no significant discontinuity: the Pharisees had exercised the predominant influence on Jewish religious life before 70, and their spiritual descendants, the rabbis, continued to do so afterward. For others, the Pharisees were an insignificant sectarian organization that disappeared in the late first century, and the rabbis and patriarchs who gradually became the leaders of the Jews had an undeniable but complex relationship with their predecessors.

---

[16] I adopt the interpretation proposed by G. Alon, *The Jews in Their Land*, p. 587, and followed by Peter Schäfer, "The Causes of the Bar Kokhba Revolt," in J. Petuchowski and E. Fleischer, eds., *Studies in Aggadah, Targum and Jewish Liturgy in Memory of Joseph Heinemann* (Jerusalem: Magnes 1981), 74–94, esp. 90–94. Also, Schäfer, *Der Bar Kochba-Aufstand* (Tübingen: Mohr, 1981), pp. 45–50. Other explanations—e.g., Graetz's view (apud Alon, *Jews in their Land*, p. 66 n. 35) that they were trying to avoid having to pay the tax of two *denarii per annum* to the *fiscus Judaicus* imposed on Jews after 70—are unconvincing.

[17] My usage here is informed by C. Geertz, "Common Sense as a Cultural System," *Local Knowledge: Further Essays in Interpretive Anthropology* (New York: Basic, 1983), pp. 73–93.

[18] W. Eck, "The Bar Kokhba Revolt: The Roman Point of View," *JRS* 89 (1999): 76–89, has now argued that the revolt spread outside Judaea, but the evidence is poor; at any rate, Galilee was certainly less damaged than Judaea by its failure.

There is general agreement, however, that the political impact of the Destruction should be seen mainly as an internal Jewish problem.[19] I would like to explain why I think that this view and the various more current refinements of it are wrong, without attempting to produce a full history of the rabbinic movement or the patriarchate.[20]

The legal and administrative implications of direct Roman rule must be taken seriously. First, when the Romans annexed a province, they subjected it to Roman law and entrusted all legal and political authority in the province to the Roman governor and his staff, and to the local city councils. They did not recognize the autonomy of the local population (except, of course, of the citizen bodies of the Greek cities, in a very tenuous way), and they did not appoint intermediaries between the "natives" and themselves—the main characteristics of the old client-kingship system, which by the later first century was an unambiguous failure. It is thus counterintuitive to think that the Romans granted official status to the patriarchs and their rabbinic protégés after 70 or 135.[21]

To be sure, the government did nothing to prevent Jews from patronizing their native legal experts for advice and arbitration. Yet by failing to recognize their jurisdiction, they made them effectively powerless to compete with the Roman courts and the arbitration of Jewish city councillors and landowners for most purposes. We may in a general way compare the Palestinian situation with the deleterious effects on the native priesthood of the (far less radical) Severan reforms of the ancient nome system in Egypt: the transformation of the old nome capitals into more or less normal Greco-Roman cities, in which both political power and religious authority were concentrated, apparently seriously undermined the financial well-being of the rural temples and the authority of their clergy.[22] For Palestine, even G. Alon, who always ascribed to the rabbis absolutely as much power and popularity as the most romantically sentimental reading of rabbinic literature would allow, admitted that in the

[19] See my review of D. Goodblatt, *JJS* 47 (1996): 167–69, for full discussion. It is only fair to point out that I contributed to what I now regard as an elementary error in my *Josephus*.

[20] Several large studies of the patriarchate have recently been published: Goodblatt, *Monarchic Principle*; M. Jacobs, *Die Institution des Jüdischen Patriarchen* (Tübingen: Mohr, 1995); K. Strobel, "Jüdisches Patriarchat, Rabbinentum, und Priesterdynastie von Emesa: Historische Phänomene innerhalb des Imperium Romanum der Kaiserzeit," *Ktema* 14 (1989): 39–77 (published 1994); L. Levine, "The Status of the Patriarch in the Third and Fourth Century: Sources and Methodology," *JJS* 47 (1996): 1–32; S. Schwartz, "The Patriarchs and the Diaspora," *JJS* 50 (1999): 208–22.

[21] These points are discussed in greater detail in my review of Goodblatt and in "Patriarchs and the Diaspora."

[22] See R. Bagnall, *Egypt in Late Antiquity* (Princeton: Princeton University Press, 1993), pp. 261–68, for an account of the decline of the temples; the connection with the Severan reform is my own. For a different approach, see Frankfurter, *Religion in Roman Egypt*, especially pp. 37–82.

second through fourth centuries, it was mainly the city councils and other urban and rural magnates who controlled the legal affairs of the Jews through a mixture of local (partly Torah-based) custom, Greco-Oriental common law, and equity.[23] In fact, the Babatha papyri may now suggest that even this view requires revision, for one of the striking facts about Babatha and company is that they apparently made almost no use of local judges but brought even trivial cases to the Roman governor.[24] If we could extrapolate from Arabia to Galilee (which is far from certain), then we should conclude that local judges and legal experts, whether rabbis, town councillors, or rural *padroni*, were less important as legal authorities than even the most skeptical reader of rabbinic literature would have guessed.

Nevertheless, even if they enjoyed little substantial authority, some might argue that the rabbis were influential in extensive circles as embodiments of Torah. By contrast, I would argue that such circles were very limited, though not wholly nonexistent. One reason for this was the partial collapse of Judaism described above. However, in order to make this argument more cogently, I need to confront head-on the common narrative of the rise of the rabbis and patriarchs, which is based on the extensive evidence of rabbinic literature. In sum, I do not disagree with the common narrative, at least in my minimalist version, while stressing that this minimalist version is a history of the rabbis and not, as is often claimed, a history of Jewish society in Roman Palestine in general.

The common narrative in its minimalist version runs roughly as follows: a rabbinic or protorabbinic movement consisting largely of former Pharisaic and/or priestly scribes, judges, and teachers began to take shape after the Destruction, perhaps mainly around Rabban Yohanan ben Zakkai and/or Rabban Gamaliel II, the latter a descendant of a prominent Pharisaic family of Jerusalem, ancestor of the patriarchal dynasty influential among the Jews until the early fifth century, and remembered by rabbinic tradition as a dynamic and powerful figure.[25] A recent study by Shaye Cohen suggests that these earliest rabbis enjoyed substantial judicial prestige, at least with respect to such inter-

---

[23] A remarkable admission that did nothing to alter the essential rabbinocentricity of his account; see "Those Appointed for Money," 382–86; though Goodman, *State and Society in Roman Galilee, A.D. 132–212* (Totowa: Rowman & Allanheld, 1983), pp. 122–26, understands the functioning of Jewish society in Roman Palestine very differently, this is basically his view, too. But note now Z. Safrai, *Haqehillah Hayehudit Be'eretz Yisrael Bitequfat Hamishnah Vehatalmud* (Jerusalem: Merkaz Shazar, 1995), pp. 77–78, who imagines that Alon *underestimated* the importance of the rabbinic courts, that, indeed, nonrabbinic courts were of no significance in Jewish Palestine—an approach characteristic of the *diadoche* of Alon.

[24] See previous chapter, note 58.

[25] This is the view I expressed in *Josephus*, pp. 170–208. In broad outline it follows Neusner; and S. Cohen, "Significance of Yavneh."

estingly backward-looking legal categories as purity and priestly gifts.[26] This prestige was not confined to Judaea but extended in a limited way even to Galilee and the Palestinian coastal cities. The Bar Kokhba revolt and the consequent massacre in Judaea were probably responsible for the fact that the rabbis of the middle and later second century, the main objects of Cohen's study, were characterized by a practically sectarian involution: they were unconcerned with and of no concern to Jews outside their own pietistic circles. Gamaliel's son, Simon, enjoyed correspondingly little general prestige.

Around the beginning of the third century, for reasons long the object of speculation and still unknown, the position of the patriarchs and rabbis began to change—a change most scholars follow rabbinic literature in attributing partly to the activities of the patriarch Judah I. He somehow became a wealthy landowner, well-connected in the increasingly prosperous Galilean cities and even, the Talmudim claim (or rather fantasize), in the Roman imperial court.[27] He or his son may have been the famous Jewish "ethnarch" referred to by Origen as behaving regally, to the point of executing criminals—though without imperial authorization. It was probably in this period, too, that the patriarchs began to claim Davidic ancestry.[28] Cohen argues that around 200 rabbinic judicial activity broadened to include issues of interest outside rabbinic circles, like civil law and Sabbath observance. Apparently, rabbinic judicial prestige was growing again, perhaps in part because the rabbinic movement left its rural Galilean exile for the cities, mainly Sepphoris and Tiberias, but also Caesarea, Scythopolis–Beth Shean, and Lydda.

The move to the cities also had significant financial implications for the patriarchs and rabbis. It connected them to long-distance trade networks and so was a necessary precondition for the loosening of their dependence on the Galilean countryside.[29] Patriarchs and rabbis could now more easily establish

[26] I would like to thank Cohen for letting me see this fundamental essay, an excerpt of which was published as "The Place of the Rabbis." The full essay was written in 1983 and has now appeared in *Cambridge History of Judaism*, 3: 922–90. See also C. Hezser, "Social Fragmentation, Plurality of Opinion, and Nonobservance of Halakhah: Rabbis and Community in Late Roman Palestine," *JSQ* 1 (1993–1994): 234–51.

[27] See Levine, "Patriarch," 654–59; note the "historicism" of the surprisingly influential article of M. D. Herr, "The Historical Significance of the Dialogues between Jewish Sages and Roman Dignitaries," *SH* 22 (1971): 123–50.

[28] See Goodblatt, *Monarchic Principle*, pp. 141–75.

[29] I would hesitate to suggest that this is reflected in Judah I's alleged deathbed instruction that he not be eulogized in the villages (because of disputes, the Talmud explains, not as helpfully as one would wish), Y. Ketubot 12:3, 34d–35a. For the routine character of interprovincial commercial contacts in the high and later Roman Empire (especially for such relations between Palestine and Egypt), see Bagnall, *Egypt in Late Antiquity*, p. 108. On the urbanization of the rabbis, H. Lapin, "Rabbis and Cities in Later Roman Palestine: The Literary Evidence," *JJS* 50 (1999): 187–207, supercedes previous discussions.

contacts outside Palestine; with a certain amount of hard selling and help from wealthy and sympathetic diasporic Jews and Roman officials, such contacts were slowly transformed into recognition of the authority of the patriarch and his protégés, who were not all rabbis, by at least some Diaspora communities.[30] Evidence for the mechanism of this development is nonexistent, but one possibility, which I do not intend to be exclusive, may be suggested.

I will argue below that in the second and third centuries the Jewish communities in the Diaspora experienced a decline comparable, and related, to the disintegration of Palestinian Jewish society in the same period. But this decline was never complete. Some communities escaped the effects of the diaspora revolt of 115–117, and had enough demographic bulk and institutional density to continue functioning, if probably in a weakened state. Such communities occasionally needed to petition the government in connection with problems raised chiefly by the conflict between their municipal obligations and those of Jewish law. The evidence for such a conflict is abundant in the first century, as we know from the writings of Josephus and Philo, and again in the fifth century, when it was one of the main issues in the legislation about the Jews in the Theodosian Code, 16.8. Though it is far sparser in the second and third, it is even then not wholly nonexistent (see chapter 6).

Petitions to the emperor were most likely to be heard if presented by a large pressure group, especially if it was represented by a well-born and well-connected grandee.[31] Thus, the Jews of the Diaspora cities had a better chance of a hearing if they presented themselves at court as "the Jews" (which is how they always appear in the Theodosian Code) and enjoyed the advocacy of a noble intermediary than if they were merely, say, "the (eminently ignorable) Jews resident in Laodicea Combusta." In the first century, the Jews of the cities had often received such help from members and agents of the Herodian family. If the patriarchs now assumed the role of Herodian-style advocates for Diaspora communities, they would have acquired political leverage (and enhanced fund-raising potential) there, not to mention visibility in the imperial court (is this the reality behind the fictional tales of the meetings of "Antoninus and Rabbi"?) and renown at home.[32]

Whatever the mechanism of the patriarchs' diasporic rise, it is surely significant that for the third century the Palestinian Talmud reports rabbinic fund-raising trips abroad, some of them presumably on the patriarch's behalf.

[30] A rabbinic *locus classicus* both for the activities of patriarchal representatives abroad and for rabbinic hostility to some of these representatives (*ilen demitmenin biksaf*, as the rabbis call them: "those appointed for money"), is Y. Bikkurim 3:3, 65 c-d.

[31] See Jones, *LRE*, 1:357–65.

[32] An isolated homily may ascribe such a role to the patriarchs, though it seems to be referring to Palestine, not the Diaspora; see Levine, "Jewish Patriarch," 659. For more on conditions in the Mediterranean Diaspora in the second and third centuries, see part 3, chap. 6.

It also reports patriarchal exercise of authority over judicial appointments. One obscure passage is sometimes thought to contain an early reference to the collection of the so-called *aurum coronarium*—the patriarchal tax—said later to have been exacted mainly from the Diaspora, but the silence of rabbinic literature apart from this passage probably indicates that in the third century it had not yet made its transformation from gift to exaction.[33] Other stories describe the classically patronal behavior of the patriarchs of the third century—the morning greetings by bands of clients and competition among the latter for access to their patron, and even gangs of toughs being employed as a "private army".[34] The rabbis were among the beneficiaries of patriarchal patronage, especially as recipients of appointments as judges and religious functionaries, mainly in Galilee, but also in the cities of Arabia, Phoenicia, Syria, and perhaps even farther afield.

In the same period the rabbis likely worked to acquire influence independent of patriarchal patronage. There is no reason to think that all or even most of the rabbinic fund-raising trips abroad mentioned in the Palestinian Talmud were undertaken on behalf of the patriarch.[35] Of special interest as a particularly blatant and problematic case of rabbinic hard selling is the account of a fund-raising trip to Emesa (Homs, in Syria) ostensibly on behalf of widows and orphans but in fact on behalf of the rabbis themselves, a piece of mischief of which one opinion quoted in the Talmud approves, ex post facto![36] The

[33] See Y. Sanhedrin 2:6, 20d = Genesis Rabbah 80:1 (ed. Theodor-Albeck, pp. 950–53), a sermon apparently attacking the fiscal rapaciousness of Judah II, though other interpretations are possible—see below; otherwise, rabbinic sources say nothing about patriarchal taxation, except for some minor involvement in the municipal taxes of Tiberias, primarily as possessing the authority to exempt rabbis from the obligation to pay them; see the discussion of Levine, "The Jewish Patriarch in Third Century Palestine," in *ANRW* II 19.2 (Berlin: De Gruyter, 1979), pp. 671–74, disregarding his unwarranted conclusion on the bottom of page 673; and see Goodblatt, *Monarchic Principle*, pp. 136–41. Why scholars have always posed the issue in the most extreme way, "when did the patriarchs acquire the authority to impose taxes?" instead of positing a gradual, halting, and uneven development from solicitation of gifts (implied by the very term *aurum coronarium*), I do not know. On *aurum coronarium*, see F. Millar, *The Emperor in the Roman World* (Ithaca: Cornell University Press, 1977), pp. 140–42.

[34] See Y. Shabbat 6:9, 8c; Y. Yoma 8:5, 45b (Germans); Y. Horayot 3:2, 47a = Y. Sanhedrin 2:1, 19d–20a ("Goths"). Rashi, ad B. Berakhot 16b, already speculated (because such gifts were common in medieval France?) that these Goths were "Antoninus's" gift to the patriarch, and remarkably enough this is reported as fact by Avi-Yonah, *The Jews of Palestine* (Oxford: Blackwell, 1976), pp. 59, 120, who also followed Rashi in regarding these slaves (?) as a private army. Levine, "Jewish Patriarch," p. 681, uses a turn of phrase whose meaning is not obvious: "(The patriarchs) employed gendarmes, but no army." For discussion, see Jacobs, *Die Institution*, pp. 43–44. On the employment of gangs by landowners, see P. Garnsey and G. Woolf, "Patronage of the Rural Poor in the Roman World," in *Patronage in Ancient Society*, pp. 152–67; and in the same volume, K. Hopwood, "Bandits, Elites, and Rural Order," pp. 171–85.

[35] See Goodblatt, *Monarchic Principle*, p. 140.

[36] Y. Megillah 3:1, 73d.

Palestinian Talmud also describes rabbinic grandees appointing their needy
fellows to communal posts, intervening with municipal governments to secure
tax breaks for friends, and interposing themselves as advocates in the trials of
ordinary Jews.[37] Some rabbis, and others on the fringes of rabbinic circles,
were acquiring visibility and prestige through their rhetorical ability, that is, by
preaching in synagogues—also reported to have been increasingly a rabbinic
concern in the third century.[38] There is a tendency in rabbinic literature, more
pronounced in the later documents, to portray some rabbis as "holy men,"
working miracles, making rain, and performing cures.[39] Rabbis also acquired
influence by offering legal advice. Though a full study of cases reported in
the Palestinian Talmud, comparable to Cohen's study of the earlier rabbinic
literature, remains to be done, most cases that came before the rabbis of the
third century seem to have originated within rabbinic circles.[40] Yet there seems
no reason to doubt the reports of the Talmud that occasionally their opinions
on some matters were sought by urban communities (even outside Palestine),
local village elders primarily in Lower Galilee, and others.[41]

In the late fourth century the patriarchs reached the peak of their power.
The Palestinian church father Epiphanius and the Theodosian Code both
indicate that the *apostole*, or *aurum coronarium*, was now collected as if it
were a conventional tax, as indeed it may have been as early as 363, when the
emperor Julian "encouraged" his "brother," the patriarch Iulus (= Hillel), to
cancel it and so free the Jews from its shackles.[42] In 399, the western emperor

[37] See, for example, Y. Sanhedrin 3:9, 21c, though the rabbi in question was Babylonian and
it is unclear where the anecdote is set. Similarly, Y. Shabbat 1:4, 3c, when a "great man" would
come to R. Jonathan's village, he would send him tokens of respect, so as to soften his heart
toward the widows and orphans. A full collection of passages in which rabbis assume the role of
intermediaries would be instructive, since this seems to me likely to have been a significant way
in which they acquired influence. Note also Y. Berakhot 9:1, 11d, about the two late-third-century
rabbis (R. Yohanan and R. Jonathan) who went "to make peace in the villages of the South"
(*me'bad shelama be'ilen qiryata dedaroma*).

[38] See L. Levine, "The Sages and the Synagogue in Late Antiquity: The Evidence of the
Galilee," in *Galilee*, pp. 209–10.

[39] See, for example, B. Bokser, "Wonder-Working and the Rabbinic Tradition: The Case of
Hanina Ben Dosa," *JSJ* 16 (1985): 42–92.

[40] Levine, *Rabbinic Class*, pp. 127–33, claims that 80 percent of cases reported in the Y concern rabbis and their families and students. But in C. Hezser's thorough analysis of the cases in
Y. Bavot (*Form, Function, and Historical Significance of the Rabbinic Story in Yerushalmi Neziqin*
(Tübingen: Mohr, 1993), pp. 396–98), 54 percent definitely concern rabbis and their connections, and in the rest the litigants are anonymous.

[41] Points similar to these are made at greater length and with full documentation by Catherine
Hezser, *Social Structure*. I thank her for discussing these issues with me before her book's publication.

[42] Julian, *epistulae* 51 = Linder, no. 13. Cohen's attempt to explain away Eusebius's mention
of *apostoloi* ("Pagan and Christian Evidence," p. 171): Eusebius does not explicitly connect them

Honorius did in fact briefly cancel the right to collect the tax,[43] as Julian had never had the opportunity to do, but in the eastern empire this right was consistently affirmed.[44] Imperial laws of the 390s seem to recognize the patriarch's jurisdiction over the *primates* (leaders) of the Jews throughout the empire,[45] who in turn were authorized to legislate and judge concerning Jewish religious, though not civil, law.[46] Epiphanius (Panarion 30.11), writing in the 370s, describes a patriarchal agent traveling through Asia Minor collecting taxes and removing archisynagogues and *azanitae* (*hazanim*) from office. The patriarchs were thus recognized by law as occupying the pinnacle of the Jewish ecclesiastical pyramid. Furthermore, by the 390s,[47] they were *viri inlustres* (the highest rank in the late imperial senate) and honorary praetorian prefects and so *in some sense* (precisely what sense is obscure, since these honors were just that) occupied a position surprisingly near the pinnacle of the Roman *imperial* pyramid, certainly ranking higher than the governors of their native province of Palaestina Secunda, who were mere *clarissimi*, members, that is, of the lowest senatorial rank.

The importance of the patriarchs in the late fourth century is confirmed by contemporary writers: for Epiphanius, the patriarch was a regal figure, complete with a *consistorium* (an advisory council, like that of the emperor), a fiscal administration, archives public and, in the church father's none too credible story, secret as well, and regents.[48] The Jewish world as ruled by him was a sort of Roman Empire in miniature but in its pre-Constantinian state —

---

with the patriarch (but he comes pretty close) and says nothing of their power in the Diaspora synagogues (though it was the obvious place for messengers from overseas to come, and even if they lacked power, why should they have lacked prestige?) seems to me unnecessary. Most likely they were what they seemed — messengers from the patriarchs trying (with ungaugeable but surely mixed success) to raise money and interest in the Diaspora synagogues. For more detailed discussions of the evidence, see S. Schwartz, "Patriarchs and the Diaspora" and Levine, "Status of the Patriarch," p. 13–6.

[43] CTh 16.8.14 = Linder, no. 30; rescission: CTh 16.8.17 = Linder, 34.

[44] So apparently CTh 16.8.15 = Linder, no. 32.

[45] CTh 16.8.8=Linder, no. 20; 16.8.13 = Linder, no. 27.

[46] CTh 2.1.10 = Linder, no. 28. See below.

[47] But probably not much earlier; Julian addresses Iulus as *aidesimotatos*, which has no administrative significance, though we would not expect technical terminology in a rhetorical context; but the mosaic inscription from the floor of the synagogue of Hamath Tiberias that calls the patriarchs *lamprotatoi* (= *clarissimi*, the lowest of the senatorial ranks) is unlikely to be much earlier than the mid-fourth century.

[48] For some salutary, if at points excessive, skepticism about Epiphanius's story, see Z. Rubin, "Joseph the *Comes* and the Attempts to Convert Galilee to Christianity in the Fourth Century C.E." *Cathedra* 26 (1982): 105–16 (in Hebrew). Contra Rubin, though, Epiphanius does not say there was a bishop *in* Tiberias but rather a bishop *near* Tiberias — which is to say that Epiphanius knew there was no bishop in Tiberias and did not know where the nearest one was in Constantine's time (Beth Shean?).

rotten at the core and on the brink of transformation. More telling, or less obviously tendentious, may be Jerome's account of the patriarch's role in the deposition and execution of a Roman governor of Palestine around 390, and Libanius's inclusion of possibly the same patriarch in his circle of high-ranking friends.[49]

Concurrently, the patriarchs' links to the rabbis seem to have weakened, or become less exclusive, continuing a process begun already by Judah I. One reason for this is likely to have been the growing importance of the patriarchs' ties to the Diaspora, where Jewish communities were once again on the rise. If it is true that one function of patriarchal agents in the Diaspora communities was advocacy, then they would have needed training primarily in rhetoric. This would have had a strong influence on the composition of the patriarchs' clientele, which in turn seems to be reflected in Libanius's correspondence. The latter testifies to a steady exchange of clients, most of them students of rhetoric, between the sophist and the patriarch.[50] There is no reason a priori why the occasional rabbinic figure might not have had such training.[51] But both rhetorical and rabbinic education were presumably sufficiently rigorous to render mastery of both rare. In fact, it is unattested. Thus, the patriarchs of the fourth century, unlike those of the third, are scarcely mentioned in rabbinic literature. Nevertheless, Epiphanius (*Panarion* 30.4) still imagined that the chief function of the *consistorium* of the patriarch was to teach him Torah; that is, he describes rabbis or rabbi-like figures as having performed a crucial advisory role in the patriarchal court, though Epiphanius's patriarch was subject to other influences as well. There may be no reason to take the account of this clumsy and slightly paranoid champion of Christian orthodoxy at face value, but it does remain likely that there were rabbis among the *primates* mentioned in the law codes. According to a law in the Theodosian Code (16.8.29), these *primates* tried to continue collection of the *apostole* after the death or deposition of the last patriarch in the 420s. Another factor in the loosening of the patriarchs' ties to the rabbis in the fourth century may be the marginalization of the curial classes (members of the city councils) of Tiberias and Sepphoris. Some wealthy *curiales* elsewhere responded to the increasingly burdensome and dishonorable character of their hereditary obligations by joining the imperial bureaus (especially in the fifth century, with the rise of Constantinople) or the Christian clergy, or by securing illegally and at great cost papers demonstrating senatorial rank and therefore providing exemption

---

[49] Jerome, *Epp.* 57.3 (CSEL 54.506). For Libanius, see the detailed commentary in GLAJJ 2, nos. 496–504. Like Jerome's, Libanius's letters indicate that in the 380s and 390s the patriarch meddled in provincial high politics.

[50] See S. Schwartz, "Patriarchs and the Diaspora" for further discussion.

[51] Notwithstanding the alleged rabbinic ban on rhetorical training, which prohibited only teaching, not study: see E. E. Hallewy, "Concerning the Ban on Greek Wisdom," *Tarbiz* 41 (1972): 269–74; Lieberman, *Hellenism*, pp. 100ff.

from curial duties.[52] It would be naive to suppose that wealthy Jews failed without exception to take either of the first two options, which would have required their conversion to Christianity. The christianization of the cities, to be discussed below, may have been to some extent an internal development produced by systemic pressures, rather than a purely foreign implantation; and a difficult Sepphorite inscription apparently commemorating a gift to a synagogue by a *clarissimus* (i.e., senatorial) *comes* called Gelasios, a descendant of archisynagogues, may provide an example of the third.[53] But for the remainder of the *curiales*, the progressive marginalization of their class in the third and fourth centuries may have forced more and more of them to seek the protection of the patriarch, further tilting the balance of the patriarchal clientele away from the rabbis. We may further speculate that this provides a partial explanation for the abolition of the patriarchate in the 420s. With the Christianization of the cities and the newly enhanced dependence of the northern Palestinian Jewish elites on the patriarch, he now for the first time in history had a power base that made him an open rival of the local government and the church.

The Limits of Patriarchal and Rabbinic Authority

This narrative is, as I suggested, unobjectionable and, with some quibbling over details, would probably be accepted by many specialists in the field, though I have intentionally made it rather more minimalist than is usual and have toned down the institutional history elements of the standard account, which I find uncongenial for reasons to be discussed below.[54] Nevertheless, as an account of the history of Jewish Palestine from 100 to 400 C.E.—as opposed

[52] On the decline of the curial classes, see the classic account in *LRE* 1.737–57, with the important qualifications of M. Whittow, "Ruling the Late Roman and Early Byzantine City: A Continuous History," *Past and Present* 129 (1990): 3–29.

[53] *CIJ* 2.991 = Lifshitz, *Donateurs et fondateurs*, no. 74, dated by Schwabe to the first half of the fifth century.

[54] A minimalist approach is not unprecedented. It was already adumbrated by Ronald Syme, "Ipse Ille Patriarcha," *Emperors and Biography* (Oxford: Clarendon, 1971), pp. 17–29. S. J. D. Cohen extended Syme's claims, arguing strongly that the explosion of interest in the patriarchate in legal and Christian and pagan literary sources in the later fourth century indicates a sudden expansion of patriarchal power, especially in the Diaspora; his assumption that patriarchal power was well established in Palestine earlier requires examination: see "Pagan and Christian Evidence," pp. 170–75. See also M. Goodman, "The Roman State and the Jewish Patriarch in the Third Century," in *Galilee*, pp. 127–39. A minimalist approach to patriarchal authority in diaspora communities is implicit also in T. Rajak and D. Noy, "Archisynagogoi: Office, Title, and Social Status in the Greco-Jewish Synagogue," *JRS* 83 (1993): 75–93; see also Strobel, "Jüdisches Patriarchat." I find it not unsurprising that a maximalist approach, in the tradition of Alon, still finds new adherents (and/or people outside Israel willing to publish their work): e.g., E. Habas [Rubin], "Rabban Gamaliel of Yavneh and His Sons: The Patriarchate before and after the Bar Kokhva Revolt," *JJS* 50 (1999): 21ff.

to an account of patriarchal and rabbinic history—it is inadequate. Archaeological remains impose the most important qualifications on this account.
Here I will briefly note that patriarchal wealth (enormous as it was) and influence (enormous as it is said to have been) left no material traces *in Palestine*,
not even as a single synagogue dedication.[55] (This is interestingly not the case
in the Diaspora.) Furthermore, though patriarchal and rabbinic authority may
have increased between 150 and 350, patriarchs and rabbis always remained
in important ways marginal, so that there is much about Palestinian society
that this change does not tell us.

Indeed, the written remains themselves offer clear indications of the con-
straints on rabbinic and patriarchal influence. In the third century rabbinic
and patriarchal authority were unquestionably limited. The rabbis and patriarchs had become more aggressive—a policy that apparently yielded real results. Yet the Palestinian Talmud itself, interested though it is in playing up
rabbinic authority, never describes the rabbis as possessing jurisdiction in the
technical sense.[56] No one was compelled to accept rabbinic judgment. The
rabbis could threaten, plead, and cajole but could not subpoena or impose a
sentence.[57] Only the Roman governor and his agents had such authority. An
eastern law of 398 quoted in Theodosian Code 2.1.10 (Linder, no. 28)—
posted when the patriarchs and their *primates* were at the height of their
power, in conditions far more amenable than those of the third century to
rabbinic judges—is of interest for what it fails to authorize. The *primates* are
granted authority only over religious law; for all other purposes the Jews are
obliged to attend regular courts (of course the state cannot, and does not
attempt to, control the use of *arbitri ex compromisso*, i.e., informal arbitrators,
and yields to them what it cannot deny, a certain de facto authority).[58] From

---

[55] The *lamprotatoi patriarchai* of Lifshitz, *Donateurs et fondateurs*, no. 76 (Hamat Tiberias)
are mentioned only as masters/patrons of a donor.

[56] My position is only a small step beyond the conclusion reached a century ago by H. P.
Chajes, "Les juges juifs en Palestine de l'an 70 à l'an 500," *REJ* 39 (1899): 39–52: "il n'existait
pas de tribuneaux au véritable sense du mot, fonctionnant d'une manière permanente. Nous
trouvons surtout des juges isolés, ayant des pouvoirs plus ou moins étendus, mais exerçant leur
action dans un domaine restreint, avec l'autorisation ou, du moins, la tolérance des autorités" (p.
52). G. Alon's subsequent "disproof" ("Those Appointed for Money," pp. 382–36), is based entirely on rabbinic passages that are exegetical, prescriptive, or found only in the Babylonian Talmud. See also J. Mélèze-Modrzejewski, apud D. Sperber, *A Dictionary of Greek and Latin Legal
Terms in Rabbinic Literature* (Jerusalem: Bar Ilan University Press, 1984), pp. 213–14. See also
J. Neusner, *Judaism in Society: The Evidence of the Yerushalmi* (Chicago: University of Chicago
Press, 1983), for the material collected rather than Neusner's comments.

[57] See, e.g., Y. Moed Qatan 3:1, 81d; the only means of compulsion Rabbi Joshua ben Levi
has is the threat of excommunication, which he refuses to use on principle; Y. Nedarim 9:4, 41c,
Rav resorts to a curse to punish a man who refused to appear before him. Though Rav was
Babylonian, the story is set in Palestine.

[58] The following remarkable passage from the early seventh century (?) *Ma'asim Livnei Eretz
Yisrael* (apparently extrapolating from a halakhah like that attributed to R. Aqiva in B. Bava Qama

the perspective of the Jewish *primates* themselves, this division of authority was highly problematic, since all law was religious law, whereas for the state, the category of Jewish religious law would, by analogy with Christian religious law, presumably have been limited to such issues as liturgical practice, *kashrut*, and so on. Marriage, divorce, guardianship, inheritance, and similar matters of critical halakhic importance were arguably outside the jurisdiction of the Jewish judges, who thus, even at the height of their post-Destruction authority, had in fact precious little jurisdiction at all.

Like the authority of the *primates*, a category I assume included rabbis, patriarchal authority, especially before the fourth century, too depended *not* on the existence of an embedded institutional structure but on something far less formal: the power of patriarchs and rabbis depended on the consensus of the ruled.[59] This is so notwithstanding the patriarchs' genuinely growing wealth and influence, claims of royal descent, and occasional displays of regal high-handedness. My emphasis on the limitations on patriarchal power disagrees with most modern accounts of the patriarchate after Judah I. But those historians who extrapolate entire institutional histories from rabbinic literature often neglect to mention the isolation of the anecdotes they depend on so heavily, or their literary function or context. A characteristic case is the common treatment of the anecdote that serves as the centerpiece of all standard accounts of patriarchal control of rural Palestinian religious life. It is worth quoting the anecdote *in extenso*:

> The people of Simonias came to Rabbi (Judah I) and said, "We wish you to give us one person who will be a preacher, judge, *hazan*, teacher of Bible and Mishnah (*safar [u]metanyan*), and will fulfil all our needs." He gave them Levi bar Sisi. They made him a big *bema* and set him upon it, and asked him, "How does an armless woman perform the *halitzah* ceremony?" and he did not answer them. "And what if, in the *halitzah* ceremony, she spat blood?" and he did not answer. They said, "Perhaps he is not a master of [legal] instruction. Let us ask him a question of *aggadah*." . . .he did not answer. They returned to Rabbi and said, "Is

---

113a—I thank Eliezer Diamond for this reference) seems relevant, but it is difficult to know how: "A gentile who comes to be judged in accordance with Jewish law may be so judged. If the judgment is tending (to favor the gentile, then he is to be judged—by the Jewish judge) according to the laws of the nations, but he may not be judged crookedly, lest the Name be desecrated. And he (the gentile) must write a *compromissum* [a document authorizing arbitration] for the judgment he is requesting" (J. Mann, "Sefer Hama'asim Livnei Eretz Yisrael," *Tarbiz* 1 no. 3 [1930]: 8). This rule is puzzling because Roman law had long since forbidden Jews to judge Christians; and it is also unclear whether the *compromissum* is required because Jewish judges are always considered *arbitri* or because their jurisdiction (de facto or de jure?) does not extend to Christians. Since the case in question is obviously civil, not religious in a narrow sense, it seems unlikely that the Jewish judge could have had formal jurisdiction of any sort.

[59] For criticism of the "institutional history" approach, see my review of Goodblatt, *The Monarchic Principle*, *JJS* 47 (1996): 167–69; and "The Patriarchs and the Diaspora."

this the intercessor we petitioned you for?"[60] He said, "By your lives! I've given you a man like myself!"... [Rabbi then summons Levi and asks him the same questions and he answers them easily.] Rabbi said, "Why did you not answer them [the villagers]?" He said, "They made me a big *bema* and sat me upon it and my spirit swelled." And Rabbi applied to him the verse, etc., and said, "Who caused you to become foolish in words of Torah? It was only because you elevated yourself through them." (Y. Yevamot 12:7, 13a)

This story is quoted in Y. Yevamot 12 because of the questions about the *halitzah* ceremony, whereby a childless widow is released from her biblical obligation to marry her brother-in-law, which are relevant to the concerns of the tractate. But the story also appears in different contexts, indicating that it circulated independently and so was probably formulated for reasons unconnected with *halitzah*.[61] In the "historical" interpretation of the story, it is often noted that the villagers had the option of rejecting an incompetent patriarchal appointee. But this would in fact have been a trivial qualification of patriarchal authority—provincials could ask the Roman emperor, whose authority is indubitable, to remove an incompetent governor, too. It is less often emphasized that the patriarch did not simply appoint a functionary; rather, the Simonians *petitioned* the patriarch. What we have here, then, is something less than a display of formal administrative authority; it is a demonstration of patriarchal prestige, which served as a guarantee to the villagers that the communal functionary would be appropriate. The patriarch was not alone in possessing such prestige. Apparently Rabbi Shimon ben Laqish (mid-late third century), among other rabbis, enjoyed it too, for the Jews of Bostra approached *him* with a request to appoint a communal functionary similar to the one requested by the Simonians.[62] What is least often observed about the story is that it is a homily, not a historical account, and one of its points is to warn rabbinic religious functionaries not to get carried away with the authority of their positions, lest in their pride they forget their Torah (and lose their jobs).[63] As such,

[60] *Haden paysuna depaysantak*—following the translation of M. Sokoloff, *Dictionary of Jewish Palestinian Aramaic of the Byzantine Period* (Jerusalem: Bar Ilan University Press, 1992), s. v. PYYSWN; correct Neusner accordingly.

[61] See also Genesis Rabbah 81:1 = Theodor-Albeck, p. 969.

[62] Y Sheviit 6:1, 36d. The language of the request is identical to that in Y. Yevamot, perhaps reflecting a standard formula. I am skeptical that there was in the third century any formal "right of *minui*," or if there was, that it had any connection with village appointments. In any case, the Palestinian Talmud occasionally mentions appointments made by nonpatriarchal rabbis, and the schematic pseudohistory of *minui* in Y. Sanhedrin 1:2, 19a admits that in its day (?) the patriarch was no longer the exclusive holder of the right. See Alon, *Jews in their Land*, pp. 719–27, and, in more detail, "Those Appointed for Money," pp. 401–10, for an attempt to read Y. Sanhedrin as real history. See also Levine, "Status of the Patriarch," 7–10.

[63] Which is not to deny the obvious fact that for the editors of the Palestinian Talmud the story's point was exclusively halakhic.

the story is important evidence that people in rabbinic circles were in the third and fourth centuries being employed as functionaries, at least in the larger and wealthier villages in Lower Galilee like Simonias, which could afford it.[64] It also rather touchingly supposes that rabbis might be overwhelmed by such unaccustomed power. But, though it significantly presupposes the patriarch's influence, it tells us very little indeed about the extent and nature of his authority and certainly fails to demonstrate that he was more influential than other important rabbis.

Likewise, Y. Hagigah 1:7, 76c, another homiletic tale, this time about the importance of Torah study for all (perhaps intended to encourage rabbis to accept positions as rural schoolmasters), is often used as "proof" that "the patriarchs" supervised rural education. What the story actually says is that one patriarch, Judah III, once sent out three rabbis to tour Palestinian villages and appoint in them (or examine) schoolteachers. In one village, finding none, they asked the villagers to bring to them the guardians of the village. When they did so, the rabbis asserted that these were not the village's guardians but its destroyers; the true guardians are teachers of Torah, as it is written, etc. Once again, the point is not historical but moral; nevertheless, this story, like the previous one, may assume the increasing importance of rabbis as communal functionaries. It may even be true that a patriarch did once (or several patriarchs did several times) send out teams to villages to inspect teachers. Can we conclude from this isolated sermon that rural Palestinian education was under the supervision of the patriarchs, *tout court*? Obviously not. In sum, the Talmudic anecdotes that scholars use to demonstrate the institutional authority of the patriarchate demonstrate at most the prestige and influence of some of the incumbents.

The Fourth Century

There is little reason a priori to think that the position of the rabbis changed, despite the elevation of the patriarchate. Many of the homiletic and legal tales in the Palestinian Talmud reflect conditions in the fourth century, and these indicate that while rabbis or people with rabbinic associations still worked, and were expected to work, as communal functionaries, teachers, and so on, sometimes in villages, their geographical diffusion was not in fact very great. Information provided by the Palestinian Talmud and the Palestinian *mid-*

---

[64] Cf. the story in Y. Megillah 4:5, 75b of Rabbi Shimon the Bible teacher/reader (*safra*) of Tarbenet, vel sim. (the text is uncertain), dismissed from his job for refusing to adopt an unlawful manner of Torah reading and subsequently praised for his obstinacy by an important rabbi. Clearly there was anxiety in some rabbinic circles about the implications of taking a post in a village—the compromises required, and so on.

rashim makes it likely that the rabbinic movement was mainly urban.[65] When villages are mentioned in the Palestinian Talmud, they are usually in the immediate vicinity of Tiberias or Sepphoris, the main rabbinic centers. Even so, it seems to me that such non-Palestinian cities as Bostra, Naveh (the main town of Batanaea), and Tyre figure more prominently in the Palestinian Talmud than even big, quasi-urban Lower Galilean villages like Arab and Beth Shearim. The densely packed Jewish population of Upper Galilee and the Golan, so important in archaeology, is hardly mentioned in the rabbinic literature at all. It is perhaps noteworthy that in one story a rabbi who ventured out of Tiberias into the Galilean countryside is said simply to have "gone outside" (*nafaq lebara*).[66] The geographical diffusion of rabbinic culture in Palestine and vicinity was thus identical with that of Greco-Roman urban culture.

The story of the rabbi who "went outside," which goes on to make the rabbi answer the locals' legal questions (incorrectly, it turns out), implies that though rabbis were not a regular presence in rural Palestine—notwithstanding their work in some big villages and occasional visits even elsewhere—they were not entirely without prestige there. It is striking that the Palestinian Talmud and *midrashim* record few complaints about rabbis being treated with open disrespect in the countryside,[67] perhaps in part because rabbinic literature tends to ignore what its protagonists were powerless to change. Or perhaps rabbis preferred to go where they knew they would be well received; the Talmud does record many instances of the rabbis' failing to intervene to stop practices of which they disapproved.[68] Nevertheless, it seems certain that they enjoyed a limited and compartmental, perhaps gradually increasing, influence.

The rabbis did not *control* anything in rural Palestine—not synagogues, not charity collection or distribution, nor anything else. But as acknowledged experts in Jewish law, protégés of the patriarch, and so on, they might be approached (and given that most of them lived in the cities, the villagers had to take the initiative) with some regularity for some purposes. By the fourth century, then, the rabbis may have lacked formal authority for the most part, but they were not without a certain compartmentalized and largely informal influence (acquired through the hard work of fund-raising, preaching, and setting themselves up as intermediaries between common folk and the powerful). Thus they constituted a limited and marginal but nevertheless discernible part of the system.

[65] See discussion in Hezser, *The Social Structure*, pp. 157–65. Hezser herself is mildly skeptical. But the matter now seems settled by H. Lapin, "Rabbis and Cities."

[66] Y. Betzah 1.4, 60c; and see Sokoloff, *Dictionary*, s. v. *br*. Neusner's translation is seriously misleading.

[67] See material collected by Levine, *Rabbinic Class*, pp. 98–133.

[68] For example, Y. Berakhot 5:3, 9c, containing several pericopae in which rabbis in synagogues witness but fail to correct what they regard as errors in liturgical practice; contrast Y.

The patriarchs of the fourth century may have been less interested in promoting their influence in the Palestinian countryside than the rabbis were.
This contradicts the common argument a fortiori about patriarchal influence;
since we know they were powerful in the Diaspora, we can take for granted
their dominance in Palestine. I would argue a different position—that the
patriarchs extended their influence in the Diaspora and in Palestine simultaneously—both from evidence and from hypothesis.

First the evidence: apart from the talmudic anecdotes discussed above,
there is remarkably little of it for patriarchal interference in rural Palestine.
With the exception of a single story that may have nothing to do with the
patriarch, all information about patriarchal fund-raising and tax collection,
and about the activities of their agents, concerns Diaspora cities.[69] The unim-
pressive epigraphical evidence for patriarchal influence is likewise entirely
diasporic: a synagogue inscription from Stobi, in Macedonia (CIJ 694); an
epitaph from Venusia, in the Basilicata, mentioning the presence at the funeral of the deceased young daughter of communal leaders of *duo apostuli et
duo rebbites* who recited *threnoi;*[70] an epitaph from Catania, Sicily, dated 383
(CIJ 1.650 = Noy, *Jewish Inscriptions,* no. 145); perhaps CIJ 719, from Argos,
Greece (see comments of Noy at 145).

Now the hypothesis: The patriarchs of the fourth century were, if the legal
and literary sources do not completely deceive us, mainly concerned with
raising money, although we have no idea what they did with it all, apart from
transforming it into senatorial rank. For this purpose, the Jewish peasants of
Palestine were of little utility. Though they were probably nearing the peak

---

Megillah 4:1, 74d, a string of anecdotes about interventions in synagogue liturgy by Rabbi
Shmuel bar Rav Yizhak.

[69] See Y. Sanhedrin 2:6, 20d = Genesis Rabbah 80:1 (ed. Theodor-Albeck, pp. 950–53): the
Jews cannot pay the priestly gifts because "the king" (in the Palestinian Talmud) or "the *nasi* (in
Gen.R.) has taken all." Even if Genesis Rabbah is correct, the reference is not to a money tax
but an impost in kind—thus not the *apostole.* Strobel's suggestion ("Jüdisches Patriarchat," p. 66
n. 209) that the story refers to rent from the patriarchal estates is attractive.

[70] For the Stobi inscription, see the discussion of Cohen, "Pagan and Christian Evidence," pp.
172–73; Venusian inscription, D. Noy, *Jewish Inscriptions of Western Europe,* vol. 1 (Cambridge:
Cambridge University Press, 1993), no. 86 = CIJ 1.611. The juxtaposition of *apostuli* and *rebbites*
seems significant, and this is furthermore the earliest case known of the use of the word "rabbi"
as a substantive rather than a title. However, the dating is controversial. *Apostuli* suggests a date
no later than c. 420, but the exceptionally "barbarous" character of the Latin orthography, as well
as the fact that other burials in the same catacomb chamber seem "late" (i.e., sixth century), have
generated some resistance to an early fifth century dating (and see now M. Williams, "The Jews
of Early Byzantine Venusia: The Family of Faustinus I, the Father," *JJS* 50 [1999]: 38–52). If the
late dating is correct, then the inscription demonstrates the otherwise unattested employment of
apostoloi either by the Palestinian academies, the Babylonian exilarchs, or an unknown authority.
See comments of Noy ad loc. All these texts are discussed in Schwartz, "Patriarchs and the Diaspora"; and Levine, "Status of the Patriarch," pp. 13–6.

of their prosperity and populousness in the later fourth century (which is to say, they had more available surplus than they were used to, did more buying and selling, and made more use of coins), the fact remains that they were still peasants with a heavy tax burden and limited (though not nonexistent) access to gold, the only stable currency in the later Roman Empire. Any attempt to exact taxes is likely to have produced small returns and generated mainly resentment. The cities of the Diaspora offered much richer pickings. The Jews in these places were probably mostly artisans and merchants, not peasants.[71] Since most personal taxes were land taxes, artisans and merchants had a comparatively light tax burden and, given their complete dependence for survival on urban markets, relatively easy access to cash.[72] The largest Jewish communities tended to be in the largest cities—easily accessible and conveniently centered on their synagogues, and possessing in some cases by the fourth century the rudiments of a loosely hierarchical organization, all of which facilitated collection.[73]

It is likely that the sources present a slightly distorted picture of the character of patriarchal authority even in the Diaspora. The laws of the late fourth cen-

[71] The evidence is almost all late antique. There were of course Jewish peasants in Egypt (CPJ passim); how typical for northern Syria were Libanius's Jewish tenant farmers? (see GLAJJ, 2, no. 495a). Note also, around the year 400, the apparently prosperous Jewish landowner Licinius in the region of Hippo Regius, whose legal entanglements with the local bishop, Victor, are the subject of a recently (1974) discovered letter of Augustine (J. Divjak, ed., Sancti Aureli Augustini Opera, sec. 2 pars. 6, CSEL 88 (Vienna, 1981) no. 8, with the comments of Helmut Castritius, "The Jews in North Africa at the Time of Augustine of Hippo: Their Social and Legal Position," Proceedings of the Ninth World Congress of Jewish Studies, B.I. (Jerusalem, 1986), 31–37); similarly on Minorca in precisely the same period (see sec. 3 chap. 6). For Jewish glassmakers at Constantinople and Emesa, see J.-P. Sodini, "L'artisanat urbain à l'époque paléochrétienne (ive– viie s.)," Ktema 4 (1979): 94; and H. J. Magoulias, "Trades and Crafts in the Sixth and Seventh Centuries as Viewed in the Lives of the Saints," Byzantinoslavica 37 (1976): 23–24; for other Jewish artisans in late antique Asia Minor at Korykos, see J. Keil and A. Wilhelm, Monumenta Asiae Minoris Antiqua, vol. 3 III (Manchester: Manchester University Press, 1931), no. 237 (shoemaker), nos. 344, 448 (perfumers), no. 607 (head of goldsmiths' guild); for Jewish merchants in the late antique Adriatic area, L. Ruggini, "Ebrei e Orientali nell'Italia Settentrionale," Studia et documenta historiae et iuris 25 (1959): 231–41. The complex question of the Jews' liability for curial service is also relevant here because in most, though not all, places such liability depended on ownership of land; see below and discussion in Linder, Jews in Roman Imperial Legislation, pp. 75–77, with his comments on the particular laws cited there; LRE 1.737ff.

[72] The only personal tax assessed on urban merchants and artisans was the much-resented but economically hardly onerous chrysargyron, instituted in the early fourth century and preceded perhaps by some sort of head tax; for a general account, see LRE 1.431; R. P. Duncan-Jones, Structure and Scale in the Roman Economy (Cambridge: Cambridge University Press, 1990), pp. 187–98; Bagnall, Egypt in Late Antiquity, pp. 153–54.

[73] That the apostole was mediated through the communal leaders explains why CTh 16.8.14, the western law of 399 forbidding collection of the tax, lists archisynagogues and elders together with apostoli as those on whom the prohibition falls. Rajak and Noy, "Archisynagogoi," 80, however, regard the law's list as blatantly erroneous.

tury take for granted, and so may have functioned to prescribe, an organized clerical hierarchy in Jewish communities, subject to the authority (*dicio*) of the patriarchs (this issue is discussed in more detail below). This clergy, however, was certainly less institutionalized than its Christian counterpart, if it existed at all; we would scarcely have guessed of its existence from the inscriptions. It was at most a thin terminological veneer imperfectly concealing, in most places, a basically self-regulating euergetistic structure.[74] In practice, this must have meant that it was harder for the patriarchs to exert control over these communities than a superficial reading of the evidence indicates. It cannot have been hard to shirk orders, and some communities would have been split or would have ignored, or been ignored by, the *apostoloi* completely. Imperial authorization of patriarchal power rarely made much practical difference.[75] It is true that *primates* actually enjoyed formal jurisdiction over religious law, but Jewish religious law was so murky and contentious a category, and it was in practice probably so unclear who counted as a *primas*, that it is hard to see why a Roman governor would have wished to get involved in trying to impose the judgment of a *primas* on an uncomplying Jew; thus, imperial authorization counted mainly as an expression of goodwill (which was not of course to be taken lightly). Furthermore, the patriarch's right to collect the *apostole* was just that, and no more: the laws, that is, never suggest that the government obligated the Jews to pay, only that the patriarch was allowed to keep what he could raise. This was no small concession: the emperors cannot have been happy to see precious metals disappear into patriarchal coffers, and this unhappiness twice found legal expression.[76] Furthermore, it is

---

[74] The fundamental discussion is now Rajak and Noy, "Archisynagogoi," who speak of the Diaspora communities as possessing a patronal structure, though this is misleading, since it is probable that the communal *institutions* depended on the wealthy (cf. P. Veyne, *Bread and Circuses* (New York: Penguin, 1990), p. 10. Euergetism is "private liberality for public benefit"); with whom individual Jews entered into relationships of dependency—assuming that charity distribution did not provide a completely adequate safety net—will be discussed below. Furthermore, Rajak and Noy are skeptical that the patriarch could have intervened in local synagogue appointments as described by Palladius, *Life of Chrysostom* (PG 47, p. 51, the patriarch changes archisynagogues at Antioch annually) and Epiphanius in his story of Joseph's deposition of archisynagogues, and so on, in Cilicia. But a letter of Libanius (*GLAJJ* 2, no. 504) indicates that the patriarch could appoint an *archon* of the Jews at Antioch, but also that the Jews could remove the man from office on their own initiative. Thus, Palladius may have been right for the 390s, but even then patriarchal authority was neither absolute nor uncontested. This would not change Rajak's and Noy's larger picture.

[75] Rajak and Noy, "Archisynagogi," 79–80.

[76] See above. Both Julian and Honorius implied that the Jews found the tax an unbearable burden; Honorius even called the patriarch *depopulator Judaeorum*—despoiler of the Jews. Clearly professional rhetoricians were at work here, as often in the law codes, and the emperors had reasons of their own for outlawing the tax. Clearly, also, some Jews were unwilling to pay. They could have been forced by the local archisynagogue, but it is hard to imagine that the apostles had any recourse if the archisynagogues themselves were unwilling to pay.

striking that some Diaspora communities (we do not know how many) actually submitted, voluntarily, to the patriarchs and came to think of their gifts as obligatory and perhaps even to allow patriarchal interference in their internal governance. But we should be careful not to exaggerate the extent of imperial privilege or patriarchal power.

In sum, I have been arguing that rabbis and patriarchs rarely wielded much formal authority. Even the patriarchs, whose history is usually written in constitutional terms, enjoyed mainly the informal prestige accruing to any great and wealthy patron with a far-flung network of important dependents, and very briefly succeeded in transforming this hard-won *auctoritas* into formal status and legal jurisdiction (which is not to deny the possibility that some Jews were impressed by their dynastic pretensions). The rabbis, for their part, never attained so high a level of official recognition, but they too, both as clients of the patriarchs and in some cases as small-scale patrons in their own right, enjoyed a certain prestige. Neither patriarchs nor rabbis, however, had much impact on the lives of Palestinian Jews. The patriarchs' main interest, especially in the fourth century, was in maintaining their ties in the Diaspora; they had little to gain from interfering in the lives of Palestinian Jews, though the latter did show them the deference due grand figures, and they are likely to have acquired a strong voice in local politics and, as suggested above, influence over the local Jewish urban elites. As for the rabbis, they too were recipients of deference due experts in Torah, but mostly they affected the lives of Palestinian Jews by serving as or advising rural religious functionaries—judges, schoolteachers, Torah readers, and the like. They seem rarely to have served such functions in Upper Galilee or the Golan; even nearer the rabbinic centers, in the villages of Lower Galilee, they were employed only by those few villages that wished, and could afford, to do so, and probably somewhat more frequently in the fourth century than in the third. There they were functionaries rather than authorities—not therefore necessarily without influence, since functionaries can transform service into control. But, as far as we are aware, whatever influence they had was ideologically compartmental and geographically restricted.

FOUR

JEWS OR PAGANS? THE JEWS AND THE
GRECO-ROMAN CITIES OF PALESTINE

I F THE RABBIS and their Torah were marginal, and the constitutional
role of the Torah was now assumed by the Roman government, where did
that leave the apparently still numerous part of post–Bar Kokhba revolt
Palestinian society that remained Jewish, however tenuously? A partial description of high imperial Jewish Palestine can be made because the evidence is
fairly abundant. What this description teaches us—that in important and surprising respects Jewish Palestine was indistinguishable from other eastern provinces—raises profound questions about the character of Jewish identity in antiquity, and about the survival of local ethnic identities under the basically
uniform surface of high imperial urban culture. My main contention will be
that the core ideology of Judaism, discussed in the first part of this book, was
preserved in profoundly altered but still recognizable form mainly by the rabbis
but had a weak hold, if any, on the rest of the Jews. Yet the Jews, or some of
them, must have retained some consciousness of being separate from their
Greco-Syrian neighbors or they could not have begun to reemerge in the fourth
century as a clearly defined, Torah- and synagogue-centered ethnic/religious
group in northern Palestine. Their neighbors may have contributed to this
sense of separation: in the middle of the second century pagan Scythopolis
(Beth Shean) adopted the suggestively overdetermined title "Nysa, also called
Scythopolis, the Holy and Inviolate, One of the Hellenic Cities of Koile Syria."
The Scythopolitans had good reasons for their cultural anxieties—the presence
of large Jewish and Samaritan communities in their city, and the importance
of people of Jewish (and Samaritan?) origin among the city's "Greeks," for
example. But presumably they were also trying to distinguish themselves from
their Jewish, and perhaps Arab, neighbors.[1] What the separate consciousness
of the high imperial Palestinian Jews consisted of remains to be discussed.

[1] For the title, see G. Foerster and Y. Tsafrir, "Nysa-Scythopolis: A New Inscription and the
Title of the City on its Coins," *INJ* 9 (1986–1987): 53–58. The suggestion that the Scythopolitans
were worried about the Jewish and Samaritan communities within the city is theirs. For pagans of
Jewish origin, the evidence is two altar bases of the second century C.E., one inscribed, "To Good
Fortune. Abselamos son of Zedokomos (or Zelokomos) the builder dedicated (this)," and the
other, "To Good Fortune. Theogene daughter of Tobias dedicated this to Zeus Akraios." Abselamos is probably but not certainly Jewish (or Samaritan), Tobias seems certain. See *SEG* 28
(1978): 1446 (but also J. and L. Robert, *BullEp*, 1964, no. 516); and Y. Tsafrir, "Further Evidence
of the Cult of Zeus Akraios at Beth Shean (Scythopolis)," *IEJ* 39 (1989): 76–77. For recent excavations at Scythopolis, see the special issue of *Qadmoniot* 27 (1994). On the "Arab" or "Semitic"

Between the Bar Kokhba revolt and the christianization of the empire, the main areas of Jewish settlement included Upper and Lower Galilee, Diospolis-Lydda and its vicinity, perhaps Joppa and some scattered settlements elsewhere on the Mediterranean coast, the Golan Heights, and the semidesert fringe of Judaea. As already suggested, Jewish settlement in Judaea proper was drastically reduced in the wake of the Bar Kokhba revolt.[2] What then became of the district is unclear, but it may not have recovered fully until late antiquity, when it began to benefit from the attention of the Christian state. What Jewish population remained in Judaea was confined to its edges: there are scattered pieces of evidence, especially but not exclusively late antique, for Jewish settlement in such agriculturally marginal villages as Zif, Eshtemoa, and Susiyah, south of Hebron. Joppa, conventionally considered Judaea's port but for most of its history a normal Levantine town with a mixed population, retained some Jewish inhabitants even after it was rewarded by Vespasian for its loyalty to Rome during the first Jewish revolt.[3] Indeed, the Jews may have been numerous and influential. The evidence is exiguous but suggestive—a set of molds for lead weights dated to the first decade of the second century, which identify as *agoranomos* (market supervisor) of the city one Ioudas son of Gozom or Tozom.[4] As *agoranomos*, Ioudas, who was obviously of Jewish origin however we construe his mysterious patronymic, was one of the city elites, probably in fact a member of the *boule*, or city council.[5] Evidence for Lydda, on the northwestern fringe of Judaea, is more abundant and will be considered below.[6]

Galilee, 135–324

Galilee was divided into two zones that were to some extent culturally distinct—urbanized Lower Galilee and unurbanized Upper Galilee.[7] While Upper Galilee had been a populous and prosperous region before 67 C.E., and

---

character of some of the Transjordanian cities, see Bowersock, "Greek Culture at Petra and Bostra," pp. 15–22; D. Graf, "Hellenisation and the Decapolis," *Aram* 4 (1992): 1–48, esp. 5–7.

[2] For a full account of the evidence for continued Jewish settlement in the district, see J. Schwartz, *Jewish Settlement in Southern Judaea from the Bar Kokhba Revolt to the Muslim Conquest* (Jerusalem: Magnes, 1986).

[3] See Isaac, *Limits of Empire*, pp. 348–49.

[4] See *SEG* 31 (1981): 1410.

[5] S. Applebaum's claim, made entirely on the basis of these weights, that there existed at Joppa multiple *politeumata* (ethnic corporations), each with its own magistrates, is unlikely: see *SCI* 8–9 (1985–1989) 138–44. The Jewish cemetery of Joppa (see *CIJ* 2.892–960) is mainly late antique, to judge from the Greek spelling and the use of such titles as *kyra* (e.g., 896) and *beribbi*. Some of the inscriptions Frey assigned to the Joppan catacombs may come from elsewhere and may be somewhat earlier—they lack "late" features, including Jewish iconography. This cemetery needs a comprehensive reexamination.

[6] In general see J. Schwartz, *Lod (Lydda), Israel: From its Origins through the Byzantine Period*, BAR International Series 571 (Oxford: Tempus Reparatum, 1991).

[7] For a general account, see Goodman, *State and Society*.

possibly after, there is a nearly complete gap in information from Vespasian's invasion in that year until the fourth century.[8] The Palestinian Talmud displays little interest in the district, and the less than extensive excavations have with some exceptions uncovered mainly late antique material—most prominently synagogues, to be discussed below. A similar situation prevails in the Golan Heights. While we have enough information to know that Upper Galilee was settled in the second and third centuries, at least partly by Jews (some rabbis came from Upper Galilean villages, and a handful of late antique synagogues were built over slightly earlier, *perhaps* synagogal, structures), little else can be said.[9]

One enigma may be noted, though. In the Upper Galilean village of Qasyon, an area especially rich in late antique synagogue remains, fairly extensive remains were found in the nineteenth century of a monumental building constructed in the second century C.E. The building resembles neither later Galilean synagogues nor contemporary Syrian temples precisely, though it has structural elements in common with both. Among the remains were a stone eagle, an altar, and a lintel bearing a rather roughly carved Greek inscription:

> For the well-being of our lords the Caesars L. Septimius Severus Pius Pertinax Augustus and his sons M. Aurelius Antoninus and L. Septimius Geta. By oath of the Ioudaioi. . .

Inside a wreath beside the main inscription is carved the name of the empress Julia Domna. Since these remains were discovered in the last century, archaeologists have disagreed about the identity of the structure: it is either an exceptionally peculiar synagogue or a slightly peculiar temple odd mainly for having been patronized by a group of self-identified Ioudaioi. (The only thing known about Qasyon otherwise is that is was the hometown of a Palestinian *amora* called R. Yohanan deQasyon, presumably in the later third century.)[10] The ambiguities of these remains, the possibility they imply of the coexistence of the retention of some sense of Jewish separateness with full participation in normative Roman imperial religious life, and this in a remote hill country village, serve as a good introduction to this chapter's discussion of the complexities of Jewishness in high imperial Palestine.

---

[8] On the Galilean economy before the revolt of 66, see S. Schwartz, "Josephus in Galilee." If we could extrapolate from the findings of D. Adan-Bayewitz, *Common Pottery in Roman Galilee* (Ramat Gan: Bar Ilan University Press, 1993) to the economy of Galilee in general, which is unlikely since there is no reason a priori to consider pottery especially useful as a tracer for general patterns of exchange, then we would learn that the two halves of Galilee were quite thoroughly integrated economically despite their cultural and social distinctness. This would be surprising and interesting. For additional discussion, see Lapin, forthcoming.

[9] See Goodman, *State and Society*, pp. 32–33.

[10] For a survey of Qasyon and an account of the controversy about it, see Z. Ilan, *Ancient Synagogues in Israel* (Tel Aviv: Ministry of Defense, 1991), pp. 57–59; on the inscription, see L.

Lower Galilee is quite well attested for the high imperial period. Rabbinic literature, especially the Tosefta and Palestinian Talmud, is filled with information. This information above all concerns Tiberias, the place of their composition, and curiously enough tends to confirm the impression created by the material evidence of the rabbis' own marginality in their main city, as we will see. Furthermore, though the city cannot be thoroughly excavated because it has been inhabited without substantial interruption since its foundation, around 19 C.E., enough small-scale excavation has been done, and enough inscriptions and coins have turned up, to give some sense of the city's public life.

Jewish Cities?

In the second and third centuries the free population of Tiberias apparently consisted mostly, or almost entirely, of people who were in some sense Jewish. Josephus, who knew the city well, was hostile to it, and considered its Judaism suspect, noted that at the outbreak of disturbances in Palestine in 66 C.E., the Tiberians massacred the "Greek" (i.e., non-Jewish) residents of the city (Life 67). Apparently they had not been numerous. Subsequently, there is little evidence for the permanent presence of "Greeks" or "Syrians." The rabbis unquestionably regarded Tiberias, along with Sepphoris and Lydda, as "Jewish," in contrast to the mainly pagan Scythopolis and Ptolemais. Probably in all these places there was a small Christian or Jewish-Christian presence, notwithstanding Epiphanius's claim (Panarion 30.11.9–10) that around 320 the cities and large villages of Galilee were entirely Jewish.[11] A single story in the Palestinian Talmud (Shabbat 16:7, 15d) mentions a *shuqa de'arama'e* (Syrian market), which operated on the Sabbath, in the Tiberian district, or suburb, of Kifra. The only other unambiguous pagans whom rabbinic literature mentions in connection with Tiberias are specialist professionals (a physician, interestingly enough female: Y. Shabbat 14:4, 14d) or itinerants (philosophers and astrologers: T. Shevuot 3:6; Tanhuma Shofetim 10). To this list should

---

Roth-Gerson, *Greek Inscriptions from the Synagogues in Eretz-Israel* (Jerusalem: Yad Ben Zvi, 1987), no. 30.

[11] The most useful collection of rabbinic sources for all these places remains S. Klein, *Sefer Hayishuv* (Jerusalem: Dvir, 1939), sub vv. The Tiberian material has been discussed in greater detail by J. Schwartz, "Hayei Yom-Yom Beteveryah Bitequfat Hamishnah Vehatalmud," in Y. Hirschfeld, ed., *Teveryah: MeYisudah ad Hakivush Hamuslemi: Meqorot, Sikumim, Parashiyot Nivharot Vehomer-Ezer* (Jerusalem: Yad Ben Zvi, 1988), pp. 103–10. In general, Goodman, *State and Society*, pp. 41–53. For rabbinic comments about *minim*, perhaps Christians, in Tiberias and Sepphoris, see A. Büchler, *Studies in Jewish History*, ed. I. Brodie and J. Rabbinowitz (London: Oxford University Press, 1956), pp. 245–74. See also the Syriac version of Eusebius, *The Martyrs of Palestine*, ed. W. Cureton (London, 1861), p. 29, where either Sepphoris (Diocaesarea) or Lydda (Diospolis) is described as entirely Jewish.

probably be added legionary troops, for although their fixed presence in or near the city is not mentioned in rabbinic literature or any other source, the Latin epitaphs of two serving troops (as opposed to veterans) found in Tiberias suggest that a detachment of the Sixth Legion Ferrata, based at Legio-Capercotna, was encamped at Tiberias.[12]

Given the likely demographic composition of the city, how are we to explain the explicitly pagan character of its material remains? First I will survey the material and then offer some brief reflections on its character.

Scholarly convention has tended to introduce a distinction between two categories of material evidence—coins and everything else—and different techniques have been used for dismissing the implications of each. Statues, both public and private, decorated furniture and tableware, mosaic pavements decorated with mythological scenes, after all, create a rather different set of problems from images on coins. The latter are commonly assumed to include more or less straightforward, and authorized, representations of the cities' "official" religious behavior—portraits of gods seated in temples, images of cultic acts, and so on.[13] Therefore, the coins can only be reconciled with the knowledge that the cities were inhabited mainly by Jews by drastic means, for example, by the invention of a historical narrative (Hadrian disenfranchised the Jews, entrusting control of their cities to pagans) not attested in any ancient source. Once the coins are dismissed, most of the other types of paganizing material can be combined with pagan-seeming imagery used in synagogues and other definitely Jewish contexts, such as the necropoleis of Beth Shearim and Rome, and discussed as aspects of the hellenization of Judaism, though, of course, the actual tools of sacrifice, several examples of which were discovered at Sepphoris, have to be attributed to pagan interlopers. The main question in that case is, How did Jews *as adherents of an ideological system that tended to frown on representations of humans, let alone of gods* defend their use of figurative art? This issue—the use of figurative, including paganizing, representation by the ancient Jews—is the topic of an old but durable debate between E. R. Goodenough and his followers and their students on the one side, and a loosely arrayed opposition on the other, of whom Michael Avi-

[12] See M. Schwabe, "Letoldot Teveryah: Mehqar Epigrafi," M. Schwabe and Y. Gutmann, eds., *Sefer Yohanan Lewy* (Jerusalem, 1949), pp. 200–251, nos. 18–9 = L. di Segni, "Ketovot Teveryah," in *Teveryah*, pp. 70–95, nos. 11–12. Also B. Isaac, *The Limits of Empire*, p. 434, who, however, in locating a detachment of the Tenth Legion Fretensis in the city, failed to notice that Aurelius Marcellinus, centurion of the Legion, was seventy-four years old when he died and had obviously (re?)settled in Tiberias after his discharge many years earlier; his epitaph thus provides no evidence for the presence of the Tenth Legion in the city. For rabbinic comments about *minim*, possibly Christians, in Tiberias and Sepphoris, see Büchler, *Studies in Jewish History*; R. Kalmin, "Christians and Heretics in Rabbinic Literature of Late Antiquity," *HTR* 87 (1994): 155–70.

[13] This is, for example, the assumption of R. MacMullen, *Paganism in the Roman Empire* (New Haven: Yale University Press, 1981), p. 25.

Yonah, the archaeologist and historian, may serve as an exemplary figure because of his tremendous influence on the interpretation of ancient Jewish art.

Avi-Yonah and colleagues were inclined to understand most paganizing art and iconography from ancient Jewish Palestine, whatever the context in which it was found, as "merely" decorative. The ancient Jews were able to utilize such threatening images in this way because sometimes they were unaware of the implications of the images, and in any case by the second and third centuries paganism had run out of steam so the images were largely free of any noisome religious content.[14] However, art with recognizably Jewish or biblical themes, even when found in the same context as the pagan, for example, on adjacent panels of a mosaic pavement in a synagogue nave, is supposed to have been profoundly meaningful. The continuing vibrancy of this school of noninterpretation is strikingly demonstrated in a recent publication on the grand Dionysiac mosaic discovered on the acropolis of Sepphoris, duly described as religiously meaningless. In an important, in many respects excellent, recent synthetic book on ancient Jewish art, Avi-Yonah's approach, clearly and programmatically described, is represented as the view of "most scholars."[15]

Goodenough adopted a different sort of judaizing approach to the material. In contrast to the Avi-Yonah school, which rabbinizes, by supposing that if an image was not likely to have been worshiped then it was purely decorative, absolutely devoid of religious meaning, and thus unproblematic from the Jewish perspective (see below on the rabbinic view of "idolatry"), Goodenough "Philonized."[16] For Goodenough, even geometric designs, rosettes, and so on, were packed with religious meaning. Nothing was simply decorative; indeed, nothing even had a subtle meaning, as being faintly evocative of secondarily religious emotions, for instance. All images used by Jews were in a more or

[14] See also E. E. Urbach, "The Rabbinical Laws on Idolatry in the Second and Third Centuries in the Light of Archaeological and Historical Facts," *IEJ* 9 (1959): 149–65, 229–45. Sometimes a mild judaizing interpretation is offered. For example, the zodiac wheel with Sol Invictus seated in his *quadriga* in the center, found in several Palestinian synagogues, represents the Jewish liturgical year; see R. Hachlili, "The Zodiac in Ancient Jewish Art: Representation and Significance," *BASOR* 228 (1979): 61–76, following Avi-Yonah. Cf. G. Foerster, "The Zodiac in Ancient Synagogues and Its Iconographic Sources," *EI* 18 (1985): 380–91; and "The Zodiac in Ancient Synagogues and Its Place in Jewish Thought and Literature," *EI* 19 (1987): 225–34; and below for further discussion.

[15] See R. Talgam and Z. Weiss, "The Dionysus Cycle in the Sepphoris Mosaic," *Qadmoniot* 83–84 (1988): 93–99. Many examples of Avi-Yonah's approach can be found in his collection *Art in Ancient Palestine* (Jerusalem: Magnes, 1981); for a characteristic case see the discussion of the imported mythological sarcophagi from Beth Shearim, pp. 268–69; Hachlili, *Ancient Jewish Art*, pp. 286–87.

[16] See E. R. Goodenough, *Jewish Symbols in the Greco-Roman Period*, 13 vols. (Princeton: Princeton University Press, 1953–68); the essential evaluation of Goodenough's work is M. Smith, "Goodenough's Jewish Symbols in Retrospect," *JBL* 86 (1967): 53–68. Goodenough was a leading authority on Philo before he began studying ancient Jewish art.

less straightforward way aspects of, and are evidence for, the popular Judaism practiced for centuries throughout the Mediterranean world. It was this same mystical variety of Judaism that, according to Goodenough, had been propounded in articulate and (semi)systematic form in the works of Philo, and against which the socially and politically marginal rabbis were for many centuries unable to prevail.

Goodenough's method consisted in part of interpreting iconographic items, which he regarded as having universal "values" (i.e., religious/emotive content) as distinct from "interpretations" (i.e., the explanations given by contemporaries) by means of introspection. Goodenough himself cheerfully acknowledged the utter subjectivity of this method and not even his greatest admirers have ever had the sheer insouciance, or rather *hutzpah*, to imitate him. But if Goodenough's art history was a failure, his fundamental historical observation based on his unchallengeably exhaustive collection of archaeological material—that there is nothing in the Talmud to prepare us for the quantity and character of ancient Jewish art and that it must therefore indicate that the rabbis were far less powerful than was normally believed—has been highly influential, including on this account. On the other hand, those influenced by Goodenough seem to have despaired of or lost interest in the task of making sense of ancient Jewish art, except to reiterate, in an almost ritualistic way, that it disproves the proposition that the rabbis controlled the religious life of the Jews.

Avi-Yonah's and Goodenough's common tendency to offer judaizing interpretations of the archaeological material was to some extent a consequence of its consensual chronology. It was generally thought that many or even most Palestinian synagogues were built in the second and third centuries, so that statuary and decorated pottery from the high imperial cities, imported sarcophagi in third-century Beth Shearim and elsewhere, and similar material, were contemporaneous with the synagogues, whose decoration often combined pagan and Jewish elements. It thus seemed reasonable to both Avi-Yonah and Goodenough to suppose that almost all the pagan iconography was used by people who were in some sense "good," Torah-oriented, if not rabbinic, Jews. Goodenough argued that the pagan imagery was the visual counterpart of Philo's use of Greek religious language and concepts to describe a profoundly hellenized but still basically "Jewish" version of Judaism, but he also acknowledged the existence of genuine syncretism, paganizing Judaism and judaizing paganism.

In the last two decades, however, the traditional chronology of the ancient synagogues has collapsed. It seems unlikely that any post-Destruction Palestinian synagogue whose remains survive much predates 300 C.E. Furthermore, scholars of Roman religion tend now to reject, or at least feel squeamish about, the nakedly teleological claim that by the second or third century Greco-Roman paganism was somehow moribund; it must on the contrary be admitted that the high imperial Palestinian cities were participants in a religious culture of enduring vitality if perhaps ever changing character.[17] These factors, I would argue, require us to regard the use of pagan objects and decoration by Jews, mainly before 350, and the incorporation of pagan iconography in synagogues, mainly after 350, as distinct phenomena. Clearly, use of identical items of pagan imagery would have had a very different meaning in synagogues in the fifth and sixth centuries, and in town squares, public baths, private houses, theaters, and temples in the second and third. Finally, the recognition that between 70 and 350, at earliest, the rabbis were marginal figures, suggests that whatever else we do we should certainly avoid Avi-Yonah's (unconsciously?) rabbinizing approach to the material. As we shall see, the rabbis' dismissal of much of the pagan material as "meaningless" was part of their attempt to cope with life in the Palestinian cities. There is no reason to suppose that their views were shared by many of their compatriots.

The Evidence

COINS[18]

Like some 500 other cities in the high imperial Roman East, Tiberias, Sepphoris, and Lydda issued bronze coins. These coins served for small-scale day-to-day transactions within the city. Since the value of bronze city coins was wholly fiduciary (unrelated to the market value of the metal) and the minting authority was the city and not the provincial or imperial governments, the coins tended not to circulate in a regular way even in areas adjacent to the city. The coins were also an important expression of local patriotism, indisputable evidence of the city's autonomy (though of course a city could not officially mint without the emperor's approval), and one of the main media for the expression of the class interests of the municipal leadership—the city councillors, great landlords, and so on. It was they who chose and commissioned the design of the coins and they who initiated the minting. This factor makes separate treatment of the coins convenient.

---

[17] E.g., MacMullen, *Paganism in the Roman Empire*, pp. 62–94; R. Lane Fox, *Pagans and Christians* (London: Penguin, 1986); North, "Development of Religious Pluralism", J. Lieu, J. North, and T. Rajak, eds., *The Jews among Pagans and Christians in the Roman Empire* (London: Routledge, 1992), pp. 174–93; and, most cogently, Frankfurter, *Religion in Roman Egypt*; M. Beard, J. North, and S. Price, *Religions of Rome, vol. 1, A History* (Cambridge: Cambridge University Press, 1998), passim.

[18] The basic corpus is M. Rosenberger, *The Rosenberger Israel Collection*, 3 vols. (Jerusalem: n.p., 1972–1977) (vols. 2–3 entitled *City-Coins of Palestine*); some discussion and additional material in Y. Meshorer, *City Coins of Eretz Israel and the Decapolis in the Roman Period* (Jerusalem: Israel Museum, 1985); for updating, see A. Kindler and A. Stein, *A Bibliography of the City Coinage of Palestine from the Second Century BC to the Third Century AD*, BAR International Series 374 (Oxford: BAR, 1987), with further information in the journal *Numismatic Literature*.

Coins were minted only occasionally, when the need arose to put more small coins into circulation or when there was something to celebrate. Meshorer's attribution of gaps in and resumptions of coinage to the vicissitudes of the relations between the city and the emperor, a concern that dominates his highly influential historical interpretations of the coinage and therefore deserves special mention, is misleading: it neglects the fact that emperors more often *reacted* to requests from cities than exercised active supervision over them—not surprisingly, given the number of "autonomous" cities in the East.[19] And, in its exclusive concentration on Palestine, Meshorer's view fails to acknowledge the contours of the evidence as a whole.[20] To be sure, emperors occasionally did reward or punish cities by, among other things, granting or suspending rights of coinage, the best-known case being Septimius Severus's behavior in the aftermath of the civil war of 193. Nevertheless, only the very largest cities produced bronze coins uninterruptedly, and gaps elsewhere must not be overinterpreted.[21]

What do the Tiberian coins tell us about the interests of the city councillors and their peers?[22] The first issue, dated to the year 81 (probably 100 C.E.), includes three distinct reverse types. (The obverse of Roman city coins almost invariably shows a portrait of the emperor, Trajan in this case, or a member of his family.) One of these depicts a palm branch flanked by cornucopias.[23] The cornucopia is a common image on city coins of all sorts but had also appeared on "Jewish" (Hasmonean, Herodian, and revolutionary) coinage, and the palm had powerful Jewish associations in ancient iconography. The *Iudaea Capta* coins issued by Vespasian to celebrate the quelling of the Judaean revolt depicted Judaea as a weeping woman seated beneath a palm tree.[24] But the other two types are pagan: one coin shows the goddess Hygieia (the personification of health) seated on a rock over a spring, holding a snake eating from a bowl—clearly a celebration of the medicinal properties of the hot springs just south of the city at Hamath.[25] The other type depicts Tyche (Fortune), an old Greek goddess often pressed into service in the Roman east as a city goddess, standing on a boat and holding a cornucopia.[26] Nine years

[19] This is the main, and probably mainly correct thesis, of Millar, *Emperor in the Roman World*.

[20] Y. Meshorer, "Sepphoris and Rome," in O. Mørkholm and N. Waggoner, eds, *Greek Numismatics and Archaeology: Essays in Honor of Margaret Thompson*, (Wetteren: Cultura, 1979), pp. 159–71, with comments of K. Harl, *Civic Coins and Civic Politics in the Roman East, AD 180–275* (Berkeley: University of California Press, 1987), p. 24, n. 34.

[21] On Severus, see, e.g., Isaac, *Limits of Empire*, pp. 359–61. For a general account of city coinage, see Harl.

[22] Rosenberger, 3: 64–67.

[23] Rosenberger, nos. 8–9.

[24] For a discussion of the palm in Jewish iconography, see Hachlili, *Ancient Jewish Art*, pp. 80–83; 256–67.

[25] Rosenberger, nos. 6–7.

[26] Rosenberger, no. 5.

later, another coin with a "Jewish" reverse (or at any rate a reverse common on earlier Jewish coins though also in other contexts, namely, an anchor) was issued, followed ten years later by a coin with a four-columned temple, with Zeus seated within portrayed on its reverse.[27] The remaining reverse types, on coins issued down to the reign of Elagabalus (218–222), depict more Tychai on boats, a winged Nike bearing a wreath and a palm branch, Poseidon holding a trident, also on a boat, and Asclepius and Hygieia, again holding snakes.[28] But in 119–120, the year in which Zeus first appeared seated in his temple, Tiberias also issued a coin with a galley but no human or divine figure on its reverse.[29]

The coinage of Sepphoris is similar, except that its Trajanic coinage—unique among Roman city coins in acknowledging the fact that the emperor himself had granted the city permission to mint—is more uniformly "Jewish" in its reverse types.[30] But later coins show the city's Tyche, as well as Zeus and possibly Athena, all in tetrastyle temples, Hera holding an incense shovel, and the Capitoline Triad (Zeus/Jupiter, Hera/Juno, Athena/Minerva) also in a temple.[31] Some of the Severan coins of the city contain on their reverse only the city's pompous titulature, presumably a reward for having supported the winner in the civil war of 193.[32] That this aniconism was not due to Jewish religious scruples (and, *pace* Meshorer, whose views on the matter have been widely accepted by Jewish historians, if not Roman numismatists, certainly has nothing to do with the activities of Rabbi Judah Hanasi) is demonstrated by the fact that the city simultaneously continued minting pagan coins.[33] The others are aniconic because Sepphoris's titulature left no room for an image. Anyway, they are only relatively aniconic: the obverse still features the emperor's portrait.

Of other coins of "Jewish" cities, Flavia Neapolis (formerly Shechem, in fact Samaritan rather than Jewish) began its coinage under the Flavian emper-

---

[27] Rosenberger, nos. 9–11. Needless to say, even the "Jewish"-style coins are problematic from the point of view of Jewish law because of the emperor's bust on the obverse. The Hasmoneans, Herod, and even the Roman procurators of Judaea, it is worth remembering, never put human images on their coins.

[28] Rosenberger, nos. 12–21; the figure identified as Asclepius by Meshorer, *City Coins* no. 86, is left unidentified by Rosenberger.

[29] Rosenberger no. 15.

[30] Rosenberger, 3: 60–63; the Trajanic coins are nos. 3–6.

[31] Rosenberger, nos. 7–18; the Capitoline Triad coin is in Meshorer, *City Coins*, no. 93.

[32] On these coins, see C. Kraay, "Jewish Friends and Allies of Rome," *ANSMN* 25 (1980): 53–57. For additional arguments against Meshorer's interpretation, see H. Lapin, *Early Rabbinic Civil Law and the Social History of Roman Galilee: A Study of Mishnah Tractate Bava Mesi'a'* (Atlanta: Scholars, 1995), p. 12 n. 28.

[33] Contrast, for example, Z. Weiss and E. Netzer, *Zippori* (Jerusalem: Israel Exploration Society, 1994), p. 8. Meshorer's presentation of this material in *City Coins* is tendentious, creating the impression that the "aniconic" coins were the last the city minted.

ors with Jewish types and then switched to pagan types at the *beginning* of Trajan's reign.[34] Lydda-Diospolis was raised to city status only after 193 and its coinage is entirely pagan, as is also the rare coinage of Joppa.[35] It may or may not be a coincidence that Sepphoris stopped issuing "Jewish" types when its name was changed to Diocaesarea (i.e., city of Zeus and Caesar) and that Lydda's elevation to city status involved a change of name, to Diospolis—city of Zeus.[36] Lydda's new name may have been intended as a compliment to the emperor Severus, whose in-laws and heirs were ancestral priests of Zeus Heliopolites (the Baal of Baalbek), a god whose image is especially prominent on the Lyddan coins.[37] But at Tiberias and Neapolis there was no comparable coincidence of change of name and of coin types.

Prima facie, all this coinage of "Jewish" cities provides evidence for the importance of the Greek gods and/or of their local Semitic equivalents in the way the leaders chose to think about and celebrate their cities. The Tiberians used images of Poseidon, Asclepius, and Hygieia to emphasize the importance to their city of the Sea of Galilee and the hot springs of Hamath, just as the Sepphorites celebrated their ancient friendship with Rome, which had survived even the revolt of 66, with images of the Capitoline Triad. This is especially striking given that the Sepphorites presumably were obliged to pay the special Jewish tax to Capitoline Jupiter (or were they? Did they cease officially to profess Judaism and thereby free themselves from the obligation to pay?), deemed by all modern historians to have been humiliating to the payers. It must again be emphasized that the coin types were items in a culture of display, little pieces of public political and religious discourse; but the display and discourse were primarily internal, the coins seen and used only within the cities. They therefore reflect the images of the cities the leaders wished their fellow citizens, not Greek neighbors or imperial officials, to see.

Do the coins imply more about the public life of the cities? It is normally assumed that gods depicted on city coins, especially in cultic situations, were beneficiaries of public worship. If so, the gods on the Tiberian, Sepphorite, and Lyddan coins cannot all be dismissed as metaphors, since all these cities issued coins showing gods seated in temples, which strongly suggests the gods were actually worshiped. To my knowledge this assumption about the relation between gods depicted on coins and municipal cults has never been examined in a systematic way and it may be best not to draw hasty conclusions about the civic religions of Tiberias, Sepphoris, and Lydda on the basis of the coins

[34] Rosenberger, 3: 5–26; the Flavian coins are nos. 1–6.

[35] Rosenberger, 2: 28–31, 76–78.

[36] Sepphoris probably adopted its new name in honor of Hadrian's visit to the province of Judaea in 130: the name is first attested on a milestone of that year; see M. Hecker, "The Roman Road Legio-Sepphoris," *BJPES* (= *Yediot*) 25 (1961): 175–86, esp. 176. The pagan coins begin under Antoninus.

[37] See Herzog, "Iulia Domna," in *RE* 19.929.

alone. Nevertheless, there can be no doubt that in all other cities of the Roman East there was at least a *rough* correspondence between coin types and public cults; furthermore, according to the admittedly unreliable Palestinian church father Epiphanius (writing shortly before 377), there was in Tiberias a temple of the deified emperor Hadrian, of all people, which some scholars have supposed is the same as the tetrastyle temple of Zeus depicted on a coin of Hadrianic date.[38] Though no structure definitely identified as a temple has yet been discovered at Sepphoris, some evidence for cultic activity has (see below). There may, in sum, be no reason *not* to think that the coins imply the existence of public pagan cults in the Jewish cities.

A common way of explaining the religious implications of the coinage of the Palestinian Jewish cities has been to suppose that Hadrian removed the city councils from Jewish control and entrusted them to Greeks, either in reaction to or in anticipation of the second Jewish revolt.[39] This is unlikely for a number of reasons. Why, for instance, does rabbinic literature record not a single complaint about the pagan oppressors who ruled the rabbis' towns even though, if the common view is right, the pagan town councillors were more religiously heavy-handed than the Herodian princes and Roman procurators who had so catastrophically misruled the Jews in the first century? On the contrary, the rabbis may have felt little affection for their cities' *bouleutai*, but they seem to have regarded them, at least by the early third century (the date of the earliest rabbinic text), as Jews.[40] Furthermore, if the appearance of pagan

[38] For example, A. H. M. Jones, *Cities of the Eastern Roman Provinces*, 2d ed. (Oxford: Clarendon, 1971), p. 278; Meshorer, *City Coins*, pp. 34–35; 112–13. Goodman, *State and Society*, p. 46, minimizes the importance of the Hadrianeum and of the coins.

[39] This was suggested by Jones, *Cities of the Eastern Roman Provinces*, p. 278. Isaac and Roll, "Judaea in the Early Years of Hadrian's Reign," transformed Jones's suggestion into a narrative: Around the year 120, Hadrian reformed the province of Judaea in the aftermath of (conjectural) disturbances there connected with the Diaspora revolt of 115–117 by introducing a second legion (this is evidently correct) and taking the city councils of Tiberias, Sepphoris, and Neapolis out of Jewish and Samaritan hands. Isaac seems to have retracted this view; at any rate, there is no trace of it in *Limits of Empire*, pp. 347–61. Goodman, *State and Society*, pp. 128–29, specifically rejects it, with somewhat vague arguments. He helpfully observes, though, that there is no reason to think Jews had ever been barred from serving on city councils. Similarly equivocal is Lapin, *Early Rabbinic Civil Law*, pp. 10–12.

[40] E.g., the *bouleutai* (city councillors) of Sepphoris who paid court to the patriarch Judah I (Y. Horayot 3:9 48c = Y.Shabbat 12:3, 13c); indeed, there are many references in the Palestinian Talmud to Jewish city councilors in Sepphoris, collected by G. Stemberger, *Juden und Christen im Heiligen Land*, p. 36; a lead weight (undated) from Sepphoris inscribed with the name of the *agoranomos* Simon; the statement attributed to the third-century rabbi Yohanan, "If you are appointed to the *boule*, let the Jordan be your boundary" (i.e., run for it), obviously presupposing that rabbis are likely to be appointed (but this probably reflects conditions of a slightly later period than the one under discussion); the references to the *kenishta deboule* (*boule* - synagogue) at Tiberias, perhaps, however, named for its location: Y. Sheqalim 7:3, 3c; Y. Taanit 1:2, 64a. Note also *SEG* 38 (1988): 1647, a lead weight from Tiberias listing two *agoranomoi*, one of whose names is illegible; the other is called Iaesaias (or -os) son of Mathias. But the weight is dated to

images on the coins is taken as proof of the paganism of the city councils, how are we to understand the mixture of Jewish and pagan types on Tiberias's Trajanic coinage? Jones (*CERP* 278) responded to this question by dismissing the pagan types as "symbolical" rather than genuinely pagan (as later types were, in his view), but this seems incorrect. Tyche and Hygieia may have been personifications, but there is no denying their status and function as real goddesses. And, conversely, if *they* could be used metaphorically by Jews, why not Zeus and Athena? And why, finally, should the emperors have taken the initiative of punishing cities that had never misbehaved, not even, apparently, at the time of the Bar Kokhba revolt? It would not be implausible to suppose that Sepphoris's remarkable name change to Diocaesarea, reminiscent of its adoption of the name Eirenopolis (Peace City) in 66, as well as Tiberias's construction of a temple of Hadrian, originated in the 130s as the city councils' way of distancing themselves from their rebellious Judaean coreligionists, just as the leaders of Shechem during the Maccabean revolt are said to have rededicated its Israelite temple to Zeus Xenios (2 Maccabees 5:22–23)—though both developments may in fact be connected to Hadrian's visit to Provincia Judaea in 130.[41] But this does not explain Tiberias's use of pagan coin types earlier nor the continuity of the pagan types and pagan city names down into the third century, as well as other manifestations of public paganism, to be discussed below, even beyond.[42]

The case of Lydda is especially illuminating. The town may have been even more completely Jewish than Tiberias; at any rate, there is almost no evidence for the permanent presence of pagans.[43] Yet when the town supported Severus in his civil war with Niger, the emperor *rewarded* the Lyddans by recognizing their urban status, granting them the name Diospolis, and allowing them to mint coins of utterly pagan type. It is necessarily the case that the town leaders had requested the changes in status and name (the new name, as suggested

---

year 43 of Agrippa II (98–99?), before the city was under direct Roman rule. Note also a weight from "Roman period" Sepphoris naming as *agoranomoi* Simon son of Aianos (= Hiyya?) and Justus son of. . . . See R. M. Nagy et al., eds., *Sepphoris in Galilee: Crosscurrents of Culture* (Winona Lake, Ind.: Eisenbrauns, 1996), p. 201. Also, *CIJ* 2.985, a Tiberian sarcophagus decorated with Jewish symbols belonging to "Isidoros *bouleutes*." See also J. Schwartz, "Hayei Yom-Yom," p. 107, arguing from rabbinic sources. Finally, a presumably Jewish city councillor from Ono, in 291 (it is unclear whether Ono was a city or a village): CPJ 3, no. 473.

[41] As was almost certainly true of Sepphoris' name change; see above.

[42] For an argument with similar tendencies that is used to explain the outbreak of the Bar Kokhba revolt, see P. Schäfer, *Der Bar Kokhba-Aufstand*.

[43] See J. Schwartz, *Lod*, pp. 87–88, who interprets some rabbinic passages as evidence for pagans and even Jewish Christians in the town in the second century (their presence is perfectly plausible regardless of the validity of these interpretations), while rightly insisting on its essentially Jewish character. Certainly this is preferable to Jones (*CERP* 278) who, unaware of rabbinic literature, inferred from the city's coinage that it was entirely pagan. Interestingly, Jones's reviser for Palestine, M. Avi-Yonah, who certainly knew better, did not correct him.

above, perhaps a piece of flattery directed at the empress) and determined the character of the coinage.[44]

In sum, it would be mistaken to explain the coinage of Tiberias, Sepphoris, Lydda, and, for that matter, Neapolis (which may present a rather different set of problems) by positing an imperially ordained change in the composition of the city councils. We must rather suppose that the city councillors were always, like the cities themselves, mostly (not necessarily entirely) of Jewish background, but that at different times in the course of the later first and second centuries they came to adopt, at the very least, important elements of the common urban culture of the Roman east, suffused though this culture was with Greek, Roman, and Greco-Semitic religion. Some of the cities may initially have been inhibited from trying to develop a distinctively Jewish style of Roman municipal public expression by the Bar Kokhba revolt, which probably generated more hostility to Judaism than the first revolt had done. But self-defensiveness alone does not explain Tiberias's (or Neapolis's) Trajanic coinage, nor the city councils' embrace of Greco-Roman urbanism long after Bar Kokhba had been forgotten, nor Lydda's indisputably voluntary adoption of the pagan style at the very end of the second century.

SEPPHORITE ARCHAEOLOGY

The very pervasiveness of pagan images in Tiberias and Sepphoris in the second and third centuries (about Lydda less is known) makes it difficult to view the culture of these places as having been imposed by outsiders on an unwilling populace, though there *were*, needless to say, Jewish opponents—among them the rabbis—who will be discussed below. Indeed, to judge from their physical remains, Tiberias and Sepphoris were normal Greco-Roman cities, with the full range of institutions and public buildings and spaces.[45] If we could be as confident about the relationship between coin types and cult as scholars usually are, then we could be quite certain that the cities' normalcy extended to their possession of pagan temples. There may, as already

---

[44] See J. Schwartz, *Lod*, p. 103, who is constrained to argue that though the emperor thought he was rewarding the Lyddans, he was mistaken, and to suppose that Severus initiated (or the change in the city's status generated?) an influx of pagans into the town, though even Severan *colonies*, which Lydda was not, did not receive colonists: see F. Millar, "The Roman *Coloniae* of the Near East: A Study in Cultural Relations," in H. Solin and M. Kajava, eds. *Roman Eastern Policy and Other Studies in Roman History: Proceedings of a Colloquium at Tvärminne, 2–3 October, 1987*, (Commentationes Humanarum Litterarum 91 (Helsinki, 1990), pp. 31–39.

[45] For Sepphoris, see S. Miller, *Studies in the History and Traditions of Sepphoris* (Leiden: Brill, 1984). Suffice it to say that Miller's city of rabbis and *kohanim* is invisible in the archaeology (though the alleged *miqva'ot* are suggestive), which is not to say that they did not exist, only that they did not predominate. See also Y. Ne'eman, "Sepphoris in the Second Temple, Mishnah, and Talmud Periods," (Ph.D diss., Hebrew University, 1993). The excavations at Tiberias are summarized in the *NEAEHL* (English edition), 1464–73 and updated in *HA* 104 (1995): 32–38 (mainly late antique).

suggested, be little reason to doubt the presence of temples in the cities despite their absence in the archaeological record. At Sepphoris, the excavations of the acropolis are incomplete, and anyway, the massive reconstruction of the city in the sixth century may well have obliterated any traces of a temple, perhaps replacing it with a church. Something like this happened at Tiberias, if we can believe Epiphanius. The church father claimed that there had been a great temple of deified Hadrian there, which the locals had attempted to turn into a bath but had never completed. This structure was subsequently (in the 320s or 330s; Epiphanius was writing at the end of the fourth century) turned into a church (Panarion 30.12). If this is so, it may imply that the christianization of the city was preceded by its judaization—hence the attempt to convert the temple into a bathhouse—a point to which I will return below.

The cities also had synagogues, mentioned frequently in rabbinic literature.[46] Tiberias had had a synagogue already in the first century (Life 277), though the structure may not have survived the destruction wrought by Vespasian in 67. In any case, possession of a synagogue was a common feature of high imperial Greek cities in general. The Palestinian Talmud claims there were eighteen synagogues in Sepphoris and thirteen in Tiberias, but there is no way to determine what period, if any, these claims may be true for; still less is it possible to guess what proportion of the population the synagogues could accommodate; in any case, they surely played a minimal role in the public life of the cities, at least before the later third century. The richly decorated synagogues discovered by archaeologists at Hamath Tiberias and Sepphoris were built in the fourth and fifth centuries respectively, not the second and third.[47]

There are in fact more archaeological traces of pagan than of Jewish worship for the earlier period; not unexpectedly, the information concerning Sepphoris is largely archaeological and that concerning Tiberias mainly comes from the Palestinian Talmud. Thus far, publications of the Sepphorite excavations have consisted mainly of tantalizing fragments; it goes without saying that comprehensive publication may produce a rather different image of the city. But in the meantime, here is what has been published:[48] a theater with

---

[46] For Sepphoris, see e.g., Y. Kilayim 9:4, 32b (eighteen synagogues in Sepphoris, as opposed to thirteen in Tiberias); Y. Shabbat 6, 8a; Y. Berakhot 3, 6a, and in general, for both places, and Lydda, too, Klein, Sefer Hayishuv, s.v. These passages may reflect conditions of the fourth century rather than the second and third.

[47] On the synagogue of Sepphoris, see Z. Weiss and E. Netzer, Promise and Redemption: The Synagogue Mosaic of Sepphoris (Jerusalem: Israel Museum, 1996); on Hamath Tiberias, M. Dothan, Hammath Tiberias: Early Synagogues and Hellenistic and Roman Remains (Jerusalem: Israel Exploration Society, 1983).

[48] Articles and annual reports since the later 1980s in IEJ, HA (= Excavations and Surveys in Israel), and so on, have concentrated on describing the structures and publicizing the spectacular mosaics. Most helpful for the small finds has been E. Meyers, E. Netzer, and C. Meyers, Sepphoris (Winona Lake, Ind.: Eisenbrauns, 1992); and R. Nagy et al., Sepphoris in Galilee; see also

a seating capacity of 4,000 to 5,000 was discovered earlier in the century and has recently been reexcavated; traces of frescoes are said to have been visible on the corridor walls, but their content is not reported.

Other structures of interest are the by now famous private house on the acropolis whose *triclinium* (dining room) floor is decorated with an exceptionally fine mosaic depicting scenes from Dionysiac mythology and cult. More recently, another domestic mosaic pavement has been discovered, depicting Orpheus in one panel and wrestlers, banqueters, and dice players in others.[49] Both of these are said to be of "Roman" date, and the excavators have dated the Dionysiac floor with implausible precision to the early third century— implausible because the dating is based on style, which is a very *imprecise* criterion for dating, even in places like North Africa, where the corpus of material is vast.[50] (Several other impressive mosaic pavements were found in Sepphoris, too, but these are late antique.) On the other hand, over twenty small bathtubs were discovered in a residential district of the city, which excavators have identified, with what justification is unclear, as *miqva'ot*.[51] If this is correct, then the population of Sepphoris in approximately the third century was either radically diverse, consisting of a mixture of paganizers and the purity-obsessed or mind-bogglingly eclectic in their Jewish observance.[52] While both options seem probable on other grounds, it is unclear why the bathtubs should not be considered simply bathtubs.

Among the few small finds of relevant date that have thus far been reported, though not yet fully published, are bronze figurines of Prometheus and Pan, several molded ceramic lamps with images on the *disci* of couples having sex, and, from the same area as the lamps, several ceramic incense shovels and a

---

NEAEHL (Eng.) 1324–28 for a helpful summary and bibliography, up to date as of 1991. I am painfully aware of the fact that not all Palestinian and Israeli excavations have been published adequately (or at all), that the storerooms of the Israel and Rockefeller Museums, as well as the archives of Israel's Department of Antiquities, are filled with items and notices of items with which I am unfamiliar. I am assuming and hoping, though, that this material will not alter the general picture substantially.

[49] See *HA* 106 (1996): 31–39, with photographs on inside cover.

[50] See K. Dunbabin, *The Mosaics of Roman North Africa: Studies in Iconography and Patronage* (Oxford: Clarendon, 1978), pp. 30–37.

[51] In a site on the Sepphorite acropolis examined by Rutgers, the *miqva'ot* fell into disuse in the course of the second century, at the same time that pig bones begin to appear among the osteological remains. Rutgers argues that this evidence for neglect of Jewish law does not imply that the high imperial residents of the site were not Jewish. See L. V. Rutgers, "Some Reflections on the Archaeological Finds from the Domestic Quarter on the Acropolis of Sepphoris," in H. Lapin, ed., *Religious and Ethnic Communities in Later Roman Palestine* (Bethesda: University Press of Maryland, 1998), pp. 179–95. For the argument that the *miqva'ot* are really bathtubs, see H. Eshel, "A Note on the 'Miqvaot' at Sepphoris," in D. Edwards and C. McCollough, eds., *Archaeology and the Galilee* (Atlanta: Scholars, 1997), pp. 131–34.

[52] For the suggestion that the *bouleutai* of Sepphoris were mainly of priestly origin, see R. Kimelman, "The Conflict between the Priestly Oligarchy and the Sages in the Talmudic Period (An Explication of PT Shabbat 12:3, 13c = Horayot 3:5, 48c)," *Zion* 48 (1983): 125–48.

small bronze altar.[53] These items were obviously used for domestic rather than civic cult or decoration; in the case of the shovels, it is unclear whether they were used at all.[54] On the other hand, not a single piece from the appropriate period with a Jewish symbol on it has been found; neither, however, has anything like the impressive public statuary found at Scythopolis and Caesarea.

TIBERIAS IN THE PALESTINIAN TALMUD

The situation for Tiberias is similar, though here even more so than in Sepphoris the great majority of the sparse archaeological remains is late antique. There is, however, a small corpus of epigraphical material of the second through early fourth centuries, in addition to the aforementioned rabbinic material. The Palestinian Talmud, which I will discuss first, is a product of the later fourth century, by which time much of the old pagan city had disappeared.[55] The Talmud itself preserves several stories about the alterations of the city, which give a good idea of the city's character before they were undertaken and are of great interest in their own right. An important collection of such stories is found in Y. Avodah Zarah 3:1, 42c, partly paralleled in B. Moed Qatan 25b. It is worth quoting *in extenso*.[56]

> When R. Nahum bar Simai died, they covered the *eikonia* with mats.[57] They said, "Just as he did not look upon them in life, so let him not look upon them in death.". . . And why was he called Nahum of the Holy of Holies? Because he never looked at the image on a coin in his life. . . .

[53] The altar is mentioned only in *NEAEHL* 1328. Weiss and Netzer, *Zippori*, p. 22, astonishingly regard the incense shovels as "Jewish" because they resemble incense shovels later depicted on synagogue mosaics! Incense was apparently burned in some late antique synagogues, but the two known censers are not shovels. The rabbis of course regarded incense burning as a type of sacrifice and so absolutely forbidden outside the Jerusalem Temple. On the incense shovels, see now Rutgers, "Incense Shovels at Sepphoris?" in E. Meyers, ed., *Galilee through the Centuries: Confluence of Cultures* (Winona Lake, Ind.: Eisenbrauns, 1999), pp. 177–98.

[54] In his article, Rutgers simply stated that there is no evidence they had been used (i.e., no clear indication of carbon deposits) but expressed more uncertainty on this point in private communication.

[55] For the date of the Palestinian Talmud, see Y. Sussmann, "Ve-shuv Li-yerushalmi Neziqin," in Y. Sussmann and D. Rosenthal, eds., *Mehqerei Talmud: Talmudic Studies* (Jerusalem: Magnes Press, 1990), 2: 55–133.

[56] The translation is mine; Neusner's is unreliable. In the source, the passage is fleshed out, as usual, with interjections, digressions, and glosses, but the basic structure of the prodigy collection is easily recoverable, especially when it is compared with the parallel in the Bavli.

[57] I leave *eikonia* untranslated; the Talmud clearly intends different things by the words *eikonion*, *tzalma*, *andarta*, and so on, but it is not clear what. Here the reference seems to be to statues or reliefs lining the street along which the funeral procession passed. For a full discussion of the sparse rabbinic material on Nahum, see Y. Florsheim, "R. Menahem (= Nahum) ben Simai," *Tarbiz* 45 (1976): 151–53. The Babylonian parallel here reads *ishte'u tzalmanaya vehavu lemahalatzaya* (the statues became smooth and were used as slabs for rolling machines), apparently having confused the "mats" (*mahatzalaya*) of the Palestinian tradition for "slabs."

When R. Aha died, the star (Venus) was visible at noon.

When R. Hanan died, the statues (*andartaya*) bent over.

When R. Yohanan died, the *eikonia* bent over—they said it was because no *eikonion* was as beautiful as he.

When R. Hanina of Berat (Bet?) Hauran died, the Sea of Tiberias split. . . .

When R. Hoshaya died, the *Kalon* of Tiberias fell.[58]

When R. Isaac b. Elyashib died, seventy lintels belonging to landlords in Galilee were uprooted—they said that they had stood by his merit.

When R. Samuel b. Rav Isaac died, the cedars of the Land of Israel were uprooted. . . .

When R. Yasa bar Halfuta died, the gutters of Laodicea ran with blood—they said it was because he had given his life for circumcision (?).

When R. Abbahu died, the columns of Caesarea wept. The Cutheans (Samaritans) said, "Rather, they were sweating. . . ."[59]

A member of the patriarchal household died and the burial cave collapsed and endangered lives.[60] R. Yosi came and eulogized him, "Happy the man who left the world in peace!". When R. Yosi died,[61] the Castellum of Tiberias fell and the Patriarch's men rejoiced. R. Ze'ira said to them, "The two events are dissimilar: there, lives were endangered, here not; there no idolatry was uprooted, here it was."

This remarkably complex collection of material deserves a fuller treatment than it will receive here. For the present purpose, one of the points of the passage is simply to demonstrate in a concise way that Tiberias was dominated by images and shrines of gods—the *eikonia* and *andartaya*, the *Kalon* and *Castellum*—which complicated things for the rabbis who lived and died there.[62] Apart from the first story, which concerns the great piety of Nahum of the Holy of Holies, the passage is a compilation of reports of prodigies. These reports presuppose, and in one case come close to stating explicitly, that the rabbis play an important role in maintaining the order of the cosmos.

---

[58] *Kalon* in Hebrew means "reproach," and it seems overwhelmingly likely that Jastrow (s.v.) was right in taking it as a cacophemistic reference to some public image of a god or a temple. Lieberman, "Emendations in Jerushalmy" *Tarbiz* 1, no. 2 (1931): 113–4, asserted that it was simply a loanword from Latin *columna*, and this assertion is taken up as fact in M. Sokoloff, *Dictionary of Jewish Palestinian Aramaic*, s.v.; but Jastrow's suggestion makes more sense in context. Neusner's translation, "palm," seems a guess or a mistake, since its etymological justification is unclear; G. Wewers, *Avoda Zara: Götzendienst* (Tübingen: Mohr, 1980), p. 91, suggests "pagan temple or whorehouse."

[59] See S. Lieberman, "The Martyrs of Caesarea," *Annuaire de l'Institut de Philologie et d'Histoire Orientales et Slaves* 7 (1939–1944): 400–401 for the emendation of *mry'yn* to *mdy'yn* (sweat).

[60] The meaning of the word translated "collapsed" (QLT) is uncertain, according to Sokoloff, but seems obvious enough from the context.

[61] *Editio princeps* reads "Yasa," but clearly "Yosi" is meant.

[62] For additional, scattered stories and laws to the same effect, much of it in Y. Avodah Zarah, see Klein, *Sefer Hayishuv*, s.v.

This may have had a polemical thrust, even beyond what some of the stories explicitly indicate. Perhaps this is especially true of the stories in which the death of a rabbi causes the collapse of an idol or pagan temple, since at the time the Talmudic passage was compiled Christians were taking most of the credit for the destruction of the public institutions of paganism in Palestine. Epiphanius claims that his hero, Joseph, turned the Tiberian Hadrianeum into a church after he had won a magical competition with the Jews. This suggestion may be partly confirmed by the fact that Eusebius also knew of the weeping columns of Caesarea but believed they were weeping for the unburied Christian victims of persecution.[63] Polemical or not, some of these rabbinic stories presuppose a conception of the universe as characterized by a precise, and hypostatized, moral economy. Whenever some good disappears from the world, a corresponding piece of evil must go, too, hence, the death of a rabbi is balanced by the collapse of an idol (by contrast, the death of one of the patriarch's men causes a near calamity!). This seems to foreshadow the much later notion that there are in each generation righteous men by whose merit God permits the world to exist.[64]

Not only do the stories, then, provide an *interpretatio rabbinica* of the prodigy, in which the death of the rabbi plays a role similar to (though inversive of) that of the mass catastrophe in pagan prodigy collections, but they may also have offered an aetiology, from the perspective of the fourth century, for the changes in the appearance, and so in the public life, of the city.[65] Another such story, reported elsewhere in Y Avodah Zarah (4:4, 43d), claims that Rabbi Yohanan, the leading rabbinic figure of Tiberias in the second half of the third century, had ordered one Bar Drusai, apparently supposed to be a pagan,[66] to remove the statues from the public bathhouse of Tiberias and destroy them.[67] The pagan destroyed all but one—which, the Talmud explains, was suspected of having been worshiped by a Jew (!). So, according to rabbinic law, destruction was not sufficient. The idol had to be discarded in a way that rendered it

[63] See K. Holum, "Identity and the Late Antique City: The Case of Caesarea," in *Religious and Ethnic Communities*, 157–60.

[64] See G. Scholem, "The Tradition of the Thirty-Six Hidden Just Men," in *The Messianic Idea in Judaism: And Other Essays in Jewish Spirituality* (New York; Schocken, 1971), pp. 251–56.

[65] On statues in pagan prodigies, see Ch. Clerc, *Les théories relatives au culte des images chez les auteurs grecs du IIme siècle après J.C.*, (Diss., Paris, 1915), pp. 45–49. In pagan prodigies, the suffering of the gods resonates with that of humans.

[66] Since the story, or the Talmud's editors, take it for granted that Bar Drusai is engaged in the act of "nullifying" the statues, that is, rendering them halakhically harmless by disfiguring them; this can be done only by pagans. On "nullification" of idols, see G. Blidstein, "Nullification of Idolatry," *PAAJR* 41–42 (1973–1974): 1–44. On Bar Drusai, see S. Friedman, "Recovering the Historical Ben D'rosai," *Sidra* 14 (1998): 77–92.

[67] Curiously, what seems to have been the central public bathhouse of the city, excavated in the 1950s, is said to have been built in the fourth century. Its floors were paved with mosaics depicting fish and animals; see *NEAEHLP*. 1466.

completely inaccessible. We may infer from the stories in our passage, though, that on the whole the depaganization of Tiberias (in the later third century?) was not the work of the rabbis. If the rabbis had brought about the transformation of the city by natural means, there would have been no need to claim that they had done so by supernatural ones.

TIBERIAN INSCRIPTIONS[68]

There is little in the inscriptions of the second and third centuries to warn us of the city's subsequent transformation. Most of the inscriptions in question are funerary, and as such require some introductory remarks. A noteworthy characteristic of these inscriptions is the absence of any discernible "Jewish" content: the deceased are not designated as *Ioudaioi*; no one thought to include in their epitaphs such biblically derived prayers as "may the memory of a righteous man (or woman) be a blessing," or "may his (or her) soul be bound in the bundle of life"; the epitaphs do not conclude with the Hebrew word *shalom*, nor do they mark the Jewishness of the deceased with such symbols as the menorah, shofar, palm branch, or rosette. All of these practices became common in Jewish epitaphs beginning in the fourth century, but Jews seem rarely to have felt constrained to mark themselves as such on their funerary inscriptions previously.

Why? Burial practice (unlike mourning ritual) was a surprisingly marginal issue in Jewish law in antiquity. The Bible offers no guidance, except by implication, and far-reaching changes are known to have occurred in Jewish burial practice in the second and first centuries B.C.E: burial in *kokhim* (long, narrow shelves dug perpendicular to the wall of the cave) was introduced, as well as the practice of ossilegium (collection and reburial of bones), which left no trace in the abundant religious polemical literature of the period.[69] The rabbis took for granted a corpus of established burial practice—which had again

---

[68] The main collections are M. Schwabe, "Letoldot Teveryah: Mehqar Epigrafi"; and L. di Segni, "Ketovot Teveryah," in Y. Hirschfeld, ed., *Teveryah*. Schwabe's restorations (not always followed by di Segni) of some of the most fragmentary texts are speculative.

[69] See R. Hachlili, "Changes in Burial Practice in the Late Second Temple Period: The Evidence from Jericho," in Y. Singer, ed., *Graves and Burial Practices in Israel in the Ancient Period* (Jerusalem: Yad Ben Zvi/IES, 1994), pp. 173–89. This failure of shifts in burial practice to be meaningfully relatable to other ideological shifts is paralleled by the Roman change from cremation to inhumation in the second century C.E. See A. D. Nock, "Cremation and Burial in the Roman Empire," in Z. Stewart, ed., *Essays on Religion and the Ancient World* (Oxford: Clarendon, 1972), 1: 277–307, arguing that the shift was not very meaningful, largely a matter of "fashion," and certainly not associated with any change in views about the afterlife; for a similar argument about the Jewish evidence, see, in the same volume as Hachlili, N. Rubin, "Secondary Burials in the Mishnaic and Talmudic Periods: A Proposed Model of the Relationship of Social Structure to Burial Practice," pp. 248–69; in general, Rubin, *The End of Life: Rites of Burial and Mourning in the Talmud and Midrash* (Tel Aviv: Hakibbutz Hame'uhad, 1997).

changed drastically in that ossilegium had mostly disappeared—but never bothered to legislate about it or denounce practices they considered objectionable.[70] Ancient Jewish burial practice had little or nothing to distinguish it from that prevalent in the eastern Mediterranean in general. While burial was no doubt deeply significant to its practicioners and probably heavily ritualized, little or nothing about it was marked as Jewish. It was only in the seventh or eighth century, when the treatise Evel Rabbati (also called Semahot) was compiled that burial formally entered the province of halakhah.[71] Burial was thus another common activity, like urban politics, that was judaized gradually, partially, and late. Standard practice was transformed into rabbinic prescription and provided with interpretation, ad hoc and unsystematic though it may have been, in light of "normative" Jewish religious beliefs. For the present purposes this late development is important because it implies that we will have difficulty determining what, if anything, a "proper" Jewish burial of the second and third centuries should look like; it also means we should not expect Jews to have provided graphic indication of their Jewishness in their burials.[72] (The earliest signs of change appear at Beth Shearim, discussed

[70] Except for the importation of the bones of diasporic Jews for secondary burial in Palestine, see Y. Ketubot 12:3, 35b. with discussion of I. Gafni, *Land, Center, and Diaspora: Jewish Constructs in Late Antiquity* (Sheffield, U.K.: Sheffield Academic Press, 1997), pp. 79–95. For archaeological surveys of burial in Palestine, see H.-P. Kuhnen, *Palästina in griechisch-römischer Zeit*, Handbuch der Archäologie, Vorderasien 2, vol. 2 (Munich: Beck, 1990), pp. 253–82; Y. Tsafrir, *The Land of Israel from the Destruction of the Second Temple to the Muslim Conquest* (Jerusalem: Yad Ben-Zvi, 1984), 2: 143–64.

[71] The common opinion dates Evel Rabbati to "post-Talmudic" times, but some consider it a genuinely Tannaitic work of the third century; see D. Zlotnick, *The Tractate Mourning*, Yale Judaica Series 17 (New Haven: Yale University Press, 1966), pp. 4–9; Lauterbach, "Semahot."

[72] Some characteristic burials of the second and third centuries: the apparently Jewish mausoleum of the later third and early fourth centuries at Kefar Giladi, in the "finger of Galilee," fifteen kilometers north of Kadesh; see *NEAEHL*, s.v., where the only mark of Jewishness is that the earliest user of the mausoleum had his name, Hezekiah, inscribed on his sarcophagus in Jewish Aramaic script; the remaining users of the mausoleum may or may not have been Jewish. The lead sarcophagi found in the mausoleum are all decorated with mythological motifs. See also Z. Ilan and A. Izdarechet, "Arbel: An Ancient Town in the Eastern Lower Galilee," *Qadmoniot* 22 (1989): 111–17 for burial caves over whose entry is carved an eagle with spread wings; V. Tsaferis, "A Monumental Roman Tomb at Tel 'Eitun," *Atiqot*, Heb. ser., 8 (1982): 23–25 for a third-century burial cave whose arcosolia are decorated with paintings of *kline*-beds, and whose walls have graffiti of gladiators, horses and riders, and so on. A Greek inscription commemorates one Ioanes, evidently Jewish. N. Feig, "Burial Caves at Nazareth," *Atiqot* Heb. ser. 10 (1990): 67–79 for first-third centuries, standard grave gifts, no iconography at all, as also at Hanita, halfway between Akko and Tyre, regarded by rabbinic literature as a Jewish settlement: see D. Barag, "Hanita, Tomb XV: A Tomb of the Third and Early Fourth Century CE," *Atiqot*, Eng. ser., 13 (1978), entire volume. Note especially the gem engraved with Poseidon's head (p. 43) and Barag's unexplained judgment that the grave was not "Jewish" (p. 56). Finally, at Givat Seled, five kilometers north-northeast of Beth Guvrin, in an enduringly Jewish region of the country, a burial cave "Jewish" in structure (the burials in *arcosolia* and *kokhim*; but *kokhim* were in use in Idumaea long before the district was Jewish) but containing a Greek inscription whose only legible words

below. The failure of Jews to inscribe pious expressions and iconographic, linguistic, and other markers of Jewish group identity on their gravestones therefore may tell us nothing about the character of their adherence to the central ideology of Judaism.

The Tiberian inscriptions, though, are characterized not merely by a predictable lack of distinctive Jewish content. They are all in Greek, and some of them contain absolutely normal Greco-Roman religious and moralistic content.[73] In their implications they thus complement and extend what we learn from the coins, the small finds, and the rabbinic literature, adding some verisimilitude to what appears abstract in the archaeology and flatly stereotypical in the Talmud. Even some of the epitaphs that lack pagan religious content are of great interest as indications of what some Tiberians thought worth commemorating about themselves and their relatives. For example, a basalt slab, now lost, probably carved in the third century, to judge from the name of the deceased and the way it is abbreviated,[74] reads as follows:

> To Aur(elius) Marcellinus, (centurion) of the Tenth Le[g(ion)] Fret(ensis), who lived seventy-four years, five months, fifteen days. Aur(elia) Bassa, his spouse and heir, to her incomparable mate, in memoriam. (Schwabe, no. 17 = di Segni, no. 10)[75]

Legionary soldiers normally served for twenty-five years after joining the army in their late teens. This means that Marcellinus, who had been an officer in the southern Palestinian legion based near Aelia Capitolina (Jerusalem), had been retired for over thirty years at the time of his death. His military service had made him rich: in the earlier third century a legionary centurion was

---

are [*theois kat*]*achthoniois*—the customary dedication to the gods of the dead: A. Kloner, "A Burial Cave from the Early Roman Period at Givat Seled in the Judaean Shephelah," *Atiqot* 20 (1991): 159–63; L. di Segni, "A Fragmentary Greek Inscription from the Givat Seled Burial Cave," ibid., 164–65, regarded the inscription as proof that the cave was pagan. For some additional examples that conform to the patterns described here, see '*Atiqot* 33 (1997), entitled *Burial Caves of the Roman and Byzantine Periods in Western Galilee*. On late antique Jewish burials in the Diaspora, see below; and L. Rutgers, *The Hidden Heritage of Diaspora Judaism* (Leuven: Peeters, 1998), pp. 83–91.

[73] The two Latin epitaphs commemorate troops who were probably garrisoned in or near the city. One of these is the only Tiberian epitaph headed with the formula D(is) M(anibus) (To the gods of the dead), but see previous note for the use of its Greek equivalent in a Jewish (?) burial cave.

[74] AVR suggests a date after 212, when the *nomen* Aurelius, assumed by the vast number of new Roman citizens, became so common that it was often abbreviated: see A. E. Gordon, *Illustrated Introduction to Latin Epigraphy* (Berkeley: University of California, 1983), p. 145 (earliest attestation of the abbreviation in 158 C.E.), 174 (vastly more common later).

[75] I follow Di Segni, who prefers the reading of *IGRRP* 3.1206, to the slightly different one of Schwabe. In the latter's reading, Marcellinus was not a soldier; but the Greek letters FRE seem to have been unambiguously present in the second line of the inscription and seem best understood as part of the legionary name. Schwabe ignores them.

paid 54,000 sesterces (13,500 denarii) per annum, a vast fortune worth some *forty* times minimum subsistence wages for a family of four; such a salary could constitute a firm basis for the attainment of equestrian rank.[76] Clearly Marcellinus's widow believed that it had also added the lustre of prestige to his life and was his most memorable accomplishment.[77] What is significant about this inscription is the banality of this sentiment in the context of the high imperial Roman east, where in smaller cities like Tiberias retired centurions and their ilk often passed for high society, and its unexpectedness in a "Jewish" context.[78]

Of equal interest is Schwabe no. 10 = di Segni no. 8, a marble plaque now lost:

> In gratitude to our deceased master Siricius, we, your home-born slaves (*threptoi* = *vernaculi*) have built this (monument).

Schwabe plausibly suggested that the slaves had been manumitted in Siricius's will and also proposed that this Siricius is somehow connected with a landmark near the entrance to Tiberias mentioned in the Palestinian Talmud (Erubin 5:1, 22b), the *nafsha disiriqin*. In fact, Schwabe thought that the building in question was the tomb of the Siricius mentioned in the inscription, but the Talmudic phrase should mean "mausoleum of the Siricii," in the plural. Once again, acknowledgments of a well-to-do former master's generosity by manumitted slaves can be found everywhere in the Roman Empire.

Rather less banal than these two is Schwabe 14 = di Segni 27, inscribed on a sarcophagus found outside the south gate of the city. This is the epitaph of a retired low-ranking officer who probably served in an auxiliary, rather than legionary, unit. Though his pay was lower (even much lower) than that of his probable near contemporary Aurelius Marcellinus, at between 18,000 and 42,000 sesterces a year, depending on the precise nature of the unit in which he had served, it still helps explain the uninhibited materialism of his epitaph, and probably placed him firmly in the ranks of the well-to-do citizens:

> Here I lie, Amandus, who has partaken of every luxury, who has lived, godlike [*isotheôs*], a great number of years, honorably having the rank of decurion of the army, having virtue [*aretê*] which lives even after death. Who has enjoyed as many luxuries among men as I? Who is so beloved of his native city [*patrê*]? I, who am always well-known among many men, whom the native city longs for, [T]i[berias?], that is, which bore me.[79]

---

[76] See M. Alexander Speidel, "Roman Army Pay Scales," *JRS* 82 (1992): 87–106.

[77] Cf. the fragmentary ivory carving of a Roman legionary troop found at Sepphoris: R. Rosenthal, "Late Roman and Byzantine Bone Carvings from Palestine," *IEJ* 26 (1976): 96–103.

[78] On the high status of legionary veterans in their hometowns, see P. Garnsey, *Social Status and Legal Privilege in the Roman Empire* (Oxford: Clarendon, 1970), pp. 245–51.

[79] See Speidel, "Roman Army Pay Scales." Some of my comments on this inscription are indebted to a conversation with Simon Goldhill.

Unlike the previous examples, this inscription has ambitions. Its second half is written in an approximation of the Homeric dialect of Greek, which was commonly used in funerary epigrams. However, even a quick glance through W. Peek, *Griechische Vers-Inschriften*,[80] demonstrates the clumsiness of this example. Nevertheless, the epigram does feature some of the conventional themes of the genre—the love of the native city for the deceased, for example. A striking feature is the repeated emphasis on luxury, *tryphê*. In pagan literary works this word has the unambiguously negative connotations of softness, effeminacy, feebleness, and so on (see LSJ sub v.).[81] Addiction to *tryphê* was thought servile. Yet in this text, written up, at any rate, by someone who had read a bit, participation in *tryphê* is presented as a praiseworthy accomplishment. It would be a mistake to attribute this sentiment to the eccentricity and ignorance of an ex-soldier in a remote provincial town, or to the ineptitude of the "epigrammatist" hired to compose the text. For notwithstanding the invariably pejorative sense *tryphê* possesses in classical texts, in funerary epigrams, including some of considerable elegance clearly composed by and for the highly literate, *tryphê* is commonly a neutral value and occasionally an admirable one. Common in epigrams is the "eat, drink, and be merry, for tomorrow you die" theme,[82] for example, in this Greek epigram from the city of Rome: "Life is good but short; light is sweet but it fails. Enjoy your luxuries [*tryphêson*] while you can, for here eternal night awaits you." In such texts, *tryphê* is morally neutral, even, implicitly, somewhat inferior to moderation; after all, the poems imply, if not for the insouciance produced by the inevitability of death, you might have been inclined to avoid luxury! But in other texts, *tryphê* is, as in our Tiberian text, a virtue, possession of which is a source of pride.[83] This epitaph, from Phrygian Apamea, in the third century C.E., is especially illuminating:

> He who lives life, lives for his friends even after his death; he who has acquired much but does not enjoy his luxuries [*tryphôn*] with his friends, such a one has died while still walking the earth and lives in the manner of corpses. But I, Menogenes, have lived luxuriously [*etryphêsa*]. . . . (Peek 1113a)

This epigram can be read as a coherent and articulate rendition of what is inchoate in the Tiberian text. If we read the Tiberian text in light of the Phrygian, it too can be seen to describe a nexus of surplus, conceived as excess, social reciprocity, and immortality. Amandus's *arete* survives his death (proba-

---

[80] Berlin: Akademie-Verlag, 1955.

[81] In Christian texts, though, the word frequently has a positive connotation, for example, it is regularly used of man's state before the Fall (see Lampe, *Patristic Greek Lexicon*, s.v.). The Christian usage is conceivably revelatory of the word's meaning in a nonliterary semantic register.

[82] E.g., J. Robert and L. Robert, *BullEp*, 1960, no. 445; L. Robert, *Hellenica* 13 (1965): 184–92; B. Lifshitz, "Notes d'épigraphie palestinienne," *RB* 73 (1966): 248–57.

[83] Peek 263 (from Dorylaeum, Phrygia, second century C.E.); Peek 1113a.

bly also an allusion to his military prowess) and Menogenes, having "lived life," still lives for his friends. But our text goes further still in attributing to Amandus a characteristic I could not find paralleled in other epigrams: Amandus's life was equivalent to a god's.[84]

Perhaps this is an idiosyncratic expression of a religious value not foreign to ancient moralists, Greek, Roman, or Jewish—a theodicy of good fortune (in Max Weber's formulation), the conviction that the fortunate ipso facto enjoy divine favor. Perhaps Amandus thought that it was precisely his enjoyment of luxury that had made his life *isotheos* (equivalent to a god's), just as his military valor had given him immortal *aretê*. Surely the display and celebration of wealth, the sharing of it with friends, clients, and the city, and the attribution to it of religious significance were essential parts of the ideological fabric of the Greco-Roman city. And it is in such a cultural nexus that the sentiments, both commonplace and unusual, that Amandus had carved on his sarcophagus belong, even more firmly and unmistakably than the epitaphs of Siricius and Marcellinus.

The content of Amandus's epitaph makes it unsurprising to find the statue of a goddess dedicated as a gift by a Tiberian called either Ismenos son of Ioenos, or Ismaelos son of Ioanes, to the Tiberian *statio* (trade office) in the Roman forum, probably in the middle or later second century.[85] Yet, a century or two later, Tiberians resident at Rome were identifying themselves as "Hebrews" and burying their relatives in the Jewish catacombs.[86]

The Villages of Galilee

Most excavated remains from outside the Palestinian cities from the second to the fourth centuries are of burials, for reasons that may have something to do with an enduring bias of Israeli archaeologists for the monumental or, alternatively, with the character of ancient village life. There are, however, important exceptions from Lower Galilean villages like er-Rama, with its big bathhouse; Capernaum, containing a variety of structures of uncertain and/

---

[84] The word *isotheos* appears not infrequently in imperial Greek inscriptions commemorating city councils' resolutions to offer emperors *isotheoi timai* "divine honors" (i.e., a sacrificial cult). See Veyne, *Bread and Circuses*, p. 308 n. 43.

[85] Schwabe 16 = di Segni 19. The stone is lost and Schwabe observed that the names as transmitted are unparalleled (though Ioenos could conceivably represent the Latin Iovinus, if the *eta* was already pronounced î) and suggested that they were mistranscribed and should be read as the common Jewish names Ismael and Ioan(n)es.

[86] *CIJ* 1.502 = Noy, *Jewish Inscriptions*, 2.561; cf. *CIL* 3 suppl. 1, 10055, from Salona, Dalmatia (in Latin, in Greek letters): *Aurelius Dionysius Iudeus Tiberiensis An XXXX, filiorum trium pater.* For the dating of the Roman Jewish inscriptions, see Rutgers, *Hidden Heritage of Diaspora Judaism*, pp. 45–71.

or controversial dating and function and Beth Shearim, with its basilica.[87] These finds confirm the impression created by rabbinic literature that the big villages of Lower Galilee were in close contact with the cities. They also conform with what Fergus Millar observed about high imperial Syria generally—the tendency of large villages to adopt the institutions and cultural norms of the cities.[88] Presumably the chief mechanism of the transformation was the ambition of the most prosperous village landowners to secure for their villages some urban prestige and even, in some cases, city status.

The most extensive nonurban remains from our period come from its very end, from the middle of the third to the middle of the fourth centuries—the period of transition from high to late empire or perhaps even a bit later.[89] These are from the big Lower Galilean village of Beth Shearim, where the most prominent feature is the vast necropolis. Although most burials in high imperial Palestine were, like those of the later Second Temple period, made in single underground chambers or very small cave complexes, twenty cave complexes were found at Beth Shearim, some of them containing hundreds of burials. From the inscriptions we know that the primary catchment of the necropolis was not only local but regional, and it included some Diaspora communities as well.[90] Also atypical of high imperial Palestinian burials is that at Beth Shearim Jewish symbols are carved and scratched almost everywhere. It seems obvious that the burial caves of Beth Shearim were used mainly by especially Torah-oriented Jews, who even in the third century remained close to the traditional symbolic center of Judaism. Indeed, if it is the case that even strongly "Jewish" Jews were often buried without the accompaniment of Jewish iconography—that despite what we are accustomed to think about such liminal moments as birth, death, marriage, and so on, death was not yet generally an occasion among Palestinian Jews for strong public affirmation of group identity—then Beth Shearim shows that the judaization of Jewish

---

[87] For er-Rama, see V. Tsaferis, "A Roman Bath at Rama," *Atiqot*, Eng. ser., 14 (1980): 66–75; for Capernaum, see *NEAEHL*, s.v.; for Beth Shearim, see below.

[88] See Millar, *Roman Near East*, pp. 17–24; cf. Goodman, *State and Society*, pp. 27–28. For other Palestinian examples, note Roth-Gerson, *Greek Inscriptions*, no. 30; L. Y. Rahmani, "A Bilingual Ossuary Inscription from Khirbet Zif," *IEJ* 22 (1972): 113–16; pace Rahmani, there is no particular reason to think the deceased had any connection with Eleutheropolis-Beth Guvrin; more likely he was head of a village council with pretensions.

[89] Z. Weiss, "Social Aspects of Burial in Beth Shearim," in Levine, *Galilee*, pp. 357–71, especially 370–1, suggests that the necropolis remained in use "well into the fifth century," though presumably he accepts the standard view that most (?) of the burials are earlier. See note 93 below for an inscription likely to have been carved in the later period.

[90] Beth Shearim is usually described as an "international" or a "central" necropolis, but this is not borne out by the inscriptions. See T. Rajak, "The Rabbinic Dead and the Diaspora Dead at Beth Shearim," in P. Schäfer, ed., *The Talmud Yerushalmi and Graeco-Roman Culture* (Tübingen: Mohr, 1998), pp. 356–61.

burial practice was now (third-fourth century) under way in some circles.[91] In the very same period the Jews of Rome also began to use large-scale communal burial places and mark their epitaphs with Jewish symbols.

Nevertheless, the circles engaged in the judaization of burial practice in the third century are likely to have still been a small minority of Palestinian Jews. Their atypicality is confirmed by the interment in Beth Shearim of many "rabbis" (whether or not they are "our" rabbis,)[92] of possible members of the patriarchal family, and of the bones of small numbers of Diaspora Jews, among whom the practice of sending bones to Palestine for secondary burial must have been restricted to the most Jewishly pious (and wealthy), despite rabbinic ambivalence regarding the practice.[93] On the other hand, the general absence of pagan iconography in the wall carvings and graffiti, and its predominance on the sarcophagi of catacombs 11 and 20 (discussed in more detail presently) hints at a certain tension between different groups of customers of the necropolis, or between the management (if there was one),[94] responsible for digging out and decorating the chambers, and some of the purchasers. Interestingly, it is in catacomb 20 that the aforementioned "rabbis" were buried, though we do not know if it was they who used the sarcophagi.

Thus, even Beth Shearim, strongly Jewish as it is, is filled with pagan iconography, most of it introduced into the catacombs in the form of decorated sarcophagi but not built in. Of the decorations actually carved and scratched on the walls, lintels, and so on, most common are the menorah and the highly traditional but utterly inscrutable rosette, ubiquitous in the Jewish iconography of the later Second Temple period.[95] Also common are graffiti of arched structures, sometimes flanked by lions, with a door, a menorah, or nothing at all within the arch. A complete glass plate decorated with a similar design, perhaps made for funerary use like the decorated gold glasses in the Jewish and

---

[91] Note also the construction outside several of the catacombs of areas of assembly, closely resembling the later apsidal synagogues in design, presumably for some sort of ritual gathering.

[92] On which, see S. Cohen, "Epigraphical Rabbis," *JQR* 72 (1981–1982): 1–17. That the "rabbis" preferred Hebrew for their epitaphs probably indicates that they felt themselves somehow connected to the Torah; see S. Schwartz, "Language, Power, and Identity in Ancient Palestine," *Past and Present* 148 (1995): 3–47.

[93] Y. Ketubot 12:3, 35b; most of the few burials identified in the inscriptions as those of foreign Jews also identify the deceased as communal officials: *Beth Shearim* 2.141 (Aidesios, gerousiarch of Antioch); 164 (Eusebios, *vir clarissimus* [!], archisynagogue of Berytos—clearly an inscription of the mid-fourth century at earliest, if *lamprotatos* has its customary meaning); 203 (Iako, archisynagogue of Caesarea in Pamphylia [?], or Iako of Caesarea Maritima, archisynagogue, [originally] from Pamphylia); 221 (Iose, archisynagogue of Sidon).

[94] For a not very conclusive discussion, see Z. Weiss, "Social Aspects of Burial in Beth Shearim," pp. 362–66.

[95] On rosettes, see R. Hachlili, *Ancient Jewish Art*, p. 80. *Menorot* were uncommon in the Second Temple period, but even so, there are several examples from funerary contexts; see Hachlili, *Ancient Jewish Art*, pp. 81–82.

Christian catacombs at Rome, was also found in the necropolis. The archway design, too, is inscrutable (it could be an image of a Torah shrine, the ark of the covenant, the arched portals typical of the necropolis, the gateway to eternal life, the gateway to the holy of holies, etc.) but apparently "Jewish."[96] In several of the catacombs (as also in Jason's tomb in Jerusalem, first century B.C.E.; Marisa, third-second centuries B.C.E.) are graffiti of boats. Is this Charon's ferry? Many Jews were buried, like Greeks, with Charon's fare in their mouths.[97] But some of the graffiti seem to be of galleys rather than ferries. Do they, then, imply a conception of the grave as a passageway, without specific reference to Greek mythology? Or do they, as some have suggested, commemorate the mercantile activities of the deceased? If so, why are no other occupations similarly commemorated? Finally, throughout the necropolis there are many crude human figures, most of them little more than stick figures, carved or scratched on the walls, among them several horses and riders in catacomb 1 and an apparent gladiator in catacomb 4. The oddest of these human figures is in catacomb 3, a relief of a man (?) with a menorah on his head. Since most of these items I find completely opaque, apart from the fact that the graffiti (as opposed to the reliefs) are undatable and some could be medieval, I will say no more about them. I have briefly described some of them precisely to convey something of the impenetrability of much of the most "Jewish" of the iconographic language of even this most "Jewish" of high imperial burial sites.

Surely the most poignant of the structural items at Beth Shearim is the lintel over the entrance to the western hall of catacomb 19.[98] Several lintels at Beth Shearim are decorated with rosettes and the like, but this one is unique in being decorated with a relief of something like a Gorgon or Medusa mask (as indicated by the prominence of the ringletted hair), resembling the Gorgon, Dionysiac, tragic and Satyr masks common on Roman sarcophagi (including one from Beth Shearim) and found carved on the door of a contemporaneous burial chamber in Jaffa.[99] To the right of the mask is scratched the

---

[96] Though obviously in some cases this is the counterpart of the common pagan image of the deity visible inside his or her schematically represented shrine. For an extensive treatment, see B. Goldman, *The Sacred Portal: A Primary Symbol in Ancient Judaic Art* (Detroit: Wayne State University Press, 1966).

[97] See Z. Greenhut, "The 'Caiaphas' Tomb in North Talpiyot, Jerusalem," *Atiqot* 21 (1992): 70–71; and see W. Horbury's discussion of the practice: "The 'Caiaphas' Ossuaries and Joseph Caiaphas," *PEQ* 126 (1994): 34–35. However, L. Y. Rahmani argued that most coins found in Jewish burials cannot be proved to have been meant as Charon's fare: "A Note on Charon's Obol," *Atiqot* 22 (1993): 149–50.

[98] *Beth Shearim* 3.81–82.

[99] For masks on sarcophagi, see Guntram Koch and Hellmut Sichtermann, *Römische Sarkophage* (Munich: Beck, 1982). For the tomb door, see *NEAEHL*, s.v., photograph. See also the discussion in L.Y. Rahmani, "Five Lead Coffins from Israel," *IEJ* 42 (1992): 82. The closest parallels to the relief from Beth Shearim are tomb decorations at Petra and Medain Saleh from a slightly earlier period: see J. S. McKenzie, A. T. Reyes, and A. Schmidt-Colinet, "Faces in the Rock at Petra and Medain Saleh," *PEQ* 130 (1998): 35–50; with an appendix by J. R. Green.

name of the owner of the hall, Socrates, and to the left, a crude graffito of a menorah. Avigad was evidently right to claim that the menorah was not made by the same hand as the mask, carved in high relief by the stonemason. He may also have been right to think that whoever carved the menorah thought the doorway looked insufficiently "Jewish," but there is no way of knowing whether this was Socrates himself, a relative of his, an official of the necropolis, or a passerby. What is significant is the initial decision to mark the chamber at its most conspicuous point with a Dionysiac mask (vel sim.), and the failure of the menorah carver to efface it.

Some of those buried at Beth Shearim used mythological sarcophagi with no detectable trace of hesitation. Some of these are of exceptionally crude workmanship, almost certainly made at Beth Shearim itself of the local *nari* (a type of chalk), decorated with carvings whose closest stylistic analogues are the reliefs on the walls of the catacombs. Some of the crudest are simple imitations of the most popular types of Roman sarcophagi, decorated, for example, with a bucranium-and-acanthus design, with eagles, shells, or simplified hunt scenes—surely all pagan in origin but not necessarily in function.[100] But two of these simple sarcophagi have unmistakably pagan images—on one, another Dionysiac mask and on another, two fully clothed and winged *Nikai* holding aloft a wreath. The use of such motifs on crude products made locally for a local market plainly demonstrates the popularity of the motifs themselves and shows that the implications of the many fragments of relatively high quality, probably imported, marble sarcophagi, found in the same catacomb and featuring a wide range of pagan themes cannot be dismissed.[101]

In a separate burial outside catacomb 11, grandly built with a facade decorated with friezes of animals,[102] the excavators found not only a fragmentary marble sarcophagus featuring reliefs of Leda and the Swan on the short side and perhaps of Achilles on Skyros on the long side,[103] but also, on a marble plaque, a Greek epigram commemorating the youth, a native of Beth Shearim, who had probably been buried in the sarcophagus. Here is the epigram.

---

[100] On the stone sarcophagi of catacomb 20, see *Beth Shearim* 3.136–64; only two of these sarcophagi have Jewish designs—a "hunt" sarcophagus that also features a rosette and another decorated with a menorah. Avigad predictably plays down the importance of the mythological themes on some of these sarcophagi.

[101] See *Beth Shearim* 3.164–73. The Leda sarcophagus from the mausoleum adjacent to catacomb 11 was found by isotopic analysis to have been made of Pentelic marble, which is consistent with the fact that it, like the marble fragments from catacomb 20, is of roughly "Attic" type; presumably, then, they are all Greek imports, like the very similar sarcophagi from Caesarea; see R. Gersht and Z. Pearl, "Decoration and Marble Sources of Sarcophagi from Caesarea," in R. L. Vann, ed., *Caesarea Papers* (JRA suppl. 5 (1992): 223–43; 234 for the Leda sarcophagus of Beth Shearim; and M. Fischer, *Marble Studies: Roman Palestine and the Marble Trade*, Xenia vol. 40 (Konstanz: Universitätsverlag Konstanz, 1998), pp. 206–7, 238–39.

[102] See reconstruction in *NEAEHL*, s.v. "Beth Shearim."

[103] Published by Avi-Yonah, *Art in Ancient Palestine*, pp. 257–69.

I Justus, Leontes' son, lie dead, son of Sappho,
I who have plucked the fruit of all wisdom
have left the light, my poor parents eternally mourning,
and my brothers, alas, in . . . Besara (= Beth Shearim).
And I, Justus, have gone to Hades . . . lie here,
with many of my people [?], for so mighty Fate willed.
Courage, Justus, no one is immortal.

It would be an amusing and instructive irony if the *sophie* whose fruits Justus plucked turned out to be the biblical "tree of life," the Torah. Although there is no way of being certain, it is perhaps more likely that it was rhetoric or some other skill. The importance of this assemblage is that it indicates something of the tastes and interests of the large landowners of a big country town in Jewish Lower Galilee. Like the elites of Tiberias and Sepphoris who put images of gods on their cities' coins and decorated their houses with rich mythological mosaics, some of the rural elites, too—and it is worth remembering that Beth Shearim was a big town that probably aspired to municipal status, which it seems never to have received—participated hopefully in the common urban culture of the high imperial east. There is in Justus's tomb no indication of his Jewishness; he may have studied Greek rhetoric. He was almost certainly buried in a sarcophagus decorated with mythological scenes, and he was certainly commemorated in a (rather rough) epigram whose only religious content is its invocations of Hades and Moira. Yet Justus "lay with many of his [Jewish? Besaran?] people." The sarcophagi from Beth Shearim catacomb 20, and perhaps the lintel in catacomb 19, show that even Jews who utilized the symbolic language of Judaism in their burials—a language that around 300, the date of most of the burials, was just beginning to develop—still participated, or aspired to participate, in aspects of the common urban culture.

The Jews and Urban Culture: A Summary

In the second and third centuries, the "Jewish" cities of Palestine and the larger villages in their vicinity were normal participants in the urban culture of the Roman east, a culture that was suffused with pagan religiosity. This participation was not forced on the cities by the emperor but was in part the response of the city elites to conditions created by the end of Jewish autonomy and the imposition of direct Roman rule, among other factors. In other words, we should neither sentimentalize nor hasten to condemn (depending on our predispositions) the decision of the city elites, for the freedom with which it was made was variously constrained: surely the violence of the Roman state played a large, if indirect, role in the "normalization" of life in the Palestinian cities.

The normalcy of life in the Jewish cities and towns seems to have extended to religion, at least in part. The evidence for the existence of municipal cults is far from negligible, though it is impossible to tell how widespread participation was. The big temple of Hadrian and other Tiberian shrines *perhaps* ceased to be used by around 300; even if this is so, however, it does not tell us anything about the extent of the citizenry's enthusiasm in, say, 170. What we can be certain about is the importance of the gods in the way some section of the cities' population thought about their own place in the city, the empire, the cosmos. When a well-to-do Sepphorite wished to display—and the culture of the Greco-Roman city was overwhelmingly a culture of theatrical display— his wealth, education, good taste, his appreciation of visual wit, his celebration of the abundance his city provided, and of the state whose peace imposed worldwide had helped make his city rich, like a seventeenth-century Dutch burgher with his still lifes, he did so by having scenes from Dionysiac mythology depicted on the floor of his dining room, where his relatives, guests, and clients would be sure to see them. When the city elites collectively desired to celebrate some of the same qualities, they did so in a similar way, by having images of the gods struck on their cities' coins and by decorating their public buildings, marketplaces, and main streets with statues and reliefs of emperors and gods. And prosperous villagers behaved no differently when they had their relatives buried in mausolea richly decorated with mythological scenes and publicly justified their death, in dactylic hexameters, by invoking the inscrutable will of Moira, not that of Israel's True Judge. Thus, entirely conventional, perhaps somewhat allegorized, Greek mythology seems generally to have replaced, or at least supplemented, the Jewish mythology I discussed in chapter 2 as a way of accounting for the operation of the universe. Or perhaps what it replaced was the Deuteronomic or covenantal ideology, also a theology of prosperity and success.[104]

I am arguing here that pagan art used by Jews had a specifically pagan religious meaning, but not necessarily a simple one. Whether or not large numbers of Jews regularly worshiped the Greek gods, their ubiquity as symbols is profoundly important as an indication of the postrevolt collapse of any normatively Jewish ideological system. Even where traces of the old system are detectable, as at Beth Shearim, a site that is transitional between high and late empire and atypical in the concentration of especially Jewishly pious people buried there, these traces still coexist with standard urban paganism. Certainly there are no grounds for a judaizing interpretation of the urban material culture, of either the dismissive or the constructive variety. The former is excluded by the very oddity involved in imagining conventionally pious Jews blithely using pagan imagery as decoration, even if urban paganism *was*

---

[104] Contrast, though, Fox, *Pagans and Christians*, p. 38, who emphasizes the "anger" of the civic deities.

"running out of steam" and the imagery in any case sometimes had an allegorical character (Dionysus = Prosperity).[105] At the very least, the imagery acquires
its meaning as decoration only by its embeddedness in a pagan religious system. Even so, we should be careful not to assume that most Tiberian or Sepphorite town councillors were Lucian-like sophisticates. Their counterparts
elsewhere in the empire often attributed real religious (or "magical") meaning
to their domestic decoration, and Tertullian could take it for granted that his
Christian readers were aware that garlands hanging on doorways were offerings to gods like Janus.[106] Thus, the decorative use of Dionysiac imagery may
have been thought an aspect of real (pagan) piety. A constructive judaizing
interpretation, of the type associated with E. R. Goodenough, is excluded by
the fact that before 300 the images never appear in a context marked as Jewish,
and when they begin to do so, as at Beth Shearim, it seems more compelling
to view the two sets of cultural markers as being in tension.

Some might be tempted to posit a class distinction in religious practice, to
suppose that paganizing was limited to the well-to-do, who needed it as a way
to show off their wealth (post-Destruction Judaism having not yet developed
effective ways of doing so) and associate themselves with the rulers. Furthermore, in a religious system built around a "theodicy of good fortune," it stands
to reason that the less fortunate would have been ambivalent—an ambivalence that may in this case have tended to favor (partial) adherence to Judaism.[107] While there may be some truth to this, it is also reductive and misleading, and it fails to explain the evidence. First of all, show off their wealth
to whom? If they were to do so effectively, their (almost entirely Jewish) audience had to be receptive; in fact, by 200 or so, the cities and some of the larger
villages already contained specifically Jewish institutions, synagogues, that
could have served as objects of the elites' euergetistic impulses, but they seem
not to have done so in a way that left material traces. Second, the elites themselves were divided, if very unequally, since it is overwhelmingly likely that
most rabbis were from well-to-do backgrounds (perhaps usually subcurial?).
Finally, we need to understand the implications of the Sepphorite mosaics,
figurines of the gods (which someone had thrown down a well), and small

---

[105] On allegorizing interpretation of mythological imagery, see A. D. Nock, "Sarcophagi and
Symbolism," in *Essays*, 606–41; and in more detail, M. Koortbojian, *Myth, Meaning, and Memory, on Roman Sarcophagi* (Berkeley: University of California, 1995), pp. 3–8, passim.

[106] See Tertullian, *De Idololatria* 15.4–5 (= J. H. Waszink and J. C. M. van Winden, eds.,
Tertullian's De Idololatria: Critical Text, Translation and Commentary [Leiden: Brill, 1987], pp.
52–53, with comments ad loc.); K. Dunbabin, *The Mosaics of Roman North Africa* (Oxford:
Clarendon, 1978), pp. 137–87. For an interpretation of the decoration on a high imperial Syro-
Palestinian lead coffin as "apotropaic," see D. White, "The Eschatological Connection between
Lead and Ropes in a Roman Imperial Period Coffin in Philadelphia," *IEJ* 49 (1999): 66–91.

[107] Cf. Gordon, "Religion in the Roman Empire: The Civic Compromise and Its Limits," p.
238.

altar. These items remind us that a sharp distinction between public and private, self-evident to us and presupposed by the hypothesis that the paganizing of the wealthy had no significant resonances down the social scale, was not a normal feature of life in the Roman city, at least not for the better-off.[108] The contents of the privately owned house were scarcely less on display than the public buildings bordering the marketplace, and the fact that they were meant to impress the (ipso facto) poorer dependents of the city elites confirms that interest in and/or adherence to the values of Greco-Roman urban culture was not limited to the rich—a point perhaps further strengthened by the seating capacity of the Sepphorite theater and by the use of pagan imagery on the crude limestone sarcophagi produced at Beth Shearim in imitation of high-quality and expensive imports made of marble.[109] We would do well to remember that civic paganism incorporated magical and paradoxical elements that partly compensated for its status as a theodicy of good fortune,[110] just as Judaism, in its covenantal form no less a theodicy of good fortune, had done in the Second Temple period: both systems cut across class lines.

These cities were, finally, not simply Greek but Greco-Roman: unlike most classical Greek cities but like other Greco-Roman cities, the Palestinian cities were oligarchies characterized by euergetism rather than democracies in which expenditure was state controlled; rhetoric was used mainly for entertainment, not politics;[111] citizenship in the city apparently did not exclude possession by individuals or subgroups of other types of formally constituted ethnic identity. Furthermore, the cities' values (their ideology) were influenced in specific ways by Rome.[112] Some of the citizens were also Roman citizens even before the universal grant of citizenship by Caracalla in 212, many had Latin names whether or not they were Roman citizens, and legionary service was an effective way of acquiring not just wealth but prestige—not unsurprisingly in cities whose population probably consisted of descendants of refugees from the devastation the legions had wrought in Judaea.

---

[108] On the Roman house as public space, see A. Wallace-Hadrill, *Houses and Society at Pompeii and Herculaneum* (Princeton: Princeton University Press, 1994), esp. pp. 17–37.

[109] For a similar observation about the romanization of Gaul, see G. Woolf, *Becoming Roman: The Origins of Provincial Civilization in Gaul* (Cambridge: Cambridge University Press, 1998), p. 81.

[110] This point is brilliantly made by Gordon, "Religion in the Roman Empire."

[111] See E. L. Bowie, "The Importance of Sophists," *YCS* 27 (1982): 31–38 (art. 29–60), on the relative unimportance of sophists (which is not quite the same as rhetoric) in city politics including, rather surprisingly, embassies.

[112] Cf. Millar, *Roman Near East*, passim.

FIVE

THE RABBIS AND URBAN CULTURE

WE HAVE ALREADY SEEN that the rabbis shared a territory with Greco-Roman urbanity.[1] They, too, were concentrated and exercised what influence they had, primarily in the "Jewish" cities of Palestine and the larger villages of Lower Galilee, and secondarily in proximate cities like Joppa, Caesarea Maritima, Akko-Ptolemais, Tyre, Sidon, Beth-Shean-Scythopolis, Bostra, and Naveh, in Batanaea. They were scarcely to be found at all in unurbanized and relatively unhellenized Upper Galilee and Golan, at least in the second, third, and early fourth centuries.[2] The rabbis, whose conviction that they constituted the true leadership of the Jewish people made them not sectarian but expansionist, probably gravitated to cities because there they had access to networks of trade, money, communications, patronage, and political power.

But Greco-Roman urban culture and its rural offshoots, permeated as it was with pagan religiosity, constituted a serious problem for the rabbis. This point requires special emphasis because so much of the best scholarship in the years since the publication of Saul Lieberman's *Greek in Jewish Palestine* has argued for the normalcy of the rabbis in the context of the high imperial East.[3] What this scholarship has demonstrated is that the rabbis were influenced by their environment. How, indeed, could they not have been? And why should they have refrained from imitating attractive or effective features of philosophical or rhetorical schools, for example? And why should we marvel if individual rabbis—the most famous, perhaps the only available, example is R. Abbahu of Caesarea—were relatively well integrated in some respects

---

[1] Most of this chapter has appeared as two articles: "Gamaliel in Aphrodite's Bath: Palestinian Judaism and Urban Culture in the Third and Fourth Centuries," in P. Schäfer, ed., *The Talmud Yerushalmi and Graeco-Roman Culture* (Tübingen: Mohr, 1998), 203ff.; and in expanded and (I think) improved form as "The Rabbi in Aphrodite's Bath: Palestinian Society and Jewish Identity in the High Roman Empire," forthcoming in S. Goldhill, ed., *Being Greek under Rome: Cultural Identity, the Second Sophistic, and the Development of Empire* (Cambridge: Cambridge University Press, 2001).

[2] The *"bet midrash* of R. Eliezer Haqappar" in Dabbura, Golan, presumably dates from the fourth century or later, though R. Eliezer himself, if identical with the *tanna* R. *Elazar* Haqappar, lived in the second and early third centuries. See J. Naveh, *On Mosaic and Stone* (Jerusalem: Sifriyat Maariv, 1978), no. 6 (in Hebrew).

[3] S. Lieberman, *Greek in Jewish Palestine* (New York: Jewish Theological Seminary, 1942); *Hellenism in Jewish Palestine*. This is a different question from that of the cultural "hellenization" of the Jews.

into the life of their cities, given that the integrative pressures exerted on them, as would-be elites, were fairly strong?

But the rabbis were emphatically *not* normal elites or subelites of the eastern part of the Roman Empire. All the efforts of scholars over the last 150 years to detect significant similarities in social role and status between rabbis and sophists, philosophers, *iurisprudentes,* or other easily recognizable high imperial types have only highlighted the fact that the rabbis were *not* sophists, philosophers, or *iurisprudentes.* One reason these parallels (and one could easily think of others that have never been suggested: certain types of pagan priests and Roman senators, for example) have not proved convincing is that the rabbis combined elements of all of these functions in a way that no one else in the Greco-Roman world did, except, mutatis mutandis, Christian bishops. This, in turn, is because the rabbis were unique in deriving their self-understanding from the Torah, which in their view was the repository of everything worthwhile. Although in reality their wisdom may sometimes have had a Stoic or Cynical tinge, their legislation may have owed something to Roman civil law, and their miracles (or miracle stories) resembled those performed by (or told about) such figures as Apollonius of Tyana, as far as the rabbis themselves were concerned, the source of all wisdom, law, and numinosity was the Torah alone. In this way they closely resembled their predecessors in the Second Temple period and rabbinic colleagues in Mesopotamia, and they were at odds with their nonrabbinic contemporaries and counterparts in the Greco-Roman cities.

Correspondingly, the search for parallels in form and patterns of thought between rabbinic and contemporary pagan and even Christian literature has yielded mainly frustration. Perhaps most promising is the very recent work of Catherine Hezser, who has detected significant formal similarities between the Palestinian Talmud and the Digest. But of course these similarities are restricted to the Talmud's legal material, and they may tell us mostly about the working methods of the editors and such social questions as the extent of the institutionalization of the rabbinic class in the late fourth century; direct influence, in either direction, is obviously out of the question. Otherwise, the search has yielded little of interest to anyone but antiquarians, lexicographers, and experts in "realia."

The rabbis cannot readily be "normalized." It must finally be admitted that the culture of the Greco-Roman city and the Judaism of the rabbis contradicted each other both essentially and in superficial detail. As far as we can tell from the surviving literature, the rabbis, no less than their Christian counterparts, largely rejected high imperial urban culture and offered their followers a radical and coherent alternative to it.[4]

---

[4] Indeed, it can even be argued that some imperial Greek elites, in their devotion to religion and the Greek past, were carving out for themselves a space in which to resist the realities of the

Yet the rabbis did live in the cities and wished to win the support of their Jewish inhabitants, whose religious behavior and thought in many cases differed in no way from those of pagans. So the rabbis, who needed to take the Pentateuchal horror of paganism very seriously in formulating their own views, also needed to develop a mechanism to allow them to live in the cities and to participate in some the the the cities' public activities, pagan though they were.[5] This mechanism, I would like to argue, was an act of misprision, of misinterpretation, whereby the rabbis defined pagan religiosity as consisting exclusively of cultic activity, affirmed, and even extended the biblical prohibitions of it, but in so doing declared the noncultic, but still religious, aspects of urban culture acceptable.[6]

To the extent that words like "problem," "mechanism," and "misprision" imply intention, I use them as metaphors. I would not care to argue that *the* rabbis, still less that specific rabbis, were conscious of the systemic tensions between Judaism and the life of the city, though of course they knew that the city posed many specific halakhic problems. Nor would I want to suggest that the act of misprision, which constitutes the foundation of the laws of *avodah zarah* ("alien worship"), was *intended* as a way of coping with Greco-Roman culture, and was not, say, the result of conventionally rabbinic ways of thinking about halakhic issues in general.[7] In the final analysis, intentions may be what is least knowable about another, and when that "other" is in fact a *group* — consisting by definition of individuals whose motivations are complex and variable — that lived in the remote past and that we know about entirely from a small and opaque corpus of texts, any attempt to recover intentions would

---

empire, the difference being that Greeks such as Plutarch and Pausanias were at least ambivalently coopted by the Romans, while the rabbis and the Christians were not, before the fourth century; see J. Elsner, "Pausanias: A Greek Pilgrim in the Roman World," *Past and Present* 135 (1992): 3–29.

[5] See M. Halbertal, "Coexisting with the Enemy: Jews and Pagans in the Mishnah," in G. Stanton and G. Stroumsa, eds., *Tolerance and Intolerance in Early Judaism and Christianity* (Cambridge: Cambridge University Press, 1998), pp. 159–72. This is one of several surprising points of convergence between our work — surprising because of a drastic difference in approach.

[6] In other words, I reject the common emphasis on the rabbis as primarily pastoral figures, who, in one view, adopted a *stringent* approach to paganism in order to protect their spiritually vulnerable flock from the encroaching religious environment (so M. Hadas-Lebel, "Le paganisme à travers les sources rabbiniques," ANRW II 19.2 [Berlin: De Gruyter, 1979], p. 398), or in another, adopted a *lenient* position in order to allow the economically vulnerable Jews to subsist in an uncaring pagan world (so Urbach, "Rabbinical Laws of Idolatry"). Apart from the problematic understanding of the rabbis' role, these blanket characterizations clearly miss the point, as is well observed by C. E. Hayes, *Between the Babylonian and Palestinian Talmuds: Accounting for Halakhic Difference in Selected Sugyot from Tractate Avodah Zarah* (New York: Oxford University Press, 1997).

[7] For a very detailed argument that this is usually what is behind the rabbinic laws of idolatry, directed mainly against the naive historicism of E. E. Urbach, see C. E. Hayes, *Between the Babylonian and Palestinian Talmuds*.

be a priori futile, if not meaningless. What I argue, though, is that the rabbis' misprision, whether they knew it or not, allowed them to live and work in the cities, the very places where they could most easily accumulate wealth, social ties, and influence. Their presence in the cities, and their interest in establishing ties with the local population, may have been a factor in keeping alive a sense of separateness among some of the Jews in high imperial northern Palestine. Furthermore, the rabbis' institutional aspirations, which provided for the Jews a clear-cut, if not at first terribly attractive, alternative framework within which to live their lives and acquire influence, were an important way in which the Jewish cities differed from those of their neighbors.

The Rabbis on Idolatry[8]

The tractate concerned with *avodah zarah* never explicitly prohibits it or prescribes a punishment for its practice. The concerns of the Mishnaic tractate are in fact at several logical removes from the mere prohibition of idol worship. This is the topic of M. Sanhedrin 7:6—a mishnah worth quoting, since it constitutes the foundation of the rabbis' approach to the issue.

> "One [i.e., a Jew] who engages in idolatry" [is to be stoned—quoting Mishnah 4]—whether he worships [the idol in its normal way], or sacrifices, or burns incense, or offers a libation, or bows, or accepts it as a god, saying, "you are my god." But if he hugs it, or kisses it, or cleans it, or washes around it, or washes it, or anoints it, or dresses it, or shods it, he violates a negative commandment [and so is merely liable to be flogged]. If he takes a vow or swears in its name, he violates a negative commandment. If he exposes (*po'er*) himself to Ba'al Pe'or—this is his [normal form of] worship; if he throws a stone at Merkulis [a dolmen sacred to Hermes-Mercury]—this is his worship.

Characteristically, the Mishnah requires *action* of its idolaters, especially cult-related action. The Mishnah arranges these punishable actions hierarchically. Most severe is the prohibition of what we may call first-order worship—worshiping a god either as he is normally worshiped by his adherents or with forms of sacrificial worship that may not in fact be customarily used for the particular god but are unambiguously cultic acts, either because they are how

[8] See *TDNT* s.v., and also the comments of G. Stroumsa, "Tertullian and the Limits of Tolerance," Stanton and Stroumsa, eds., *Tolerance*, pp. 173–84. The Greek word is found only in Christian sources, as a katachresis for paganism, though it has a precise Jewish parallel in the rabbinic *'avodat 'elilim* (idol worship); I use it as a functional equivalent of the nonkatachrestic term *'avodah zarah*. Hadas-Lebel, "Le paganisme," is a full discussion of the specific pagan practices mentioned in Avodah Zarah; see also the analyses of the tractate in G. Blidstein, "Rabbinic Legislation on Idolatry: Tractate Abodah Zarah Chapter I," (Ph.D. diss., Yeshiva University, 1968); and in Hayes.

the Jewish God demanded to be worshiped, according to the book of Leviticus, or because they are elements in a Mediterranean cultic *koine*. *Everyone* knows that pouring a libation is a cultic act. Finally, and most interestingly, in this category, the acclamation of a god (I take this to be explanatory of the clause it follows: we can tell if someone "accepts" a god only if he has acclaimed him) also counts as first-order worship. Next, and less severely punished, is second-order worship, characterized not as ambivalence about a god or as acts indicating ambivalence, but as unambiguous acts of reverence for an idol that stop short of full worship,[9] or their verbal equivalent—the oath, that is, a speech act that unambiguously indicates belief but does not amount to acclamation. The Mishnah's final category is the ambiguous act, which looks like an expression of disrespect but is actually a first-order cultic act. It is not entirely clear what punishment the Mishnah prescribes in this case: perhaps an effort is to be made to detect the intentions of the actor. It is characteristic that one "case," that of Ba'al Pe'or, is presumably derived entirely from biblical narrative with no known correlate in Syro-Palestinian religious life of the second century, while the other seems a reference to a piece of common Palestinian folk piety, notwithstanding its Latin name.[10] For the rabbis, the world of the Hebrew Bible was at least as real as the world in which they actually lived.

The Mishnah's basic law of "idolatry" is founded on two principles. The first of these is that only cultic actions (including speech) matter and the second is that pagan worship is primarily directed at fetishes. Though both of these principles are derived from Pentateuchal law, they reflect a rather reductive reading of it. The Bible prohibits not just acts associated with the worship of strange gods in the form of idols but also a wide range of activities associated only peripherally with pagan cult, including "having other gods" (Exodus 20), whatever that may mean. To be sure, M. Sanhedrin is primarily concerned with court procedure, not paganism, so it does not legislate about beliefs, about speech that ambiguously expresses belief in other gods, about what attitude Jews should have to the ethos and physical trappings of paganism, in sum, about how one should cope with the realities of a life in which the images of gods, places associated with gods, items offered to gods, and the people who worship them were absolutely everywhere.

Such subtler issues do, however, constitute the main concerns of M. Avodah Zarah: how, the tractate asks, to avoid any semblance of participation in or collusion with pagan cultic activity, how to treat items associated or suspected of being associated with such activity (especially images and wine),

---

[9] Indeed, as far as some pagans were concerned, bathing and dressing the images of gods were acts of profound devotion requiring the presence of a priest; see Clerc, *Culte des Images*, p. 33.

[10] See Hadas-Lebel, "Le paganisme," pp. 403–5 for a different view. For a remarkable explanation of "*po'er et 'atzmo leba'al pe'or*," see Sifre Numbers (ed. S. Horowitz), pisqa 131.

how to treat images of the gods in general, and how to cope with aspects of city life objectionable for other than religious reasons—various types of entertainments, for instance, and the building of gallows (M. Avodah Zarah 1:7)?

In trying to make sense of the rabbis' view of paganism, it may be best for us to begin with a story in M. Avodah Zarah 3:4, which is unusual in the context of the Mishnah in that it lacks any clear legal content. In fact, it may appear in the Mishnah for no other reason than that one of its protagonists quotes Deuteronomy 13:18, which is quoted also in the previous Mishnah. However, in my view, M. Avodah Zarah 3:4 also articulates the meta-legal principles that underlie rabbinic legislation on *avodah zarah* as a whole in a way that highlights their contrast with the sort of rigoristic interpretation of the Pentateuch that may have prevailed in some contemporary nonrabbinic circles and had almost certainly been widespread among the Jews before 70, in prerabbinic times.[11]

> Proklos ben Philosophos[12] asked Rabban Gamaliel in Akko, when they were bathing in the bath-house of Aphrodite, "It is written in your Torah, 'let nothing of the *herem* [roughly equivalent to "sacer"—a status the Pentateuch ascribes to any object associated with idolatry] remain in your hand' (Deuteronomy 13.18); why then are you bathing in the bath-house of Aphrodite?" He said, "One may not respond [to questions about Torah] in a bath-house." When they went out, Rabban Gamaliel said, "I did not enter her territory; she entered mine. You do not say 'the bath-house is made as an ornament for Aphrodite,' but 'Aphrodite is made as an ornament for the bath-house.' Furthermore [*davar aher*], if you were given much money, you would not[13] enter your temple naked, having just ejaculated, and urinating before the goddess. And yet here she is set over the drain and everyone urinates before her. It is written 'their gods' [probably an allusion to Deuteronomy 12:3: "you shall dismember the idols of their gods"]—in cases where they are treated as gods they are forbidden, when they are not they are permitted."

[11] S. Kanter, *Rabban Gamaliel II: The Legal Traditions* (Ann Arbor: Scholars, 1980), pp. 175–77, misreads the story as a report of Gamaliel's halakhically objectionable behavior as revised by a sympathizer, comparable to the complex of material in M. Berakhot 2:5–7. But in M. Avodah Zarah Gamaliel's behavior is precisely not objectionable in terms of rabbinic halakhah, only in terms of the sort of rigoristic reading of the Pentateuch the rabbis are trying to distance themselves from.

[12] Or in the better MSS, the unconstruable PLSLWS: see D. Zlotnick, "Proklos ben PLSLWS," in S. Friedman, ed., *Saul Lieberman Memorial Volume* (New York: Jewish Theological Seminary, 1993), pp. 49–52, for an attempted construal. For the text of the tractate, see D. Rosenthal, "Mishnah Abodah Zarah: Critical Edition with Introduction" (Ph.D. diss., Hebrew University, 1980), esp. 2: 40–43.

[13] MSS Cambridge, Kaufmann, and Parma omit "not" and presumably read the statement as a rhetorical question.

Proklos and His Question

By the time of the compilation of the Mishnah and associated documents, there were real pagan critics of the Hebrew Bible and its Jewish and Christian interpreters, Celsus and Porphyry, for example. But at least some of the learned pagans who sparsely populate the pages of rabbinic literature seem to function as safe mouthpieces for the expression of the rabbis' own concerns about their version of Judaism.[14] The pagans' questions thus tend to have a coherence and rigor that the rabbinic responses (which, as products of profound systemic tensions, often combine laxity and overdetermination) lack. Proklos begins by quoting a verse that, when read in its biblical context, is not precisely relevant. Deuteronomy 13:13–19 concerns an Israelite town whose inhabitants have been seduced into the worship of strange gods. Yet in their expansion of the biblical laws of idolatry, the rabbis themselves removed verse 18 from its context and understood it as a foundation for the laws of idolatry in general, with no necessary connection to the seduced Israelite city. For example, the rabbis derive from the verse the rules that an Israelite's idol must be destroyed in such a way as to make impossible any potential contact even with the fragments, and that monetary benefit derived from idolatry must likewise be destroyed without a trace. Thus, when "Proklos" uses the verse, oddly, to demonstrate the impropriety of Rabban Gamaliel's behavior, his use conforms to that of the rabbis elsewhere. By your standards, Proklos is made to say, this bath is *herem*, which means that whether or not you destroy it, you may not use it; why then are you here?

This powerful question reveals several anomalies at the very core of the rabbinic treatment of paganism. How, in the first place, could the rabbis simply ignore the images that decorated both private and public spaces in the cities and larger villages? It is true that the rabbis demanded going to tremendous lengths to avoid even indirectly encouraging pagan worship. The tractate opens by prohibiting the conduct of business with a pagan for three days before his festival, apparently so that he would not offer thanks to his god for his success.[15] One may not even walk toward a city whose inhabitants are celebrating a festival (1:5); since pagans are assumed to be constantly pouring libations, their very contact with wine is enough to render it forbidden. Yet in other circumstances, they seemed to have little objection to images. Not only is it permissible to enter places decorated with images of the gods, such as

---

[14] Modern treatments of this issue, in their single-minded attention to the identification of the real identity of the interlocutors, are characterized by the most naive pseudohistoricism; on "Antoninus and Rabbi," see above; on the "Rabbi Yosi and Matrona" stories, T. Ilan, "Matrona and Rabbi Yose," *JSJ* 25 (1994): 18–51; on Gamaliel and Proklos, A. Wasserstein, "Rabban Gamliel and Proclus the Philosopher," *Zion* 45 (1980): 257–67.

[15] M. Avodah Zarah 1:1, following Rashi, ad loc., who was himself extrapolating from the editorial response to the opinion of R. Judah at the end of the Mishnah.

public baths, and use inexpensive items decorated with unambiguously pagan symbols (3:3), but it is also permissible to derive benefit from idols assumed not to have been worshiped (4:4; cf. T. Avodah Zarah 5:3–4) or idols that have been abandoned, slightly disfigured, or, in one opinion, simply sold, by a pagan (4:5–6). Indeed, a Jew may unhesitatingly enjoy a garden or bathhouse that belongs to a pagan temple, as long as no expression of gratitude to the priests is required (4:3). The later rabbinic collections go further, in some cases, making explicit what the Mishnah leaves unsaid: images, even of the gods—in paintings, mosaics, the carvings on such household items as "Delphic" tables—are expressly permitted, provided they are simply "decoration." How could the rabbis so blatantly ignore the tenor of the Pentateuchal laws, with their apparently unconditional opposition to images, and of general biblical thought?

Gamaliel's Response: A Doctrine of Mere Decoration

In their discussions of this Mishnah, the Talmuds focus on Rabban Gamaliel's refusal to answer Proklos in the bathhouse. This refusal foreshadows the Mishnah's argument that the bath, with its naked, urinating patrons, is unsuitable for religious activities, such as pagan sacrifice and Torah study. The Talmudim observe that Gamaliel's very refusal to answer was a piece of Torah study and so should have been forbidden! We will not let this characteristic paradox detain us, though, since what follows is of greater interest. What can Gamaliel have meant by saying that the goddess entered his territory, and not vice versa? Rabban Gamaliel's first response is indeed difficult to understand, but it may in fact mean no more than that bathhouses are for bathers, not worshipers, so the goddess, not the bather, is the intruder. As the Babylonian Talmud observed in its comment on this Mishnah, this sort of argument is palpably inadequate, even from the perspective of rabbinic law, let alone that of biblical prescription. But this very inadequacy explains why additional responses are given.

The second and third clauses should, I believe, be taken as complementary: together they produce a kind of "doctrine of mere decoration." The pagans themselves would say that Aphrodite in the bath is secondary, a mere ornament—indeed, they themselves do not hesitate to stand before her naked, behavior they would not countenance in their own temples. An idol is only a god, and so subject to (our attenuated version of) the biblical prohibitions, if it is treated like one. If it is erected in a bathhouse or, by extension, used to decorate tableware, or simply neglected, it is perfectly acceptable.[16]

---

[16] My argument here about the rabbis' creation of the category of the decorative is functionally similar to Halbertal's claim ("Coexisting with the Enemy") that with the laws of *avodah zarah* they created a "neutral space" in which Jews and pagans could coexist.

The phrasing of R. Gamaliel's response—you pagans say, "Aphrodite is made as an ornament for the bath," you pagans would never think of behaving in a temple as you do in the bath—indicates that the Mishnah is not simply ignoring the nature of real-life paganism in a quest for formal exegetical precision. Rather, it claims to be shaping its interpretation of the biblical laws around its understanding of paganism. And for good reason. The Pentateuchal text itself does not in fact constrain the rabbis' view of paganism. On the contrary, the rabbis could, for instance, have taken the Pentateuchal exhortations about divine unity (Deuteronomy 6:4; Exodus 20:1–5) as legal prescription and understood them to prohibit any practice that seemed to contradict it, such as the noncultic use of images. Instead of reading in an exclusive way the verses prohibiting the representation of animal, human, and divine creatures ("thou shalt not make an idol nor any image. . . .thou shalt not bow down to them nor worship them" [Exodus 20:3–5; Deuteronomy 5:7–9] = do not make them or have them if they have been or will be worshiped, but otherwise, you incur no penalty), they could have read them inclusively, as their predecessors before 70 C.E., when the Jews rigorously avoided figurative art, had done. They could, in sum, have prohibited everything associated with paganism. After all, the stakes were high: Israel's God was a jealous God (Exodus 20:5; Deuteronomy 5:9). Instead, the rabbis imagined that pagan religiosity consisted exclusively of cultic acts directed at fetishes, and they interpreted the biblical prohibitions accordingly (though it must be said that some aggadic—nonlegal—passages indicate a more subtle appreciation of pagan religiosity).

What would a pagan have thought of the rabbis' view of his religion? Clearly the rabbis supposed that Proklos was convinced by R. Gamaliel's arguments, and no doubt few pagans would have denied the importance of figural representation and the centrality of sacrifice in their religious life. Some, furthermore, would have regarded the deity's image as its embodiment, at least under some circumstances. But others would have claimed that the individual gods were only aspects of the divine, all legitimately worshiped because, as the fourth-century poet Symmachus put it, "it is impossible that there is only one road to so great a mystery."[17] Such thoughtful pagans might have regarded the rabbis' theology of paganism as unhelpfully reductive: even homespun statuettes that would never receive a cult might be thought to contain a spark

---

[17] See MacMullen, *Paganism in the Roman Empire*, pp. 59–60; A. D. Nock, "Studies in the Graeco-Roman Beliefs of the Empire," in Z. Stewart, ed., *Essays on Religion and the Ancient World* (Cambridge: Harvard University Press, 1972), p. 40. In some aggadic passages, the rabbis evince a more nuanced grasp of pagan religiosity. See B. Avodah Zarah 54b–55a, with partial parallels in Mekhilta deRabbi Ishmael, pisqa 65 and Mekhilta deRashbi, Yitro (Ex 20:5), with discussion in M. Halbertal and A. Margalit, *Idolatry* (Cambridge: Harvard University Press, 1992), pp. 26–27.

of the divine, even if only because they turned men's minds to piety.[18] And even essentially decorative images, like Aphrodite in the bathhouse, Dionysus on the mosaic pavement of the city councillor's triclinium, the Capitoline Triad on the city coins, all had real religious meaning, or at very least were meaningful as decoration only within a pagan religious scheme. Aphrodite may have been thought present in the bath that housed her image, not *in* the image itself but as patron goddess (or for the more skeptically inclined, as the allegorical personification) of physical pleasure.[19] Even such decorative representations underlined the omnipresence of the gods; they also underlined what seems at first glance to be an essential difference between Jewish and Greco-Roman, indeed, general eastern Mediterranean, religiosity. The latter had long been characterized by a slippage between impersonal natural or social forces and personified deities, which allowed people to view Fortune or Youth as gods deserving of worship, and Aphrodite and Zeus as metaphors for human social relations, while yet remaining gods, all of them readily representable. Their images, even when not meant as objects of cult, were unambiguously part of an ethos of paganism. I would add here parenthetically that apart from the issue of representation, Judaism was not as remote from its environment as we, and the rabbis before us, might like to think, for the Jews, too, had endowed natural and social forces with personality and made them not gods, perhaps, but demigods or angels.

I am trying, in sum, to problematize the rabbis' creation of the category of the purely decorative; this is necessary because the rabbinic category resonates all too closely with our own preconceptions. It is, for instance, perfectly obvious that the Gorgon's heads and classicizing busts that decorate the facades of the apartment buildings on the Manhattan avenue where these pages were written have no religious meaning whatever, and it is all too easy to suppose that the comparable deployment of similar iconography in a Roman town of the third century did not either. But on closer examination, the decoration of the buildings proves deeply meaningful. The residents of the street sense that they live in a neighborhood with depth and resonance, not with classical antiquity but with the near past of baroque Rome and nineteenth-century Paris. The street does not feel as if it had been built up hastily in the 1920s on the ruins of workers' quarters to accommodate a rising bourgeoisie. Even residents who have never visited Paris or Rome cannot miss the implications of the classicizing decorations and Berniniesque façades. The street is grand but restrained, its inhabitants substantial but unaddicted to excess. Here, the images of the gods indeed have no religious meaning, but their status as cultural signs is unmistakable. The rabbis' world was, in contrast to ours, pervaded with gods. To take for granted the "naturalness" of the rabbis' dismissal

[18] Clerc, *Culte des Images*, p. 38.
[19] See the extensive discussion in Dunbabin, *Mosaics of Roman North Africa*, p. 137–87.

of the significance of their commonplace material representation, as all modern scholarship has done, is not only problematic per se but ignores the evidence from rabbinic literature itself (discussed below) that at least some rabbis recognized that decoration was never *merely* decorative.

What motivated the rabbis' radical misinterpretation of Greco-Roman paganism? It is of course impossible to say. But we may at least note that their formalism, their taxonomists' aversion to ambiguities, and their consequent creation of categories whose correspondence to social realities is loose are all characteristic of their treatment even of issues far less freighted with consequence than paganism. If we knew nothing about the context in which the rabbis produced and compiled the laws of idolatry, it is unlikely that we would sense anything strange about them.

By suggesting, following C. E. Hayes,[20] an internalist rationale for the laws of idolatry, I am rejecting the sort of naïve historicizing contextualization that has dominated modern interpretation. For example, E. E. Urbach, in a celebrated article, argued that the rabbis' leniency about certain categories of images was intended to ease the lot of the economically challenged Jews by permitting them to deal in slightly damaged idols.[21] Not only is this implausible (how much demand was there for slightly damaged idols?) and apologetic (since it is intended to demonstrate that the rabbis of the Mishnah were more enlightened than their contemporary Tertullian), but it also makes what I consider the error of regarding rabbinic legislation as unproblematically binding on all the Jews. But rabbinic legislation was utopian in that it was directed at a nation that no longer existed, and whose former members had no reason to recognize the laws' authority over them. It was also inner-directed in that its primary context was the rabbinic study house, increasingly institutionalized in the course of the third century. Hayes's argument that we take seriously the inner dynamics of rabbinic law is convincing.

That said, there is evidence from rabbinic literature itself that at least some of the rabbis were uncomfortable with the implications of their formalism; they were not unaware that their own views represented an attempt to mediate between the absolute aniconism and rejection of paganism demanded by a rigoristic reading of the Pentateuch (and characteristic of standard pre-Destruction Jewish practice) and the pervasive presence of images of the gods in their own world. Some rabbis are supposed to have sensed that even halakhically innocent images are problematic and to have avoided possessing or even looking at them. We have already encountered the Palestinian Talmud's admiration for R. Nahum bar Simai—Nahum of the holy of holies—who

---

[20] *Between the Babylonian and Palestinian Talmuds.*

[21] "The Rabbinical Laws of Idolatry." For discussion of additional examples, see Hayes, *Between the Babylonian and Palestinian Talmuds*, pp. 2–24; see also S. Stern, "Images in Jewish Law in the Period of the Mishnah and the Talmud," *Zion* 61 (1996): 397–419.

never looked at an image in his life, not even if it was only stamped on a coin.[22] The Palestinian Talmud also reports a series of stories concerning rabbis who were reluctant to pass before public statuary (Y. Avodah Zarah 3:13, 43b). The stories all conclude with the rabbis' giving in at the urging of Rabbi Yohanan (but, quite literally, closing their eyes to the images as they passed), but they still *may* reveal that the Mishnah's formalism does not tell the whole story. We may, however, wonder whether these stories were not retrospective creations of the later fourth century, when the Talmud was compiled, idealized projections made by rabbis who no longer knew what it was like to live in a pagan city. The same may be true of the story of R. Yohanan's instruction to one Ben Drusai to destroy the presumably wholly unproblematic statues in the Tiberian bathhouse (Y. Avodah Zarah 4:4)[23]—the same R. Yohanan who is reported elsewhere to have permitted to the Jews of Bostra a spring whose waters were used in the local cult of Aphrodite (Y. Sheviit 8:11, 38b-c) and to have permitted Jews to pass through the shade of a sacred grove that had encroached on public land (B. Avodah Zarah 48b) on the grounds that what is public cannot be prohibited—a rule whose legal rationale is unclear.[24]

Whether or not the rabbis were aware that their legislation was accommodative is in the final analysis impossible to determine. What seems clear is that it *functioned* as accommodation. I am suggesting that although the rabbinic

[22] A minority opinion, whose precise meaning is obscure, not mentioned in the Mishnah, attributed in two sources to R. Judah (second century C.E.), prohibits looking at *dioqna'ot*, or *eikoniot* (Sifra, Kedoshim parashah 1, sec. 10; Y. Avodah Zarah 3:1, 42b; T. Shabbat 17[18].1, where it is quoted anonymously), but this had no impact on general rabbinic halakhah; R. Nahum's refusal to look at *eikoniot*, whatever precisely they are, is presented as supererogatory. R. Nahum himself was for the rabbis a shadowy, almost legendary, figure: see Florsheim, "R. Menahem (= Nahum) ben Simai."

[23] On this story, and on the identification of Ben Drusai with the Ben Drusai who lent his name to an important category of Sabbath law, see Friedman, "Recovering the Historical Ben D'rosai."

[24] See G. Blidstein, "R. Yohanan, Idolatry, and Public Privilege," *JSJ* 5 (1974): 154–61. I have not followed his interpretation of Y. Sheviit 8:11, 38b-c: "R. Shimon b. Lakish was in Bostra and saw them sprinkling a certain Aphrodite [*mezalpin lehada Aphrodite*]; he said to them, 'is it not forbidden?' He went and asked R. Yohanan, who told him in the name of R. Shimon b. Yehozadak, 'that which belongs to the public cannot be forbidden.'" Blidstein followed Lieberman, *Hellenism in Jewish Palestine*, pp. 132–33, who read *mezalpin behada Aphrodite*, "were bathing *in* that (bathhouse? of) Aphrodite." But in this case it is puzzling that neither R. Shimon b. Lakish nor R. Yohanan is made to quote the Mishnah. (The same objection rules out what would be syntactically the simplest interpretation: that R. Shimon saw Jews sprinkling water on an idol and declared it forbidden but was overruled by R. Yohanan. Sprinkling water on an idol is explicitly forbidden by M. Sanhedrin; see above). Furthermore, *mezalpin* without the reflexive pronoun (*'al garmehon*) does not mean "bathe" but "sprinkle." The interpretation given in the commentary attributed to R. Elijah b. Solomon, the *gaon* of Vilna, is preferable: R. Shimon b. Lakish saw the Bostrans sprinkling water drawn from a spring on a statue of Aphrodite and wished to forbid the spring to the Jews of Bostra, drawing an analogy from the Mishnah's prohibition of a barrel of wine from which a libation has been offered.

laws of idolatry may have as their primary context the rabbinic study house, and so they may have been motivated by the internal dynamics of rabbinic law, they may also be seen as part of a larger social process. Having moved to the cities and having decided to set about acquiring the authority that they believed the Torah had granted them, the rabbis could not have maintained the purely rigoristic approach to idolatry that they presumably had inherited from their pre-Destruction Pharisaic and priestly predecessors. At most, the persistence of individual extremists in or near rabbinic circles (or at least the rabbinic recounting of stories about such men and about the miraculous destruction of public statuary) kept pure aniconism and separatism alive as ideals, by definition generally unattainable. But the universalization of such attitudes among the rabbis of the second and third centuries would have reduced them to existing in complete isolation from the rest of Palestinian Jewish society. Their modified rigorism, with its uncompromising rejection of anything remotely connected to pagan cult,[25] but acceptance of most noncultic manifestations of Greco-Roman pagan culture, permitted them to live and function in the cities.

On the other hand, there is reason to believe that some rabbis, even apart from the patriarchs, took more liberties than the codified halakhah allowed. We know, for instance, that Hamat Gader, the hot springs near Gadara, was a favorite resort of some rabbis in the third and fourth centuries, yet we also know that the place was thoroughly pagan in character. Not only did all the springs and baths have mythological names, but the annual festival that took place there, as well as the common practices of incubation and commemoration of miraculous cures, clearly indicate that the hot springs were not simply a winter resort but also functioned as a shrine to Asclepius and Hygieia.[26] The Mishnah admittedly permits the use of baths and gardens owned by temples, but it is hard to see how a bath that *was* a temple could have been permitted. The willingness of some rabbis to patronize a place like Hamat Gader demonstrates what we might have supposed anyway—a greater diversity of rabbinic behavior (and opinion?) than the rabbinic sources indicate.

[25] Even this was to some extent modified by, or in tension with, another rabbinic principle, *darkei shalom*, "the ways of peace," which requires Jews to treat pagans far better than the letter of the law would lead one to expect. Thus, in towns with mixed population Jews are required to support the pagan poor, care for their sick, comfort their mourners, and so on. R. Ammi (early fourth century) is said to have almost permitted some Jews of Gadara (or "weavers": *garda'e* or *gadra'ei*) to attend a pagan's (wedding? religious?) celebration, but to have been dissuaded by a colleague, R. Ba (Y. Avodah Zarah 1:3 = Y. Gittin 5:9, 47c).

[26] See Y. Hirschfeld, *The Roman Baths of Hammat Gader: Final Report* (Jerusalem: IES, 1997). The rabbinic passages are collected in Klein, *Sefer Hayishuv*, s.v. "Hamat Gader = Hamat." The mosaic inscriptions from the fifth-century synagogue indicate that the resort remained popular among Jewish visitors even after it was thoroughly christianized; see Naveh, *On Mosaic*, nos. 32–35.

Conclusion

Despite the evidence for their integrationist ambitions, and for some flexibility, rabbis were nevertheless marginal. I have been arguing that with the progressive centralization of the Roman Empire in the first century, the Jewish polity, which imposed and maintained and depended to some extent for its legitimacy on the core Jewish ideology discussed in part 1 and mediated between the imperial state and the Jewish subject, failed. With its failure, Judaism shattered. There may have been little groups apart from the ones that later coalesced as the rabbis which tried to keep the Torah alive after the failed revolts of 70 and 135, despite its loss of constitutional status. There are, for example, tantalizing hints about a priestly group at Sepphoris in the third century and even later. But of all these conservative groups, the rabbis seem to have been the most successful.

But even they were not dominant. In fact, no self-consciously Jewish group was—only the Romans and their local agents, the city councillors, almost all of whom may have been of Jewish origin. In other words, in the wake of the revolts, Jewish society disintegrated. In practice, Palestinians of Jewish background in the second through fourth centuries had two core ideologies to chose from (to use a series of crude but heuristically serviceable metaphors). The more influential, authoritative, and, it must be emphasized, even religiously compelling was the ideology of the Greco-Roman city, culturally Hellenic, religiously pagan, ostensibly nonparticularistic, rendered prestigious by its association with the peace and prosperity of the high empire, and probably reconcilable, if only with difficulty, with retention of a variety of other mildly discredited ethnic identities. A citizen of Caesarea might be a proud Roman citizen, too, but also a Jew, a Samaritan, a Christian, or a Syrian, in addition to thinking of himself as being in some sense Greek. If he took his municipal responsibilities seriously, though, his Jewishness or Christianity would necessarily have been attenuated, for the public life of the city was pagan to the core.

What Palestinian Jews had (but most other co-opted nations lacked) was the sense, which some of them had partly internalized, that life ought to be lived differently, a sense embodied in the rabbis, who preserved a profoundly altered but still recognizable version of Judaism. The rabbis were not authorized by the state and had little glamor after the revolts. Nevertheless, to the extent that some probably very small number of Jews had internalized Judaism in a fairly comprehensive way, with many others retaining a looser attachment to it, the rabbis did have a few followers and probably slightly larger numbers of occasional supporters. This loose periphery of supporters is likely to have consisted of people who in most respects lived normatively Greco-Roman lives and whose Jewishness was strictly compartmentalized (e.g., perhaps they refrained from eating pork and circumcised their sons but participated without hesitation in public festivals).

We should view the population of urban and suburban Jewish Palestine (and let us remember that we know next to nothing about the least urbanized areas during this period) as situated along an ideological continuum. At one extreme are people who, though of Jewish origin and probably in some sense ethnicity (they must have known that they were living in "Jewish" towns, even if only because their "Greek" neighbors sometimes reminded them), were to all intents and purposes standard Greco-Roman pagans. At the other are hardcore representatives of Judaism, mainly the rabbis. Most Jews were caught in between, though the evidence clearly indicates that the two poles were unequal in their attraction. Most Jews seem to have lived mainly as pagans and looked primarily to the Roman state and the city councils as their legal authorities and cultural ideal, but even they may have retained some sense of being not quite fully Greek—(un?)like their insistent neighbors in Scythopolis. Others may have been eclectic, living in some respects as pagans and in others as Jews, occasionally supporting and consulting rabbinic figures for some purposes, perhaps by the third century helping in the construction of synagogues, but most often ignoring them. Or they may have been people whose primary identity was Jewish and, like the rabbis themselves, may often have regarded their accommodations with the dominant culture with unease.

It is possible that the balance began to shift by the end of the third century. We have seen that there is some evidence for a growing anxiety in Jewish Palestine about public paganism around 300. Perhaps this should not be pressed, but it may be no coincidence that the Palestinian rabbinic movement attained its greatest numerical extent, that the patriarch began his rise, and probably that the city councils began their decline all in the same brief period around 300. Whether or not the Palestinian Jews did take a step toward judaizing their public—and private—lives in the decades before Constantine's conquest of Palestine in 323–324, it is certain that with the christianization of the empire, the character of Jewish life changed dramatically.

PART III

SYNAGOGUE AND COMMUNITY FROM 350 TO 640

SIX

CHRISTIANIZATION

IN THIS PART of the book I attempt to describe some aspects of the novel and distinctive Jewish culture that emerged in late antiquity (c. 350–640) as the integrative ideology of the Jews. In this chapter I will argue that one of the main causes of the rejudaization of the Jews was the christianization of the Roman Empire. This process (and it must be emphasized that christianization was a process, not a moment, which cannot be regarded as in any sense complete before the reign of Justinian [527–565], if then)[1] affected the Jews in two ways. First, it tended to *marginalize* them. As religion assumed ever more importance in social relations in late antiquity, Jews were gradually excluded from the networks of patronage that held the empire together.[2] The Jews had two possible ways of responding: continued integration at the cost of conversion to Christianity or continued adherence to Judaism (its component communities increasingly inward turning and possessing their own discrete social structures) at the cost of withdrawal.

Second, christianization, and what is in social-historical terms its sibling, the emergence of religion as a discrete category of human experience—religion's *disembedding*—had a direct impact on the Jewish culture of late antiquity because the Jewish communities *appropriated* much from the Christian society around them. That is, quite a lot of the distinctive Jewish culture was, to be vulgar about it, repackaged Christianity. Much more importantly, the dominant forms of Jewish social organization and patterns of expenditure in late antiquity, the local community and the synagogue (its chief material manifestation), were constituted by appropriative participation by Jews in the common late antique culture. This point will be argued in detail later in this section.

Before proceeding with these arguments, I will pause very briefly to consider in a bit more detail what it is I am trying to explain. The remains of northern Palestine in late antiquity are very different from those of the second and third centuries. Most prominent among the late antique remains are syna-

---

[1] See, e.g., Averil Cameron, *The Mediterranean World in Late Antiquity, AD 395–600* (London: Routledge, 1993), pp. 57–80; P. R. L. Brown, *The World of Late Antiquity* (London: Thames & Hudson, 1971), passim. This point requires special emphasis as a corrective to much of Jacob Neusner's work on the Palestinian Talmud and the *midreshei aggadah*—to take just one example, *Judaism in Society.*

[2] For this sense of marginalization, see the fundamentally important first chapter of A. Avidov, "Processes of Marginalisation in the Roman Empire" (Ph.D. diss., Cambridge University, 1995).

gogues, which, we may infer, were found in all but the very smallest settlements. The rise of the synagogue will be discussed in detail below; for now
we may observe two of its chief implications. The first is that some version of
Judaism apparently now reemerged as an important feature of Jewish life, and
the second is that Jewish religious life was organized in local, partly autonomous, and self-enclosed communities, as has just been suggested. The synagogue remains also introduce us to the beginnings of a dynamic, novel, and
distinctive religious culture. They provide evidence of the development of
a specifically Jewish iconography and art, which in turn are obliquely and
complicatedly related to a renewed literary culture, whose remains include
the Palestinian Talmud, the Midrash collections, the massive quantities of
innovative liturgical poetry produced in the sixth century and following,
called *piyyut*, a magical/cosmological literature including the Hekhalot books,
the Sefer Yezirah, and the Sefer HaRazim, as well as the beginnings of a
medieval-style halakhic literature.

I have been careful not to write of a late antique Jewish *society* because
the Jews in late antiquity (unlike in the later Second Temple period) were
fragmented politically, socially, and economically. Though loosely bound together by a complex and varied religious ideology, they lacked any sort of
institutional centralization, especially after the end of the patriarchate, around
425. This ideology may have come to provide Jewish life everywhere with a
certain sameness, just as it did in the Middle Ages. Even in northern Palestine,
where there was a concentrated Jewish population, routine social and economic relations may not have been marked as Jewish, and there may have
been no way of excluding Christians and pagans from the networks created
by such interactions. Alternatively, such networks as existed may, even if separated by religion, have been too localized to contribute to the integration of
a still large regional population. In sum, it may be more useful to think about
a late antique Jewish *world* than a society.[3]

Judaism and Christianity in Late Antiquity

Though it is not my intention to present a synthetic reappraisal of the history
of the Jews in the later Roman Empire, my argument—that Jewish life was
transformed by Christian rule—has important implications for the wider history of the Jews in the later Roman Empire, which I shall consider briefly

---

[3] See B. Musallam, "The Ordering of Muslim Societies," in F. Robinson, ed., *The Cambridge
Illustrated History of the Islamic World* (Cambridge: Cambridge University Press, 1996), pp. 164–
207, who uses the concept of the Islamic world to describe the similarly fragmented not-quite
society of the high Middle Ages.

here. Since the days of Heinrich Graetz it has been common to view the history of the Jews in late antiquity as one of inexorable decline, from the flourishing postrevolt revival of the Jewish polity under the Severan emperors to the horrors of the Middle Ages, a decline that had, however, only a superficial effect on the inner constitution of Jewish society.[4] The old characterization of the Severan period is no longer tenable. Nor would many historians nowadays be willing to view the Middle Ages in Graetz's terms, at least not without serious qualification. But the traditional view of Jewish life under the Christian emperors is undeniably powerful. No one could reasonably deny that the state and its various retainers sometimes displayed hostility to the Jews in the first through third centuries: the writings of pagan intellectuals are rife with it, and the brutality of the suppression of the three Jewish revolts goes without saying. But hostility to Jews and Judaism certainly reached an unprecedentedly high pitch in late imperial Christian writing, and this hostility was increasingly reflected in imperial legislation, as well as in an ever increasing number of local acts of persecution and violence.

On the Jewish side, there is, despite this slight sense of embattledness in literature thought to have been written or compiled in the fourth and fifth centuries, the Palestinian Talmud and the *midrashim* Genesis and Leviticus Rabbah (perhaps literature from the Diaspora, if we had any, would convey a different impression).[5] But later midrashim and the early piyyut, mainly products of the sixth century, are suffused with defensiveness and aggressive opposition to Christianity and the state that supported it, indeed, with a strong sense of gloom. Some Jews had unhappily internalized Christian triumphalism and believed, as the payyetan Yannai put it, that the lamps of Edom (Rome, i.e., Byzantium) burned brightly while those of Zion were about to flicker out.[6] So it is unsurprising that in the sixth and seventh centuries the historical apocalypse apparently experienced a revival in some Jewish circles (although the surviving Hebrew apocalypses are probably later; at the very least, they were heavily reworked in the Islamic period).[7]

Even before the theory of decline was systematically attacked, starting in the 1970s, it received occasional criticism. Most interesting is the characteristi-

---

[4] See the discussion in J. Cohen, "Roman Imperial Policy toward the Jews from Constantine until the End of the Palestinian Patriarchate," *Byzantine Studies/études Byzantines* 3 (1976): 1–29.

[5] Perhaps the *Collatio Legum Mosaicarum et Romanarum* is such a work, but its schematic character makes it difficult to interpret; see Rutgers, *Hidden Heritage*, pp. 235–84.

[6] Z. M. Rabinovitz, *The Liturgical Poems of Rabbi Yannai* (Jerusalem: Mossad Bialik, 1987), 2: 37. On Yannai's gloom and hostility to Byzantium and to Christianity, see H. Schirmann, "Yannai Ha-payyetan: Shirato Ve-hashqafat Olamo," *Keshet* 23 (1964): 56–59.

[7] See Y. Even-Shmuel, *Midreshei Ge'ulah: Pirqei Ha-apoqalipsah Hayehudit Mehatimat Hatalmud Habavli Ve'ad Reshit Ha'elef Hashelishi* (Jerusalem: Mossad Bialik, 1953), for these texts.

cally iconoclastic argument of Yitzhak (Fritz) Baer that there was no golden age of Roman-Jewish relations in the high empire, that, on the contrary, the state was generally hostile to the Jews and even sometimes persecuted them, just as it did the Christians.[8] This argument was based not on direct evidence (which is nonexistent),[9] but on the observation, in my view correct, that as a body, professing Jews were hardly more assimilable in the pagan than in the Christian Roman state; it implies that the situation of the Jews in the latter was basically unchanged.

The reaction of the 1970s and 1980s approached the issue from a different direction.[10] It is no coincidence that this was a period of intensive archaeological exploration in Israel and the occupied territories, and of the beginnings of the systematic questioning of the old consensus about the role of the rabbis and the normative status of their literature in post-Destruction Jewish Palestine. The new approach to rabbinic literature allowed scholars to adopt an exaggerated form of Saul Lieberman's hypothesis of rabbinic acculturation (viz., rabbinic assimilation) and simultaneously to dismiss the rabbis as marginal. So, the argument goes, the rabbis' particularism, which would have predisposed the Jews to a state of hostile separation from Christian Roman society, may be a mirage and in any case had little impact on the Jews in general. The new archaeological exploration suggested that starting in the third century the Jews, especially in Palestine, experienced a period of unprecedented prosperity and demographic growth, and they engaged in extensive cultural borrowing from their pagan and Christian neighbors. This seemed to imply that Jewish-Christian relations in late antiquity were generally friendly—a view paradoxically strengthened by, for example, the contents of John Chrysostom's ferocious Sermons against the Jews. These consist mainly of the priest's warnings to his flock to resist the attractions of the synagogues and the Jewish festivals, combined with vituperative attacks on the Jews. One of the harbingers of this reevaluation of the Jewish experience in late antiquity,

---

[8] "Israel, the Christian Church, and the Roman Empire," SH 7 (1961): 84–86. By contrast, J. Juster had argued (Les juifs dans l'empire romain [Paris: Paul Geuthner, 1914], 1: 44) that the inability of the church fathers of the second and third centuries to provide concrete legal proof for their repeated contention that the Jews were persecuted demonstrates that they were not.

[9] Or nearly so: see S. Lieberman, "Palestine in the Third and Fourth Centuries," Texts and Studies (New York: Ktav, 1974), pp. 112–53 (= JQR 36–37 (1946): 329–70); for a direct response to Baer, see Lieberman, "Redifat Dat Yisrael," in D. Rosenthal, ed., Studies in Palestinian Talmudic Literature (Jerusalem: Magnes, 1991), pp. 369–80 (= S. Baron Jubilee Volume, ed. S. Lieberman [Jerusalem: AAJR, 1974], 3: 213–46).

[10] The large bibliography on this issue will be cited below as needed. The "friendly" hypothesis underlies much non-Israeli archaeological publication; for an influential example, see E. Meyers and J. Strange, Archaeology, the Rabbis, and Early Christianity (Nashville: Abingdon, 1981). Also important have been several books by Robert Wilken, especially John Chrysostom and the Jews: Rhetoric and Reality in the Late Fourth Century (Berkeley: University of California Press, 1983).

the medievalist Jeremy Cohen's account of "imperial policy" toward the Jews from Constantine to Theodosius II, was unconnected with either the Neusnerian or the archaeological revolutions. Cohen acknowledged his debt to Salo Baron and his intention to refute the "lachrymose" view of late antique Jewish history promoted by Graetz, Dubnow, and (it must be said, to a far lesser extent) Juster, and argued that the Christian emperors were basically sympathetic to the Jews, and their laws tended to protect their rights and privileges.[11]

In what follows, I would like to alter the terms of the debate. First of all, both the traditional and the revisionist accounts seem partly correct. There can be no doubt that as the interests of the state and the orthodox church gradually and incompletely converged, the state became increasingly hostile to Jews. Local persecutions, forced conversions, seizures of synagogues, and so on, which violated the letter but not always the spirit of the laws, may have been somewhat less common than has often been thought (surprisingly few are attested in contemporary sources), but they undoubtedly occurred.[12] Stroumsa and Millar were right to argue that what distinguished Christian from pagan emperors was the Christians' conviction that they possessed the unique religious truth—a conviction that could only make life difficult for the Jews, in the end.[13]

There is, however, no denying the prosperity demonstrated by archaeological discoveries, nor the extent of the Jews' practice of appropriating cultural items great and small from their Christian environment. But it is far from obvious how these facts can be used to argue that Jewish Christian relations were basically friendly, or, what is far less likely, that Jews and Christians were still not fully differentiated in late antiquity. But presumably peaceful coexistence may have been the norm in some places (see below on Minorca).

[11] And note also T. Braun, "The Jews in the Late Roman Empire," SCI 17 (1998): 142–71.

[12] For a perhaps too skeptical view, see G. Stemberger, "Zwangstaufen von Juden im 4. bis 7. Jahrhundert: Mythos oder Wirklichkeit?" in C. Thoma, G. Stemberger, and J. Maier, eds., Judentum—Ausblicke und Einsichten: Festgabe für Kurt Schubert zum Siebzigsten Geburtstag, (Frankfurt/Main: Peter Lang, 1993), pp. 81–114. Stemberger comes down firmly on the side of mythos, and it must be admitted that the stories of forced conversions tend to be found mainly in noncontemporary sources and function as foundation myths of churches, in a way that arouses suspicion. But Stemberger's question is too narrow. For a broader view, see the works cited in the following note.

[13] G. Stroumsa, "Religious Contacts in Byzantine Palestine," Numen 36 (1989): 16–42; F. Millar, "Jews of the Greco-Roman Diaspora Between Paganism and Christianity," in J. Lieu, J. North, and T. Rajak, eds., Jews among Pagans and Christians in the Roman Empire (London: Routledge, 1992), pp. 97–123; also, Z. Rubin, "Christianity in Byzantine Palestine: Missionary Activity and Religious Coercion," Jerusalem Cathedra 3 (1983): 97–113. By contrast, the pagan Roman state established a set of behavioral norms, adherence to which might result in a subject's successful integration. Many of these norms were in conflict with Jewish practice, but other aspects of Jewish practice were of no interest to the state. The Christian state regarded Judaism as simply wrong.

We should also consider the likelihood that the failure of many Jewish con-
verts to Christianity to sever their family ties completely (as some laws and
many church canons imply, just as others suggest that Jews sometimes persecuted their former coreligionists) may have created important groups of people characterized by religious lability, a phenomenon well attested among
elements of the imperial aristocracy.[14] We will encounter an example of this
phenomenon below.

I would like to press the argument further. We should not be debating
whether some preexisting Jewish polity declined or prospered, or think only
about relatively superficial cultural borrowing conducted by two well-defined
groups. In my view, we should be looking for *systemic change*: the Jewish
culture that emerged in late antiquity was radically distinctive and distinctively
late antique—a product of the same political, social, and economic forces that
produced the no less distinctive Christian culture of late antiquity. In this
chapter I will defend this position, and in the remainder of this book I will
provide a more detailed account of some aspects of the distinctive Jewish
culture of late antiquity.

The Third Century

There are scattered hints that some of the characteristics of late antique Judaism were beginning to emerge in the later third and early fourth centuries,
before the conversion of Constantine to Christianity. We have already seen
that the Jewish cities may have begun to lose their pagan character then, and
that the patriarchs were beginning to grow in prominence. It is also thought
that several archaeologically attested synagogues in the Palestinian countryside were constructed in the late third century, though this view is now under
attack.[15] Here I will attempt only a partial explanation; I would emphasize
that whatever the causes of these changes, they were still very small in scale
in the late third century.

It is generally supposed that one of the most important effects of the "crisis
of the third century" was the decline of the curial classes. Contrary to what was

---

[14] See the material collected in the appendices of J. Parkes, *The Conflict of the Church and
the Synagogue: A Study in the Origins of Antisemitism* (London: The Soncino Press, 1934, reprint
New York: Hermon, 1974), especially the church canons (pp. 381–88) and the mainly undatable
but suggestive professions of faith extracted from Jews on baptism, pp. 394–400. On the religious
lability of some elements of the aristocracy, in Peter Brown's view especially characteristic of the
later fourth century, less so later, see Brown, *Authority and the Sacred: Aspects of the Christianisation of the Roman World* (Cambridge: Cambridge University Press, 1995).

[15] Note also the *synagoge Ioudaion* of Oxyrhynchus mentioned in a papyrus of 291: *CPJ* 3,
no. 473.

once believed, this decline was probably neither steep nor terminal in the third century. The curial classes remained important for centuries thereafter, and the massive legislation about the city councils incorporated in the second book of the Theodosian Code offers no unambiguous evidence for a steady decline, as opposed to imperial interest in the city councils' smooth functioning.

Nevertheless, it is not unlikely that city councils throughout the empire came under pressure in the later third century as silver coinage was debased because the councillors were responsible for the collection and transmission of most taxes, and the emperors continued to demand payment in undebased silver. That in general they were not able to bear the traditional expenses imposed upon them by the culture of euergetism is generally thought confirmed by the decline in the number of dedicatory inscriptions, taken as indications of expenditure on public construction and festivals. But this cannot be the only reason for the general decline in epigraphy—the vast majority of it funerary—in the third century.[16]

We have no direct information about the fate of the curial classes of Jewish Palestine in the later third century. But it would not be implausible to connect the retreat of paganism in the Jewish cities with the decline of the *curiales* for the simple reason that there, as elsewhere, municipal religions were expensive to maintain. Such a retreat may have favored the counterculture, in the form of the patriarchs and their rabbinic protégés. And the decline of the city councils may also explain why starting around 300 the patriarchs began to have at their disposal young Jewish men of Greek education to serve as agents. In their newly straitened circumstances, some city elites may have found it advantageous to seek the patronage of the patriarchs. Perhaps the same factor may also explain the first rural synagogues, built by villagers who increasingly felt left to their own devices.

We should consider other factors, too: the slow and incremental growth in the influence of patriarchs and rabbis as a result of their own aggressive self-promotion; the increasing importance of religion as a discrete category of existence as the emperors belatedly confronted the alarming spread of Christianity;[17] indeed, the same sorts of (mainly unknown) factors that favored the spread of Christianity. To repeat, though, the changes in Jewish Palestine in the late third century are only poorly attested and, if they occurred, were far from amounting to the systemic transformation that is well attested for the fourth century and following. It is to this process that we now turn.

---

[16] See S. Mrozek, "À propos de la répartition chronologique des inscriptions latines dans le Haut-Empire," *Epigraphica* 35 (1973): 13–18; R. MacMullen, "The Epigraphic Habit in the Roman Empire," *AJP* 103 (1982): 233–46.

[17] See J. B. Rives, "The Decree of Decius and the Religion of Empire," *JRS* 89 (1999): 135–54.

Laws[18]

A discussion of late imperial legislation in regard to the Jews will introduce us to a crucial set of ideological and social changes. It has been commonly thought since the days of Jean Juster, if not earlier, that such legislation was characterized by tension between the emperors' conservative tendency to continue to view the Jews as a licit collectivity, which enjoyed the full protection of the state and the right to practice its peculiar customs without disturbance, and their growing, theologically based conviction that those Jews who persisted in their religion were living a lie.[19] As the interests of the state became ever more closely identified with those of the church, especially from the reign of Theodosius I on, the legal position of the Jews declined. They increasingly suffered various disabilities: they were barred from service in the army and the government bureaus, forbidden to own slaves and build synagogues, and so on. As early as the later fourth century, imperial constitutions might classify (licit) Jews with (illicit) heretics and pagans for limited purposes.[20] By the early sixth century, this occasional similarity of status was approaching identity. It is tempting to view the condition of the Jews in the sixth century through the prism of the Christian Middle Ages. And yet, even under Justinian, Judaism, unlike paganism and heresy, was never declared illegal (nor was it in medieval Christendom).

This standard analysis seems mainly correct, as far as it goes, but it needs to be qualified and supplemented. We must, first, beware of translating the laws into human action in any simple way. Roman imperial laws were usually, though not always, reactive—responses to conditions brought to the emperor's attention by administrators or private citizens. Once issued, laws were technically applicable everywhere, but there is ample evidence that they were not, indeed could not be, everywhere enforced, that in some cases the emperors were lax about enforcing laws they themselves had made, even when they had the means to do so.[21] A concentration of constitutions and rescripts (imperial

---

[18] The best recent treatment by far is A. Linder, *The Jews in Roman Imperial Legislation* (Detroit: Wayne State University Press, 1987); some bibliographical but not conceptual updating of J. Juster's classic but now badly outdated book (*Les juifs dans l'empire romain*) may be found in A. M. Rabello, "The Legal Condition of the Jews in the Roman Empire," ANRW 2.13 (Berlin: DeGruyter, 1980, pp. 662–762.

[19] Or alternatively that both positive and negative legislation had a theological foundation (e.g., Rabello, "Legal Condition," 693).

[20] E.g., CTh 16.7.3, 383; Const Sirm 12, 407; CTh 16.5.44, 408; Const Sirm 14, 409, etc. And see Avi-Yonah, *Jews of Palestine*, pp. 213–20.

[21] The "classic" though possibly fictional case is that of Arcadius and the temples of Gaza in 400—see *Vita Porphyrii* 41; for a perhaps too optimistic discussion of the authenticity and date of this work, see H. Grégoire and M.-A. Kugener, *Marc le diacre: Vie de Porphyre évêque de Gaza* (Paris: Les Belles Lettres, 1930), introduction. But see now Z. Rubin, "Porphyrius of Gaza and

responses to legal questions sent by private citizens) on a certain issue around a certain date can inform us about the emergence of certain social tensions, and it can tell us how the emperor and his entourage tried to resolve such tensions. Perhaps we can even speak in some cases of rather loose and evanescent imperial policies, always modified by the need to pacify conflicting special interests.[22] But we cannot write social history from prescription. So, for example, it is important to note, as all scholars have done, the ever shriller rhetoric of imperial legislation about the Jews, in part because deepening imperial hostility, and the episcopal hostility that influenced it, are important per se as expressions of official ideology. But it is not legitimate to infer from either rhetoric or law alone that the conditions of Jews everywhere correspondingly deteriorated.

Even when understood in these more modest terms—as oblique reflections of social concerns and/or as expressions of imperial will—the laws about the Jews in the Theodosian Code are not at all conservative. By their very existence they constitute a significant innovation because they imply that by the late fourth century, the Roman state consistently regarded the Jews as a discrete category of humanity. I am suggesting that the state had not done so, at least not consistently, between the first and the fourth centuries. This suggestion is related to but rather different from the argument of the previous section of this book—that the Palestinian Jews did not enjoy autonomy in the high empire—and requires some additional argumentation.

While it is true that Julius Caesar, Augustus, and their Julio-Claudian successors recognized the right of the Jews to live according to their own laws, emperors after 66, or 135 C.E., seem rarely, if ever, to have passed laws concerning the Jews or to have had anything like a Jewish policy. The Jews had no legal "personality" or, at most, a rather thin and ephemeral one.[23] Martin Goodman argued, by contrast, that changes in imperial policy regarding the tax to the Jewish fisc in the first thirty years after its imposition in 70 constituted an attempt by the state to define the boundaries of the Jewish community. Thus, by trying to collect the tax from nonprofessing Jews and from gentiles (or, according to Goodman, Jews) who observed Jewish customs without formally converting (or acknowledging a formal connection) to Judaism, Domitian opted for a broad, "ethnic" definition, while Nerva made profession of Judaism the essential characteristic of Jewish identity (for the purposes of

---

the Conflict Between Christianity and Paganism in Southern Palestine," in A. Kofsky and G. Stroumsa, eds., *Sharing the Sacred: Religious Contacts and Conflicts in the Holy Land* (Jerusalem: Yad Ben Zvi, 1998), pp. 31–66, for an even more optimistic evaluation.

[22] See J. Harries, *Law and Empire in Late Antiquity* (Cambridge: Cambridge University Press, 1999), pp. 77–98.

[23] Contrast K. L. Noethlichs, *Das Judentum unter der römischen Staat: Minderheitenpolitik im antiken Rom* (Darmstadt: Wissenschaftliche Buchgesellschaft, 1996), pp. 76–90.

tax collection) and thereby contributed significantly to an alleged centuries-long shift of Judaism from ethnicity to religion.[24]

But this thesis seems implausible.[25] One of the abuses Domitian's "harshness" had made possible was *calumnia*, or denunciation (Suetonius, *Domitian* 12.2). Since he tried to collect the tax from people who for various reasons kept their Jewishness secret, it was now possible to inform on such "Jews" and thereby make them liable to the tax. That Nerva abolished such delation, as legends inscribed on some of his coins assert, does not automatically mean that he changed the rules in other respects. Nonprofessing Jews may still have been liable, though it would obviously have been harder to enforce such liability in the absence of delation, and some writers of the later second century do admittedly associate the tax with profession of Judaism. Even if Nerva did restrict the tax to professing Jews, then, we may infer from Suetonius's account, he would have simply been restoring the practice that had existed before Domitian's reign. What this most likely meant was that Nerva, probably like Vespasian and Titus before him, simply left determination of liability to the Jews themselves. Or perhaps collection was sold to an agent who, once again, was likely to be Jewish (and wealthy) or to have worked in close collaboration with Jews, since Jews are likely to have known who was liable to pay. In any case, sporadic imperial concern about liability for the Jewish tax hardly amounted to an enduring effort by the state to determine the boundaries of the Jewish community, the more so since there is no evidence for any further imperial interest in the question of liability after Nerva's death in 98. Indeed, the history of the tax after the middle of the second century is obscure, to say the least.

Similarly, sources of the second, third, and early fourth centuries, legal and otherwise, preserve remarkably little information about relations between the Roman state and the Jews.[26] The eccentric (so he later seemed) Christian Syriac writer Bardesanes claimed in his treatise *On Fate* (or, *On the Laws of the Regions*), composed in the later second or early third century, that (para. 43–44, my translation):

> All the Jews who received the Law through the hand of Moses circumcise their
> male children on the eighth day, and do not await the arrival of the stars, and do
> not observe the law of the region (in which they live), and the star which rules
> that region does not control them. But whether they are in Edom or Arabia or
> Greece or Persia, in the north or the south, they observe that Law given to them

[24] Goodman, "Nerva, the *Fiscus Judaicus*, and Jewish Identity," *JRS* 79 (1989): 40–44.

[25] Even aside from the fact that I am not fully convinced that such a shift, which Goodman takes for granted (following the arguments of S. Cohen: see the articles collected in his *Beginnings of Jewishness*), ever really occurred—at least not in quite the way that Goodman assumes.

[26] I am excluding the fictions of the Historia Augusta and the equally fictional stories of "Antoninus and Rabbi" in the Palestinian Talmud. Both reflect fourth-century conditions, if anything.

by their ancestors, and clearly do not do so because of their horoscope. For it is not possible that Ares rises for all the Jews who circumcise on the eighth day, so that iron crosses over them and their blood flows [44]. Wherever they live they do not worship idols and one day a week they and their children refrain from all work, from all building, from every journey, from buying, from selling; they do not slaughter animals on the seventh day, do not light fires, do not try cases. There is to be found among them no one whom Fate can command on the seventh day to be found innocent or guilty in a trial, to demolish or build, or to do anything that men who have not accepted this Law do.

Bardesanes is contrasting the Jews with the Arabs, for his interlocutors and audience not ethnographic exotica but part of their personal experience (*de-qariba lekon den detehezun hada*). As is well known, when the Romans seized (*ahdu*) Arabia, they abolished all the Arabs' earlier laws, especially their practice of circumcision. They failed to do the same to the Jews, Bardesanes implies.[27]

What Bardesanes left implicit was stated more openly by his African contemporary Tertullian: No one, the church father wrote (*Apologeticum* 21.1), should imagine that just because the Christians use the Hebrew scriptures, they are trying to draw on the the prestige of the older and more famous, *or*, Tertullian adds parenthetically, *at any rate, legal*, religion; in fact Christianity has nothing in common with Judaism. Scholars have tended to interpret Tertullian's comment more positively than its context warrants; indeed, scholars who argue for the essential friendliness of Roman–Jewish relations (give or take a few massacres) use Tertullian's phrase (*religio licita*) as a shorthand characterization of early and high imperial Roman policy. But Tertullian never implies that the legality of Judaism was a matter of state policy. On the contrary, Judaism is legal only in the sense that no one has ever bothered to declare it illegal, unlike Christianity.[28] Indeed, earlier in the same work,

---

[27] Bardesanes's assertion that the Jews all observe their own laws (the same claim is made about all the groups discussed in the ethnographic section of the treatise) is an aspect of his argument that the stars may control human passions but not their actions; humans have free will and so are subject to divine reward and punishment. If Bardesanes had admitted that people do not all observe their national laws, he would have had to admit the possibility that their behavior might be influenced by their horoscopes.

Bowersock, *Roman Arabia*, p. 79 n. 12, suggests that Bardesanes's comment refers not to the annexation of Arabia in 106 but to that of Mesopotamia by Septimius Severus.

[28] See Baer, "Israel, the Christian Church, and the Roman Empire," 84–86; cf. Hippolytus, *Refutatio Omnium Haeresium*, ed. M. Marcovich (Berlin: De Gruyter, 1986), p. 351: some Roman Jews, having been attacked in their synagogue by a Christian scoundrel, argue successfully before the urban prefect that "the Romans have permitted us to read our ancestral laws publicly." See also P. Garnsey, "Religious Toleration in Classical Antiquity," in W. J. Sheils, ed., *Persecution and Toleration*, Studies in Church History 21 (Oxford: Blackwell, 1984), p. 9, who characterizes the standard Roman approach to foreign religions as "toleration by default," since there was nothing the state could do about them. He claims that Judaism was the exception to

Tertullian describes what is probably the Jewish tax as the fine Jews are compelled to pay for their observance of the Jewish laws (*Apol* 18.9). This may not be meant entirely literally but may nevertheless reflect a common understanding of the relationship between those Jews who insisted on maintaining their separateness and the state: they were, barely, tolerated, and taxed.[29]

Other information on the status of the Jews in the high empire comes from much later legal sources. Two of the leading jurists of the early third century, Ulpian and Modestinus, preserved, respectively, fragments of a constitution and a rescript concerning the Jews, both extant in the Digest. According to Modestinus, Antoninus Pius had permitted the Jews to circumcise their sons, but not others (Digest 48.8.11; Linder, no. 1), while Ulpian wrote that Severus and Caracalla had "permitted those who follow the Jewish *superstitio* to acquire honors [i.e., serve as decurions], but also imposed on them such obligations [i.e., *munera publica*, liturgies] as do not harm their *superstitio*."[30]

The comments of Bardesanes and Tertullian may be taken to mean that the Jews were generally left to their own devices after 135, while the two legal fragments indicate that the Jews retained some of their traditional exemptions, *at least in theory.* For we must wonder why, if the state's intervention to preserve Jewish privileges was anything other than sporadic and ad hoc, there are so few laws (and no stories to speak of) about the conflicts between these privileges and the Jews' civic obligations—in sharp contrast to the situation in the first century. To be sure, our information is very incomplete. But why has rabbinic and Christian literature so little to report? Perhaps because the Jews' traditional privileges were in fact widely recognized and thus rarely generated conflict and new legislation.[31] But it would be very surprising if city councils throughout the eastern part of the empire suddenly acquiesced in a legal situation so disadvantageous to them—in that the Jews' traditional privileges had exempted them from many civic duties—after having resisted it for centuries previously.[32] Perhaps, rather, in many places the Jews themselves were disinclined to press their privileges, that is, they were willing to perform

---

this rule, but the evidence is all from the late republic and the first century of the empire. See also J. Rives, *Religion and Authority in Roman Carthage from Augustus to Constantine* (Oxford: Clarendon, 1995), pp. 234–49.

[29] Though a literal interpretation is not impossible—see E. M. Smallwood, *The Jews under Roman Rule* (Leiden: Brill, 1981), p. 345; cf. Origen, *Epistula ad Africanum* 28a (PG 11, col. 81).

[30] See commentary of Linder for interpretation; *superstitio* may be value-neutral, something like "religion."

[31] So F. Blanchetière, "Le statut des juifs sous la dynastie constantinienne," in E. Frézouls, ed., *Crise et redressement dans les provinces européennes de l'empire* (Strasbourg: AECR, 1983), p. 128; Rabello, "Legal Condition," pp. 686–90, argues that the silence of the sources is accidental and even that such lost legal collections of the third century as the "Codex Gregorianus" and the "Codex Hermogenianus" had separate chapters on the Jews.

[32] See Garnsey, "Religious Toleration," 11.

liturgies even if they "harmed their religion," and so on, much as many Palestinian Jews in the same period conformed without noticeable hesitation to the cultural and religious norms of city life.[33]

In sum, for most purposes, the Jews were subjects and later citizens like all others, not in any meaningful way a separate category of humanity. We may in general compare them to such groups as the priests of the Egyptian temples and Gallic religious experts, still in existence, still occasionally asserting traditional privileges, but much reduced, by a combination of official apathy and official hostility. In this reduced state, such people were not thought immune to the salvific power of Roman *civitas* and *humanitas*.[34] Similarly, the state tacitly allowed the Jews to do more or less as they pleased—a benefaction that the Jews either often declined or their neighbors almost never bothered to challenge. Perhaps the Roman state felt it could leave the Jews alone because it had already stamped out their religion in 70 C.E.; all that was left was a set of largely inoffensive private *mores*.[35] In any case, the state expressed little interest in the inner constitution of Jewish corporations (e.g., in the rights and privileges of their leaders) or in determining the legal and social boundaries between Jews and others. Indeed, there is reason to believe that, at least after the universal grant of Roman citizenship in 212, the state did not recognize the legal existence of the Jewish corporations at all.[36]

[33] Apart from the evidence cited in the last section for Jews in municipal office, see *CPJ* 3, no. 474: Aurelius Ioannes, most likely Jewish, gymnasiarch at Karanis, in 304. Were the Jews exempted from the imperial cult and/or the requirements to sacrifice imposed especially during the sporadic persecutions of Christianity? Remarkably, there is almost no ancient information on this question at all. A possible exception is Y. Avodah Zarah 5:4: "(Why is the wine of the Samaritans forbidden?. . .) Some would say that when King Diocletian came here [to Palestine], he decreed that all the nations must offer libations, except the Jews; the Cutheans [Samaritans] offered libations and so their wine was forbidden. Some would say, etc." What should we make of this? Probably it is one of several stories invented to explain the otherwise inexplicable prohibition of Samaritan wine. Even if it has a "historical kernel," it may have nothing to do either with the imperial cult or with the persecution of Christians (so Baer, "Israel, The Christian Church, and the Roman Empire," 119–28: Diocletian visited Palestine in 286 but did not persecute the Christians until 303). Modern scholars are divided over whether the Jews were exempt or not—see Juster, 1.339–54; Rabello, "Legal Condition," pp. 703–4; Smallwood, *Jews Under Roman Rule* pp. 539–44; Rives, "Decree of Decius," 138. Perhaps some Jews were able to convince local authorities that they did worship the emperor, in their own way, in the synagogues (why not? who knew what went on in there anyway? and why doubt the Jews if they were upstanding citizens otherwise?); other Jews may have participated.

[34] See, in general, Frankfurter, *Religion in Roman Egypt*; Woolf, *Becoming Roman*, pp. 206–37.

[35] See, pending publication of James Rives's discussion of this issue, G. Bohak, "Theopolis: A Single-Temple Policy and Its Singular Ramifications," *JJS* 50 (1999): 6–7; and note Cassius Dio's oddly periphrastic comment (37.17.1) that the Jews, though frequently persecuted in the past, have now (early third century) so grown in number that they have achieved the right to express their beliefs freely (*es parrhesian tes nomiseos eknikesai*).

[36] See CJ 1.9.1, dated 213, which denies to the *universitas Iudaeorum* of (Syrian?) Antioch the right to recover in court a legacy left them by one Cornelia Salvia; since the senate had not long

All this changed in the later fourth century. The emperors now explicitly recognized the Jews as a legitimate religious organization, with a clergy whose authority and privileges approximated those of the Christian clergy, and with the right to police their own boundaries of membership without state interference. This recognition should be seen not as traditionalism but as an innovation of the 380s and 390s, which in the end helped redefine the relation between the Jews and the state in a radical way (see below). Admittedly, the legislation of the late fourth century and following was no less reactive than that of earlier periods; the emperors were responding in part to changes in the position of the Jews in cities that were increasingly dominated by Christians. Whatever strategies the Jews had developed to cope with life in the pagan cities were, we may infer, no longer working. If these strategies consisted in part of religious eclecticism, as they had in high imperial Palestine, then it is easy to understand why: to be eclectically Jewish and pagan marked you as a successful accommodationist; but to be eclectically both Jewish and Christian marked you as a heretic.[37]

Recognition and Its Limits

The structural tension between the growing religious exclusivity of the Christian Roman cities, and the desire of some hitherto integrated Jews to retain a sense of separation, demanded assiduous imperial response. The emperors did so by both empowering and marginalizing the Jews, in effect declaring that the Jews were for most purposes a unique category of humanity, like neither orthodox Christians nor pagans and heretics, who were gradually outlawed. Some of the elements of official recognition have already been discussed in connection with the patriarchs. In brief, laws of the 380s and following consistently regard the Jews as constituting a religious community with an authoritative and privileged clergy. This clergy was based in local communities throughout the empire but derived its authority from its dependency on the patriarchs, who for several decades were ardently patronized by Theodosius I, Arcadius, and those who ruled on behalf of the child emperor Theodosius II. The patriarch's privileges were limited in a law of 415, and under unknown circumstances abolished about ten years later, perhaps with the death of Gamaliel "VI" (the identity and chronology of the patriarchs of the fourth and early fifth century are very obscure). Though the emperor, not the re-

---

before affirmed the right of *collegia licita* to claim legacies, this law probably implies that the Jewish community of Antioch, and by extension Jewish communities in general (?), had no legal standing. See the comments of Linder, no. 3. The suggestion of Rabello that the *universitas Judaeorum* was not the Jewish community (who, then?), is apologetic special pleading.

[37] A status far more dangerous than Jewishness, as a glance at the laws in CTh book 16 demonstrates.

maining Jewish officials, then inherited some of the patriarch's privileges, most importantly, the right to collect the so-called *aurum coronarium*, or *apostole* (CTh 16.8.29), there is no reason to think the Jewish *primates* were entirely stripped of their recognized authority over the Jews. At any rate, most of the laws granting them such authority were retained in the Codex Justinianus, promulgated over a century after the end of the patriarchate.

Several laws of the 390s are of special interest because their backgrounds are easy to reconstruct. They may thus enable us to learn something of the social pressures that helped precipitate this change. For example, in the case of CTh 16.8.8 (Theodosius I to Tatian, praetorian prefect of the East, Constantinople, 17 April 392), a group of Jews who had been expelled from the Jewish community in an unknown eastern location by the decision of the local communal leaders appealed to the provincial court, which restored them to their community; apparently the expelled Jews, by misrepresenting the facts of the case, had secured a favorable imperial rescript, whose decision the Roman judges were legally constrained to follow. In the law in question (not a rescript addressed to the injured *primates* but a constitution issued to a high imperial official), the emperor rectified the situation and concluded by recognizing the *primates'* jurisdiction over their own religion (*sua de religione sententiam*).

We would like to know more. Where did this incident occur? Why and how were the Jews expelled from their community, and how, precisely, did the decision of a Roman court secure their readmission? But for our purposes the law is important even without such details, indicating as it does the existence (though not the extent of the diffusion) of the partly self-governing Jewish community, which offered enough to its members that expulsion from it was something to be avoided. It implies the existence of a class of Jewish leaders, though as we have seen we should probably not assume that this class was well defined. And finally this law shows that the emperors recognized the existence and legal rights of the community and its leaders, as well as its authority to establish its own boundaries. But the law also implies a limitation: the Jews are a *secta*, followers of a *religio*, and their primates' authority is limited to the religious sphere.

This implication is spelled out in two laws of roughly the same period. The first of these is of interest because it supplements one of the other implications of the law just discussed, that the legal separation of the Jews from their neighbors suited the interests of (the? some?) Jews. In CTh 13.5.18, a law of 390 issued by Theodosius I to the governor of Egypt, it is the non-Jewish (presumably mainly Christian) citizens who benefit from the Jews' separation. The municipal, or perhaps imperial, administrators in Alexandria, or another Egyptian town, were in the habit of holding the local "corpus Iudaeorum" collectively responsible for the transport of grain to the capital cities (or rather, some share of it, presumably), in violation of the previous practice, in which the liturgy was incumbent on the college of ship owners. The emperor prohibits the innovation on the grounds that it is illegal to oblige small traders and other poor people to transport grain and, conversely, to reduce the obligation of the wealthy. In other words, when it comes to their *civic* obligations, the Jews do not constitute a separate body but remain citizens. The same conclusion emerges clearly from the emperors' repeated insistence that Jews, other than their clergy, are obliged to serve on city councils—the insistence presumably implying that in many places the Jews managed to avoid such service, which was both an honor and a burden.

The tension between Jews as a separate body and Jews as Roman citizens, and the related recognition of the Jews as members of a *religion*, is expressed most clearly in a law given by Arcadius to Eutychianus, praetorian prefect of the East, in 398 (CTh 2.1.10). Here the Jews are obliged to subject themselves to Roman laws, as well as Roman courts, in matters that pertain not to their superstition but to *forum, leges et iura*, that is, civil law. The law continues by recognizing the right of Jewish religious judges to serve as arbitrators in civil cases, a right, as already indicated, the emperor was in no position to deny. This may reflect the difficulties that some Jews may have had in distinguishing between religious and civil cases, but it does not subvert the principle that as far as the state is concerned, the Jews are separate from other citizens primarily with respect to their religion.

Marginalization

Neither the pagan nor the Christian Roman Empire was founded on an ideology of pluralism.[38] What changed under Christian rule was the emperors' promotion of *religious* uniformity—as opposed to cultural uniformity containing a diffuse and rather vague religious component. Notwithstanding what has just been said, many laws already in the fourth century move far in the direction of identifying Roman citizenship with orthodox Christianity. This theme emerges in an edict Theodosius I issued at Thessalonica in 380, shortly after his accession (CTh 16.1.2), in which he declared his desire that all his subjects "shall practice the religion which the divine Peter the Apostle transmitted to the Romans. . . . the religion that is followed by the Pontiff Damasus and by Peter, Bishop of Alexandria," that is, post-Nicene orthodoxy. Others were inevitably marginalized in the state ideology, however insistently the emperors declared their legality and their Romanness.

In the case of the Jews, marginalization took the form of actual legislation, not just general declarations, which are unlikely to have had any practical results except to inform them, along with the remaining nonorthodox, of the

---

[38] See Garnsey, "Religious Toleration," and in general Rives, *Religion and Authority*.

state's hostility, and the aforementioned insulting rhetoric (which is by the way not universally used in the laws). Several laws seem intended to prevent Jews from exercising any authority over Christians; hence, starting in 404, a series of laws remove Jews from service as imperial officials.[39] Likewise, the oft repeated prohibition of Jewish ownership of Christian slaves started under Constantine as an extension of the traditional Roman taboo against circumcision, since it was assumed that Jews would circumcise their male slaves (CTh 16.9.1; Const. Sirm. 4; issued 335). But it came to be an expression of opposition to the subjection of Christians by non-Christians.

Other laws seem to have different motivations. The emperors, before Justinian (see Novella 37, issued 535), consistently stated that synagogues may not be seized by Christians and destroyed or turned into churches. But starting with CTh 16.8.25 (Constantinople, 423; cf. 16.8.27, given several months later; Theod. Nov. 3, 438) they also forbade construction of new synagogues— perhaps a concession to the apparently numerous bishops and monks who opposed the imperial protection of synagogues. The prohibition of synagogue construction provides us with an important warning about the functioning of the law because, as is well known, the great age of synagogue construction in Palestine was in the fifth and sixth centuries, precisely the period when such construction was illegal.[40]

Social Consequences of Marginalization

The progressive marginalization of the Jews (of which the laws are an important manifestation) was not simply a matter of expulsion from government bureaus and military office, and theologically motivated prohibitions against synagogue construction. The laws, both the apparently friendly and the restrictive ones, can be viewed as components of a structural shift, in which the relations between the Jews and the state were radically redefined. The increasing importance of religion affected the structure and composition of the patronage networks that held the empire together. Although Peter Brown has

---

[39] CTh 16.8.17, Rome, 404, removing Jews and Samaritans from service as *agentes in rebus*, and all other imperial service; CTh 16.8.24, Ravenna, 418, prohibition of Jews as *agentes in rebus, palatini* and military officers, but permission of advocacy; Jews already in nonmilitary service shall not be expelled; Const. Sirm. 6, Aquileia, 425, Jews and pagans removed from government service and advocacy, "ne occasione dominii sectam venerandae religionis inmutent" (lest [Christians], because of the Jews' rule over them, exchange the venerable religion for a sect); Theodosii (II) Novellae, 3, Constantinople, 438, Jews and Samaritans barred from all government offices, including that of *defensor civitatis*; CJ 1.5.12, Constantinople, 527, all nonorthodox barred from civil and military offices. But Jews of the curial class were consistently liable for service as decurions, unless they were members of the clergy.

[40] Cf. Theophanes the Confessor, *Chronographia*, ed. De Boor, 1:, 102.

recently revised his classic argument about the importance of "holy men" as patrons in the late empire, by admitting that the traditional elites were never really fully replaced, and that the gulf between the bishops and the leading ascetics was not as wide as he had supposed, his more general point, about the potential utility of religious authority for the acquisition of prestige, and of dependents, seems unchallengeable.[41] We should perhaps suppose that one of the corollaries of this change was that the Jews' position in the conventional patronage structures was becoming increasingly unstable.[42] Indeed, the laws can quite easily be read as an attempt by the emperors to create for the Jews an alternate structure, in which the Jewish commoners are dependent on their *primates*, who are dependent on the patriarch, who is dependent on the emperor. Other avenues are *gradually* shut down (we will see presently that the emperors were in some cases trying to slow, to control, what was in some places a violent and disorderly process), and aristocratic Jews in turn are barred from acting as patrons to Christians and others.[43]

It is tempting to understand the well-known story of the conversion of the Jews of Minorca in 418, as told in the *Letter of Bishop Severus on the Conversion of the Jews*, as an example of how this shift could be played out in life. In brief, the arrival of the relics of St. Stephen on the island in 417 sent the inhabitants, especially Severus and the people of Iamona, his entirely Christian see, into such a state of religious enthusiasm that they attacked the large and socially prominent Jewish community of Magona, the larger of Minorca's two towns, and in effect compelled them to convert to Christianity. If we stand back a bit from this ominous story, we can easily grasp its broader importance. The leaders of the Jews of Magona were also the leading citizens of the town, its *patroni* and *defensores civitatis*,[44] well connected even in the

---

[41] See P. Brown, "The Rise and Function of the Holy Man in Late Antiquity," *JRS* 61 (1971): 80–101 = *Society and the Holy in Late Antiquity* (London: Faber, 1982), pp. 103–52; "The Rise and Function of the Holy Man, 1971–1997," *JECS* 6 (1998): 353–76.

[42] Venantius Fortunatus, Carmina v.5.17–20, composed c. 576 to celebrate the forced conversion of the Jews of Clermont in the Auvergne: plebs Arverna etenim, bifido discissa tumultu,/ urbe manens una non erat una fide./ Christocolis Judaeus odor resilibat amarus/ obstabatque piis impia turba sacris. This is quoted by B. Brennan, "The Conversion of the Jews in Clermont in AD 576," *JThS* 36 (1985): 328.

[43] Cf. the following passage in Pesiqta deRav Kahana (ed. S. Buber, 139b), a text of perhaps the sixth century: "the nations of the world count Israel and say, 'How long will you go on being killed for your God, and giving up your souls for Him? . . . How much pain does He inflict on you! . . . Come, join us, and we will make you *duces*, *eparchs*, and *stratelatai*.' And Israel enters its synagogues and study houses, and takes the Torah scroll, and reads in it . . . (then, at the End of Days) Israel says before the Holy One, Blessed Be He, 'Master of the Universe, if not for the Torah scroll which You wrote for us, the nations of the world would long since have corrupted us (so that we ceased to worship) You.' "

[44] The post was created in the 360s to protect the weak from the depredations of the powerful, and so the *defensores* had themselves to possess considerable *auctoritas* (CTh 1.29.1, 3). They were supposed to be nominated by the city council and the bishop, and, as of 409, were supposed

central government. One of the Jewish leaders was the son-in-law of Litorius, an important, rather surprisingly Jewish (or ex-Jewish) imperial official, the governor of the Balearics.[45] The climax of the story is the conversion of Theodorus, "even now" patron of the city, former *defensor* and leader of the Jews. Apparently his position had been unproblematic previously, but the intrusion of Severus and his followers into the affairs of Magona had made it untenable. His conversion is fairly openly described as an attempt to recover his prestige and power, and it is a successful attempt.[46] Theodorus publicly promises to convert and is given a tumultuous and heartfelt welcome by his Christian fellow citizens: "some ran to him affectionately and caressed his face and neck with kisses; others embraced him in gentle arms, while still others longed to join right hands with him or to engage him in conversation" (16.17–18).This story can be used to confirm the hypothesis that in broad terms, and in ideology if not always in practice, the Jews of the Roman Empire were given a choice—they could live as socially isolated communities, with internal hierarchies of dependence, under the protection of the emperor, or they could be integrated into the social fabric of the cities, but only as Christians.[47] The story also informs us that it was not uncommon in late antiquity, at least for a time, for Jews to have it both ways—to function both as discrete communities and as components of their towns—a situation I believe was relatively uncommon in the second and third centuries.[48] It is worth adding that Severus's forcible conversion was a violation of imperial laws, which consequently can be seen as not always successful attempts to regulate an often violent and disordered reality.

---

also to be orthodox Christians (CJ 1.55.8). For discussion, see S. Bradbury, *Severus of Minorca: Letter on the Conversion of the Jews* (Oxford: Clarendon, 1996), pp. 32–34.

[45] On the remarkable career and problematic religious identity of this man, see Bradbury, *Severus*, 34–37.

[46] 16.24–25, a Jew who has already converted tells the panic-stricken Theodorus, "If you truly wish to be safe and honored and wealthy, believe in Christ, as I too have believed. Right now you are standing and I am seated with bishops; if you should believe, you will be seated and I will be standing before you."

[47] Cf. the discussion in P. Brown, *The Cult of the Saints: Its Rise and Function in Latin Christianity* (Chicago: University of Chicago Press, 1982), pp. 102–5, which attempts, not very convincingly, to account for the marginalization of the Jews and others in terms tacitly borrowed from Mary Douglas. See the criticism of Carlo Ginzburg, "La conversione degli ebrei di Minorca (417–418)," *Quaderni Storici* 79 (1992): 277–89. I am not suggesting, of course, that *individual* Jewish communities, even apart from that of Minorca, were actually given such a choice: on Clermont and Orléans, in 576 and 585 respectively, see Brennan, "The Conversion of the Jews."

[48] The tendency of late antique Jews, especially but not exclusively in the western empire, to bury their dead without separation from Christians, but in graves marked iconographically as Jewish, may serve at least as a metaphor for, if not a proof of, the diffusion of this transitional condition; see the important discussion in Rutgers, *Hidden Heritage*, pp. 83–91. This phenomenon is attested even in Palestine; and note also *Beth Shearim* 2.164, the epitaph, probably of the later fourth century, of an apparent *vir clarissimus*—a low ranking senator—who was also an archisynagogue in Beirut.

But we should be careful. First of all, the story itself: while there now seem no grounds for suspecting the authenticity of the *Letter of Severus*,[49] its veracity is a different matter. Some episodes are questionable, the author knows too much about his characters' thoughts and motivations, and some of the characters are almost certainly invented.[50] But the letter is a social historian's dream, filled with plausible yet unexpected details about the social life of Magona. Perhaps this fact alone should impose restraint. But perhaps, too, it gives the story the value of a good historical novel: regardless of its truth, the story may still be useful as garnish or illustration, especially since its author apparently really did live on Minorca in the early fifth century.

How common were such events on Minorca? The ample evidence for the destruction of synagogues or their reconsecration as churches suggests at least that the episode was not unique, and the boom in synagogue construction elsewhere provides evidence that some Jews took the option of turning inward, of constituting themselves as religious communities, presumably protected but marginal.[51] We should certainly suppose, though, that the ideological shift in relations between the Jews and the state, which can be read with perhaps misleading ease in the law codes, masked messy social realities. For one thing, in real life, the process of marginalization proceeded at different rates in different places. Though the Jews of Magona were excluded from the system in the early fifth century, in Venusia, a rather similar sort of small town in Calabria (now Venosa, in the Basilicata), we hear of a Jewish *patronus civitatis* as late as the sixth century.[52] The "barbarian" law codes and church councils even later continue to prohibit many types of intimacy between Jews and Christians—intimacies that we may take as tracers for relations of social dependency.[53] It may be significant, though, that such references are far more common in the West than in the East, where, in relatively stable conditions, there may have been a closer connection between state ideology and social

[49] This is the main, and convincing, argument of the introduction of Bradbury, *Severus*; Stemberger, "Zwangstaufen," pp. 86–90, is characteristically inconclusive, while most historians have tended to assume the work's authenticity and essential veracity without discussion.

[50] See again the discussion of Bradbury, *Severus*.

[51] On the Palestinian synagogues, see below; the vast majority of Diaspora synagogues were built in the same period; see Rutgers, *Hidden Heritage*, pp. 125–35.

[52] See Noy, *Jewish Inscriptions*, 1, #114; for the date, see M. Williams, "The Jews in Early Byzantine Venusia: The Family of Faustinus I, the Father," *JJS* 50 (1999): 47–48. For an aristocratic Samaritan family at Scythopolis in the sixth century, whose members included *patroni civitatis* and even a Constantinopolitan senator who attained the illustrate, i.e., the highest senatorial rank (but who may have been Christian), see L. di Segni, "The Samaritans in Roman-Byzantine Palestine," in H. Lapin, ed., *Religious and Ethnic Communities in Later Roman Palestine* (Bethesda: University Press of Maryland, 1998), pp. 65–66. The legal position of Samaritans was somewhat different from that of Jews, as di Segni notes.

[53] See the summary presentation of this material in Parkes, *Conflict of the Church and the Synagogue*, pp. 379–86.

reality, though even there, the insistence that Jews exercise their curial responsibilities kept the door open to limited integration. Finally, the tendency to form inward-turning, partly self-enclosed religious communities was strongest in Palestine, where there remained a concentrated Jewish population. Even there, though, as we will see, there is evidence for conversion to Christianity, especially in the later fifth and sixth centuries. And it can scarcely be denied that throughout the East, the state's bargain with the Jews—protection in return for withdrawal—*began* to break down in the reign of Justinian.

Appropriation

What constituted the ideology that integrated the late antique Jewish world? First, it did *not* consist of the prescriptions and attitudes of the rabbis, though there is some evidence that they were assuming greater importance starting in the sixth century. Though the rabbis continued to exist and to have followers in late antiquity, certainly benefiting in the end from the marginalization of the Jews and their rejudaization, they themselves remained marginal in the Jewish world. Marginal, but not totally insignificant. Rabbinic Judaism was no more a completely discrete entity in late antiquity than it had been in the second and third centuries. The rabbis were constantly engaged with the attempt to assimilate and control the Jewish "little tradition," which explains their endorsement of the synagogue, but their ambivalence about some of its most striking characteristics (e.g., its decoration) and their no-less-pronounced ambivalence about the local religious community and the patriarchate. This engagement probably demonstrates a sustained attempt on the part of some rabbinic circles, already observed for the third century, to establish a foothold in the Jewish world, and to reach some sort of modus vivendi with nonrabbinic Jewish *primates*. One indication of the growing success of the rabbis' accommodative strategies in the sixth century is the emergence of the piyyut—its form borrowed from a popular type of Christian liturgical poetry of the period, its mood suffused with a sort of hieratic mystification that seems almost stereotypically Byzantine, but its content heavily and, it seems to me, sometimes self-consciously and even polemically rabbinic (though there may have been nonrabbinic piyyutim that did not survive).[54]

The Judaism that most late antique Jews shared was no less a product of christianization than the fact of their reemergence as a discrete religious entity. In the following chapters I will concentrate on what I regard as the most significant characteristic of late antique Judaism—the rise of the synagogue

---

[54] Or perhaps several of them do; see M. Sokoloff and J. Yahalom, *Jewish Palestinian Aramaic Poetry from Late Antiquity* (Jerusalem: Israel Academy of Sciences and Humanities, 1999), pp. 39–45.

and the local community which now became the chief organizing institutions of Jewish life and remained so until 1800; indeed, in an attenuated and altered form, down even to the present. In what way was this development a product of christianization?

The local Jewish community had certainly existed in the Diaspora as early as the third century B.C.E. But where we know about such communities, they turn out to have been simply a special manifestation of a general phenomenon. Groups of immigrants in Egypt, and elsewhere in the Hellenistic world, though they enjoyed a high level of integration in their environment, often formed compartmentalized corporations in order to preserve elements of their traditional cults by building temples dedicated to their national gods. The Jews were similarly integrated, and they formed similar corporations. Like the others, they built holy places—but synagogues, not temples—dedicated to the God of Israel. Some of these Jewish corporations appear to have been more durable than other ethnic corporations, and the fact that they built synagogues and not temples may help explain why. The corporations for which we have evidence were those that had internalized to some extent the monism and exclusivism of Torah-centered Judaism, and so they are likely to have remained more separate from their neighbors than other ethnic corporations. But some non-Jewish groups were probably as durable as the Jews (we know of a temple of Qos-Apollo in Hermopolis, Egypt, still functioning along traditional lines four centuries after its foundation in the second century B.C.E. by a group of Idumaean immigrants),[55] and it must always be recalled that the evidence favors the most separatist of the Jews—others would be unrecognizable (all these issues are discussed in more detail below). In any case, such corporations are very different from what is normally meant by a Jewish community.

In late antiquity, the local community became the predominant form of religious organization in rural Palestine, where it had never before been significant, as we know from the remains of synagogues discovered by archaeologists. What this development surely implies is the emergence of the local community as a full-blown social institution—no longer just a practical response to a set of perceived needs, as earlier in the Diaspora, but something freighted with significance, particularly, as we happen to know, religious significance, in its own right; it reflects, in sum, a comprehensive reorientation of Jewish life. These points are confirmed by the emergence, attested in inscriptions placed in late antique synagogues, of a new, ideologically loaded language used to refer to the community. The local community is now the Holy *Qehillah* or *Qahal* (roughly, congregation or assembly), or the Nation

---

[55] See E. Kornemann and P. Meyer, *Griechische Papyri im Museum des Oberhessischen Geschichtsvereins zu Giessen*, vol. 1 (Leipzig-Berlin: Teubner 1910–1912), no. 99; F. Zucker, *Doppelinschrift spätptolemäischer Zeit aus der Garnison von Hermopolis Magna* (Berlin, 1938), 13.

('*am* or *laos*), and in some places possibly even Israel—terms that in their original scriptural context refer to the community of Israel as a whole.

There are important gaps in our knowledge about these local religious communities. For example, we know nothing about the role of charitable foundations. They were an essential part of the medieval and modern Jewish community and are sporadically attested in rabbinic literature. But they are never mentioned in inscriptions and are invisible in archaeology.[56] But we do know that one of the main tasks of the community was to build and maintain a synagogue, which even in small villages was likely to be an elaborate structure decorated with surprising luxury and urbanity. Why did Jews begin to imagine their villages as loci of religious meaning and spend so much of their presumably unabundant surplus capital to construct monumental commemorations of their local religious autonomy?

Obviously, in the absence of detailed information we cannot answer such a question satisfactorily. But certain factors may be profitably considered. It is generally and plausibly thought that the great period of synagogue construction in Palestine, probably around 350–550, was also a period of unprecedented prosperity in Syria and Palestine. It is often considered a period when the village economy was unusually independent of urban influence, and unusually highly integrated—a view that seems to me far more speculative, based as it is on highly ambiguous archaeological remains, but especially on a single celebrated passage in Libanius's Eleventh Oration. Prosperity should mean that more surplus was available for rural construction projects, and rural economic integration can help explain the large-scale presence in the ancient synagogues of nonlocal items, although there is good evidence that many of these items came from cities or were made by craftsmen who did. If we accept this scenario, then we might conclude that the local community and the synagogue reflect an attempt by well-to-do villagers (who clearly were the main funders of the community and its institutions) to institutionalize local loyalties that increasingly lacked a real material foundation. At a time when most people's social connections were elsewhere, the old patrons felt the need to stress, by public commemoration, their honor and generosity all the more strongly.

But we should be careful of exaggerating the effects of the economic boom. It certainly did not benefit every town and village equally and, in any case, was not significant enough to alter the fact that in nucleated settlements, most social and economic relations presumably remained local. If, then, the religious community was deeply embedded in the rural economy and social structure, which were *basically* unchanged from what they had been previously,

<hr>

[56] With the remotely possible exception of the famous "godfearers" inscription from Aphrodisias: see J. Reynolds and R. Tannenbaum, *Jews and Godfearers at Aphrodisias*, Cambridge Philological Society Supplementary Volume 12 (Cambridge: Cambridge Philological Society, 1987), pp. 26–28. But Tannenbaum's interpretation is very implausible.

why did the community emerge only in the fourth century and following? In response, I would suggest that a purely socioeconomic approach is insufficient (as we should have expected in any case) because it leaves unanswered the question, Why synagogues? And why the community?

What we are actually witnessing is a change that, though it certainly had important social and economic causes and effects, was essentially cultural, and was not restricted to the Jews. As we will see, the entire Palestinian, and Syrian, landscape changed in late antiquity. The great period of synagogue construction was also the great period of church construction. The many important similarities and differences in detail between the village church and the village synagogue, as well as in the ideological factors that justified their construction (see below), cannot conceal the gross similarity in pattern: both Jews and Christians came to view the small settlement as religiously important and to some extent self-contained. Both acted on this idea by producing monumental construction and public writing that commemorated both the religious self-determination of the town or village and the generosity and piety of relatively well-to-do donors. Both synagogues and churches testify to the spread of the Greco-Roman urban culture of euergetism to the countryside and to the various transformations of that culture. And both point to the growing importance of religion in the self-understanding of the villagers. From the rise of the synagogue, we learn of the importance of appropriation in the construction of the novel Jewish culture of late antiquity. In the chapters that follow, I will examine these developments in greater detail.

SEVEN

A LANDSCAPE TRANSFORMED

Cities

THE LANDSCAPE of high imperial Palestine was dominated by the pagan city. It was there that wealth was concentrated, and there that patterns of expenditure generated by the Greco-Roman ideology of euergetism resulted in the production of monumental structures and public writing.[1] These were rare outside the city, but where they existed they were unambiguously derived from urban models—bathhouses and basilicas, marked with inscriptions in Greek. In Syria, large villages had long been important, and in the high empire, many aspired to be cities of the standard Greco-Roman type.[2] Smaller villages on the whole lacked monumental construction and public writing, except occasionally for monumental grave complexes.

By the fifth and sixth centuries, the landscape had been transformed. The cities remained important; indeed, some of them grew. Aelia Capitolina, a backwater in the high empire, became, as Christian Jerusalem, a metropolis with a population estimated at 50,000–80,000. Negligible desert settlements, such as Sobata, Mampsis, and Nessana, grew and some of even became cities—small (Elusa, the largest of the Negev settlements and the only one among them that was unambiguously a city, is thought to have had a population of about 10,000) and chaotically laid out, but cities all the same.

Jerusalem and the Negev cities were unquestionably anomalous. The tremendous growth of the former was obviously due to its importance in Christian theology; it was second only to Constantinople as an ecclesiastical center. The growth of the Negev cities is more problematic: recent surveys show that the northern Negev as a whole was surprisingly densely inhabited in the fifth and sixth centuries, and probably later. The well-known sites were all surrounded by villages and farmsteads, and winepresses are extremely common. The area as a whole is comparable to the limestone massif of northern Syria, another agriculturally marginal region that flourished under the later Roman Empire at a time when the density of population in adjacent, rainier areas was at its maximum.[3] The presence at Nessana, which was perhaps no more

---

[1] See G. Woolf, "The Roman Urbanization of the East," in S. Alcock, ed., *The Early Roman Empire in the East* (Oxford: Oxbow, 1997), pp. 1–14.

[2] See Millar, *Roman Near East*, pp. 17–23.

[3] See G. Tate, *Les campagnes de la Syrie du Nord* I, Institut français d'archéologie du proche-orient, Bibliothèque archéologique et historique 133 (Paris: Paul Geuthner, 1992).

than a village, of a caravansarai with ninety-six beds suggests something about the role of a possibly expanding commerce in the growth of the region.[4] It may at least be suggested that cultural changes (e.g., the sedentarization of desert tribes perhaps connected to their christianization) played a role, too.[5] Evidence for the growth of other Palestinian cities is more ambiguous: the walls of Caesarea and apparently Tiberias were extended, some formerly uninhabited districts of Scythopolis and Sepphoris became residential, and so on. But the consensual view that on the whole the urban population of Palestine increased in the late empire, an aspect of a general increase in population, seems entirely plausible.[6]

Less controversial is the transformation in character and physical appearance of the cities: where they had once been pagan in appearance, they were now Christian, though in many places older structures continued to be maintained and used. The Palestinian cities thus participated in changes that occurred throughout the eastern empire. Pagan temples were destroyed or turned into churches, theaters and amphitheaters fell into ruin or were filled in with market stalls or private houses, *agorai* and other public spaces became cramped bazaars and residential districts.[7] Monumental construction certainly did not cease and was not restricted to churches. The Tiberians built a new bathhouse in the fourth century, and the Sepphorites built lavishly decorated public buildings and a classical-style colonnaded street in the fifth.[8] But in general there was massively more public expenditure on religious buildings, and, conversely, much less expenditure on other types of public buildings than there had been previously.[9]

Though some of the Palestinian cities were notorious, at least among church fathers, for their resistance to Christianity—Gaza, Raphia, and Petra because of their inveterate paganism, and Tiberias and Sepphoris because of

[4] See C. J. Kraemer Jr., *Excavations at Nessana, vol. 3, Non-Literary Papyri* (Princeton: Princeton University Press, 1958), no. 31; on trade, see the discussion on pp. 26–28.

[5] On the Negev settlements, see the important discussion of C. Foss, "The Near Eastern Countryside in Late Antiquity," JRA suppl. 14 (1995): 225–31.

[6] See the surveys of Palestinian cities in Y. Tsafrir, *Eretz Israel*, pp. 317–32; Y. Dan, *The City in Eretz-Israel during the Late Roman and Byzantine Periods* (Jerusalem: Yad Ben Zvi, 1984), pp. 51–68. In general, Dan assumes more growth and provides slightly higher population figures, but his disagreements with Tsafrir are minor. For Sepphoris see, pending publication, the annual surveys in HA in the 1990s, and note also the comments of Netzer and Weiss, *Promise and Redemption*, pp. 9–10. For Tiberias, see the report of Y. Hirschfeld in HA 104 (1995): 32–38, and the discussion of Hirschfeld and G. Foerster in *NEAEHL*, s.v.

[7] However, see Foss, "Near Eastern Countryside," 226, who revives the view that urban planning broke down only in the seventh and eighth centuries.

[8] On the Tiberian bathhouse, see Y. Hirschfeld, "Tiberias," in *NEAEHL* 1466–67; on Sepphoris, Z. Weiss, "Sepphoris," in *NEAEHL* 1327.

[9] See Tsafrir and Dan; on the transformation of the late antique city, see M. Sartre, *Bostra: Des origines à l'Islam* (Paris: Paul Geuthner, 1985), pp. 119–39; H. Kennedy, "From Polis to Madina: Urban Change in Late Antique and Early Islamic Syria," *Past and Present* 106 (1985):

their Judaism—they all eventually became Christian or, rather, Christians came to predominate and the bishops to play leading roles in municipal affairs.[10] Tiberias and Sepphoris are not known to have had bishops before 449, but the partial reconstruction of the latter in the fifth and sixth centuries was in part a monument to the glory of the Church—so an inscription informs us.[11] Nevertheless, the coastal and Decapolitan cities retained some of their traditional diversity. Their populations included, in addition to Christians, Jews and probably dwindling numbers of Samaritans and pagans until the Muslim conquest.

Tiberias and Sepphoris, too, retained Jewish populations. Tiberias was of course the home of the patriarchs until the 420s, which obviously inhibited the spread of Christianity there, notwithstanding Epiphanius's fantasy about the patriarchs' crypto-Christianity. It apparently remained the center of the rabbinic movement in Palestine, and of the explosive literary production (the Palestinian Talmud, the Midrash collections, the *piyyut*, etc.) associated with it until and even for several centuries after the Muslim conquest.[12] Whether the Jews remained a majority in this period is unknown. It is surely noteworthy, though hardly probative, that the only synagogue remains so far discovered are in the northern and southern outskirts of the city (though the Talmud mentions a *kenishta deBoule*, presumably located in the center of the city).[13] Similarly, the insistence of the excavators that Sepphoris retained a Jewish majority under the late empire is baseless (though not necessarily false).[14]

Only during this period can we be certain that the Jewish inhabitants of the cities built synagogues. Though it would be perverse to doubt that there were synagogues in Tiberias, Sepphoris, and Caesarea earlier, the earliest archaeological remains of an urban synagogue—perhaps of any synagogue—in post-Destruction Palestine are from Hamat Tiberias, probably constructed in

---

141–83; M. Whittow, "Ruling the Late Roman and Early Byzantine City"; A. Zeyadeh, "Urban Transformation in the Decapolis," *Aram* 4 (1992): 101–15.

[10] See Dan, *City*, pp. 14–17, on paganism; 90–102, on the role of the bishops; on the Jewish cities, Epiphanius, *Panarion* 30; Theodoret of Cyrrhus, *Church History* 4.22 = GCS 44.260.

[11] On the bishops, see Avi-Yonah, *Jews of Palestine*, p. 168; contra Z. Rubin, "Joseph the Comes," Epiphanius, *Panarion* 30. 4.5 (= GCS 25.339) is very careful not to say that Tiberias had a bishop, either, it would seem, at the time of the writing in the 370s, or of the dramatic date of his story, in the reign of Constantine. On the reconstruction of Sepphoris, see E. Netzer and Z. Weiss, "Sepphoris, 1991–2," *IEJ* 43 (1993): 190–96; the Duke University excavators claimed that the faunal remains from the city changed from mainly sheep and goats in the high empire to mainly pigs in the sixth century: E. Meyers, C. Meyers, and K. Hoglund, "Sepphoris," *IEJ* 45 (1995): 68–71.

[12] See R. Brody, *The Geonim of Babylonia and the Shaping of Medieval Jewish Culture* (New Haven: Yale University Press, 1998), pp. 100–109.

[13] Kenishta deBoule: Y. Sheq. 7:5, 50c (the story assumes the central location of the synagogue), Y. Taan. 1:2, 64a; synagogues of Tiberias: Hirschfeld, "Tiberias," 1468–70.

[14] See Weiss and Netzer, *Promise and Redemption*, p. 9.

the early or middle fourth century.[15] Rather surprisingly, the urban synagogues (unlike the prayer house of first-century Tiberias described by Josephus, Life 277) are invariably small structures, frequently situated in remote or inconspicuous locations. The synagogue complex of Hamat Tiberias measures only 13 by 15 meters, the newly discovered synagogue of Sepphoris is 20 by 8 meters, and the main hall of one of the largest, that of Hamat Gader, measures 13 by 13.9 meters—approximately the same size as most rural synagogues.[16] No counterpart has yet been discovered in Palestine to the massive, centrally located synagogue of Sardis.[17]

The urban synagogues did differ from the rural ones, though: there seem often to have been more than one per settlement (two are known from Tiberias, Sepphoris, and Scythopolis), and they occasionally used Greek in inscriptions.[18] Furthermore, urban synagogues were often much more lavishly decorated than rural ones: they tended to make more use of marble, and several, most strikingly those of Hamat Tiberias, Sepphoris, and Gaza, are decorated with magnificent figurative mosaic pavements. Nevertheless, they seem on the whole contemporaneous with the rural synagogues, and apparently they did not serve as models for the latter, unlike urban churches, which were imitated by architects in the Christian countryside. Though the essential structure and many of the motifs of the pavement of the synagogue of Hamat Tiberias were taken up in later synagogues, there is no evidence of direct imitation. The ideological underpinnings of the urban synagogues, as revealed in the inscriptions, likewise bear comparison with those in the countryside (see below). There is, in sum, no physical evidence for a city-based hierarchy of synagogues in late antique Palestine, a point that will be discussed in more detail below.

Villages

The transformation of the landscape of rural Palestine in late antiquity was if anything even more striking than that of the cities. The countryside was now packed with nucleated settlements, ranging in population from several hundred to several thousand inhabitants. If the surface surveys may be trusted (and though they are questionable in every detail, they *may* cumulatively paint a plausible picture of the true situation, especially since they correspond so

[15] See Dothan, *Hammath Tiberias*, pp. 66–67.

[16] For a full list of the dimensions of the synagogue remains, see Hachlili, *Ancient Jewish Art*, p. 148.

[17] See A. T. Kraabel, "The Diaspora Synagogue: Archaeological and Epigraphic Evidence since Sukenik," ANRW 2.19.1, pp. 483–88.

[18] Contrast Naveh's mainly rural corpus of Aramaic inscriptions and Lifshitz's mainly urban corpus of Greek inscriptions.

well with the well-attested situation in northern Syria), many more such villages existed in late antiquity than at any earlier period.[19]

One novel characteristic of these villages was, if we follow a recent suggestion of Benjamin Isaac, that while as late as the early mid-fourth century they were commonly inhabited by mixed populations of pagans, Jews, and some Christians, there was a tendency later toward religious separation.[20] Most villages came to be either Jewish or Christian, or perhaps pagan. As early as the 370s Epiphanius could regard the largest settlements of Galilee, Tiberias, Sepphoris, and Capernaum as exclusively Jewish, though this is likely to be a polemical exaggeration.

By about 500, the pattern of separation was clearly defined, and it is confirmed by another fundamentally important novelty of the late antique rural Palestinian landscape: all but the very smallest villages had at their center, often set in a paved square, a monumental, purpose-built, stone religious building.[21] In fact, villages usually had either churches or synagogues, not both. There were exceptions. Some were like the extremely large village of Capernaum, located in the heart of Jewish Galilee, but also a Christian pil-

---

[19] See M. Kochavi et al., *Judaea, Samaria, and the Golan: Archaeological Survey, 1967–68* (Jerusalem: Keter, 1972), and the important discussion in H. Lapin (forthcoming) containing a complete survey, analysis, and criticism of surface surveys of late antique material in Israel and the territories; see also Y. Hirschfeld, "Changes in Settlement Patterns of the Jewish Rural Populace before and after the Rebellions against Rome," *Cathedra* 80 (1996): 3–18 — noting the scattered evidence for farmsteads in late antique Judaea and Samaria, and the absence of such evidence for Galilee (implying, Hirschfeld believes, that the Jewishness of the Galileans, which meant that they were organized in communities, required them to live in nucleated settlements). This is an interesting phenomenon, which requires some sort of explanation. But Hirschfeld overlooks the obvious point that even in Judaea most people lived in villages, not on farmsteads. Note also J. Pastor's point in response to Hirschfeld that the evidence for late antiquity is continuous with that of the Second Temple period: farmsteads were never common in Galilee and never absent from Judaea and Samaria ("Why Were There No Jewish Farmsteads in Galilee?" *Cathedra* 84 [1997]: 175).

[20] B. Isaac, "Jews, Christians, and Others in Palestine: The Evidence from Eusebius," in *Jews in a Graeco-Roman World*, pp. 65–74; on the separation of Jews and Christians, see M. Aviam, "Christian Settlement in Western Galilee in the Byzantine Period" (master's thesis, Hebrew University, 1994).

[21] It is less clear whether Galilean villagers, like those in northern Syria in the later fifth century, also built substantial, often heavily decorated stone houses — one of the striking characteristics of the region surveyed by Tchalenko. The evidence of the Meiron excavations suggests that on the whole they did not, but Meiron may have been abandoned before 500, when Syria reached the peak of its prosperity (E. Meyers et al., *Excavations at Ancient Meiron, Upper Galilee, Israel, 1971–72, 1974–75, 1977* (Cambridge: ASOR, 1981), pp. 50–65; 158–61, on the abandonment of the site). In general, Galilee gives the impression of having been less prosperous than the northern Syrian limestone massif, but this impression may be false: the limestone massif was a marginal area, inhabited mainly under Roman rule and abandoned once and for all in the early Middle Ages. Galilee has been continuously inhabited, and ancient stone structures are in general unlikely to have survived later inhabitants' need for building materials.

grimage site. Others were Jewish villages that became Christian, perhaps like
er-Rama, in western Galilee.[22] A very few villages had two churches or two
synagogues (Kefar Baram, for example), probably the result of the synoecism
of two originally separate settlements.

The precise numbers of churches (there were many hundreds)[23] and synagogues (commonly said to be around 100 or 120)[24] indicated by the remains
are impossible to establish because in many cases the remains are merely
suggestive. For example, many of the Upper Galilean sites surveyed by Z. Ilan
yielded only fragments of monumental structures. Some or all of these could
indeed have been from synagogues, as Ilan assumed, especially since earlier
observers had documented what they regarded as the remains of synagogues
at many of the sites. But many could just as well have been from churches,
or the large stones may have been brought from elsewhere for use in later
structures.[25] Notwithstanding the many doubtful cases, though, patterns of
geographical distribution emerge clearly: the churches were heavily concentrated in Judaea and in the district of Akko-Ptolemais, northwest of Upper
Galilee, while the synagogues were concentrated in eastern Galilee and western Golan. In western Galilee, the Carmel region, the Beth Shean Valley,
and southern Judaea, there were looser concentrations of both churches and
synagogues.[26]

Dates

There were certainly many more such structures than have been discovered.
Given the small size of the settlements in which some of the buildings were
found, it seems reasonable to follow the consensus of archaeologists and historians in concluding that by the later fifth or early sixth centuries, almost every
village in Palestine, except perhaps the very smallest, had either a church or
a synagogue.[27]

Unlike the Jews, the Christians tended to record the dates of construction
and renovation of their religious buildings in dedicatory inscriptions. (The

[22] On the christianization of some Jewish villages in southern Judaea, see J. Schwartz, *Jewish Settlement*, pp. 107–9.

[23] Ovadiah lists 265 sites in *NEAEHL*, but many of these were pilgrimage sites and monasteries that contained more than one church.

[24] See Levine, "Synagogues," in *NEAEHL*.

[25] See Z. Ilan, "Survey of Ancient Synagogues in Galilee," *EI* 19 (1987): 170–207.

[26] See most conveniently the maps in Y. Tsafrir, L. DiSegni, and J. Green, *Tabula Imperii Romani: Iudaea-Palaestina* (Jerusalem: Israel Academy of Sciences and Humanities, 1994). Similar maps appear in *NEAEHL*.

[27] E.g., Y. Tsafrir, in *Ancient Churches Revealed* (Jerusalem: Israel Exploration Society, 1993),
p. 4; D. Urman, *The Golan* (Oxford: BAR, 1985), p. 93.

Jews' general failure to date synagogues and graves is a puzzling fact that will not detain us here.) So we know that the great age of rural church construction in Palestine was the middle and later fifth century, with considerable activity continuing through the sixth. The buildings were remarkably uniform—overwhelmingly apsidal, and later triapsidal, basilicas, though a small number were octagonal. In both cases, the models were the great Constantinian urban and pilgrimage churches.[28]

By contrast, the dating of the synagogues is, as I have already suggested, controversial and their architecture was, uncontroversially, highly varied.[29] What is often forgotten is that the controversy about dating attaches to only one category of synagogues. Otherwise, there is general agreement on several important issues. First, the basic version of the old tripartite typology (Galilean/"broadhouse"/apsidal basilica) elaborated by Avi-Yonah from the work of Kohl and Watzinger and Sukenik can no longer be maintained, since many of the synagogues discovered since the 1960s have failed to conform to any of the old categories. Second, even those who retain an early dating for the "Galilean" type do not deny a late antique date for the other types, and presumably would not hesitate to depend on stratigraphy and other ostensibly objective criteria to date synagogues that conform to no type. In sum, even followers of Avi-Yonah would have to admit, if they applied their own methods rigorously, that the synagogue did not reach its maximal diffusion until the fifth or sixth centuries. In practice, though, Israeli scholars, who are now almost alone in believing that the Galilean synagogues were built in the later Severan period (and even among them consensus is breaking down; see below), tend to regard them as already an essential component of the Jewish village.[30] The matter is thus worth a brief discussion.

[28] Tsafrir, *Ancient Churches Revealed*, pp. 2–16. There is no corpus of (the hundreds of) Palestinian church inscriptions, though they will presumably be included in the data-base/corpus now being prepared at Tel Aviv University. Meanwhile, most convenient, though seriously out of date, is M. Avi-Yonah, "Mosaic Pavements in Palestine," in *Art in Ancient Palestine*, pp. 283–382, supplemented by A. Ovadiah and R. Ovadiah, *Hellenistic, Roman, and Early Byzantine Mosaic Pavements in Israel* (Rome: L'Erma di Brettschneider, 1987). For a discussion of the dated inscriptions, see L. Di Segni, "Epigraphic Documentation on Building in the Provinces Palaestina and Arabia, Fourth-Seventh Centuries," in J. H. Humphrey, ed., *The Roman and Byzantine Near East*, (JRA suppl. 31 (1999)): 149–78.

[29] A few synagogues are dated: that at Nabratein to 562 (see below); Gaza, 508 (Lifshitz, *Donateurs* 73a = CIJ 2.967); an inscription from Ascalon dates a gift to the synagogue there to 604 (Lifshitz, *Donateurs* 70 = CIJ 2.964); the mosaic pavement at Bet Alfa was made in the reign of Justin (Naveh, *Al Psefas* 43); the reasons given by most commentators for preferring Justin I (reigned 518–527) over Justin II (567–578) are inadequate. For a convenient set of plans of Palestinian synagogues, see Hachlili, *Ancient Jewish Art*, pp. 144–47.

[30] E.g., Z. Safrai, *Jewish Community*. Strikingly, even L. Levine, who rejects the old typology, nevertheless regards it is indubitable that the synagogue functioned as the central institution in Jewish communities (i.e., presumably, towns) "everywhere" in the second and third centuries: *The Ancient Synagogue* (New Haven: Yale University Press, 2000), pp. 171–72. Even among

One of the most serious problems with the old chronology was a piece of information long known but easily dismissed because of its uniqueness. A dedicatory inscription carved on the meticulously classicizing lintel of the supposedly early synagogue at Nabratein unambiguously dates the construction—not restoration—of the synagogue to the 494th year after the Destruction, that is, c. 562.[31] This fact, as Naveh long ago observed, should have caused archaeologists more unease than it apparently did.[32] Recently, in another blow to the old typology all the more serious for having been delivered by an Israeli archaeologist, concerning synagogues regarded as "early" (mid-late third century) by their American excavators, it has been argued that the synagogues of Gischala and Horvat Shema were actually built in the fourth century.[33]

There is no question, though, that the major blow to the early dating of the Galilean type synagogue was the discovery of thousands of low-denomination bronze coins of the fourth and early fifth centuries beneath the floor of the synagogue of Capernaum—a flagship example of the type. In fact, such deposits (which must be distinguished from treasury hoards) are commonly found in the excavation of ancient synagogues; whatever their purpose may have been, they were certainly intentional.[34] In most such cases, archaeologists have not hesitated to draw the obvious conclusion: the synagogue was constructed after the date of the latest coin in the deposit. But deeply ingrained conservatism and loyalty to Avi-Yonah as chief representative of the new tradition of Israeli archaeology (combined perhaps with a mild suspicion of the Franciscan excavators—a suspicion in fact justified by the questionable quality

---

scholars who retain the old typology, "early" has become subtly later in the past few decades; one no longer reads about second-century synagogues. It should also be noted that consensus is beginning to dissolve even among Israeli scholars: see below for E. Netzer's recent redating of several Galilean-type synagogues to the fourth century. R. Hachlili, a prominent follower of Avi-Yonah in most respects, has now discarded his chronology of the synagogues in favor of an approach based on regionalism; see her contribution to S. Fine, *Sacred Realm: The Emergence of the Synagogue in the Ancient World* (New York: Oxford University Press, 1996), pp. 98–111. But the majority of Avi-Yonah's students in Israel remain faithful, for reasons that seem to me to have more to do with the sociology of the Jewish studies establishment there than with anything else.

[31] It seems to me likely that the inhabitants of Nabratein would have used an erroneous chronology like that of the Seder Olam Rabbah, rather than the more accurate tradition preserved by the Christian chronographers, to date the destruction of the Second Temple. For discussion of Nabratein, see Levine, *Ancient Synagogue*, pp. 298–99.

[32] *On Mosaic*, p. 31, for the inscription; p. 4, for discussion of dating. Naveh rather precociously regarded the old typology as discredited already in this book.

[33] See E. Netzer, "The Synagogues in Gischala and Khirbet Shema: A New Look", *EI* 25 (1996): 450–54. I have recently heard it argued by the American archaeologist Jody Magness that these synagogues were built in the sixth century.

[34] See, e.g., Z. Ilan, "The Synagogue and Bet Midrash of Meroth," in R. Hachlili, ed., *Ancient Synagogues in Israel, Third through Seventh Centuries CE*, BAR International Series 499 (Oxford: Tempus Reparatum, 1989), pp. 21–41, esp. p. 27

of much of their work) were not the only reasons, important as they were, for the Israeli archaeologists' denial of the obvious in the case of Capernaum.

In a major recent article, Z. U. Maoz offered three kinds of argument in support of the old chronology.[35] The first two, from stratigraphy and history, need not detain us. His stratigraphic arguments for dating synagogues like those of Meron and Gischala to the early third century appear at first glance, at least to the nonarchaeologist, to have a certain rough plausibility; but in fact they are only rationalizations, amounting to no more than the claim that the stratigraphy can be reconciled with a dating to the early third century, not that it makes such a dating likely. Maoz's argument about Capernaum—that the synagogue was built elsewhere in the early third century and then moved, stone by stone, to its present site in the fifth—is special pleading[36] (though I have recently heard it publicly praised, if not precisely endorsed, by Mordechai Aviam). The argument from history may be unhesitatingly dismissed, depending as it does on the supposition that Rabbi Judah I was in effect king of the Jews—a supposition derived from a misreading of both rabbinic literature and the works of Origen. The final argument, from style, is more compelling. The resemblance of the Galilean synagogues to buildings constructed in the second and third centuries, especially the southern Syrian shrines surveyed by Butler around the turn of the century, is undeniable, and Maoz fortifies this main point with a good deal of circumstantial detail, the truly novel aspect of his article.[37] But even this is unconvincing in the end. Why should the resemblance of the synagogues to the Syrian shrines prove that they were built at the same time? The shrines, after all, probably remained in use into the fifth century, and some of them are standing to this day. Some Galilean villagers, when they decided to build synagogues, may have wished them to look appropriately "sacred." Before the fifth century, the only available models were the shrines built (and still maintained) by the pagan villagers in the neighboring districts; monumental churches, later an important model for synagogue builders, were still rare. Once in use for synagogues, there is no reason the Galilean style should not have remained in use through the sixth century.[38] An important component of the old chronology, it is worth remembering, is a view no longer tenable since the emergence of late antiq-

[35] "When Were the Galilean Synagogues First Built?" *EI* 25 (1996): 416–26.

[36] This argument has now been published in English: "The Synagogue at Capernaum: A Radical Solution," in *Roman and Byzantine Near East* 2: 137–48.

[37] Much of which, though, consists of results of studies of architectural features that posit excessively specific chronologies of the sort one would have imagined long since discredited.

[38] As even Y. Tsafrir admitted, in an earlier attempt to salvage the old chronology; see "The Synagogue at Meroth, the Synagogue at Capernaum, and the Dating of the Galilean Synagogues: A Reconsideration," *EI* 20 (1989): 337–44. But he regarded the definitely late examples, e.g., at Meroth, to be characterized by crudity of workmanship, a view refuted by the synagogue of Nabratein.

uity as a discrete field of study (and therefore lives on as a prejudice), that is, that high-quality "classical" architecture and design were impossible after the middle of the third century and that therefore high quality implies an early date, and crudity a late date. In reality, apparent differences in quality tell us more about social and economic differences, or differences in esthetic sensibilities or religious predispositions, or about the prejudices of scholars, than about chronology.

A Booming Economy?

Since the classic study of G. Tchalenko, it has been commonplace to explain the explosion in construction in Syria and Palestine in late antiquity by supposing that there was an economic boom between the fourth and sixth centuries; more recently it has been argued that the era of prosperity continued even beyond the middle of the sixth century, to the very eve of the Muslim conquest.[39] Tchalenko argued that the boom was related to the rise of olive monoculture in some areas, but this view now needs to be qualified.[40] It has more recently been suggested that the boom was fueled by developments outside the traditional eastern Mediterranean economy, especially in Arabia, the evidence for which is that pre-Islamic Arabic poems sometimes mention products imported from Syria.[41] The influence of the rise of Constantinople on the Syrian economy should also be considered.

In addition to factors that affected Syria generally, Palestine was the beneficiary of Christian theology, which led to extensive investment by the emperors and other grandees in ecclesiastical and monastic foundations. But Avi-Yonah was right to be equivocal about the effects of Christianity on the Palestinian economy. Much Christian investment had only short-term consequences; for example, church construction created only brief spurts of demand for labor. And much investment was absolutely unproductive: all the silver plate depos-

[39] See G. Tchalenko, *Villages antiques de la Syrie du nord*, 3 vols. (Paris: Paul Geuthner, 1953–1958); for reservations about some of Tchalenko's conclusions, see G. Tate, "La Syrie à l'époque byzantine: Essai de synthèse," in J.-M. Dentzer and W. Orthmann, eds., *Archéologie et Historie de la Syrie ii* (Saarbrücken: Saarbrücker Druckerei und Verlag, 1989, pp. 96–116. For arguments that the boom lasted into the seventh century, see M. Whittow, "Ruling the Late Roman and Early Byzantine City."

[40] Tate, *Les campagnes*, demonstrated that the limestone massif had been inhabited since the first century, that its economy depended heavily on grain culture and livestock, and that the villages in the region were more traditionally rural—more agriculturally oriented, less planned, less economically diverse—than Tchalenko had supposed. Nevertheless, he too attributed the burst of construction in the late fifth century to the production of olive oil, marketed not internationally but mainly to the surrounding cities.

[41] See Sartre, *Bostra*, pp. 119–39.

ited in the great churches came ultimately out of the taxpayers' pockets and benefited only the invaders who plundered it.[42]

The remains of churches and synagogues are among the most important evidence for a boom in northern and central Palestine. In the aggregate, the construction seems to imply the availability of unexpected quantities of surplus in what we might have supposed was a standard rural subsistence economy. And both churches and synagogues were often built and decorated—sometimes surprisingly lavishly—by artisans from urban workshops who probably expected to be paid in cash.[43] For example, though marble fixtures and mosaic pavements were more common in urban than in rural synagogues, they were not unknown in the latter. Marianos and Aninas, who signed their names to the mosaic of the Bet Alfa synagogue in Greek, also made part of the floor of the Samaritan synagogue of Scythopolis: probably they were based there.[44] Likewise, Rusticus, the stonemason who built the synagogue of Dabbura, in the western Golan, signed his name in Greek and is likely to have come (despite his name!) from Caesarea Philippi or Akko (Naveh, *On Mosaic*, no. 7). This would imply the easy availability of not only surplus but also gold coins. A surprising level of monetization, which conforms with Tchalenko's hypothesis that the economy of rural late antique Syria was heavily market-oriented, is also implied by the coin "treasuries" (which may in fact be private funds) discovered in at least thirteen synagogues.[45]

But we should not underestimate the extent of communal exertion involved in the construction, and the likelihood that it was often done piecemeal over many years. Here, the mosaic of the Bet Alfa synagogue is once again instructive, for the dedicatory inscription on it states, if it has been correctly read, that the villagers had to collect and sell one hundred *se'in* of wheat in order to pay the mosaicists, and this in a village only six kilometers—an hour's brisk walk—from Scythopolis, the capital of Palaestina Secunda.[46] As to the synagogue treasuries, though some are very rich, most of them contain only bronze coins, which had no stable value. In some cases the treasury hoards were the result of centuries of collection.[47]

---

[42] See M. Avi-Yonah, "The Economics of Byzantine Palestine," *IEJ* 8 (1958): 39–51.

[43] Gifts commemorated in inscriptions are almost always in cash or at least are evaluated in cash.

[44] See L. Roth-Gerson, *Haketovot Hayevaniot Mibattei Keneset Be'eretz Yisrael* (Jerusalem: Yad Ben Zvi, 1987), p. 33.

[45] See A. Kindler, "Donations and Taxes in the Society of the Jewish Villages of Eretz Israel during the Third to Sixth Centuries CE," in *Ancient Synagogues*, pp. 55–59.

[46] See Naveh, *On Mosaic*, p. 43, for this interpretation of the inscription.

[47] The largest hoard, at Meroth, contained 485 coins, of which 245 were gold, of various denominations, with a value estimated at 17,874 folles, or 2,235 man/days of work. The bulk of the coins are dated from the reign of Anastasius (491–518), to that of Phocas (d. 609), six are from the fourth century, and additional coins were added to the treasury until 1193. See Ilan, "Synagogue and Bet Midrash of Meroth," 30–31.

In sum, it is not unlikely that late antiquity was a period of unprecedented prosperity in Palestine, as in Syria. But this alone cannot explain the burst of synagogue and church construction. Contrary to what some scholars have assumed, there is no reason to think that most Jewish villagers before the fifth century regarded a synagogue as an essential component of their settlement. And the Bet Alfa mosaic at least warns us that even in late antiquity, the construction and decoration of a monumental building was no trivial matter for a village. The source of surplus needed for the construction of the synagogues may well have been a strong economy, but the choice of how to use it has no necessary connection with the economy per se.

EIGHT

ORIGINS AND DIFFUSION OF THE SYNAGOGUE

THE SYNAGOGUE was not invented in late antiquity. By the time it reached the point of its greatest diffusion, it had been in existence for at least eight hundred years. What follows is intended as a warning against overestimating the social and cultural importance of the synagogue before late antiquity.

Such a warning is necessary because Judaic scholars are often overly concerned with origins. In one recent article, "the problem of the synagogue's origin" is declared "one of the most important issues in the history of the Jewish people." And the "invention" of the synagogue, that is, of institutionalized communal participatory prayer and study without a sacrificial cult, is sometimes said to have constituted a revolution, not just in Judaism but in religion in general.[1] The synagogue was, in this view, one of the most important elements of Judaism's alleged "democratization," to use Shaye Cohen's term, in the Second Temple period.[2]

There is nothing wrong a priori in trying to recover originary moments. Aside from their inherent interest (which I think even the most analytically inclined historians could not honestly deny), they may help us, if only in some small way, to understand the dynamics of change. Nevertheless, there is something disquieting in allowing narratives of origins to dominate accounts of the history of an institution or an ideological system, as it has to some extent in the case of the synagogue. For such a narrative tends to presuppose that genesis determines destiny—an essentialist notion that, if not entirely false, is surely simplistic.

From the perspective of a history concerned with the questions of how past societies functioned and why they changed, the obsession with origins, even when they are not unrecoverably obscure, as those of the synagogue are, is problematic for two additional reasons. First, at its point of origin a phenomenon may have been little more than a subcultural, or even a personal, peculiar-

---

[1] R. Hachlili, "The Origin of the Synagogue: A Re-assessment," *JSJ* 28 (1997), 34; S. Cohen, "Pagan and Christian Evidence," p. 160: "The invention of the synagogue was a revolutionary step in the development of ancient Judaism, indeed, of ancient religion generally." See already M. Hengel, "Proseuche und Synagoge: Jüdische Gemeinde, Gotteshaus, und Gottesdienst in der Diaspora und in Palästina," in G. Jeremias, H.-W. Kuhn, and H. Stegemann, eds., *Tradition und Glaube: Das frühe Christentum in seiner Umwelt, Festgabe für Karl Georg Kuhn zum 65. Geburtstag* (Göttingen: Vandenhoeck & Ruprecht, 1971), p. 158. And note Levine, *Ancient Synagogue*, p. 1.

[2] E.g., S. Cohen, *From the Maccabees*, p. 22, 66–68; and so in almost every one of the many collections of essays about the ancient synagogue that have appeared in the past fifteen years.

ity, of no special importance in the society that generated it. There may, for instance, have been several synagogues in first-century Palestine, but few Jews had regular contact with them and there is little justification for giving them an important role in an account of first-century Palestinian Jewish society.

Second, because phenomena at their point of origin are usually small-scale, they are inexplicable. This is because societies, even "primitive" ones, are so complex and quirky that we can begin to make sense only of gross shifts: the smaller the scale of the phenomenon, the less useful the usual historians' (or social scientists') tools are in explaining it. For example, we can at least speculate usefully about the causes, progress, and consequences of the christianization of the Roman Empire in the fourth and fifth centuries, but about the origins of Christianity, scholars can be safely said to have drawn a blank, and certainly not for lack of industry.

In sum, the invention of the synagogue was "revolutionary" only in terms of a deeply problematic genetic narrative, one in which ideas and institutions float free of their social context, so that their first appearance, rather than their maximal diffusion, is what really matters. That the synagogue came into being sometime in the Second Temple period does not tell us as much about Jewish society, then, as has often been claimed. In my view, it is the diffusion of the synagogue that demands more careful consideration, for we can only speak meaningfully about it, and with some hope of being right, when it becomes a significant factor in Jewish society. Origins and the process of diffusion must be addressed because we need to know what it is we are talking about when we talk about the synagogue and the community, and we need furthermore to discuss the dynamics of their diffusion in order to see if we can determine when and why they began to attain more than marginal significance. In this chapter, I will argue that this did not occur before the fourth century.[3]

Origins: Prayer House and Community in Ptolemaic Egypt

There is no way of determining whether the synagogue began as a response to the Josianic reforms of the late seventh century B.C.E., the Babylonian exile in sixth century, the rise of the Jewish Diaspora in the centuries that followed,

[3] Contrast Levine, *Ancient Synagogue*, who seems to set the diffusion of the synagogue in the Hellenistic period, or at any rate very early in the synagogue's history. He regards it as universal, in both Palestine and the Diaspora, starting in the first century, at latest. Levine is trying to be careful not to infer the nonexistence or unimportance of the synagogue from the absence or paucity of evidence for it. But this leaves changes in the character and quantity of the evidence unexplained and turns the relative neglect of the institution by almost all literary sources before the fourth century into a mystery. It has seemed preferable to me, at least in this case, to try to follow the contours of the evidence, in particular because there are excellent reasons to posit the rise of the synagogue in the fourth century and following.

or as a Palestinian expression of hostility to the temple and priesthood, all theses that have been proposed by modern scholars. Nor do we know whether it originated in one place—rural Egypt, say, the location of the earliest evidence—and spread, or developed independently in several different places. Nor, finally, can we tell whether the fact that synagogues might be called by various names—*synagogé, proseuché, sabbateion,* and on rare occasion even *hieron* or *naos*—implies that the synagogue originated in several different institutions whose functions took centuries to coalesce, or rather that the single institution had from the start a variety of functions or simply a variety of names.[4] In the absence of information, there seems little point in continuing to debate these issues.

The most we can say is that buildings called *proseuchai* (sing., *proseuché*), a term later definitely applied to synagogues, were erected by Jewish ethnic corporations in some Egyptian villages as early as the third century B.C.E.[5] It is worth pausing briefly to consider the case of Ptolemaic Egypt because only here does the evidence permit us to do more than guess about the nature of the Jewish community before late antiquity. Let us, then, begin with the *proseuché.*

The term, first of all, is peculiar, since it means simply prayer or vow, not prayer house, yet in the inscriptions that serve as our only evidence for the institution, it unambiguously designates a building. The word *proseuché* also provides the only hint of what went on in the buildings, but this exiguous fragment of information is deeply significant for several reasons. All ethnic corporations in Ptolemaic Egypt (and in other places where we know about them, e.g., Delos) cultivated the worship of their ancestral gods. Although pagans built temples—*naoi* or *hiera* in Greek—some Jews did not. We cannot in fact be certain that sacrifices were never offered in the *proseuchai.*[6] After all, in some ways they were very like temples: the Jews sometimes called them "sacred precincts," one of the *proseuchai* may have had the sort of monumental gateway typical of Egyptian temples, and one Jewish corporation claimed for its *proseuché* the right of *asylia,* or inviolability, a right generally restricted to temples.[7] Yet these Jews refrained from using the word "temple," which implies very strongly that unlike their predecessors at Elephantine they had

---

[4] For a comprehensive, though rather positivistic, survey, see Levine, *Ancient Synagogue,* pp. 19–41.

[5] See Horbury-Noy, nos. 9, 13, 22, 24, 25, 27, 28, 117, 125.

[6] S. Cohen, "Pagan and Christian Evidence," p. 163.

[7] Horbury-Noy, no. 125; J. Gwyn Griffiths, "Egypt and the Rise of the Synagogue," in D. Urman and P. Flesher, eds., *Ancient Synagogues: Historical Analysis and Archaeological Discovery* (Leiden: Brill, 1995), 1: 3–16; S. Fine, *This Holy Place: On the Sanctity of the Synagogue during the Greco-Roman Period* (Notre Dame, Ind.: University of Notre Dame Press, 1997), pp. 25–26.

at least partly internalized the Deuteronomic insistence on the uniqueness of the temple of Jerusalem.

Not all the Jewish residents of Hellenistic Egypt had done so, however. Apart from those who offered sacrifices at the Oniad temple in Heliopolis (who may have argued that their activities were not a violation of the Torah but merely an emergency measure, necessitated by the defilement of the Jerusalem temple by Antiochus IV and/or the Hasmoneans), some self-described Jews made offerings to "the (anonymous Jewish? temple's?) god" at a temple of Pan.[8] How numerous such Jews were, and how widespread the *proseuché* was, it is impossible to know.

The other implication of the term is that at some early period in the history of the institution in Egypt, prayer and not Torah study or reading—or for that matter periodic assembly for basically secular purposes—was the activity most closely associated with it.[9] Only in the first century can we be certain that Torah reading became a regular activity in at least some prayer houses or synagogues, since it is mentioned by Philo, Josephus in *Against Apion*, in the Acts of the Apostles, and in a dedicatory inscription from a first-century synagogue in Jerusalem (see below).[10]

The construction of the Hellenistic Egyptian prayer houses was usually a group project, so the inscriptions claim. Generally, they read something like, "The Ioudaioi in Village X made this *proseuché* for the Most High God on behalf of King Y and Queen Z." A few commemorate gifts by individuals. In

---

[8] Horbury-Noy, nos. 121–24. In Onias's letter to the king and queen, quoted by Josephus, the priest expresses his disapproval of the multiplicity of "temples" built by the Egyptian Jews and claims that his temple will replace them (*Ant* 13.64–68). The argument sounds Deuteronomic but continues by observing that the multiplicity of temples is wrong because it disunites the Jews. In any case, the temples are presumably prayer houses, and Onias's letter a forgery; see G. Bohak, "Joseph and Aseneth' and the Jewish Temple in Heliopolis," (Ph.D. diss., Princeton, 1994), pp. 73; 120–24.

[9] Contrast the puzzling comments of J. Mélèze Modrzejewski, *The Jews of Egypt* (Philadelphia: Jewish Publication Society, 1995), pp. 95–96, based on Levine, "Second Temple Synagogue." See also Levine, "From Community Center to 'Lesser Sanctuary': The Furnishings and Interior of the Ancient Synagogue," *Cathedra* 60 (1991): 36–84 (cf. *Ancient Synagogue*, pp. 124–59, 291–356): the title summarizes the argument. On the significance of the term *proseuche*, and the importance of prayer as opposed to Torah reading, see Hengel, "Proseuche und Synagoge," p. 162.

[10] In fact, prayer is scarcely mentioned in sources of the first century (except in the Dead Sea Scrolls and in Pseudo-Philo, *Liber Antiquitatum Biblicarum* 11.8), which has led some scholars to conclude that it did not occur in the synagogues then. This silence is intriguing, but I am not sure its implications can be pressed. For recent discussions of this issue, see R. Langer, "Revisiting Early Rabbinic Liturgy: The Recent Contributions of Ezra Fleischer", *Prooftexts* 19 (1999): 179–94; P. van der Horst, "Was the Synagogue a Place of Sabbath Worship before 70 CE?" in S. Fine, ed., *Jews, Christians, and Polytheists in the Ancient Synagogue: Cultural Interaction during the Greco-Roman Period* (London: Routledge, 1999), pp. 18–43. Van der Horst also offers compelling criticism of H. C. Kee's view that there were no synagogues in Palestine before 70, and of H. McKay's view that Jews did not conduct communal worship on the Sabbath before 200 c.e.; Levine, *Ancient Synagogue*, pp. 124–59, deemphasizes prayer but does not deny that it occurred.

one case, the "makers" are identified as "the Jews in Athribis" and Ptolemy, son of Epikydes, the local police chief (Horbury-Noy 1992, no. 27). When compared with late antique synagogue inscriptions or even with some contemporaneous inscriptions from foreign temples in Egypt that provide lists of contributors, though, these are strikingly opaque about the funding of the building. Perhaps lists of contributors were made but have not survived. The mention of an apparently non-Jewish *euergetes* in one case would be interesting if its implications could be generalized;[11] also noteworthy is the fact that all the prayer houses, like all Egyptian temples, were dedicated to the royal family and so commemorated (wishfully?) the Jewish corporations' alliance with the Ptolemies—an important theme also in some Egyptian-Jewish literature of the same period, like the *Letter of Aristeas*. But the prayer house inscriptions tell us little about the structure of the groups that built them.

What seems clear, though, from the papyri of Ptolemaic Egypt is that adherence to Judaism made little difference from the perspective of civil law. To make a long story short, the inhabitants of Ptolemaic Egypt were divided into two categories for legal purposes—the native Egyptian majority and the privileged minority of immigrants and their descendants. The latter, who naturally included the Jews, were deemed "Hellenes," regardless of their ethnic origins. The Hellenes theoretically had the right to use their *politikoi nomoi*, that is, the laws of their native cities or countries, but in fact a sort of Greco-Egyptian common law soon developed and came to prevail. The Jews thus had the right to use the laws of the Torah, which were their *politikoi nomoi*, but the extant papyri provide only a single more or less secure reference to a Jew's exercise of this right—an allusion to a divorce performed according to the *politikoi nomoi* of the Jews (i.e., by the husband's unilateral repudiation of his wife). This reference appears, significantly, in a document from a suit brought by the wife for a monetary settlement in accordance with *Greek* law (*CPJ* 1.128). The legal historian J. Modrzejewski, for all his diligence and ingenuity, was able to find no further trace of Jewish civil law in the papyri of Ptolemaic Egypt.[12] It may be worth adding, though, that some as yet unpublished Heidelberg papyri may refer to Jewish courts administering justice in the Egyptian countryside. If this proves to be correct, what I have written will require some revision, though not complete reversal, since the general pattern is unaffected by a single exceptional case.[13]

At least in the countryside, then, Jews generally seem to have married, divorced, lent each other money, and sued each other, in accordance with

---

[11] There seem no grounds for Modrzejewski's near certainty (p. 94) that Ptolemy was Jewish.

[12] *Jews of Egypt*, pp. 107–19.

[13] Personal communication from Roger Bagnall; Modrzejewski knows of these papyri but has not discussed them in the 1997 paperback edition of his book published by Princeton. They will be published by James Cowey.

Greco-Egyptian common law, not Jewish law. Modrzejewski was so intent on finding evidence of the Jewish *politikoi nomoi* in the papyri because he had argued that the Torah was translated into Greek, at royal initiative, to serve as such. He had in mind the parallel case of the translation into Greek in the third century of the Egyptian laws compiled originally at the command of Darius I. But the parallel is imprecise: Egyptians were compelled to patronize Egyptian courts and submit to judgment in accordance with Egyptian law, whereas Jews had the right, but were not compelled, to use their own laws. (The Jewish *politeuma*, a totalizing corporate structure similar to the medieval community, is now generally regarded as an invention of modern scholarship based on elementary misinterpretation of the evidence.)[14]

Nevertheless, despite the mainly negative evidence of the papyri, all from the Egyptian countryside, Modrzejewski's ingenious thesis should not be dismissed out of hand. There may well have been Jewish courts in Alexandria, where the texture of Jewish life was inevitably different from that in the countryside because of the density of the Jewish population, the constant flow of immigration from Palestine, and so on. But even there, Jews were never formally obliged to patronize their own courts, and it is unclear how many of them ever felt under any pressure to do so. Philo, writing toward the beginning of the period of Roman rule in Egypt, informs us that the Jews of his native city had attitudes toward Jewish law ranging from careful adherence to complete apathy, and yet all of them were Jews, at least as far as Philo was concerned, and none are said to have suffered any penalties for their disbelief or practical neglect.[15]

In sum, in several places in Ptolemaic Egypt, Jews constituted voluntary ethnic corporations, one of whose activities was the construction and maintenance of buildings devoted to the worship of their ancestral God through prayer. Whether or how they observed Jewish law in other ways is unknown, but the ethnic corporations seem not to have had control over most of the Jews' legal activities. The corporations were voluntary, compartmental institutions, concerned primarily with cultic activities. It is overwhelmingly likely that not all Jews in rural Egypt formed corporations or patronized prayer houses; in some places the Jews may have been too few, in others, too diffident, and in still others they may have had ways of expressing their Judaism that we cannot recognize. In all these respects, the Jews were no different from other groups of immigrants in Hellenistic Egypt.

---

[14] The essential criticism is provided by C. Zuckerman, "Hellenistic *Politeumata* and the Jews: A Reconsideration," *SCI* 8–9 (1985–1988): 171–85.

[15] For discussion, see A. Mendelson, *Philo's Jewish Identity* (Atlanta: Scholars, 1988), pp. 51–62; G. E. Sterling, " 'Thus Are Israel': Jewish Self-Definition in Alexandria," *Studia Philonica Annual* 7 (1995): 1–18.

The First Century

For the first century there is fragmentary and scattered evidence for prayer houses or synagogues and the corporate structures that sustained them for various parts of the eastern Mediterranean, including Palestine. Most important are references to synagogues and prayer houses in literary works. Philo gives the impression that synagogues were a fully naturalized part of Jewish religious life in Alexandria in his day (early first century C.E.) and states that the service featured a reading from the (Greek) Torah.[16] In *Antiquities*, book 14, Josephus quotes letters and decrees, mostly from the later first century B.C.E., that concern the rights and privileges allegedly enjoyed by some Jewish settlements in Asia and on the islands in the Aegean—documents that if not authentic, are at least plausible forgeries (*Ant* 14.185–264).[17] Most concern the right of the Jews to use their own laws, and so suggest that there were in each of these cities groups of Jews who constituted corporations. Here as in Egypt, the corporations had mainly a cultic function. Though some of the documents acknowledge the Jews' right to have their own courts, most simply allow the Jews to assemble to conduct their sacred rites, and to be free from civic obligations on their holy days. Some of the documents, in specifying the character of the Jews' rites, speak of prayers, and a few in addition mention sacrifices; two allow the Jews to build prayer houses (one actually uses the word *proseuché*, the other, a periphrasis). Remarkably, the most commonly mentioned ritual activities are neither prayer nor sacrifice but common meals and fund-raising. Torah reading is not mentioned. If these documents are taken seriously, they show that even in places where the Jews constituted ethnic/religious corporations, the corporations were not in every case synagogue- and Torah-centered, though they were in some places, and everywhere the Sabbath played a role in the life of the corporations.[18] The importance of

---

[16] See especially *De Specialibus Legibus* 2.60ff.; *Vita Mosis* 2.213ff.; *De Somniis* 2.123–24; H. Weiss, "Philo on the Sabbath," *Studia Philonica Annual* 3 (1991): 88–89; Hengel, "Proseuche und Synagoge," pp. 162–63.

[17] For a detailed commentary on these documents, see Ben Zeev, *Jewish Rights in the Roman World*.

[18] For a full discussion, see S. Cohen, "Pagan and Christian Evidence," 165ff. See also G. Kippenberg, "Erstrebenswertes Prestige oder falscher Schein: Das öffentliche Ansehen des gerechten in jüdisch-frühchristlichen Auseinandersetzung," in G. Kippenberg and G. Stroumsa, eds., *Secrecy and Concealment: Studies in the History of Mediterranean and Near Eastern Religions* (Leiden: Brill, 1995), pp. 203–24. A renovated house of the first century B.C.E., discovered on Delos, may have been a synagogue—it contained dedications to the Most High God, like the Egyptian synagogues, but also apparently statues and lamps decorated with pagan imagery. Did it belong to Jews, Samaritans (who formed a separate organization on the island), or God fearers? See L. M. White, "The Delos Synagogue Revisited: Recent Fieldwork in the Graeco-Roman

common meals shows that the corporations had an egalitarian aspect, though there is no way of determining the frequency of the meals, and so whether they actually performed a significant redistributive role and loosened thereby the individual members' dependence on the patronage of the city elites. Perhaps they were primarily a symbolic expression of solidarity and had insubstantial social and economic effects. It must once again be stressed that there is no reason to think that all the Jews living in an Asian city participated in the local Jewish corporation, nor that every Jewish settlement had a corporate structure of any sort.

Acts of the Apostles may indicate that synagogue- and Torah-based communities were increasingly common in Asia and Greece by the later first century.[19] If this were true, it could perhaps be seen as a result of the integrative pull of the Herodian state. But we should perhaps be wary of the current tendency to take Acts seriously as a description of reality—more a counsel of desperation (what other evidence is there?) than a methodological advance.

Palestine[20]

A corollary of my discussion of first-century Jewish Palestine in part 1 of this book is that the local community was insignificant there as a mode of social and religious organization.[21] Villagers—the vast majority of the population— did not view themselves as constituting religious corporations, at least not in any way that has left traces either in literature or archaeology. God and his subordinate deities may have been everywhere, but they were to be pacified not primarily by villages but by individuals, families, the priesthood of the Jerusalem temple, and similar intermediary figures.

Yet communities did exist, most conspicuously, sectarian communities.[22] Such communities may have influenced the development of the local Jewish

Diaspora," *HTR* 80 (1987): 133–60. For general discussion, Levine, *Ancient Synagogue*, pp. 74–123.

[19] See especially Acts 15:21: James tells the Jerusalem church that Moses has those who read him "every Sabbath in the synagogue in every city [*polis*]." Note also Philo, *Leg ad Gaium* 370–71, a highly rhetorical passage which takes for granted that the synagogue was fairly widespread in cities.

[20] See in general L. L. Grabbe, "Synagogues in Pre-70 Palestine: A Re-assessment," *JThS* 39 (1988): 401–10; Levine, *Ancient Synagogue*, pp. 42–73.

[21] This point is made already by M. Weinberg, "Die Organisation der jüdischen Ortsgemeinden in der talmudischen Zeit," *MGWJ* 41 (1897): 589–91; by contrast Y. Baer, "The Origins of the Organization of the Jewish Community of the Middle Ages," *Studies in the History of the Jewish People* (Jerusalem: Israel Historical Society, 1985), p. 62 (= *Zion* 15 [1950]: 3) claimed that the local community was "immanent" in Judaism (which is not to say that it was always widespread or highly developed or ideologized; for Baer, these are characteristic of the community only in late antiquity)—the weakest element of this fundamental and brilliant article rarely cited by ancient Jewish historians.

[22] Which I believe Baer, "Origins," p. 68 (= 9), was mistaken to conflate with the local community.

community, but mostly perhaps in peripheral ways. The common meals of the Asian Jews remind us that even local Jewish communities might assume sectarian or collegial trappings.[23] Indeed, these have never been totally absent in any Jewish community, even if the participants have been unaware of their implications.

Of greater interest, though, are the first-century Palestinian synagogues, apparently nonsectarian, which may imply the existence of some limited and specialized religious corporations with a partly local character. The New Testament mentions synagogues in Capernaum, Nazareth, and Jerusalem, and the Synoptic Gospels take for granted the presence of synagogues at least in relatively large settlements (*komopoleis*, "village-cities," presumably what we would call towns: Mark 1:38–39; in the Lukan parallel, "cities": 4:43–44; in Matthew 9:35, "cities and villages"). But caution is in order: although the synagogues in Nazareth and Capernaum figure as the scenes of important stories in all the Gospels and so need to be taken seriously (and there were unquestionably synagogues in Jerusalem), other mentions of synagogues appear in "redactional" passages and thus reflect the efforts of the authors of the Gospels to provide traditional stories and sayings with settings they considered realistic. But the authors of the Synoptic Gospels all lived in the Diaspora, and it is presumably no coincidence that the Gospel writer with the strongest interest in the Diaspora, Luke, mentions synagogues most frequently. Nor is it coincidental that John, the Gospel most likely to have been composed in Palestine, mentions the synagogue only once, in connection with Capernaum (6:59), as in the Synoptics.[24] (The silence of Paul may also be noted.) In sum, the Gospels may show that there were synagogues in some of the largest villages, at least in Galilee. But the silence of John, not to mention of Josephus, and for the most part of archaeology (see below), warn us against supposing that they were widespread.[25]

The "synagogue of Theodotus" in Jerusalem, whose existence is attested in a Greek inscription, was almost certainly built at least in large part to serve

[23] Cf. Philo, De Vita Contemplativa 80–1, and J. E. Taylor and P. R. Davies, "The So-Called Therapeutae of *De Vita Contemplativa*: Identity and Character," *HThR* 91 (1998): 10, passim; on common meals, see Baumgarten, *Flourishing of Jewish Sects*, pp. 91–100.

[24] The other possible mention, 18.20, seems more likely to refer to "assemblies." John furthermore believed that the Jews had decided that believers in Christ should be *aposynagogoi* (expelled from the *synagoge*: Jn 9.22; 12.42; 16.2). But as Schrage acutely observed (see next note), this refers to expulsion not from a local community/synagogue, but from the Congregation of Israel as a whole. In that case—whether the world was in common use, despite being unattested elsewhere, or is a Johannine invention—it is likely to reflect either the Septuagint's normal usage of the word *synagoge* to translated '*edah* or *qahal*, in the sense of all Israel, or perhaps an environment, presumably either sectarian or diasporic, in which the local *synagoge* was in effect coextensive with Isreal.

[25] The evidence on the synagogue from the New Testament is assembled by W. Schrage, "*synagoge*," in *TDNT* 7.830–38. For some rather positivistic discussion, with up-to-date bibliography, see Levine, *Ancient Synagogue*, pp. 43–49.

pilgrims from the Diaspora.[26] The Jewish inhabitants of the coastal cities, unsurprisingly, conformed to patterns that were emerging elsewhere in the urban Roman east, that is, some of them formed in some cases synagogue-centered communities. Josephus (who mentions no rural synagogues in Palestine) informs us that a synagogue in Caesarea contained holy books and that the procurator Florus deemed the removal of these books from the synagogue by the Jews at the outbreak of the Great Revolt an act of sacrilege. Levine suggested that Florus regarded the scrolls as among the protectors of the city, presumably because he thought the God of Israel was one of the city's patron deities, and the scrolls were somehow representations of the God (as statues were of the Greek gods), or were necessary for securing the God's goodwill.[27] Did the Jews share Florus's view? If so, what would this imply about the relationship between the Torah scroll and the building that housed it?[28]

Josephus also mentions a prayer house, a "huge building," in Tiberias where Jews congregated on the Sabbaths (Life 276–79).[29] Tiberias must be mentioned separately from the coastal cities because its population was mainly Jewish before the outbreak of the revolt and almost entirely so afterward. But we know next to nothing about the religious life of the city before the second century. The city's constitution was Greek, but there is no way of knowing whether, as later, the Jews conducted a public religious life of pagan character, or whether they thought of themselves as constituting simultaneously the citizen body of a Greek city and a Jewish religious corporation, or several such corporations; or perhaps Jewish religious practices were somehow incorporated into the civic constitution. Josephus mentioned the rebels' destruction of the Herodian palace, decorated with figurative paintings (Life 65–67) but says nothing of their destruction of temples, shrines, or idols. Were there none or were they destroyed (unremarked by Josephus) along with the

[26] See CIJ 2.1414; Lifshitz, Donateurs, no. 79; Roth-Gerson, no. 19, with extensive discussion. The inscription makes special mention of the construction of guest rooms for foreign visitors, complete with plumbing, attached to or somehow associated with the synagogue. Note also the emphasis on Torah study, to the exclusion of prayer, as the chief function of the synagogue. I am assuming, incidentally, that notwithstanding the strictures of H. C. Kee, "Early Christianity in the Galilee: Reassessing the Evidence from the Gospels," in Galilee, pp. 3–14, which are too vague to evaluate, the Theodotus inscription predates 70 or at least 132. The presence of a synagogue in Aelia Capitolina, or Christian Jerusalem, and the existence of a substantial Jewish pilgrimage, would be surprising, though they are not impossible.

[27] See War 2.285–92; Levine, Caesarea under Roman Rule (Leiden: Brill, 1975), p. 30, including note 198.

[28] For an account that attempts to answer this question, though it does not mention the incident at Caesarea, see Fine, This Holy Place, pp. 28–32.

[29] In Life 134, Josephus writes that Jesus b. Sapphias, archon of Tiberias during the revolt, brought a Torah scroll to the hippodrome of Tarichaeae, not far from Tiberias. Had he taken it from the synagogue of Tarichaeae? Of Tiberias? Did he own it? Was a Torah scroll kept for some reason in the hippodrome of Tarichaeae?

city's Greeks (Life 67)? Was Josephus, committed as he was to what we might call religious pluralism, embarrassed by and thus silent about their destruction?[30] The synagogue, finally, played a role in the city's public life during the revolt, but had it done so earlier?

This last consideration inescapably evokes the alleged archaeological synagogues of first-century Palestine, at Masada, Herodium, Gamala, Jericho, and Qiryat Sefer, the first two said to have been built by the rebels who occupied the fortresses, the third located in a fortified royal town whose largely military population may have rebelled against Rome and Agrippa II in 66.[31] (The fourth is part of a Hasmonean-Herodian palace complex, and the fifth is located in a settlement of unknown character; the identification of these remains as synagogues is even more problematic than that of the remains at Masada et al.) The identification of these structures rests on circular reasoning: each contains a large assembly hall, and each was located at a site whose occupants were presumably Jewish—what could they be but synagogues?[32] However, though the reasoning is circular, the conclusion is not necessarily false.

If the conclusion is true, then the structures have some important implications. First, synagogues already possessed their most distinctive feature, shared to the best of my knowledge only by Mithraea and to a limited extent churches: the congregation assembled in a large room that had no completely separate space for a clergy, in contrast to Near Eastern and many classical temples (including the temple of Jerusalem), in which the people assembled in a courtyard while the priests officiated within. At Gamala, benches were built into the walls, which presumably left the floor free for ritual activity, which was thus entirely surrounded by the observing congregation. This in turn implies that there was an officiant, as in later synagogues.[33] The location of the synagogues, if that is what they are, may imply some connection (but what?) between them and the interests and activities of the Jewish rebels of 66.[34] Alternatively, it may imply a connection between the synagogue and a sense of autonomy or self-enclosure, for in first-century Palestine, synagogues were apparently found mainly in cities and fortresses (or only in cities, if the archaeological structures are not in fact synagogues).

[30] On Josephus's pluralism, see *Josephus*, pp. 175–200.

[31] On Gamala, see S. Cohen, *Josephus in Galilee and Rome: His Vita and His Development as a Historian* (Leiden: Brill, 1979), pp. 160–69; on these synagogues, see Grabbe, "Synagogues in Pre-70 Palestine"; and Levine, "Second Temple Synagogue." The structures at Jericho and Qiryat Sefer are partially published in *Qadmoniot* 1999.

[32] Levine, *Ancient Synagogue*, pp. 51–69, expresses doubt only about Jericho.

[33] See L. Levine, ed., *Ancient Synagogues Revealed* (Jerusalem: Israel Exploration Society, 1981), pp. 19–41.

[34] Perhaps rebel groups had a heightened sense of fellowship: Bar-Kokhba's men addressed each other as "brother"; see Y. Yadin, "Expedition D," *IEJ* 11 (1961): 47; B. Lifshitz, "The Greek Documents from Nahal Seelim and Nahal Mishmar," *IEJ* 11 (1961): 60–61; perhaps Benoit, Milik, and De Vaux, *Les Grottes de Murabba'at*, no. 45.

The Second and Third Centuries and the Rabbis[35]

Despite the absence of archaeological evidence, it is certain that synagogues existed in second- and third-century Palestine.[36] One possible explanation for their absence from the record is that though the institution quickly spread in the wake of the Destruction, the synagogues were not monumental but, like Christian churches of the same period, were situated mainly in private dwellings. If this were so, however, we should expect that at least in some places, the private houses would have been "monumentalized" in the fourth century—a development that leaves detectable material traces and is in fact attested for several Diaspora synagogues. But such a development is almost unknown in Palestine; the only example that I am aware of is the so-called Bet Leontis, in Beth Shean, a private dwelling transformed into a synagogue in the *sixth* century.[37] The monumental village synagogues seem to have been built from scratch. It is more plausible to suppose that the synagogue was still not widespread in the second and third centuries, that it was found, as earlier, only in the largest settlements.[38]

[35] I thank Catherine Hezser for her comments on this section. T. Zahavy quotes and briefly discusses all mentions of synagogues in the Mishnah and Tosefta, and also lists their counterparts in the Palestinian Talmud, in *Studies in Jewish Prayer* (Lanham, Md.: University Press of America, 1990), pp. 45–84; the Tannaitic material is discussed in more detail in Fine, *This Holy Place*, pp. 35–59. The latter is problematic in several fundamental ways, apart from its incompleteness (though parts of the discussion are unobjectionable): the Mishnah and Tosefta are not treated separately but are thought simply to reflect the views of the *tannaim*, as if the documents were unaffected by editorial intervention; Fine believes that fundamental to the Mishnah and Tosefta is the sense that the post-Destruction period is essentially different from the time of the Temple and that in the former, the synagogue was, for the rabbis, the centrally important institution of Jewish life. No doubt the rabbis *did* regard the post-Destruction period as different, but the Tannaitic corpora strikingly and pointedly fail ever to articulate such a notion (which is found only in a single baraita, i.e., an allegedly Tannaitic statement quoted in the Babylonian Talmud). It is obvious that in the worldview of the documents, the synagogue was of little importance: its existence was taken for granted, but it is mentioned only a handful of times and treated in detail only in the passages discussed below. For the Tannaitic corpora, the Temple, not the synagogue, continues to stand at the center of Jewish life. The most important account remains Baer's, "Origins."

[36] On Qasyon, see previous section. Outside Palestine, the synagogue at Dura is securely datable to 244 C.E.; but most Diaspora synagogues were constructed in the fourth century and following: see L. Rutgers, *Hidden Heritage*, pp. 125–35.

[37] On the archaeology of the Diaspora synagogues, see "Diaspora Synagogue," with some updating by L. M. White, "Delos Synagogue"; and White, "Synagogue and Society in Imperial Ostia: Archaeological and Epigraphical Evidence," *HTR* 90 (1997): 23–53; and see the extensive survey by L. V. Rutgers in Fine, *Sacred Realm*, pp. 67–95; and Fine, *Hidden Heritage*, pp. 97–124; on the Bet Leontis, see N. Zori, "The House of Kyrios Leontis at Beth Shean," *IEJ* 16 (1966): 123–34.

[38] Contrast Levine, *Ancient Synagogue*, pp. 165–72, who tries to explain away the paucity of rabbinic, and the absence of archaeological, evidence for the synagogue in the second and third centuries.

That synagogues existed in the second and third centuries is certain be-cause they are mentioned in the Mishnah and the Tosefta. The latter, espe-cially, incorporates enough circumstantial detail in its discussion to make it almost impossible to imagine that the synagogue was a purely theoretical con-struct. The Palestinian Talmud also reports stories about third century rabbis' dealings with synagogues, not all of which are likely to be anachronistic. The Mishnah and Tosefta also provide us with what we may consider the earliest theoretical account of the synagogue's character, the sources of its holiness, and its relationship with the townspeople who used and maintained it.

The same works also provide some *very* limited evidence for the existence of the religious community, or rather occasionally seem to have thought of the Jewish town as a partly self-enclosed locus of religious obligation. The main manifestation of this view, aside from their association of the synagogue and the town, is that they briefly discuss communal charity requirements. But on the whole, the Mishnah and Tosefta seem not yet to have considered the possi-bility that the community was an appropriate subject of legislation or a signifi-cant locus of religious meaning.[39] We will see that even the Palestinian Talmud, which was compiled at a time when the synagogue and community were be-coming well established and frequently refers to them in passing, has still not entirely assimilated their existence. It has, for example, a remarkably impracti-cal conception of communal ownership—necessarily more so than the con-ceptions that prevailed in reality. Its avoidance of the word *qahal*, except in its biblical sense of the Congregation of Israel at a time when village communities were regularly using it to refer to themselves, is perhaps intentional.[40] We will see below that the rabbinic conception of the synagogue and the Jewish town differed in important ways from those implied by the physical remains.

Redistribution

Like its contemporary, the democratic constitution of the classical Greek city, the Pentateuch is implicitly opposed to the institution of patronage. Rather, imagining Israel as an egalitarian community, it prescribes a complex of redis-

---

[39] See Baer, "Origins," pp. 1–18.

[40] See Baer, "Origins," p. 8. The Babylonian Talmud sporadically mentions a *qahala qadisha di bi-Yerushalem*. Gaonic tradition regarded this as identical with the *edah qedoshah* (no location given) mentioned once in the Palestinian Talmud in no discernible context (Y. Maaser Sheni 2:4, 53d); there it is identified as the common designation (though it appears nowhere else in the Talmud) for two rabbis of the late second century. Qohelet Rabbah 9.9 attributes a wisdom saying to the *edah qedoshah* and then notes, following Y.M.S., that this is the name for two rabbis, who were so called because they devoted a third of their time to prayer, a third to study, and a third to manual labor. The representation in a text of approximately the sixth century of this enigmatic entity in terms manifestly derived from coenobitic monasticism is of great interest, but it is unlikely to tell us anything about the actual *edah qedoshah*, if any. At most, these shadowy traditions may inform us of the persistence or reemergence of the ideologically loaded language

tributive laws incumbent on every male Israelite—an occasional tithe of crops, the obligation to leave parts of fields for the poor, the provision of interest-free loans, and periodic cancellation of debts and redistribution of land (roughly, that is, the program of the protodemocratic tyrants of the Greek cities).[41] The obvious intention of these laws is to avoid the proliferation of relationships of dependency within the community of Israel: "for the children of Israel are *my* slaves," God says (Leviticus 25:55), not, as the rabbinic exegetes helpfully added, the slaves of slaves (B. Qiddushin 22b). And though the Pentateuchal legislators acknowledged that debt bondage continued to exist, they tried to limit its effects (Exodus 21).

The local community has no place in the Pentateuch's redistributive program. Like Israel's relationship with God, redistribution is personal and national. In the main, the Mishnah and Tosefta retain the Bible's emphases, refining, sometimes mitigating, sometimes extending, always complicating, its legislation concerning the poor tithe, the septennial cancellation of debts, the leaving of corners of fields, and the provision of interest-free loans. In all these cases, the rabbinic legislation is directed at the individual Jew as member of the nation of Israel; the local community does not enter into the discussion. Of course, the nation of Israel no longer had any real existence, and many of the rabbinic laws had no conceivable practical application. That there was any mechanism for the collection and distribution of the poor tithe after 135, for instance, is unlikely, to say the least. But the rabbis' utopian vision, their Israel of the mind, was remarkably like that of the authors of the Pentateuch: Israel as a single nation united by their obedience to, their exclusive relationship of dependency with, their one God.

Yet there are in the Mishnah and especially in the Tosefta the beginnings of the idea that the town ('*ir* in rabbinic Hebrew)[42] constitutes a meaningful religious entity. This conception in no way emerges from rabbinic exegesis of the Bible, so its appearance may constitute an attempt, clearly at this stage halting and ambivalent, to assert control over an institution that by the third century was becoming important in their circles. It may be no coincidence that it was in just this period that rabbis or, perhaps more accurately, men at the fringes of the rabbinic movement were beginning to work as religious functionaries in the larger country towns (see chapter 3), and the majority of the rabbis began to live in the cities, both places in which communities and synagogues were concentrated.

---

of the sectarian community in or near rabbinic circles at a time when it was being widely adopted by the local community; cf. M. Avot 3:6. For some rather harmonistic discussion, see S. Safrai, "The Holy Assembly of Jerusalem," *Zion* 22 (1957): 183–93.

[41] As was long ago observed by Morton Smith, *Palestinian Parties*, pp. 96–112.

[42] On the meaning of the term (a nucleated nonurban settlement and, less certainly, a "villa," that is, a large farmstead), see the discussion in Safrai, *Jewish Community*, pp. 34–38.

The Mishnah's main deviation from the Pentateuch's redistributive program is in its discussion of the *kuppah* (lit., "box" or "chest") and the *tamhui* (lit., "cooking pot"), charitable funds whose precise character the Mishnah does not specify (M. Peah 8:7–9). In fact, though the second part of the Mishnah's discussion seems to concern impoverished local townspeople, the Mishnah never says that the local poor have priority over others, nor that the people have any special obligation to contribute to local funds. Indeed, 8:7 specifies the *itinerant* poor as the main clients of the *kuppah* and *tamhui*. The Mishnah is also atypically homiletic: "Whoever does not need to take but takes will not pass from the world until he becomes dependent on his fellow creatures; and whoever needs to take but does not, will not die of old age until he supports others from what is his" (8:9). Such moralizing may be an attempt to compensate for lack of real control; or, like the emphasis on the itinerant poor, it may reflect an urban environment whither itinerants would tend to gravitate, and where even the local poor might be unknown to the charity distributors. Indeed, the Mishnah may be legislating here primarily for groups consisting of rabbis and their close followers, who lived mainly in cities, and for them the distribution of charity may have been less a redistributive than a publicistic strategy.

A slightly different picture emerges from the parallel passage in the Tosefta (Peah 4:8–21). It is, in the first place, massively more detailed than the Mishnah. Some of the detail simply adds specificity; for example, where the Mishnah states that the itinerant pauper who spends the Sabbath is to be given food for three meals, the Tosefta specifies that he is to be given (in addition to bread, presumably) oil, beans, fish, and vegetables (which seems remarkably generous). This type of expansion is characteristic of the Tosefta. The same passage also provides details about the differences between the *tamhui* and the *kuppah*; for example, the former is open daily and the latter functions only on Fridays. But here the Tosefta introduces a distinction that is foreign to, indeed, contradictory of, the Mishnah: the *tamhui*, which apparently provides only the most basic sustenance, is open to all the poor, while the *kuppah* serves "only the poor in its own town." (In the Mishnah, both funds seem to be intended for itinerants.) Similarly, T. Gittin 5[3]:4–5 presupposes the primarily local character of charity distribution: "In a town which contains both Israelites and gentiles, the *parnasim* collect from both Israelites and gentiles, because of the ways of peace; they support (both the Israelite and) the gentile poor, because of the ways of peace; they eulogize the gentile dead, and console the gentile mourners, and bury the gentile dead, because of the ways of peace."[43] Finally, T. Megillah 2[3]:15 states the matter most explicitly: "An individual who pledged charity in his town gives it to the poor of his town; in a different town, he gives it to the poor of that town; *parnasim* who pledged

---

[43] Cf. also T. Demai 3:16; T. Bava Metzia 11:23.

charity in their town give it to the poor of their town; in another town, they give it to the poor of that town." This rule simultaneously asserts the essentially local character of charity collection and imposes a significant limitation on the importance of the *'ir*, that is, the community.

While the Palestinian Talmud occasionally describes rabbis of the later third and fourth centuries serving as charity collectors (*gabba'im* or *parnasim*),[44] the Tosefta still takes it for granted that charity collection is not under rabbinic control: "At first they said that a *haver* (literally, associate) who is made a *gabbai* is expelled from his *havurah*, but then they said that while he is a *gabbai*, he is not trustworthy [i.e., is not permitted to be a *haver*], but when he ceases to be a *gabbai*, he is trustworthy" (T. Demai 3:4). On the common assumption that all rabbis were *haverim*,[45] this rule effectively bars rabbis from serving as *gabbaim* and implicitly assumes that there was no substantial overlap between the groups and that rabbis had no influence over appointments of *gabbaim*. Why did the rabbis keep their distance? Perhaps because charity collectors had to deal with the *'am ha'aretz*—people who were careless about the laws of purity and priestly gifts; such dealings are forbidden for *haverim*. Perhaps also because a suspicion of dishonesty adhered to *gabbaim*, as to tax collectors. T. Bava Metzia 8:26 may confirm the second suggestion without excluding the first: "The repentance of *gabbaim* and tax-collectors is difficult: they may return [scil., what they have extorted] to acquaintances, but the rest they must use for the public good."

The Synagogue in the Mishnah and Tosefta

The Mishnah attributes religious importance to the town in only two connections: it ambiguously and fleetingly implies that public supplicatory fasts during droughts are conducted by towns,[46] and it acknowledges, in its brief discussion of the issue, that synagogues are built and used by towns.[47] Its discussion of the public fast is equivocal: the bet din (court) is required to decree public fasts, apparently for the entire nation, if rain has not fallen by 1 Kislev (M.

---

[44] Levine, *Rabbinic Class*, pp. 162–67; Hezser, *Social Structure*, pp. 270–73.

[45] Levine, *Rabbinic Class*, p. 55 n. 56; M. Beer, "On the Havura in Eretz Israel in the Amoraic Period," *Zion* 47 (1982): 178–85; see, however, Hezser, *Social Structure*, pp. 74–75.

[46] On this see H. Lapin, "Rabbis and Public Prayers for Rain in Later Roman Palestine," in A. Berlin, ed., *Religion and Politics in the Ancient Near East* (Potomac: University of Maryland Press, 1996), pp. 105–29. For more detailed discussion, see D. Levine, "Communal Fasts in Talmudic Literature: Theory and Practice" (Ph.D. diss., Hebrew University, 1998).

[47] T Bava Metzia 11:23 adds: "Townspeople may compel one another to build a synagogue, and to buy scrolls of the Torah and the Prophets, etc." Also, M. Berakhot 4:7, perhaps implying a connection between some sort of local autonomy and the obligation to commemorate the special sacrifices on Sabbaths and festivals. But the Mishnah's language is unusual here and its interpretation is difficult.

Taanit 1), and the ceremony of supplication is to be graced by the the presence of the patriarch and the "father of the court" (the patriarch's deputy in the rabbinic scheme: M. Taanit 2:1), though the Mishnah assigns them no further role.[48] Yet the same Mishnah notes that the ceremony of supplication begins when "they (who?) bring the ark into the town square," and the prayers are led by "the oldest among them (whom?)." It is tempting to think that the editors have juxtaposed two conceptions of the public fast, the national and the local, without trying to reconcile them.[49] Indeed, public fasts described elsewhere in rabbinic literature are usually local, town-based rituals, not decreed by any central body or presided over by the patriarch.[50] The Tosefta, for example, in a discussion that closely parallels the Mishnah, acknowledges the local character of the ritual, for in its version, the bet din, the patriarch, and his deputy are not mentioned, and the supplicatory prayers are led by the oldest of the town elders and by the *hazan* of the synagogue (T. Taanit 1:8, 14). The Mishnah has apparently once again, as in the case of charity collection, transformed what in real life was a locally based religious act into a national one.[51]

The Mishnah discusses the synagogue incidentally, in the context of its legislation concerning the production and use of holy books (M. Megillah 3[4]). In elaborating on the inherent and nontransferable sanctity of the Torah scroll, the Mishnah for the only time clearly acknowledges the town and the synagogue as loci of limited sanctity:

> Townspeople who sold the town square may buy with the proceeds a synagogue; a synagogue—they may buy an ark; an ark—they may buy wrappings (for scrolls); wrappings—they may buy scrolls (of the Prophets—see Rashi ad loc.); scrolls— they may buy a Torah scroll. But if they sell a Torah scroll, they may not buy scrolls; scrolls—they may not buy wrappings; wrappings—they may not buy an ark; an ark—they may not buy a synagogue; a synagogue—they may not buy a square. The same rules apply to the money remaining (either, after the licit transactions are complete, or, from funds raised for the purpose of the purchase).[52]

[48] Jacobs, *Die Institution*, p. 87, ascribes their presence in this Mishnah to the work of a glossator.

[49] Cf. Lapin, "Rabbis and Public Prayers for Rain," p. 112. The Mishnah allows for local fasts, but only in the case of a localized drought or plague (M. Taanit 3:1).

[50] Which is not surprising, considering the various and broken topography of Palestine and the wide local variations in annual rainfall that result: see D. Ashbel, in the *Israel Pocket Library Geography* (Jerusalem: Keter, 1973), 94–111. See Y. Taaniyot 1:1, 63d, and passim throughout the tractate; 2:1, 65a: "R. Yosah said, 'the public fasts which we make are not really fasts, because the patriarch is not with us.'" For a full listing of such stories, see D. Levine, *Communal Fasts*, 254–72.

[51] Cf. M. Taanit 3:3–4, which states explicitly that towns declare fasts, but also 3:7, where the "elders" (of the "high court") do so.

[52] Cf. discussion in Fine, *This Holy Place*, pp. 38–40.

If the commentators were right to read this Mishnah as a *locus classicus* of the legal principle *ma'alin baqodesh ve'eyn moridin* (one raises up in sanctity, and one does not lower), as they seem to have been, then the Mishnah is proposing that the religious property of the community falls into a neat hierarchy of sanctity.[53] The essential principle is that the Torah scroll alone is inherently and immutably sacred—a point elaborated on not only in the continuation of the Mishnah but also in the Tosefta's expansion of this Mishnah. For the Tosefta recognizes that a synagogue is in fact merely a building, an ark a cabinet, and Torah wrappings pieces of fabric, which acquire sanctity (if at all; see below) only by an act of dedication or through the intention of the maker. The Torah scroll alone is sacred in itself and cannot be desacralized. The Talmud debates elsewhere whether scrolls written without the proper intentions (e.g., by Christians or magicians) are considered holy for halakhic purposes (do they, for example, "render the hands impure"? May they be rescued from a fire on the Sabbath?), but no one could deny their potency.[54] But a cloth, according to the Tosefta, becomes sacred only when its owner donates it for use as a Torah wrapping; and if he has merely lent it to the synagogue, its return to his possession desacralizes it.

Though intention and dedication are the formal mechanisms by which an item enters the state of sanctity, the source of sanctity, the Mishnah strongly implies, is proximity, physical or conceptual, to the Torah scroll.[55] This is obviously why inexpensive and easily produced items like wrappings and cabinets are holier than the synagogue structure itself. It is of some interest that the Mishnah seems to ascribe a minimal level of sanctity to the town square. This could conceivably be understood to imply that the Mishnah regards communal ownership, not just proximity to the Torah scroll, as conferring sanctity, thereby acknowledging the claims of communities to be holy societies whose possessions are all holy. Such a conception is reflected not only in the language of later Palestinian synagogue inscriptions, in which the townspeople call themselves "holy communities," but also in inscriptions from the Diaspora, some of them roughly contemporary with the Mishnah, in which communal treasuries, for instance, are often designated "most holy" (see below). It would be rather surprising to encounter the traces of such a conception in the Mishnah, despite its acknowledgment (3:1) that the communally owned

---

[53] For an alternative Mishnaic hierarchy of sanctity, centered on the Temple rather than the Torah, see M. Kelim 1:6–9. On Tannaitic views of "sacred space," see B. Bokser, "Approaching Sacred Space," *HTR* 78 (1985): 279–99.

[54] A point made repeatedly in Y. Shabbat 16:1, 15c. Though one may not save amulets containing quotations of biblical verses from a fire on the Sabbath, a magician who destroyed his amulets because he feared being caught by a rabbi, was regarded as a worse sinner for having destroyed his work than for having produced it in the first place; also, T. Shabbat 13:4.

[55] See Fine, *Sacred Realm*, pp. 24–25.

synagogue is holier than the privately owned.[56] The Talmudim and the commentators were thus probably right to read this law in conjunction with M. Ta'anit 2:1: the town square is holy because the Torah scroll is brought there during droughts for the ceremony of supplication (see above).

Communal Ownership

The Mishnah acknowledges that synagogues may be either communally or privately owned, but it has no theory of what communal ownership entails.[57] It quotes R. Meir's disapproval of the sale of a public synagogue to an individual (even, we must assume, if the individual intends to use it as a synagogue) but seems to reject this view by reductio ad absurdum. The Palestinian Talmud, however, introduces two contradictory approaches to communal ownership, both of which it seems to accept:

> Rabbi Shmuel bar Nahman said in the name of Rabbi Jonathan: "That which [the Mishnah] says (that is, that it is possible to sell a synagogue) applies only to a privately owned synagogue; but it is forbidden to sell a publicly owned synagogue because it is possible to argue that someone from the end of the earth owns a share of it." But have we not learned (in the Tosefta): "It happened that R. Elazar b. R. Zadok purchased the synagogue of the Alexandrians and did what he wished with it"? Rather, the Alexandrians (apparently not a local community but a limited corporation of Alexandrian immigrants elsewhere) had built the synagogue with their own funds (and so counted for legal purposes as a private individual).

This opinion, which explicitly contradicts the Mishnah, is based on an oddly primitive conception of communal ownership: it views the community as a set of individuals or, rather, a partnership, not a corporation with a constantly shifting membership consisting of whoever is living in a town at a particular time, a conception that would allow the community to *act*.[58] Since, in this view, the heirs of the builders of the synagogue are still its owners and they have presumably scattered undetectably to the winds, any sale necessarily lacks their approval and so is invalid. The inadequacy of this view, not only

---

[56] Presumably on the principle of *berov 'am hadrat melekh* (the glory of the king is in the multitude of the people, or the more the merrier), as the commentators observe.

[57] See Baer, "Origins," pp. 6–8.

[58] Contrast the cunning reworking of the same material in B. Megillah 26a: "Rabbi Shmuel bar Nahmani said in the name of Rabbi Jonathan, 'The teaching of the Mishnah [that a synagogue may be sold] refers only to the synagogues of villages; but the the synagogues of cities may not be sold because people come to them from all over, and so they belong to the general public (and not just the Jews of the city).'" Baer, "Origins," p. 67 (= 8) observes that rabbinic halakhah never abandoned its conception of the community as a partnership rather than a corporation, while simultaneously assuming, describing, or even prescribing corporate-style behavior on the part of the community.

as an interpretation of the Mishnah but as a practical approach to communal ownership, is obvious.[59] It may generally be compared to the neglect of the corporation in Roman law before late antiquity (though, significantly, late imperial law began to develop a theory of the corporation precisely to cope with problems created by the rise of the parish, that is, the local religious community).[60] There is, however, no way of telling how Jewish towns behaved in reality. That synagogues were usually built, as the inscriptions inform us, by a combination of communal exertion and private benefaction may have complicated matters. A wealthy benefactor in Macedonia, around 300 C.E., threatened his community with fines if they altered the synagogue he had donated without the approval of his heirs, but his threat demonstrates his powerlessness to control the community's behavior, and perhaps also the absence of a legal foundation for any attempt to do so.[61] Be this as it may, communities presumably had some way of disposing of their property in a manner acknowledged to be legal, notwithstanding the view of the Palestinian Talmud.

The palpable crudeness of the Talmud's theory of communal ownership probably indicates that its formulators or editors were, even in the fourth century, uncomfortable with, or basically unconcerned about, the community as a legal entity. In the following *halakhah*, the Talmud discusses laws of agency that implicitly contradict the opinion of R. Shmuel b. Nahman and concludes that seven townspeople are empowered to represent the town in the sale of a synagogue, provided the townspeople have not expressed a priori their disapproval of such an action (cf. Digest 3.4.2). This at least implies, following the Mishnah, that the town may act as a legal corporation, but in fact the Talmud here proposes no theory to replace that of R. Shmuel b. Nahman.

An Economy of Sanctity

Are there restrictions on the rights of the synagogue's purchaser? That is, does the synagogue retain its sanctity after it has been sold?

---

[59] The common rabbinic concepts of *reshut harabbim* and *reshut hayahid* refer not to ownership but to accessibility.

[60] Only two brief titles in the Digest, 3.4 and 47.22, concern corporations, and they evince no great conceptual sophistication—though Ulpian could at least assert that in (some types of?) corporations, "that which is owed to the collectivity is not owed to the individual" and vice versa; that is, the corporation has some legal personality apart from its individual members (that Ulpian is apparently referring to cities here, not *collegia*, makes little difference). On corporations in Roman law, see L. Schnorr von Carolsfeld, *Geschichte der juristischen Person, vol. 1, Universitas, Corpus, Collegium im klassischen römischen Recht* (Munich: Beck, 1933); C. Saumagne, "Corpus Christianorum," *RIDA* 7 (1960): 437–78.

[61] See CIJ 1.694, with comments of Lifshitz; but, pace Lifshitz, there is no suggestion here that the donor ascribed ownership of the building to the patriarch.

"They may sell the synagogue only on the condition that the new owners must return it on demand;" so said R. Meir. The sages say, "they may sell it in perpetuity (and the new owners may use it for any purpose) except as a bathhouse, a tannery, a ritual bath [bet hatevilah], or as a urinal." R. Judah says, "They may sell it to be a courtyard, and the purchaser may do with it as he pleases."

The opinion attributed to R. Meir suggests that the synagogue retains some of its sanctity even after its sale, that the site itself has a kind of inherent sanctity. This conforms in a rough way with the common conception, traceable inscriptions dating from the third century B.C.E. to the seventh century C.E., that the synagogue is a holy place, very much like a temple (see below). But aside from the isolated view of R. Meir, the Palestinian rabbis seem generally to have embraced such a conception only with serious qualifications.[62] The Palestinian Talmud seems to accept the view of R. Judah recorded in the following Mishnah that a ruined (as opposed to a sold) synagogue retains some trappings of sanctity. But the Mishnah itself, and the Tosefta following it, promote the view that there are few or no restrictions on what the purchaser may do with a synagogue. It would, according to "the sages," be disrespectful to transform the former synagogue into a urinal or tannery. In the Tosefta's version of this rule, R. Judah, who believed the purchaser's rights were unrestricted, and the sages were in *essential* agreement; the sages only forbade use of the site as a urinal, and so on, as long as it continued to be called "the synagogue." In other words, neither the sages nor R. Judah believed the synagogue, once sold, retained any substantial residual sanctity. Rather, the sanctity of the synagogue was in effect transferred to the money the townspeople received from the sale. The synagogue's sanctity is thus, in the standard rabbinic view, not inherent in the place but is a formal attribute, conferred and removed by the actions of the townspeople.

Some Complications

We have already seen that the Mishnah's legislation is frequently characterized by tension, sometimes explicit, sometimes subtle, untheorized, perhaps even scarcely conscious, between what may have been popular conceptions

---

[62] Note also the *beraita* quoted at B. Shabbat 32a: "R. Ishmael b. Elazar says, 'For two sins do the *'ammei ha'aretz* die, because they call the holy ark *'arona'*, and because they call the synagogue *'bet ha'am.'*" The former usage is attested in inscriptions (see Levine, "Sages," p. 212 n. 61), the latter is not. *Arona* may be objectionable because it is the name of the ark of the Temple or perhaps because it is the normal word for coffin (any explanation is rendered difficult by the fact that R. Ishmael himself calls the synagogue ark *aron haqodesh*), and *bet ha'am*, instead of *bet hakeneset*, because *'am* should refer to the people of Israel as a whole, not the members of a local community. Notwithstanding R. Ishmael's usage here, Tannaitic (but not Amoraic) sources normally call the synagogue ark *tevah*, that is, box or bookcase; see Levine, "From Community Center," 71 n. 182.

and practices, and rabbinic formalism. This is true also of M. Megillah 3. Though no law in the Mishnah contradicts the hierarchy of sanctity described in the first Mishnah, the laws that follow interestingly fail to discuss anything but the synagogue. Though the ark and the Torah wrappings are holier, the second and third *mishnayot* give the unmistakable impression, by failing to discuss them, that there is after all something special about the synagogue— a status implied not by the Mishnah's laws but by its rhetoric.

As is often the case, the Tosefta completely subverts this Mishnaic tension but introduces a new one of its own. First, it presents, in a way that conforms with the Mishnah's hierarchy, more detailed discussion about the synagogue's furniture than about the synagogue itself (T. Megillah 2[3]:13–16). Indeed, its agenda differs from that of the Mishnah. The Tosefta is concerned primarily with laws of dedication, with the question of how the act of donation transforms common objects into sacred ones, whereas the Mishnah is concerned with the sanctity of the synagogue. That the synagogue is sacred, the Tosefta simply assumes.

In fact, the Tosefta may go even further in subverting the Mishnah by presenting a view that the synagogue is not really sacred after all or, at any rate, that the Mishnah's notion that its sanctity is transferred to the proceeds of the sale is incorrect: (2[3]:12):

> R. Menahem ben R. Yoseh says, "[if they sold] a synagogue, they may not purchase the town square" (this view accords with that of the Mishnah). R. Judah said, "When does this statement apply? Only if the *parnasim* of the town have not made with the townspeople a prior condition [to purchase the square, for example]; but if the *parnasim* have made such a condition, then they can use [the funds] for anything they wish."

On the face of it, the statement attributed here to Rabbi Judah utterly contradicts the laws of the Mishnah, for if there is a hierarchy of sanctity in which the synagogue ranks higher than the town square, and if the principle of *ma'alin baqodesh* is correct, then how can a mere statement by the *parnasim* legitimate the sale of the synagogue to purchase something less holy? Some medieval commentators (e.g., Nachmanides and R. Shlomo ibn Adret) argued that Rabbi Judah's law implied that the synagogue was not sacred in any sense, that it was a mere *tashmish mizvah* (an item used in the performance of a commandment), comparable to a *lulav*. Others, however, rejected what appears to be the plain meaning of the Tosefta in an attempt to harmonize it with the Mishnah and read Judah's comment as a reaction not to that of R. Menahem ben R. Yoseh but to the final clause of the first Mishnah ("The same rules apply to the money remaining"). If this were so, then R. Judah's statement would constitute only a small qualification of the Mishnah's law. This harmonistic interpretation was preferred by Lieberman, not to mention

Maimonides, and surely deserves serious consideration, but it is hard to avoid the feeling that it does excessive violence to the text.[63]

Yet the continuation of the Tosefta reveals tensions of its own. Whatever reservations the corpus may manifest about the sanctity of the synagogue, it is striking that it repeatedly uses language associated with the Jerusalem temple in its discussion of synagogue dedications.[64] Thus, in 2:13, it states: "If one makes an ark or scroll wrappings, as long as *gavoah* has not yet used them, a *hedyot* is permitted to use them." *Gavoah*, "the exalted," is the term the rabbis normally use to refer to the temple establishment, in contrast to the *hedyot*, borrowed from the Greek *idiotes*, a lay private citizen. In light of this, halakhah 16 is particularly odd, at least rhetorically:

> If a gentile dedicated a beam to a synagogue, on which was inscribed "[dedicated] to God" (that is, the tetragrammaton was inscribed on the beam), they examine him; if he says, "I donated this beam to *heqdesh* (the temple treasury)," they hide it (i.e., in a *genizah*, and do not use it); if he says, "I donated it to the synagogue," they scrape off the name, hide the shavings, and may use the remainder. Objects belonging to *gavoah* may be used by a *hedyot* as long as *gavoah* has not yet used them, etc.

What is striking here is the tension between the anxiety that temple and synagogue not be confused, manifest in the law of the beam inscribed with the name of God,[65] and precisely the same confusion in the law that immediately follows.

Though the various tensions that characterize the rabbinic discussions of the synagogue—the occasional slippage between the formalism of rabbinic theory and the presumably popular, nonrabbinic sense that synagogues are rather like temples, in sum, the messiness of rabbinic discourse—need to be taken seriously, it still may be possible to accept some of the generalizations about rabbinic conceptions of "sacred space" described by the late Baruch Bokser. In his view, the rabbis' conception was founded on two principles, the first of which is that God is present everywhere and therefore every place is *potentially* sacred; the second principle is that the one *actual* holy place, the site of the Jerusalem temple, is still in fact holy but no longer functioning. The rabbis thus "overcame the loss of the sacred center ... (by finding) alternative centering objects, in particular the Torah. ... They made the center mobile, enabling individuals to enter it by reading or studying the laws of the cult."

[63] See Lieberman, *Tosefta Kifshutah*, Moed, 1151–53, upon which my discussion is based.
[64] This issue is discussed at length by Fine, *This Holy Place*, pp. 41–59.
[65] Also interesting is the rabbis' assumption that a pagan might not know the difference between a temple and a synagogue.

The holiness of places outside the temple "needs to be activated. . . . The Rabbis preserved the idea of sacred space in a manner that enabled the group to function without a single center."[66]

The Rabbis, the Synagogue, and the Community

It is obvious that neither the synagogue nor the community were rabbinic inventions, and unlikely that the rabbis played a role in their diffusion.[67] That the existence of the community is scarcely acknowledged in the Mishnah and is only slightly more evident in the Tosefta probably conforms to the fact that its diffusion was still very restricted in the third century. Nor was the synagogue common. The Mishnah takes it for granted that it could be found only in the *'ir*, the large town; villagers would have to come to town to participate in public religious ceremonies, such as the reading of the scroll of Esther (M. Megillah 1:1).

But even later, the rabbis' embrace of these institutions was half-hearted. They rejected the widespread conception of the local community as a "holy congregation," a miniature Israel, and of the synagogue as a holy place, both well attested in inscriptions. They suspected the honesty of communal officials, though by the later third century they began themselves to serve in such positions. Though there is little evidence for rabbinic opposition to the synagogue as such, as the strenuous efforts of scholars to discover traces of such opposition demonstrate, they certainly disapproved of much that went on in specific synagogues. Some anecdotes in the Palestinian Talmud inform us that public feasts, conducted in the synagogues, were still an important feature of communal life (e.g., Y. Sanhedrin 3:2, 26b), yet both the Tosefta and the Palestinian Talmud regarded them as forbidden (T. Megillah 2[3]:18; Y. Megillah 3:3).[68] Other anecdotes report the rabbis' disapproval of liturgical practices they encountered in synagogues (Y. Berakhot 5:3, 9c). Though many passages in the Palestinian Talmud unambiguously—indeed, perhaps a bit too insistently—regard the synagogue as the most appropriate place for prayer (e.g., Y. Berakhot 5:1, 8d–9a), others remind us that the synagogues the rabbis had in mind were not the standard local synagogues, but their own. How else are we to understand the law forbidding Jews from Haifa, Beth Shean, and Tivon to lead the prayers (because of what the rabbis regarded as their impre-

---

[66] "Approaching Sacred Space," 298–99.

[67] My conclusions in this section agree in the main with Levine, "Sages and the Synagogue"; and see *Ancient Synagogue*, pp. 440–70.

[68] Cf. Naveh, *On Mosaic*, no. 110, supplemented by Naveh, *EI* 20 (1989): 305, no. 2, an inscription from a synagogue in Qasrin in the Golan commemorating the construction of a banquet room.

cise pronunciation of Hebrew), obviously not an option in the synagogues of Haifa, Beth Shean, and Tivon (Y. Berakhot 2:4, 4d)?

Rabbinic literature provides evidence of the rabbis' gradually intensifying attempt to regulate synagogues and communities. By the fourth century rabbis probably preached in synagogues, at least in some places, fairly frequently. The occasional employment of rabbinic figures as religious functionaries, schoolteachers, and charity collectors has already been discussed. Yet we should be careful not to infer too much from this. As we will see later, there is little evidence that the rabbis' exertions had much impact before the sixth century. By the fourth, some rabbis were claiming proprietary rights over synagogues: as embodiments of Torah, they belonged to the synagogues and the synagogues to them. But a story the Talmud tells to illustrate this point serves mainly to underline its ambiguity. The rabbis themselves may have been the only ones aware of their proprietary claims (Y. Megillah 3:3).

> R. Berechiah came to the synagogue of Beth Shean and saw a man washing his hands and feet in the fountain. He said to the man, "This is forbidden to you." The next day, the same man saw the rabbi washing his hands and feet in the fountain. He said to him, "Rabbi! It is permitted to you, but to me it is forbidden?" The rabbi responded, "Yes." The man said, "Why?" The rabbi responded, "So said R. Joshua b. Levi, 'Synagogues and study houses belong to the sages and their disciples.' "

NINE

JUDAIZATION

THE DIFFUSION of the synagogue is evidence for judaization. By this I mean the reemergence of some version—altered but recognizable—of the ideological complex described in part 1 of this book as the ordering principle of the public life of most Jews. These qualifications are necessary because we have no way of knowing, for late antiquity as for the Second Temple period, how Jews actually lived their day-to-day lives, to what extent they conformed to Pentateuchal prescription. The synagogue remains and other artifacts provide excellent evidence for the symbolic importance of the Torah, but for only certain aspects of the lives of the Jews.

How are we to reconcile the claim that in late antiquity Judaism served to integrate the Jews with the obvious diversity of the synagogue remains, as well as the fragmentation of Jewish religious life implied by their very existence? I would argue that, as in the case of the literary remains of the Second Temple period, here too the diversity of the particular artifacts has drawn attention from the larger pattern. Clearly, by about 500 almost all Jewish villages, though they regarded themselves as religiously discrete, participated in a common ideology; all utilized surplus capital to build and maintain synagogues, all had placed the Torah at the the physical and perhaps symbolic centers of their world, and all regarded themselves as constituting "Israel," or rather an agglomeration of discrete Israels. We may not be able to speak of *a* Jewish state or polity, but we can speak of the beginnings at least of a Jewish world, a collection of little Jewish polities loosely bound together into a community of shared symbols and discourse that, however diverse in their details, nevertheless served to mark them off from their (by now) mainly Christian neighbors.

The Centrality of the Torah

We have already seen that the reading or study of the Torah may not have been an original part of of the synagogue's program. Whether the earliest communities possessed Torah scrolls and, if so, whether they kept them in the prayer houses, is unknown. Presumably, they were fantastically expensive, especially if written on parchment, which is, once again unknown, and this may argue against their general diffusion. It is certain, though, that by the first century Torah reading was widespread as part of the synagogue service, though there is no way of knowing if it was yet universal and if the scrolls were often kept in the synagogue. Josephus even claimed that the practice of Torah reading was instituted by Moses (*AgAp* 2.175). Josephus also reported that there were many holy books among the spoils of Jerusalem, which Titus allowed him to keep (*Life* 417–18). Were these all from synagogues, or does the story suggest that the well-to-do priests and functionaries of Jerusalem might own copies of their own (which should hardly come as a surprise)? Did their post-Destruction successors, among them the rabbis, also possess personal copies of the holy books?

The Mishnah, we have just seen, believed the synagogue's sanctity was derived entirely from the Torah scroll—a view apparently shared by some members of John Chrysostom's Antiochene flock in the late fourth century.[1] This implies that all synagogues possessed scrolls. The Mishnah likewise takes it for granted that the Torah was read in the synagogue on Sabbaths and holidays (M. Berakhot 4:4; M. Megillah 3), though it does not yet describe a regular weekly lectionary cycle, still less a regular cycle of supplementary readings from the Prophets, though it presupposes the practice of prophetic readings. It was only at the very end of antiquity that the lectionary cycle began to acquire some regularity in Palestine, and even then, there were many local variations.[2]

There may be little reason to doubt the implications of the Mishnah in this case, and in fact no scholars have done so. But perhaps some qualifications are in order. The first is that we simply cannot be certain, in the absence of external confirmation, that Torah reading was universally practiced and that all synagogues possessed scrolls. Once again, the expense of the Torah scroll may have prevented some communities from owning one, though they may still have aspired to do so. It may be best to suppose that by the third century, the Torah scroll was deemed a regular feature of the synagogue, even if not every synagogue had one. (Certainly in the fourth and fifth centuries the *image* of the Torah shrine was a fixed component of synagogal iconography; see below.)

In the fourth to sixth centuries, as the synagogue itself was reaching its maximal diffusion in the Palestinian countryside, the scroll was gradually given an increasingly central place in the structure of the synagogue—a development paralleled in the Diaspora in the same period. That is, though it was

---

[1] John Chrysostom, *Discourses against the Jews* 1.5.1–8.

[2] See Shinan, in Fine, *Sacred Realm*, pp. 132–33. In Babylonia, by contrast, the cycle achieved something like its present form by the time of the Amoraim, at least among the Amoraim; see now S. Naeh, "Sidrei Qeriat Ha-Torah Be-eretz Yisrael: Iyyun Mehudash," *Tarbiz* 67 (1998): 167–87.

uncommon before the fifth century for synagogues to be built with fixed Torah shrines, many older synagogues were then renovated to have one installed.[3] By the sixth century, furthermore, many synagogues were built with apses— a feature borrowed from the basilical church but adapted for use as a niche for scrolls. Many such synagogues also had chancel screens, sometimes finely carved in marble, in front of the apses (another borrowing from ecclesiastical design), often produced in the same workshops as the church screens. The precise interpretation of this development is unclear; perhaps it is even unwise to attempt one.[4] It seems obvious, though, that the construction of a special area for the scroll, the gradual establishment of zones of special sanctity around it, and the concomitant limitation of the congregation's access to it mark a transformation in the popular conception of the Torah and/or of the notion of sanctity.

There are other indications, too, that the Torah came to possess an ever increasing numinosity, reflected in regularly performed ritual. Philo and Josephus claimed that the Torah was *studied* in the synagogues. Though this claim normally appears in an apologetic context (the Jews, unlike the Greeks, actually know their laws because they are obliged to study them every week), its persistence at least raises the possibility that it was true for some places, as is weakly confirmed by the fact that in Alexandria, the Torah was apparently read in Greek alone, the language of common speech. But the Palestinian Talmud and other late antique Palestinian writings indicate that something very different happened in the synagogues in the fourth century and following: not study but a highly ritualized performance.[5] The reader would read a verse from the scroll (recitation from memory was forbidden); another functionary,[6] who was required to stand beside the reader, would then improvise (not read, though written texts were available) a translation into Aramaic. The Talmud itself regarded this practice, called *targum*, as a ritual reenactment of the giving of the Torah on Mount Sinai.[7] This is why the reader was not permitted

---

[3] For a survey, see Hachlili, *Ancient Jewish Art*, pp. 166–92; Levine, *Ancient Synagogue*, pp. 291–356.

[4] See J. Branham, "Vicarious Sacrality: Temple Space in Ancient Synagogues," in D. Urman and P. V. M. Flesher, eds. *Ancient Synagogues: Historical Analysis and Archaeological Discovery* (Leiden: Brill, 1995), 2: 319–46, and in greater detail, "Sacred Space in Ancient Jewish and Early Medieval Christian Architecture" (Ph.D. diss., Emory, 1993), for an attempt, with responses of Fine. See also Hachlili, *Ancient Jewish Art*, pp. 187–91.

[5] My discussion is informed by S. Fraade, "Rabbinic Views on the Practice of Targum, and Multilingualism in the Jewish Galilee of the Third-Sixth Centuries," in *Galilee*, pp. 253–86, the most sophisticated treatment of this issue I am aware of.

[6] So I assume he was, notwithstanding Fraade, "Rabbinic Views," pp. 261–62.

[7] For the rabbis, the practice also resonated with what some of them regarded as the second giving of the Torah, reported in Nehemiah 8, according to which Ezra and his assistants read the Torah out to the people *meforash*, which the rabbis understood (probably correctly!) to mean, "with translation"; see S. Schwartz, "Language, Power, and Identity," 12 n. 14.

to act also as translator: "just as the Torah was given through an intermediary, so it must also be read through an intermediary." This is why, also, the rabbis were less concerned (not to say unconcerned) about the text's comprehensibility than about the correct performance of the rite. When Rabbi Simeon, the *safar* (i.e., probably schoolteacher but also general religious functionary) of Tarbenet, was asked by the villagers to read half verses of the Torah in the synagogue, rather than full verses, in order to help the children understand, he refused, with the approval of the rabbis, and so was dismissed (Y. Megillah 4:5, 75b, and see above).

This story once again reminds us not to be too quick to assume that rabbinic practices were universally followed. Even in this Talmudic tale, the villagers are obviously not committed to the rabbinic practice of Torah reading, and we have no way of knowing how the Torah reading was performed where *targum* was not practiced. But in synagogues with fixed shrines, raised platforms in front of them, and chancel screens, we can be fairly certain that it was *performed*.

We may also note here, while reserving detailed discussion for later, one of the most striking characteristics of the novel liturgical poetry of the sixth century, the *piyyut*. In the liturgically central part of the payyetanic performance, the *qerovah* (i.e., the versified version of the *tefillah* or *amidah*)—complex and allusive manipulation of the week's Torah lection has replaced all other concerns. To put it differently, in the *qerovah* the Torah reading has encroached on and almost overwhelmed the rest of the liturgy.

The Emergence of a Jewish Iconography[8]

Every ancient synagogue that has come to light, provided its remains are sufficiently extensive, was more or less elaborately decorated, whether primarily on its facade or within.[9] The fragments of painted plaster that have been found in some excavations remind us that though they do not survive, in some synagogues walls and ceilings, not just pavements, may have been decorated. The famous painted synagogue of Dura Europos may thus have had counterparts in Palestine. Though some of the surviving decoration resists even the most elementary interpretive efforts (what are we to make of Odysseus on the floor

---

[8] This section appears in a slightly different version as "On the Program and Reception of the Synagogues Mosaics," in L. Levine and Z. Weiss, eds., *From Dura to Sepphoris: Studies in Jewish Art and Society in Late Antiquity* (JRA suppl. 40, 2000) pp. 165–81; for a different approach, see Levine, *Ancient Synagogue*, pp. 561–79.

[9] For a full survey, see Hachlili, *Ancient Jewish Art*, pp. 234–365; as a collection of material and formalistic observations, this work is unsurpassed. In her interpretations, though, she follows the Avi-Yonah school.

of the Bet Leontis, or the gladiator on the floor of the Meroth synagogue,[10] images not uncommon in domestic decoration but, it seems to us, quite out of place in a synagogue?), much of it is part of a fairly limited iconographic repertoire that, however precisely we explain it, indubitably functioned to mark as "Jewish" the place or the object in or on which it was found. Of this repertoire, some is straightforwardly Jewish in content: glyptic and mosaic images of *menorot, lulavim*, Torah shrines, incense shovels, or biblical scenes (also used by Christians)—the binding of Isaac at Sepphoris and Bet Alfa, Noah's ark at Gerasa, Daniel in the lions' den, much damaged but still discernible, at Susiyah.[11] Other components of the iconographic repertoire— pairs of lions guarding narthices or arks, zodiac circles with Sol Invictus at the center inscribed in squares featuring personifications of the seasons at the corners—have no obvious Jewish content but appear repeatedly in synagogues and rarely or never elsewhere.[12] Still other common images appear occasionally in synagogues but are not restricted to them, for example, not quite nature scenes—mosaic "carpets" of animals (some of them saddled or caged) and vegetation framed by grape vines, derived from the still life, agricultural, and hunt scenes that decorated the floors and walls of the houses of wealthy Romans—Nile scenes, and so on, which are common also in the decoration of churches and private houses. These images are in fact more typical of church than of synagogue decoration, for in the preiconoclastic period, Christian iconography still consisted very largely of themes taken over from domestic decoration with little alteration.[13]

There had been a paltry and enigmatic Jewish iconographic language in the Second Temple period and immediately following, all the more difficult to interpret for being largely nonrepresentational. This featured such items as rosettes and arches and perhaps the *menorot* that decorated some lamps produced in Judaea immediately after the Destruction. But the first appearance

---

[10] See S. Mucznik, A. Ovadiah and C. Gomez de Silva, "The Meroth Mosaic Reconsidered," *JJS* 47 (1996): 286–93; on Bet Leontis, see Roussin, cited below.

[11] There is no convenient recent reference work in English listing and discussing the synagogue remains (the books of Hüttenmeister and Reeg, and Marilyn Chiat, are out of date); the *NEAEHL* has separate entries for many of the sites discussed, and much information can be found in Levine, *Ancient Synagogue*; Hachlili, *Ancient Jewish Art*; and in A. Ovadiah and R. Ovadiah, *Hellenistic, Roman, and Early Byzantine Mosaic Pavements*. Most convenient is a Hebrew publication: Z. Ilan, *Ancient Synagogues*.

[12] An apparently non-Jewish example of the zodiac motif has now come to light in a bathhouse of approximately the fifth century on the Aegean island of Astypalaea, excavated in the 1930s and never published but recently seen by Ruth Jacobi: see her brief note, "The Zodiac Wheel from the Greek Island of Astypalaea," *Qadmoniot* 118 (1999): 121.

[13] See E. Kitzinger, *Israeli Mosaics of the Byzantine Period* (Milan: Collins/UNESCO, 1965), pp. 8–15; in general, A. Grabar, *Christian Iconography: A Study of its Origins* (Princeton: Princeton University Press, 1968). On the zodiac circles, see especially Foerster, "Zodiac in Ancient Synagogues."

of parts of the later repertoire is over the ark of the synagogue of Dura Europos, constructed in 244 C.E. A bit later, *menorot* were commonly carved on the walls of the catacombs of Bet Shearim, along with a repertoire of other items that differ both from the later synagogue iconography and from the funerary iconography of the Second Temple period.

Traditionally, the very existence of representational synagogue decoration — featuring images derived from Jewish religious life and biblical stories and also borrowed from pagan, secular, and Christian sources, all jumbled together — has been regarded as problematic. How could Jews ignore the Second Commandment, or why, in a more nuanced version of the question, did they now interpret it laxly after having interpreted it rigoristically in the Second Temple period? How could they juxtapose *lulavim*, or biblical scenes, with images of Sol Invictus derived directly from the iconography of late Roman paganism? How could descendants of the Jews who had risen up against Herod when he installed a golden eagle over the entrance to the Jerusalem temple install stone carvings of eagles over the entrances to their own synagogues?

These conventional concerns do indeed merit attention. Clearly, general Jewish attitudes toward representation were very different in late antiquity from what they had been in the first century and earlier. But we must remember the implications of the revised chronology of the synagogue. Although there are few traces of representational art in Jewish Palestine in the first century, the second and third centuries were rich in it, and it was without exception pagan in character, as we have seen. What we need to understand, then, is not so much the emergence of representational art among the Jews, already an old story by 350, as the emergence of a *Jewish* representational art.

Ancient Jewish Art in Context

It is generally acknowledged that most ancient synagogue art is symbolic. Whereas Roman temples were often decorated with reliefs more or less naturalistically portraying scenes of sacrifice, the images used to decorate synagogues (and churches) bear only an oblique relationship to what occurred in the buildings.[14] Apart from the function that the synagogue art shares with the naturalistic decoration of pagan temples — marking the "otherness," the concentrated sanctity, of the space they occupy — it seems intended to convey a religious message that stands outside of the images themselves yet was somehow intelligible to the congregants who viewed it.[15]

---

[14] Cf. J. Elsner, *Art and the Roman Viewer: The Transformation of Art from the Pagan World to Christianity* (Cambridge: Cambridge University Press, 1995), pp. 190–210.

[15] For the conceptual background of this paragraph, see N. Bryson, *Word and Image: French Painting of the Ancien Régime* (Cambridge: Cambridge University Press, 1981), pp. 1–28; cf. Grabar, *Christian Iconography*, pp. 7–30.

How precisely are we to recover this message? Here consensus breaks down. Programmatic readings of ancient synagogue art usually depend on texts. Of course, texts are indispensable for the interpretation of ancient art, especially the symbolic decoration of synagogues and churches: it is mainly texts that provide us with entrée into the ethos and cultural assumptions of the patrons, producers, and viewers of the art. Furthermore, the special status of some texts for Jews and Christians, and the fact that the art frequently refers to these texts quite directly, make recourse to them inescapable. Any approach to the interpretation of such pavements as those at Sepphoris, Bet Alfa, Gaza, Susiyah, and many others must begin with the Bible. But there are many nonbiblical elements in these pavements, and in any case it seems clear that the pavements are more than simply evocative of the biblical text. Consequently, many art historians depend on additional corpora of texts to supplement the Bible when they interpret the art. The nearly universal reliance on rabbinic texts for this purpose raises special problems.

Interpreters of Jewish art have as a matter of course adopted the methods used by classical and early Christian art historians. The latter concern themselves mainly with elite products—monuments produced by emperors and senators, art that decorated public and private buildings commissioned by, at the very least, local aristocrats, the decorations in churches like those at Ravenna or in the great monastic centers. (Scholars rarely attempt more than the most modest and general interpretation of nonelite products, such as the mosaic pavements of small parish churches.) Emperors, senators, decurions, the leading bishops, and ascetics were the people by whom and for whom the surviving classical and patristic literature was produced. It is perfectly reasonable to assume that the literature reflects, if only roughly and indirectly for the most part, the cultural assumptions of the patrons, and in some cases even the audiences, of the art. Its interpretation remains a complex and necessarily imprecise undertaking, but it is not, obviously, a misguided one.

But there are no ancient Jewish counterparts to the Ara Pacis, the Ravennate churches, or the monastery of St. Catherine at Mount Sinai, and the domestic art commissioned by the curial classes of the cities of high imperial Galilee so obviously participates in the ethos of empire wide Greco-Roman culture that it is not clear in what sense it can be considered Jewish. By contrast, no patrons of late antique Jewish funerary or synagogue art can be definitely connected to any corpus of literature except the Hebrew Bible. There is no way to know, a priori, whether the intentions of the patrons and the assumptions of the viewers are best sought in the Palestinian Talmud, the *midrashim*, the Hekhalot, the *piyyut*, Sefer Harazim, and related magical material, the late antique apocalypses, or indeed the works of Philo and the later Platonic tradition. Or they may have been incorporated in literary works that do not survive, in a body of lore that was never committed to writing, or all of the aforementioned. Some of these works may provide evidence for the varie-gated, even conflict-ridden *reception* of the art (for late antique Jewish litera-ture is very diverse) but not the motivations of those who commissioned it.

There are strong reasons for rejecting a rabbinizing approach to the inter-pretation of the synagogue art, reasons provided mainly by the synagogue remains themselves. It is well-known that the ancient synagogues often vio-lated rabbinic rules by facing in the wrong directions, having their entrances in the wrong places, being decorated with images forbidden by the rabbis, such as those of the ubiquitous seven-branched menorah or of gods holding scepters and orbs.[16] But such violations may not in fact be terribly significant in themselves: some can be explained away by clever exegesis of rabbinic laws, and the rest might be attributed to the ignorance or recalcitrant eccentricity of a handful of synagogue patrons.[17]

A more compelling objection to rabbinizing readings of the synagogue art is that the rabbis and the synagogue builders had very different notions of the sacred—a suggestion that may be understood as a modification, a toning down, of Goodenough's extreme contention that the synagogue art and the rabbinic texts are evidence for utterly different varieties of Judaism.[18] The very idea, apparently universal among the Jews by about 500, that a synagogue should be housed in a special building, indicates the distance of the villagers from the rabbinic ideology discussed above. In fact, the essential "otherness" of the synagogue was overdetermined; it was marked not only by the monu-mentality of its structure but *invariably* in other ways as well. Every synagogue so far discovered is decorated, either on its facade or within, with iconographic indications of sanctity. In some cases these decorations are not specifically Jewish in content. Eagles, wreaths, and vines, carved on the facades of several synagogues, were also the standard decoration of the Syrian pagan shrines surveyed early in the last century by Butler, and they seem to be markers of a kind of generic sanctity.[19] Even geometric mosaic carpets common in syna-gogue decoration and simple wall paintings resembling the so-called first style of Pompeii, for which there is some evidence, mark the synagogue interior as "other" because of their disorientation of the viewer's sense of space and sur-face.[20] Types of decoration that in their original domestic context had been expressions of a mildly subversive wit became in late antique synagogues and churches adjuncts of spirituality.

[16] See Levine, "Sages and the Synagogue," pp. 215–18.

[17] The most recent attempt to defend the synagogue art in terms of rabbinic halakhah is Stern, "Figurative Art."

[18] See *Jewish Symbols*, 12: pp. 40–49, for his most concise statement of the issue.

[19] H. C. Butler, *Syria: Publications of the Princeton University Archaeological Expeditions to Syria in 1904–5 and 1909*, 9 vols. (Leiden: Brill, 1907–1949).

[20] Cf. N. Bryson, *Looking at the Overlooked: Four Essays on Still Life Painting* (Cambridge: Harvard University Press, 1990), pp. 17–59.

Most synagogues, though, utilized elements of the specifically Jewish iconographic language just discussed. Whatever precisely the elements of this language may have meant to the people who used and contemplated them, they clearly served as indications of the sacred; it would, I hope, be uncontentious to suggest that the sanctity of the synagogue was somehow embodied in its decoration, that it was not only the Torah scroll that made the place holy, as in the rabbinic scheme, but the character of the synagogue's structure and art.

Some of the motifs used in synagogue decoration—especially *menorot*, arched structures, and *lulavim*—were also used to decorate small objects such as stone plaques, lamps, glasses, plates, and rings. Such items may often have been used in synagogues, and they were certainly used in tombs; sometimes the same motifs were carved on tombstones. If these items were also used in homes, which is unknown but not unlikely, they would have lent them a kind of diffuse sanctity. For the rabbis, the home was ritually charged: blessings and prayers were constantly recited, meals echoed, if only faintly, the sacrificial cult, commandments were observed even in the bedroom. We do not know if nonrabbinic Jews shared this view, but to the extent that it is foreshadowed in the Hebrew Bible and was common, *mutatis mutandis*, in the Jews' Christian environment,[21] the notion that a diffuse sanctity pervades the home is likely to have been widespread and thus marked, in nonrabbinic style, iconographically.

In sum, there is little justification for a rabbinizing approach to synagogue art, which is not to deny that rabbinic texts may occasionally help explain peculiar details of the art. The explosive diffusion of the synagogue itself, no less an overdeterminedly holy place than the consecrated church (though there is no evidence for a formal ritual of synagogue consecration), warns us against a rabbinizing approach. The synagogue's sanctity was inherent and constituted in part in the structure and decoration of the building. All of this is dramatically at odds with what we know of the rabbis' ambivalence (not straightforward hostility) to figurative representation.[22] But more to the point, it reflects an attitude to the sacred that has little in common with the rabbis' formalism.

On the Program of the Sepphoris Mosaic

In the following pages I discuss one aspect of Ze'ev Weiss's reading of the recently discovered mosaic pavement of the Sepphoris synagogue. This is the most fully elaborated programmatic reading of a synagogue mosaic that I am

---

[21] Cf. E. D. Maguire, H. P. Maguire, and M. J. Duncan-Flowers, *Art and Holy Powers in the Early Christian House* (Urbana: University of Illinois Press, 1989), pp. 1–33; Elsner, *Art and the Roman Viewer*, pp. 251–70.

[22] See Stern, "Figurative Art."

aware of.[23] Indeed, many treatments of synagogue art are content to describe, compare, and (often dismissively) discuss the "meaning" of individual motifs, especially zodiac circles. In view of what I have already written, there is little reason to discuss the consequences of Weiss's assumption that the rabbinic corpus constitutes the best set of texts through which to view the Sepphoris mosaic—which is not to deny the importance (indeed, in a limited way even the validity) of Weiss's work on the pavement. Rather I want to examine a more fundamental assumption, which he shares with most interpreters of ancient Jewish art.

Weiss argues that the pavement conveys a clear, simple message. The panels nearest the entrance, containing scenes from the book of Genesis, "symbolize the promise for the future implicit in the story [of the patriarchs]." The central panel, the zodiac circle, "symbolizes God's power as sole ruler of the universe and creation." As to the remaining panels, which depict a series of little scenes taken from the account of the consecration of the Tabernacle in Exodus 28 and following, and, closer to the bema, the familiar image of an ark flanked by *menorot* and other ritual objects:

> The . . . combination [of images on the panels] represents man's basic needs—
> bread, fruit and meat—and within the context of this structured iconographic
> scheme, conveys a clear eschatological message. These elements were selected
> . . . to express the hope that just as God had filled the world with abundance in
> the past, by virtue of the Temple cult, so would He redeem His people in the
> future, rebuild the Temple, cause the Shekhina to dwell there, and return prosper-
> ity to the world. This eschatological message, which expresses the world view and
> religious aspirations of the Jews of the Land of Israel, is a theme that runs through-
> out the rich fabric of the entire mosaic. (Weiss, *Promise and Redemption*, p. 38)

Let us leave aside some of the particular problems with this reading—its romanticism (*all* the Jews of the Land of Israel?), its inevitability (is it possible to imagine an identifiably Jewish iconographic scheme that, in a post-Destruction context, could not be read as suffused with the pathos of loss and therefore as looking ahead to redemption?). Let us attend instead to a more basic issue. What, specifically, is the epistemic status of Weiss's reading, and of others like his? What, precisely, is he trying to reconstruct? Is he suggesting that the intentions of the patrons alone are recoverable, while tacitly admitting that the reception of the art may have been complex and shifting? Or is he arguing that the art had a stable meaning, known not only to the patrons but to all viewers, and somehow transmitted across the generations in which the synagogue was in use?

---

[23] See Netzer and Weiss, *Promise and Redemption*. Other attempts at programmatic reading include J. Wilkinson, "The Beit Alpha Synagogue Mosaic: Towards an Interpretation," *JJA* 5 (1978): 16–28; L. Roussin, "The Beit Leontis Mosaic: An Eschatological Interpretation," *JJA* 8

If, as seems to be the case, Weiss is suggesting that the pavement had a single stable meaning, then he is necessarily supposing that its elements constituted a kind of code, that the iconography had a fixed set of significations readily accessible to all worshipers. This could be the case if we were to suppose that the art was somehow closely connected to the ritual and liturgy of the synagogues, so that these functioned to convey the meaning of the art to the viewers. The supposition of a connection between art and liturgy is by no means implausible and will be explored below. But it seems overwhelmingly unlikely that the Palestinian liturgy of late antiquity was stable in any way. On the contrary, the great period of synagogue construction was also, as far as we can tell, a period of unprecedented liturgical dynamism, characterized in some places by gradual rabbinization, probably almost everywhere by a tendency toward professionalization, and the development and spread of the *piyyut*, among other things; in any case, according to the consensual view, even the rabbinic liturgy of the fifth and sixth centuries was characterized in Palestine by a marked lack of fixity.[24] Not only did the liturgy vary from community to community, but even within communities, prayer leaders were expected to improvise their prayers. If the mosaics conveyed a single message to their viewers, then that message must have been fixed by some means other than the liturgy.

However, the variety of late antique synagogue decoration, the fact that identical pavements have never yet been discovered, argues strongly against the supposition that the art constituted a kind of iconographic code. Many pavements have a roughly similar design, and many more use similar motifs in distinctive and unpredictable ways. That the same are used individually to decorate small objects and tombstones in itself implies the existence not of a code but of a loosely constituted and unstable symbolic language, multivalent or vaguely evocative rather than straightforwardly denotative. A useful counterexample is the Mithraic tauroctony, the complicated scene of the god slaying a bull found, with only minor variations, at the focal point of every Mithraic shrine in the Roman Empire. The elements of this remarkably consistent image obviously do constitute an iconographic code, known in principle to every initiate (if not to modern scholars), which almost certainly refers to the central mysteries of the cult. Conversely, the stability of the Mithraic iconography implies the essential unity and stability of Mithraic ritual.[25]

(1981): 6–19. For Goodenough (*Jewish Symbols* [1953], 1: 241–53), the Bet Alfa mosaic represents the ascent of the soul—a predictable reading but perhaps less implausible here than usually.

[24] For general accounts, see S. C. Reif, *Judaism and Hebrew Prayer* (Cambridge: Cambridge University Press, 1993), pp. 146–52; I. Elbogen, *Jewish Liturgy: A Comprehensive History* (Philadelphia: Jewish Publication Society, 1993), pp. 205–47; J. Heinemann, *Prayer in the Period of the Tannaim and Amoraim* (Jerusalem: Magnes, 1984).

[25] See Elsner, *Art and the Roman Viewer*, pp. 211–21. For the image, see M. Vermaseren, *Corpus Inscriptionum et Monumentorum Religionis Mithraicae*, 2 vols. (Hague: Martinus Nijhoff,

We may illustrate the implausibility of Weiss's ascription of stable meaning to the iconography by examining his treatment of one section of the pavement. His interpretation of the panels drawn from the Abraham stories as suggesting God's promise to Israel, and thus his interpretation of the pavement as a whole, depends heavily on his identification of the heavily damaged panel nearest the narthex as the angels' visit to Abraham and Sarah. It must be admitted that this identification, suggested to Weiss by the juxtaposition of the angels' visit and the binding of Isaac in the apse mosaic of the Church of San Vitale in Ravenna, is very attractive. The only readily construable piece of the panel shows the top of a hooded, almost certainly female head (which is almost identical to the [female] personification of Winter in the zodiac panel), situated in a rectangular structure. Although this structure seems more like a doorway than a tent flap (as required by the biblical story, and in contrast to the more obviously tentlike entrance Sarah stands in at Ravenna),[26] there is only one other biblical story in which such a scene would be expected, that I can think of—the story of Jephthah and his daughter, that is, the other biblical narrative, aside from the binding of Isaac, of human sacrifice. Though Jephthah's daughter, like the female figure on the pavement but unlike Sarah, lived in a house, not a tent, I hesitate to suggest that the mosaicist was trying to represent this strange and not readily interpretable biblical tale, though the possibility should perhaps not be excluded; nor should the possibility that the damaged scene is not drawn from a biblical story.

This fragmentary scene is, as already suggested, crucial to Weiss's interpretation of the pavement as a whole. Without the angelic visitation, there is no divine promise, only a scene of primeval sacrifice or of a righteous man's submission to God's will. (Indeed, even the angelic visitation should perhaps be understood as an image of offering.) Plausible as Weiss's identification of the scene on the fragmentary panel is (and he must wish it was more than merely plausible), his interpretation of the juxtaposed scenes of the angelic visitation and the binding of Isaac, though perfectly acceptable in itself, strikingly contradicts his own assumptions about how the art conveyed meaning. The same scenes, for example, must have had a different sense in Ravenna, where they constitute part of an utterly different kind of decorative program. And how does the absence of the "promise" theme affect the meaning of the

---

1956), passim, especially plates; see also R. Gordon, "Franz Cumont and the Doctrine of Mithraism," in J. R. Hinnells, ed., *Mithraic Studies: Proceedings of the First International Congress of Mithraic Studies* (Manchester, U.K.: Manchester University Press, 1975), pp. 215–48; R. Beck, "Mithraism since Franz Cumont," ANRW 2.17.4, pp. 2002–15 (Berlin: DeGruyer, 1981).

[26] A wall mosaic unambiguously depicting this same scene from the Church of Santa Maria Maggiore in Rome offers some support to Weiss's interpretation, for here Sarah stands in an entrance whose framework is rectangular, with the fabric hanging from the transverse of the doorframe held open by cords; see the photograph in Goodenough, *Jewish Symbols* 3 (1953) fig. 1.

pavement of the Bet Alfa synagogue, which is otherwise very similar to that of Sepphoris? If two pavements use almost the same repertoire of images to tell different stories, if, that is, the images themselves have no stable meaning, how can Weiss's reading of the Sepphorite art be correct?

A New Programmatic Reading

The evident instability of the images' meaning suggests the need for a different type of programmatic interpretation, more modest in its claims and more complex in its results. We may as well admit at the outset that we cannot recover the intentions of the mosaic's patrons. We do not know who they, or the other congregants, were, what, if anything, they are likely to have read or heard read aside from the Hebrew Bible, what it was that shaped their intellectual and religious environment. The synagogue art cannot be approached in the same way, with the same pretense to certainty, as the contemporaneous art of such imperial foundations as the churches of Ravenna or monastic/ pilgrimage centers such as St. Catherine's near Mount Sinai, whose social, intellectual, political, and religious contexts are relatively well known. Though the quantity of surviving late antique Jewish texts is considerable, none of these texts can be connected with certainty to the synagogue art, as already suggested.

Nevertheless, it may be worth trying to suggest a kind of minimalistic programmatic interpretation, which the texts are likely to have appropriated and reacted against. After all, everyone, patrons and viewers, saw the same sweep of images when they entered the synagogue. The impression created by this experience may have been relatively unspecific—the pavement may first of all have produced a mood, not told a story. But the mood, if not the story, was shared. How then to proceed?

The Physical Setting

The interiors of many synagogues, which often required artificial lighting, were riotous.[27] Floors and walls were decorated with brightly colored mosaics and paintings, columns were topped with ornately carved capitals, and the congregants faced elaborate stone arks sometimes, though apparently not al-

---

[27] Z. Ilan, "Survey of Ancient Synagogues," 171, observed that oil presses have often been discovered in the immediate vicinity of synagogues and suggested that they were used primarily to provide ritually pure oil for lighting the synagogue. Synagogues frequently had *menorot* and/ or polycandela. Windows may in some cases have been arranged to highlight features of the interior (e.g., at Dura Europos, the ark was in constant sunlight): see A. J. Wharton, *Refiguring the Post Classical City: Dura Europos, Jerash, Jerusalem, and Ravenna* (Cambridge: Cambridge University Press, 1995), p. 31. Palestinian synagogues have generally not survived to the level of the windows.

ways, covered with embroidered cloths[28] and flanked by metal or stone *men-orot*.[29] For city dwellers, such a concentration of visual stimulation was not unfamiliar; bathhouses and other public buildings, and some private houses, were similarly colorful. The fifth-century Sepphorite could see in his city not only his rather magnificent little synagogue but also the "Nile Festival" mosaic in a public building (whose function is unknown); and perhaps the probably fourth-century Orphic mosaic in a nearby private house was still visible.[30]

Villagers, though, lived surrounded by nature, a delicate and tenuous green a few months of the year, but otherwise severe brown and gray. There may have been a few large houses in the village, but most dwellings were small (dwarfed by the synagogue) and undecorated.[31] To enter the synagogue was to leave the world of the village and enter a place alive with color and filled with evocations, first of all, of Jewishness, and of a general numinous sanctity, but also (and we should not minimize this element) of wealth and urbanity. Even in an urban setting, such as Sepphoris, the synagogue interior featured a remarkable and distinctive assemblage of visual stimuli. The art of the synagogue would never have seemed routine to its viewers: it was always the object of careful scrutiny.

Apparently the Galilean-type, and some other, synagogues had relatively simple interiors but grand gabled façades. In some cases these were decorated with friezes of the standard Jewish symbols, while elsewhere the decoration consisted of such less obviously Jewish symbols as eagles, wreaths, vines, animals, or mythological creatures.[32] The monumental doorway was thus a kind proscenium arch, which framed the "otherness" of the interior space and, where the lintels were decorated, gave the congregant some notion of the character of this otherness—its "Jewishness" or its general sacrality, for eagles, wreaths, and so on, were standard features of the decorated facades of southern Syrian temples. Such synagogues (which one entered facing the back of the

---

[28] See Hachlili, *Ancient Jewish Art*, pp. 191–92.

[29] See Levine, *Ancient Synagogue*, pp. 333–36. Such *menorot* have been found primarily in Judaea, but also at Hammat Tiberias and at Merot, in Upper Galilee.

[30] For these mosaics, see *Hadashot Arkheologiyot* 99 (1993): 12–4; 106 (1996) 31–39, with color photographs inside the front cover.

[31] As far as the report indicates, there is no trace of either wall painting or figurative mosaic in the big house excavated at Meiron: see Meyers, Strange, and Meyers, *Excavations at Ancient Meiron*, pp. 50–72.

[32] On the monumental doorways of the Galilean-type synagogues and their implications, see Levine, "From Community Center," 41–45. Eagles, wreaths, and so on, marked the place as sacred, though not necessarily as Jewish. This fact, in Levine's view, explains B. Shabbat 72b, a story of a man who mistook a temple for a synagogue. Jewish symbols were not commonly carved on the facades of Galilean synagogues, but were elsewhere; it now seems unlikely that the zodiacs once thought to have been carved on the façades of seven Galilean and Golanite synagogues (see Levine, "From Community Center," 64–65) are what they originally seemed (I thank Lee Levine for this observation).

hall, so that the first thing to come into view were benches where fellow congregants sat) usually were paved in stone, not mosaic, but may have had frescoes on their walls.[33]

Other synagogues were entered at the rear of the hall. It is not clear whether in such synagogues wooden benches, or perhaps straw mats, were set on the mosaic pavement of the nave facing front, or whether people sat only along the walls or in the aisles.[34] A priori, the latter option seems more plausible, if only because it would restrict wear to the relatively inexpensive and easily repaired geometric aisle mosaics. Sepphoris may be a special case because it had only a single narrow aisle, which may not have been able to accommodate all the congregation; some may therefore have had to sit (or stand?) in the nave. However, the rather crude repairs to the nave mosaic are concentrated in the area in front of the bema, where liturgical activity was naturally concentrated; there is no evidence of wear elsewhere, as far as I can tell. This seems to imply that the nave was not much used by the congregation for seating or standing, unless it was protected by a carpet or mats (but even so, the mosaic would have become worn). In any case, one certainly saw, upon entering, first of all the narthex mosaic, then, if the nave was clear, a sweep of images leading up to the officiant, who stood before the ark at the front of the hall. This sweep of images is, as suggested above, an important stabilizing element in the interpretation of the pavements because it is an inescapable sensory reality, visible to every congregant, regardless of status, as long as the pavement was in place.[35]

In many such synagogues the nave floor featured a design that had three fixed elements: the zodiac circle toward the center of the nave and, at the front, a scene containing a Torah shrine, flanked by *menorot, lulavim, etrogim,* and incense shovels, with additional elements in some places (e.g., Daniel in the lions' den at Susiyah and Na'aran). The third shared scene, of lions or other large animals protectively flanking an inscribed wreath, appears in different places in the pavements. At Hammat Tiberias and Bet Alfa, the animals are closest to the narthex, but at the latter, where they are a lion and a bull, they rather oddly have their backs to the entrant, and additional lions, if that is what they are, guard the ark, while at Sepphoris, the lions guard not the entrance but only the ark, and they hold bull's heads in their paws, a motif used also in the lintel frieze of the synagogue of Horvat Ammudim. Such animals are often designated "heraldic" in the scholarship but may be more accurately regarded as apotropaic or protective. It may be relevant to mention

---

[33] On the likelihood that Galilean-type synagogues (as well as others) were decorated with frescoes, see Hachlili, *Ancient Jewish Art*, p. 224; add to Hachlili's list the Meroth synagogue: Z. Ilan and I. Damati, *Meroth: The Ancient Jewish Village* (Tel Aviv: Society for the Protection of Nature, 1987), p. 49 (pl.); and Levine, *Ancient Synagogue*, pp. 336–40.

[34] Levine, "From Community Center," pp. 45–47, is inconclusive.

[35] I owe this point to Natalie Kampen.

an amulet from the Cairo *genizah* in which a pregnant woman invokes the sign of Leo (*mazal aryeh*) to protect her from evil spirits.[36]

In some of the synagogues, the next panel contains a biblical scene or several at Sepphoris,[37] but at Na'aran, the corresponding panel contains a vine-scroll pattern peopled with animals. It is perhaps significant that the earliest pavement, that of Hammat Tiberias, has no such scene but moves directly from the guardian lions to the zodiac circle. In all the synagogues, these circles, which occupy the center of the nave and are usually the largest panel, have certain commonalities. The circles are inscribed in squares that feature at the angles personifications of the seasons drawn without significant modification from Roman domestic decoration (the seasons do not necessarily line up with the appropriate quadrant of the zodiac, which argues against the view of Hachlili and others that the synagogue zodiacs were intended to function as a kind of liturgical calendar); all except Sepphoris contain at the center a representation of Sol Invictus riding a quadriga, once again derived directly from Roman iconography. Though the Sepphorites did not hesitate to have human and even mythological figures (Sagittarius is depicted as a centaur and, as at Hammat Tiberias, several other figures—most prominently Gemini—appear to be nude) depicted in their synagogue, Sol apparently aroused anxiety—a strong argument, if any were needed, against the view of Urbach and his followers that Jews even earlier were simply unaware of what representations of the gods denoted.[38]

Aramaic and Greek tend to prevail in synagogue inscriptions, but the zodiac circles invariably feature inscriptions in Hebrew, perhaps because it was understood to be the language of creation, of the cosmos, or of God. In any case, the use of Hebrew marks the zodiac as somehow special.[39] At Sepphoris, too, the signs and the seasons are marked in Hebrew, but the seasons are marked in Greek as well (perhaps because the seasons belong also to the earth?), and the quadriga circle is surrounded by a narrow band containing a dedicatory inscription in Greek. The Sepphoris zodiac is also unique in identifying the signs of the zodiac with months (thus Libra is marked both *moznayim* and Tishri, Scorpio both '*aqrav* and Marheshvan, and so on) and here the signs of the zodiac do line up correctly with the seasons represented in the angles of

[36] Leo is also asked to "stand and pray and beseech for her in front of the King of all kings . . . so that all kinds of demons be driven away from her." See Naveh and Shaked, *Magic Spells and Formulae*, genizah text no. 10.

[37] Weiss and Netzer, *Promise and Redemption*, p. 32; on biblical scenes in general, see Hachlili, *Ancient Jewish Art*, pp. 287–300. Hachlili somehow states as fact that "the scenes had in common the illustration of the theme of salvation and were associated with prayers offered in time of drought [!] . . . there was no intention of using these themes for symbolic or didactic purposes."

[38] Urbach, "Rabbinical Laws of Idolatry."

[39] See S. Schwartz, "Language, Power, and Identity," 31–35.

the square. This identification of the zodiacal signs with the months is, in fact, rather odd. Assuming that the Sepphorites in the fifth century used for liturgical purposes something like the periodically intercalated lunar calendar common in the Near East (and still in use as the Jewish liturgical calendar), the months actually fail to correspond precisely to the zodiacal signs, in some years in quite a significant way.[40] The introduction of the month names into the design may thus be another hint of anxiety, an attempt to tame a symbol that some people found problematic because of its obvious associations with astrology.

In all the synagogues but Sepphoris, the next panel after the zodiac contains the ark flanked by *menorot* and associated symbols. This panel in fact mirrored the real scene that stood before it, since it seems likely that synagogue arks were normally flanked by menorot (notwithstanding the strictures of the rabbis), remains of which have been found in several places.[41] But it was a distorting-mirror effect, for the mosaic panels always add elements that seem intended to heighten the evocation of the temple cult already present in the use of actual seven-branched menorot in the synagogue. Represented on the pavements, floating alongside the menorot, are *lulavim, shofarot,* and incense shovels.[42] Though the rabbis authorized the use of lulavim and shofarot outside the temple (i.e., in synagogues), in the Pentateuch their association with the cult is unmistakable and there is no way of knowing if they were actually used in nonrabbinic synagogues. The incense shovel is certainly strongly associated with the cult. Though incense apparently was burned in some synagogues, the two extant censers I am aware of are not shovels.[43] In Bet Alfa, the

---

[40] Yet Jewish astrological texts, which seem on the whole somewhat later than the mosaics, persistently identify the signs and the lunar months, though the months play no role at all in their horoscopic calculations; see, e.g., Sefer Yezirah 5:2; Beraita deMazalot, chapter 1 (see S. A. Wertheimer and A. J. Wertheimer, *Batei Midrashot* (Jerusalem: Ktab Wasepher, 1968), 2: 12; the text, indebted to both rabbinic and Ptolemaic cosmology, has been attributed to Shabbatai Donnolo, a southern Italian physician and magician of the tenth century: see G. Sarfatti, "An Introduction to Berayta De-Mazzalot," *Bar-Ilan* 3 (1965): 56–82); Pesiqta Rabbati, ed. M. Ish-Shalom [Friedmann], (reprint Vienna: Kaiser, 1880 Tel Aviv, 1963), 95–96 (on the vexed question of the dating of this text—conceivably any time between c. 400 and the high Middle Ages, see H. Strack and G. Stemberger, *Introduction to the Talmud and the Midrash* [Minneapolis: Fortress, 1992], pp. 325–29).

[41] See Hachlili in Fine, *Sacred Realm*, p. 111.

[42] This mirroring effect is already present in the synagogue of Dura, where over the aedicula is a painting of the Temple ark, with images of the menorah, lulav, and etrog to the left, and, to the right, an aqedah scene. See C. Kraeling, *The Synagogue* (= A. R. Bellinger et al., *The Excavations at Dura Europus, Final Report* VIII, pt. 1) (New Haven: Yale University Press, 1956), pp. 54–62; Goodenough, *Jewish Symbols* 9 (1964): 68.

[43] For the incense burner from Sepphoris, see above; it is not necessarily "Jewish"; the other is from late antique Egypt and is marked with a menorah; see Fine, *Sacred Realm*, p. 87, fig. 4.18, catalogue no. 2, an entry that is a masterpiece of equivocation—explicable by the fact that for the rabbis, burning of incense was the halakhic equivalent of animal sacrifice.

ark has standing on each half of its gabled roof a peculiar bird, plausibly identified as a representation of the cherubim. At Sepphoris, the evocation of the temple cult is heightened by the intervention of four panels between the zodiac circle and the ark scene, all of them straightforward representations of cultic prescriptions from the Pentateuch, marked (like the binding of Isaac at Bet Alfa, the Daniel scenes at Na'aran and Susiyah, Noah's ark at Gerasa, but, curiously, not the other biblical scenes at Sepphoris itself) with the appropriate biblical verses.

Interpretation

What are we to make of this? The floors (except perhaps the poorly preserved floor at Usfiyeh/Husefa) tend to suggest a movement from the world, in idealized form—nature scenes, scenes from biblical narrative—through the heavens (the zodiac circle),[44] to the temple cult, and back to the reality of the synagogue. It may be worth pointing out, though perhaps not too much should be made of it in light of the paucity of the evidence, that the two most popular scenes from biblical narrative are primal scenes of worship—the binding of Isaac, the story of the prototypical sacrifice, and Daniel in the lions' den, a story of immediately efficacious prayer offered by someone without access to the temple, now destroyed.[45] Such an interpretation, at least of the binding of Isaac, is slightly strengthened by the location of the same scene in the synagogue of Dura Europus, directly over the ark, where it shares a panel with a depiction of the temple and associated objects. The scene seems, in fact, to have a similar meaning in the Church of San Vitale in Ravenna, where it is juxtaposed with the scene of the angelic visitation of Abraham and Sarah. The biblical scenes may somehow be meant to represent the activities of the congregants. Perhaps all the images taken together should lead us to think of the synagogue as a kind of reflection of the heavens or a microcosm.[46] Our prayers are not simply dim echoes of a long-defunct sacrificial cult but are in fact (we hope) its equivalent. There is

[44] For Hachlili, the zodiac symbolizes the Jewish liturgical calendar—a problematic view because calendar mosaics were commonplace and easily adaptable to Jewish needs; why then use the zodiac, whose relation to the Jewish liturgical calendar is far from obvious? For Foerster ("Zodiac in Ancient Synagogues," p. 225), "the primary intention [sic] was to represent the sanctity and blessing inherent in the divine order of the universe [this is practically a quotation of Donnolo—S.S.], expressed in the images of the seasons, the zodiacal signs, the months, and the heavenly bodies which bring with them the renewal of nature, growth, and crops" (my translation). For Weiss and Netzer, it symbolizes God's intervention in history, at least at Sepphoris.

[45] Cf. Goldman, *Sacred Portal*, p. 56; Grabar, *Christian Iconography*, pp. 7–30, for a similar interpretation of the same scenes in a Christian context.

[46] See Foerster, "Zodiac in Ancient Synagogues," p. 227, for a discussion of Josephan and Philonic echoes of this theme, which he also sees in the synagogue mosaics.

perhaps still a cult performed on high (as some apocalyptists thought) in which we participate through our actions below.

The movement from the world, from actual scenes of worship, or of nature, to the cosmic realm (not an easy movement, guarded as it is by fierce creatures, reminiscent of the guardians of the heavens in the Hekhalot texts), *within the space of the synagogue,* may also reflect, or be reflected in, the increasing ritualization and professionalization of the liturgy, the increasingly elaborate performance associated with it. These synagogues, that is, are not *loci* of undifferentiated sanctity, like the generally slightly earlier "Galilean" synagogues, where the markers of sanctity are *apparently* confined to the façade. Such developments—the differentiation of the sanctity of the synagogue interior, and the ritualization of the liturgy—are suggested by the tendency in the fifth and sixth centuries increasingly to mark off, to block general access to, the most potent space in the synagogue, that surrounding the ark, and perhaps in a rather different way by the rise of the *piyyut.* Both may imply a service conducted by a clergy and a basically passive congregation; both, and the pavements as well, imply a service increasingly pervaded by an aura of hieratic mystification.

Of course matters were not so simple. Some synagogues were decorated with only single components of the common scheme. Others featured several of the elements but in a different order or had altogether different types of decoration—geometric patterns, birds, nature scenes, or narrative scenes not easily identified. This decorative variety strengthens our reluctance to suppose that the synagogue images worked as a kind of simple code, which we could break with enough effort and if only we knew more. Even in the synagogues that did use the common scheme, the reception of it was infinitely more complex than I have just suggested. For example, the congregant who visited the synagogue repeatedly for many years certainly had occasion to reflect on the components of the decoration individually. That some of these components were used to decorate graves and a variety of small objects confirms the notion that they could be meaningful even in isolation. Furthermore, in view of the importance of astrology in late antique Judaism in general, as indicated in the Hekhalot texts and magical books like the Sefer Harazim, it is not surprising that the commissioners of the Sepphoris mosaic would have been anxious that the zodiac might be used as a horoscopic aid, in a way that abstracted it from its artistic context in the synagogue pavements. Indeed, a liturgical poem discovered some years ago among the Cairo genizah documents in the Cambridge University Library, peculiar for having been composed in Aramaic, may confirm that zodiac circles were sporadically used as such. For this poem, composed to be recited on the Sabbath preceding the new moon of Nisan (the beginning of the year, according to Exodus 12), is nothing more than a versified horoscope.[47] Indeed, since this text is a *lunar* horoscope, the juxtaposition of month names and zodiacal signs at Sepphoris may even have been meant to *facilitate* its use as a horoscopic aid!

Rabbinization

Thus, the ancient synagogues as a group seem to embody a different notion of sanctity from that evident in rabbinic texts. The synagogue seems often to have constituted an unearthly realm, a reflection of the heavenly temple, an inherently sacred space, and the community that built and maintained and attended the synagogue regarded itself as a holy congregation, an Israel in miniature (see below). The rabbis, by contrast, regarded the synagogue as primarily a place of Torah, which belonged to *benei* Torah, a place whose sanctity was a formal derivative of the physical presence in it of the Torah scroll; as to the sanctity of the community, the rabbis never bothered to try to theorize it and in general had little interest in it. The Torah was, as we have seen, important in the actual, nonrabbinic synagogues, and it may have grown in importance as time went on. But it was embedded there in a type of religiosity that apparently owed little to the rabbis' "covenantal nomism," and quite a lot to general late antique (i.e., Christian) conceptions of the sacred.

Caution is in order, however. Varieties of religiosity can coexist in the same social group; indeed, even if inherently contradictory, they can function complementarily. Specifically, there is some reason to think that the rabbis came to play an increasingly important role in late antique Jewish society, especially in the sixth century, though there is no reason to believe that they were an essential part of the picture until the Middle Ages. In late antiquity, where they were influential they normally supplemented, subtly shaped, and were shaped by, rather than replaced, local varieties of Judaism. Next I will discuss some physical and literary artifacts of this complex social interaction.

Physical Remains: Anxieties of Representation

The Sepphorite zodiac, made in the fifth century, reminds us that for some Jews in late antiquity, the very act of figural representation, if not problematic per se, had its problematic aspects; in the sixth and early seventh centuries, Jews in some places began plastering over the painted walls of their synagogues, laying flagstones, or geometric mosaics, over figurative mosaic pavements, and sometimes even gouging out the eyes or in other ways disfiguring

---

[47] See J. Greenfield and M. Sokoloff, "Astrological and Related Omen Texts in Jewish Palestinian Aramaic," *JNES* 48 (1989): 201–14.

the human or divine figures portrayed on their synagogue floors.[48] In the following section I will discuss a case of sixth-century Jewish iconophobia.

There is no reason a priori to consider ambivalence about representation a tracer for rabbinization. It is true that the rabbinic documents themselves express ambivalence about representation; and it is true as well that some of the specific contents of synagogue art were prohibited, or at least deemed problematic, by the rabbis. But nonrabbinic Jews might have had reasons of their own for avoiding figural representation. Those of the Second Temple period had been far more rigorous in their avoidance of figural art than the rabbis were, and a case could surely be made for regarding the evidence for a move away from figural representation among the Jews in the sixth century as part of a general late antique and early medieval Near Eastern tendency toward iconophobia—presumably an aspect of the more or less self-conscious rejection of the Greco-Roman ethos or aesthetic as a cultural model in favor of ideological systems whose central concerns often involved renunciation or subordination of the body.[49]

Sometimes the Jewish ambivalence toward images has a distinctly rabbinic character. The Rehov synagogue, which in the fourth and fifth centuries was decorated with friezes of lions, was decorated in the sixth and seventh with a geometric mosaic pavement but, most famously, with a vast mosaic inscription that closely parallels a series of rabbinic texts concerning the sabbatical year.[50] In any case, the growing aniconism should perhaps be taken together with

[48] See Hachlili, *Ancient Jewish Art*, pp. 371–72; D. Amit, "Iconoclasm in Ancient Synagogues in Eretz Israel," *Proceedings of the Eleventh World Congress of Jewish Studies*, Division B, vol. 1 (Jerusalem: World Union of Jewish Studies, 1994), Hebrew section, pp. 9–16; Levine, *Ancient Synagogue*, pp. 340–43.

[49] For an account emphasizing the shared elements in Jewish, Christian, and Muslim iconophobia and proposing a (perhaps excessively) specific hypothesis about how they came to be shared, see P. Crone, "Islam, Judeo-Christianity, and Byzantine Iconoclasm," *Jerusalem Studies in Arabic and Islam* 2 (1980): 59–95. Crone also assumes that Judaism was inherently iconophobic. Perhaps; but the Jews were a different matter. Elsner argues that the stylistic shift visible in late antique Christian art reflects the art's new status as normative and exegetical, as opposed to descriptive. Such a shift, arguably characteristic of contemporaneous Jewish art as well, should allow anxieties about the act of pictorial representation to come to the fore (or may indeed be somehow generated by them); see *Art and the Roman Viewer*, pp. 190–245.

[50] Naveh, *On Mosaic*, no. 49. For a summary of the archaeology of the Rehov synagogue, see F. Vitto in *NEAEHL*, s.v.; the most extensive discussion of the inscription is Y. Sussmann, "A Halakhic Inscription from the Beth-Shean Valley," *Tarbiz* 43 (1973–1974): 88–158, concerned mainly with its relations to rabbinic texts. To the more puzzling and difficult questions, What were the purpose and function of the inscription? Saul Lieberman devoted an assertive paragraph ("The Halakhic Inscription from the Beth-Shean Valley," *Tarbiz* 45 [1975–1976] 1: 54–55). That the inscription "was intended to publicize the pertinent halakhot to the local Jewish inhabitants" (in Aaron Demsky's English formulation, "The Permitted Villages of Sebaste in the Rehov Mosaic," *IEJ* 29 [1979]: 182) rests on a series of assumptions, for example, about the extent of literacy in rural Palestine, about the social structure of synagogue dedications, and about the diffusion of halakhic rigor, which cannot withstand scrutiny.

the contemporaneous rise of the *piyyut* and the appearance of collections of *ma'asim*, handbooks for Jewish judges trying cases according to rabbinic law.[51] Jewish aniconism may have been part of a widespread tendency but, like its Christian and Muslim counterparts, it had its own dynamics. We ought to recall here a point made earlier: for the rabbis, the sanctity of the synagogue was marked not architecturally and iconographically but by the presence of the Torah scroll; regardless of the details of their attitude toward figural decoration, they seem to have been entirely apathetic toward the idea, which prevailed among Palestinian Jews in the fourth and fifth centuries, that the sanctity of the place could be meaningfully conveyed through its structure. It is plausible to attribute to rabbinic influence, or at least to the same complex of factors that favored the growth of rabbinic influence, the fact that *some* other Jews began to question this idea in the course of the sixth century.

En Geddi

The mosaic pavement of the sixth-century synagogue of En Geddi is the locus classicus for the Jewish anxiety about representation.[52] The nave is paved with a geometric carpet design that has at its center a kind of square emblema, in which is inscribed an octagon; in the octagon is inscribed a circle. The arrangement is not unlike that of the zodiac circle that appears in the corresponding location in other synagogues. But here, instead of personifications of the seasons, the angles of the square feature pairs of peacocks pecking at grapes.[53] Within the circle are four birds, two of them with peculiarly elongated and curved necks. In front of the apse, instead of an ark flanked by *menorot*, there is still another bird. Yet the quadripartite scheme discussed above is preserved in the En Geddi synagogue, but in a startlingly different form. It has been moved from the nave to the aisle, and its order has been altered. Most remarkably of all, it is not pictorial, but verbal, an inscription:

(Panel 1, closest to the ark but directed away from it) Adam Seth Enosh Mehallalel Jared / Enoch Methuselah Lamech Noah Shem Ham and Japheth

(Panel 2, in Hebrew) Aries Taurus Gemini Cancer Leo Virgo / Libra Scorpio Sagittarius Capricorn and [sic] Aquarius Pisces / Nisan Iyar Sivan Tammuz Av Illul [sic]/ Tishri Marheshvan Kisliv [sic] Tevit [sic] Shevat/ and Adar Abraham Isaac and Jacob. Peace / Hananiah Mishail [sic] and Azariah. Peace on Israel

---

[51] For a survey, see Brody, *Geonim of Babylonia*, pp. 109–13.

[52] According to Z. Ilan, *Ancient Synagogues*, p. 321, the village, including the synagogue, was destroyed soon after 540; cf. D. Barag, "En-Geddi: The Synagogue," in *NEAEHL*.

[53] For similar design from the much earlier (early third century?) "House of Orpheus" at Volubilis, in North Africa, see C. Kondoleon, *Domestic and Divine: Roman Mosaics in the House of Dionysos* (Ithaca: Cornell University Press, 1995), pp. 248–49.

(Panel 3, in Aramaic) May Yosi and Azrin and Haziqin sons of Halfai be remembered for good. / Whoever causes faction between men and their fellows, or recounts / slander about his fellow to the nations ['amemayah], or steals / the property of his fellow, or whoever reveals the secret of the village [qarta] / to the nations[54]—may He whose eyes wander through all the land (cf. Zechariah 4:10; 2 Chronicles 16:9) / and who sees what is hidden, may He set His face against such a man / and his seed, and uproot him from beneath the heavens / and let all the nation ['amah] say, Amen and Amen, Selah.

(Panel 4, in Aramaic) Rabbi Yosi ben [sic] Halfai, Haziqin bar Halfai—may they be remembered for good, / for they did very much for the name of the Merciful One.

Peace. (Naveh, On Mosaic #70; my translation)

Despite its disarrangement, this inscription is quite obviously a verbal representation of the common decorative scheme discussed above. The first panel stands in for the biblical scene, and the second for the zodiac circle, the signs identified, as at Sepphoris, with the lunar months. What follows in the second panel is not a continuation of the first panel's biblical genealogy; rather, it is likely to be the counterpart of the prototypical scenes of worship found at Susiyah, Naaran, Sepphoris, and Bet Alfa. Hananiah, Mishael and Azariah, like their associate Daniel, are the types of successful (i.e., immediately answered), prayer, and Abraham, Isaac, and Jacob, perhaps of sacrifice, the activity Genesis most frequently reports of them. The third panel is puzzling by any criteria. That it begins with a short dedicatory inscription is unproblematic, since dedicatory inscriptions are frequently found in the corresponding position on the figural pavements. It is of great interest that the donors chose to have their names placed in the inconspicuous aisle, not in the nave. They presumably believed that their names belonged with the most potent evocation of the synagogue's sanctity, the zodiac scheme, even if this evocation was now somewhat discredited. The third panel is odd because where we would expect some verbal allusion to the ark and menorot, we have instead a curse. This curse bears a loose resemblance to those inscribed on amulets produced in the same period, collected by Naveh and Shaked.[55] Like many of them, it uses an allusion to a biblical verse as a periphrastic way of referring to God, and it concludes not just with a single "amen," but "amen, amen, selah." The rhetoric is rather different, though, perhaps in part because it is, unlike the amulets, a public text, as the inscription itself acknowledges ("let all the nation say"). Perhaps invocations of angels, a feature of most amulets but absent

---

[54] For a speculative interpretation of this curse, see S. Lieberman, "A Preliminary Note on an Inscription from En-Geddi," *Tarbiz* 40 (1971): 24–26.

[55] *Amulets and Magic Bowls*; and *Magic Spells and Formulae*.

here, were considered improper in a public text. In any case, the third panel's resemblance to contemporaneous amulets may offer a key to its presence in this inscription, for amulets were often deposited in the apses of ancient synagogues, either in or near the ark.[56] Thus the En Geddi inscription may be evoking the apsidal assemblage of the synagogue by miming its contents. It may be worth adding that the periphrasis used for God comes from the prophet Zechariah's vision of the *menorah*, and so may serve as another very indirect evocation of the synagogue apse. I suggest this with diffidence, because if this is what the Engeddites wished to do, why did they not quote a relevant portion of the Torah—surely a more obvious evocation of the contents of the apse? Were they squeamish about having it stepped on?

For the present purposes though, what is important, even rather poignant, about the En Geddi pavement is the tension it implies between the old and the new, the continuing embrace of the potency of the zodiacal iconography, but its quite literal marginalization, for that matter its literalization, its reduction to writing.[57]

The *Piyyut*

The *piyyut* offers unambiguous evidence for the rabbinization of liturgical practice in sixth century Palestine. All extant Hebrew *piyyutim* are constructed around the armature of the rabbinic liturgy as prescribed in Mishnah, Tosefta, and Yerushalmi Berakhot. Starting with the work of Yannai, in the sixth century, all are packed with allusions to rabbinic laws and exegesis (and it scarcely matters for our purposes whether these allusions were to written texts or unredacted "traditions"); frequently, as their Babylonian critics noted, the *piyyutim*

[56] See comments on Naveh-Shaked, no. 10 (Horvat Rimmon), no. 11–13 (Maon-Nirim, all found in the apse), no. 16 (apse of Meroth synagogue)

[57] I suggest here with diffidence, and in a footnote only, that the uniquely schematic and nonnaturalistic style of the Bet Alfa mosaic, which is roughly contemporaneous with that of En Geddi, may be the product of a similar sort of anxiety about physical representation. This point could be made more strongly (1) if there were any reason to believe that Tzori was wrong to think that the nave mosaic of the northern synagogue of Beth Shean, executed in classicizing style, was not the work of Marianos and Hanina, who signed their name to an apparently later, very poorly preserved, mosaic in a sideroom of the synagogue ("The Ancient Synagogue in Beth Shean," *EI* 8 [1967] 149–67); and (2) if we could be certain that Ernst Kitzinger (*Israeli Mosaics*, p. 15) was right to suggest that Marianos and Hanina had some role in producing the pavements of the Monastery of Lady Mary, again in Beth Shean, and again in an utterly different style from the Beth Alfa pavement. These considerations would suggest that Marianos and Hanina were not lively rustic naifs, as they are normally represented, but highly competent metropolitan artisans, who in the Bet Alfa mosaics were fulfilling the wishes of their employers. But this must remain a suggestion.

are little more than versified summaries of rabbinic halakhah and exegesis.[58] However, we have no idea how widespread the *piyyut* was in sixth century Palestine, so its value as evidence for rabbinization is limited. Furthermore, some recently published Aramaic *piyyutim* may provide evidence for the existence of a nonrabbinic version of the practice, though the dating and function of these texts are for the most part unknown.[59] Be this as it may, Hebrew *piyyutim* were unquestionably performed in some synagogues, so examination of them can enrich our understanding of the synagogues and their functioning. Indeed, the *piyyut* can help us reconstruct some aspects of what must have been the kaleidoscopic reception of the synagogue art.

I will present two *piyyutim* that seem plausibly readable as reflecting the decoration of the synagogues: first, Yannai's *qedushta* for Numbers 8, which uses the menorah as its main conceit, and then a well-known anonymous *qinah*, perhaps one of the earliest *piyyutim* (following the common assumption that anonymity and rhymelessness imply early date) to be constructed around the signs of the zodiac. It should be unnecessary to add that there is no way to prove that these *piyyutim* and others like them really were understood by their audience as commenting on the synagogue art; I am, however, suggesting that the assumption that they were explains a great deal not only about the *piyyutim* but also about the art.[60]

A few preliminary remarks about the chronology and social history of the *piyyut* are in order, in part because we need to consider whether the audience of the *piyyut* is likely to have understood it at all.[61] It may be worth noting

---

[58] See Rabinowitz, *The Liturgical Poems of Rabbi Yannai*, 1: 55–68, and in greater detail, the same author's *Halakha and Aggada in the Liturgical Poetry of Yannai: The Sources, Language, and Period of the Payyetan* (Tel Aviv: Alexander Kohut Foundation, 1965).

[59] See Yahalom and Sokoloff, *Jewish Palestinian Aramaic Poetry*, pp. 39–45. It is furthermore my impression that as a group the Aramaic *piyyutim* are more closely linked thematically to the synagogue art than their Hebrew counterparts. Further study of these remarkable poems may produce more certainty.

[60] Cf. Shinan in Fine, *Sacred Realm*, pp. 146–48; Y. Yahalom, "The Zodiac in the Early Piyyut in Eretz-Israel," *Mehqerei Yerushalayim Besifrut Ivrit* 9 (1986): 313–22.

[61] The most sustained treatment of this question is S. Elitzur, "The Congregation in the Synagogue and the Ancient Qedushta," in S. Elizur [sic] et al., eds., *Knesset Ezra: Literature and Life in the Synagogue, Studies Presented to Ezra Fleischer* (Jerusalem: Yad Ben Zvi, 1994), pp. 171–90, who confirms an old suggestion of Fleischer that *qedushta'ot* of the "classical" (i.e., pre-Islamic) period tend to start with complex and allusive language and grow gradually simpler, with complexity reemerging only in the *silluq*—the poetic version of the *qedushah*. She follows Fleischer in supposing that this variety of tone constitutes the *payyetanim's* attempt to appeal to a broad audience. While preferable to the view that "everyone" could understand the *piyyut*, it still seems to me to overestimate the extent to which a large and probably mainly Hebrew-less audience could make sense of the poems. Even the simpler stanzas assume extensive knowledge from memory of the biblical text, not to mention the Hebrew language. The recently published Aramaic *piyyutim*, usually composed in relatively simple language with many similarities to that of the synagogue inscriptions, are suggestive—if only more were known about their function and dating; see Yahalom and Sokoloff, *Aramaic Poems*.

that the social history of the *piyyut* is still largely unexplored. The *piyyutim* are a relatively recent discovery, and the scholarship on them has been largely concerned with such basic issues as textual criticism, attribution, prosody, and generic history.[62] What follows should be considered tentative.

The *piyyut* is an artifact of the professionalization of liturgy in some Palestinian synagogues, for it is a type of poetry produced by a newly emerged professional class, the *payyetanim* (*piyyut* is a hebraized back formation of the Greek loan word *payyetan = poietes*, or poet). In brief, it seems that starting in the sixth, or possibly the fifth, century, some Palestinian synagogues began employing poets whose job it was to compose a new cycle of liturgical poetry for each Sabbath and holiday.[63] This development may be seen as the institutionalization, perhaps under the impact of a similar development among Christians, of the practice of liturgical improvisation that had prevailed in at least some Palestinian synagogues—a practice that had favored employing the eloquent and learned as prayer leaders.[64] In the eighth century and following, the *piyyut* was taken up in communities under Palestinian influence, for example, in Egypt and Asia Minor. By then, though, a certain conservatism

---

[62] Even J. Yahalom, *Poetry and Society in Jewish Galilee of Late Antiquity* (Tel Aviv: Ha-kibbutz Ha-me'uhad, 1999), has mainly these traditional concerns, despite its title.

[63] See Schirmann, "Yannai Ha-payyetan"; Yahalom, "Piyyut as Poetry"; Levine, *Synagogue*, p. 119. In fact, the "Bach-at-Leipzig" model, as Schirmann and Yahalom characterized it, can be demonstrated only for Yannai and Rabbi Shimon bar Megas (see Yahalom, *Liturgical Poems of R. Simon bar Megas* [Jerusalem: Israel Academy of Sciences and Humanities, 1984], p. 13).

As to the date of the development of the *piyyut*, the reviser of I. Elbogen, *Jewish Liturgy*, pp. 220–21 (apparently H. Schirmann), argues that "we can no longer distinguish between a period of statutory prayers and a period of *piyyut* that followed"—a statement true, if at all, only if we imagine *piyyut* purely as a literary form rather than as a literary form embedded in a social practice, and furthermore adopt a kind of genetic fallacy according to which the classic *piyyut* was already present in its sources. For what Elbogen's reviser means is that Hebrew poetry was written before the sixth century that featured some elements characteristic of the *piyyut*, e.g., use of archaizing periphrasis. There is no evidence that the *piyyut* as social practice, or even as full-blown literary form, existed before the fifth or sixth century. *Au contraire*, the silence of Y. Berakhot and Y. Megillah seems decisive.

The earliest *payyetanim* are thought to have been Yosi ben Yosi and Yannai; for their dates, see A. Mirsky, *Yosse ben Yosse: Poems* (Jerusalem: Mossad Bialik, 1977), pp. 8–14; and Rabinowitz, *Liturgical Poems of Rabbi Yannai*, 1: 45–54.

[64] At least this is how Palestinian rabbinic texts describe it, and they are followed by most modern scholars; see, e.g., Yahalom, "Piyyut as Poetry," pp. 111–12; R. Scheindlin, *The Gazelle: Medieval Hebrew Poems on God, Israel, and the Soul* (New York: JPS, 1991), pp. 13–18. E. Fleischer, *Shirat Hakodesh Ha'ivrit Biyemei Habeynayim* (Jerusalem: Keter, 1975), pp. 47–54, suggests a different trajectory of development; prayer, in his view, had not been improvised but fixed in an infinity of local variants; thus, much as in modern synagogues, the congregation recited the prayers and the leader then repeated them. After several centuries, boredom set in (!), so some prayer leaders, especially those in the synagogues connected to the rabbinic *yeshivot*, began to compose new liturgies, which they performed while the congregation continued to recite the traditional liturgy. Fleischer was apparently disturbed by the congregational passivity implied by an improvisational liturgy.

had set into the liturgy, so that older *piyyut* cycles were frequently reused—fortunately for us, because this guaranteed their preservation, at least long enough to be deposited in the genizah of the Palestinian synagogue of Fustat (Old Cairo).[65] It was there that massive quantities of late antique and early medieval Palestinian *piyyut* came to light at the end of the nineteenth century, material previously almost wholly unknown because in the high Middle Ages, the Babylonian rabbinic hostility to the *piyyut* prevailed throughout the Jewish world, so that the old *piyyut* cycles largely fell into desuetude.

It is not known how widespread the *piyyut* was in sixth century Palestine. It seems a priori likely that only wealthy urban communities could afford the services of a full-time *payyetan*, as was true also of professional cantors in the nineteenth and early twentieth centuries in eastern Europe amd America, or professional organist/choir masters in the eighteenth century in western Europe. But there is no reason why rural communities should not have occasionally commissioned *piyyutim* for special occasions, or that, like famous orators during the high Roman Empire, famous *payyetanim* might not occasionally have gone on tour.[66] Perhaps there were also semiprofessional *payyetanim* working outside the cities, like the homespun *ba'alei tefillah* and church organists of later periods, but their works, if any, have apparently not been preserved, so we know nothing of them.

The *piyyutim* were usually composed in Hebrew, are characterized by an obscure and allusive style, and make frequent use of neologisms.[67] The striking formal resemblance of some *piyyutim* to the *kontakion*, a type of Christian liturgical poetry written in Greek and, like the *piyyut*, introduced in the sixth century, would benefit from a more thorough examination than it has so far received.[68] What is certain, though, is that some of the *payyetanim* were intellectuals of the first rank, masters of biblical and rabbinic lore, allusions to which often seem the main point of their work. The *piyyut* is above all a learned poetry that could be fully appreciated only by the highly educated and highly refined.

This point requires emphasis, since it is often assumed that the *piyyut* was in general readily comprehended by its real audience, the men (and women and children?) who attended synagogues in places like Tiberias, Sepphoris, Caesarea, and Bet Shean-Scythopolis in the sixth and seventh centuries.[69] At first glance, this is a fair point: after all, why use *piyyutim* if few people under-

---

[65] See Fleischer, *Shirat Haqodesh*, pp. 14–22.

[66] For similar speculation, see Fleischer, *Shirat Haqodesh*, p. 54.

[67] See in general J. Yahalom, *Poetic Language in the Early Piyyut* (Jerusalem: Magnes, 1985).

[68] See H. Schirmann, "Hebrew Liturgical Poetry and Christian Hymnology," *JQR* 44 (1953): 123–61; Yahalom, "Piyyut as Poetry," pp. 121–25. Schirmann was mainly interested in arguing that Romanos the Melode, the main composer of *kontakia*, who was allegedly of Jewish origin, was influenced by the *piyyut*; but the chronological issues are at present unresolvable.

[69] See, e.g., Rabinowitz, *Liturgical Poems*, pp. 72–76; Yahalom, *Poetic Language*, pp. 12–13; Schirmann, "Yannai Ha-payyetan," p. 50 (with reservations).

stood them? But the *piyyut* was not simply read: it was performed, probably almost always sung, sometimes with choral accompaniment, as part of the larger performance that constituted the synagogue service as a whole.[70] We must not forget that the synagogue service was, among other things, entertainment,[71] a commodity always hard to come by in antiquity, and all the more so in the fifth and sixth centuries, when rhetorical, theatrical, and athletic performances were no longer available, and even horse racing was coming under increasing attack. The *piyyut* and the sermon (and there is no reason to see them as mutually exclusive), as well as their Christian counterparts, were the functional equivalents of the sophistic performance, and we have no more grounds for thinking that the *piyyut* was generally fully understood than that most of Libanius's audience grasped the dense webs of classical allusion that constitute his speeches.

The real reception of the *piyyut* must have been complex. There must have been in every large Jewish settlement, and more so in places like Tiberias, with its long tradition of rabbinic study, small numbers of highly learned men who really could grasp the allusions of a poet like Yannai; for such people, indeed, the enigmatic character of the songs must have provided much of the pleasure to be derived from them. Perhaps Fleischer was right to suppose that the *piyyut* originated in synagogues connected with rabbinic academies. If we may trust Jerome, and the implications of rabbinic literature, Jewish primary education in late antiquity consisted in part of memorization of the Bible.[72] People with such an education constituted a larger part of the *piyyut*'s audience, and such people, provided they remembered something of what they had learned, may have understood some of the poetry, especially the simpler sections analyzed by Elitzur. But probably most of the audience had little or no education and only a poor grasp of Hebrew, which was no longer spoken.[73] Such people may naturally have had little control over the employment of a *payyetan* in their synagogue, but to the extent that they considered the payyetanic performance more than merely tolerable, they may have regarded the musical elements of the performance as primary, or have responded, no less than their wealthier and more educated fellow congregants, to the atmosphere of numinous mystification surrounding the *piyyut*, which was an important aspect of its performance. We should, however, acknowledge the important

---

[70] Fleischer, *Shirat Haqodesh*, pp. 134–36. Fleischer notes that the evidence for extensive use of choirs begins with Qiliri, probably at the very end of our period.

[71] Cf. Fleischer, *Shirat Haqodesh*, p. 51. Note also the account, from a medieval genizah document, cited by Rabinowitz, *Liturgical Poems*, p. 74, mentioned here for the sake of illustration: one Yom Kippur, a cantor from Damascus performed a *piyyut* composed by the great philosopher and poet Ibn Gabirol in such a stirring manner that when he finished the crowd shouted, "Encore! Encore!" The cantor, according to his own account, was then inspired by God to improvise additional stanzas—this at a time when liturgical improvisation was no longer practiced.

[72] See S. Krauss, "The Jews in the Works of the Church Fathers," *JQR* 6 (1894): 231–33.

[73] See S. Schwartz, "Language, Power, and Identity," pp. 12–9.

argument of Shulamit Elitzur (n 61) that *qedushtaot* of the "classical period" usually contained several relatively simple stanzas that even the moderately well-educated could probably more or less understand. Nor should we ignore the likelihood that people *discussed* payyetanic performances, and such discussions may have helped the uneducated get the gist of the contents of the *piyyutim*.[74]

Qerovah of Yannai for Numbers 8[75]

(I) By day we grope like blind men/ and by night we feel our way like the sightless/ and we say, "The Lord is my light (Micah 7.8), and a lamp for the pathway of my feet" (cf. Palms 119:105).

The branches of the menorah/ were broken with wrath/ and the city which was as a light to all/ lo, it is darkest of all.

Search Jerusalem by lamplight/ and we shall see ten *menorot* (2 Chronicles 4:7)/ which were arranged within it/ precisely set near the menorah of the Faithful.[76]

They will see her power,/ those who hear the vision of her greatness [in this *piyyut*?];/ she is entirely of pure gold/ and on her head is a bowl, as it is written (Zechariah 4:2), "He said to me, 'What do you see,' and I said, 'I saw a menorah entirely of gold with a bowl on its head and its seven lamps were upon it, seven, and seven attached to the lamps which were on its head.' "

(II) Light which shows and makes seen/ of action and of deed/ You instructed to the humble [i.e., Moses]/ and his eyes flowed.

With Your finger You showed him/ with Your mouth You instructed him/ in Your dwelling You entrusted to him/ as an artisan You taught him.

. . . ./ [etc. The poem continues with a detailed description of the menorah, drawn from biblical and rabbinic sources.]

(III) The lamps of Edom (the Christian empire) grew strong and numerous/ the lamps of Zion were swallowed up and destroyed.[77]

---

[74] Some *payyetanim*, most prominently Qiliri, delighted in displays of virtuosity that were almost certainly wholly incomprehensible, even to the most learned and attentive members of the congregation. Qiliri's *qerovah* for the Sabbath before Purim (its first lines are: Atz qotzetz ben qotzetz/ qetzutzai leqatzetz/ bedibbur mefotzetz/ retzutzai leratzetz/ letz bevo lerotzetz, etc.) was notorious for its incomprehensibility even in the Middle Ages, and yet it was exceedingly popular—one of the few ancient *piyyutim* to survive long enough to have been included in the standard modern liturgies. See Yahalom, *Poetic Language*, pp. 16–18.

[75] See M. Zulay, *Piyyute Yannai* (Berlin: Schocken, 1938), pp. 188–89; Rabinowitz, *Liturgical Poems*, 2: 35–40, with commentary. The translation is my own.

[76] I.e., of Moses—the very menorah mentioned in the week's Torah lection; cf. Y. Shekalim 6:4, 50b.

[77] A similar conceit appears also in Midrash Tadshe, chapter 2, a medieval collection that like the *piyyutim*, often draws on lost *midrashim*: " 'And he made ten golden menorot' (2 Chr 4:7),

The lamps of Edom were mighty and flared forth/ the lamps of Zion flickered and were extinguished.

The lamps of Edom pass before every pit (?)[78]/ the lamps of Zion were set back.

The lamps of Edom, their brilliance is clear/ the lamps of Zion were darker than black.

The lamps of Edom were laden and brimful/ the lamps of Zion fell and shattered.

The lamps of Edom were honored and attended/ the lamps of Zion were constrained by force.

The lamps of Edom glow for a corpse (i.e., Jesus)/ the lamps of Zion are forgotten like a corpse. . . .[the MS breaks off, and resumes with fragments of the *silluq*; the last stanza of the *silluq* is largely preserved].

(IV) . . . [the heavenly bodies (identified here with the angels)] arise at night/ to declare Your faith by night/ trembling like slaves before You/ those who are made according to Your plan/ who run alongside the wheels of Your chariot/ who face the surfaces of Your throne/ but see not the likeness of Your face/ but rather the luster of the light of Your face/ surrounded by snow and fire/ and its wheels [of the divine chariot] are burning fire/ and a river of fire is drawn out before it/ from which they [the angels/heavenly bodies] are created/ and through which they pass/ but their light avails You not/ for it was You who lit the lamps/ You who make the lights/ who create the heavenly bodies/ who bring forth the constellations/ who spread out the stars/ who light the light of the sun/ who cause to shine the luster of the moon/ which runs to the light of the sun/ who cause the sun to shine/ and Mercury to scintillate/ who set Venus in its place/ who correct the moon-star/ who illuminate the light of Jupiter/ who enrich the splendor of Saturn/ who make red the light of Mars/ and all of these are lamps in the heavens/ and You wished to light lamps on earth/ like. . .the appearance of the tent of heaven/ was made the likeness. . .[of the Temple?]. . .[the MS breaks off]

The first stanza resembles the midrashic *petihta*, or proem, in that it uses a prophetic text to illuminate a Pentateuchal one, which is, however, implied rather than quoted. In doing so, it also uses the common exegetical technique of reading the biblical text into the present, conceived as an episode in the historical mythology of the nation of Israel: with the destruction of our temple and holy city we live in darkness, yet those who persist in hearing of its past

---

corresponding to the Ten Commandments, and each menorah has seven lamps—for a total of seventy, corresponding to the seventy nations; and whenever the lamps burn the nations are restrained, but as soon as the lamps were extinguished, the nations prevailed"; see A. Epstein, *Beiträge zur jüdischen Alterthumskunde* (Vienna: C. D. Lippe, 1887), pp. xvii–xviii.

[78] Perhaps, following Rabinowitz, *Liturgical Poems*, "reach every corner," an allusion to the spread of Christianity.

glory, by listening to the biblical readings and their poetic adaptations, will yet see its restoration. The vision of Zechariah, which closes the stanza, symbolized, according to the prophet's angelic guide, the victory of Yahweh's spirit—at the End of Days, as all later interpreters believed.

The first stanza is in all likelihood meant as introductory, for what follows begins with a straightforward ecphrastic expansion of the biblical description of the menorah, different from its ultimate models in Greek rhetoric only in that it is written in rhyming Hebrew. The third stanza, finally, returns to the gloom of the present, tacitly accepting the worldview of Christian triumphalists by contrasting the glory of the Byzantine empire with the debasement of Israel.[79] This stanza is an alphabetic acrostic, and the manuscript breaks off after the letter *nun*, four lines before the end of the poem. The last of the surviving verses may indicate that a change is about to occur, and the poem will conclude with the punishment of the Christians and the restoration of Israel. The menorah is thus used in this poem as a symbol of the historical myth of Israel, a myth of Israel's past glory, its present degradation, and its future restoration, which awaits especially those who continue to remember, to witness performances of, the myth (*shom'ei hezyon godlah*).

However, the menorah also serves, in the *silluq* (i.e., the final extant stanza) as the earthly counterpart of the heavenly bodies, identified with the angels. The notion that our liturgy corresponds to an angelic or a planetary liturgy is a commonplace of the *silluq*, for the *qedushah* (i.e., the *sanctus*), which forms the core of the *silluq*, has as its main theme that Israel joins with the angels in their praise of God. The divine chariot, an allusion to the first chapter of Ezekiel, also inescapably evokes the solar chariot of the synagogue mosaics; but in this poem, the subordination of all the heavenly bodies, especially the sun, to God is given repetitive (one might almost say, polemical) emphasis. The angels do not serve here even as intermediaries; instead they are the heavenly counterparts of the menorah. When humans conform to God's will by lighting the menorah, they imitate God in his creation of the heavenly lights. In this way, the cosmic imagery of the synagogue is tamed by subordinating it completely, in an ecstatic litany, to God's will and Israel's action (but its past action, for the menorah is no longer lit).

In several extant *piyyutim*, the zodiac is pressed into service directly to testify to Israel's past and its future restoration.[80] Best known of these is an anonymous

---

[79] On this stanza, see Yahalom, *Poetry and Society*, pp. 73–75.

[80] *Qerovot* for the first day of Passover and the eighth day of Tabernacles, which contain prayers for dew and rain, respectively, conventionally mentioned the signs of the zodiac (equated with the twelve tribes of Israel and the months). But this practice is first attested in the work of R. Elazar Qiliri (fl. c. 600), and its subsequent transformation into a topos (with, naturally, less and less connection to the realia of the synagogue) may have been due to his influence; see E. Fleischer, "Lekadmoniot Piyyutei Hatal (Vehageshem): Kerovah Kedam-Yannait Ligevurot Hatal," *Kobez al Yad* 8 (1975): 91–139, especially 107.

alphabetic *piyyut*, sometimes thought "preclassical" (i.e., fifth rather than sixth century) because of the absence of rhyme and the relative simplicity of its language.[81] This poem was composed for the fast of the Ninth of Av, which commemorates the destruction of both temples. It is one of the rare late antique *piyyutim* still used liturgically and thus appears in every Ashkenazic prayer book:[82]

> So by our sins was the temple destroyed, and by our iniquities was the sanctuary burnt;/ in the land joined together[83] they wove elegies, and the heavenly host lifted its voice in dirges// How long will there be weeping in Zion and mourning in Jerusalem!
>
> The tribes of Jacob wept bitterly, and even the signs of the zodiac shed tears,/ the banners of Jeshurun bent their heads, and the Pleiades and Orion, their faces darkened// How long will there be weeping in Zion and mourning in Jerusalem. . . .
>
> Aries first wept with embittered soul because his lambs were led to slaughter/ Taurus let its cry be heard on high because we were all pursued to our necks.// How long, etc.
>
> Gemini appeared divided because the blood of brothers was spilled like water,/ Cancer sought to fall to earth because we fainted from thirst.// How long, etc. . . .
>
> We offered a sacrifice and it was not accepted, and Capricorn cut off the ram of our sin offering,/ merciful women boiled their children, and Pisces averted his eyes.// How long will there be weeping in Zion and mourning in Jerusalem!
>
> We forgot the Sabbath with back-turning hearts, so the Almighty forgot all our merits./ Be greatly zealous in avenging Zion, and grant the populous city [Jerusalem, Lamentations 1:1] of Your light!// Take pity on Zion, and build the walls of Jerusalem!

Here the signs of the zodiac are made to mourn the downfall of Israel as described in the book of Lamentations, in a way that mirrors the mourning of Israel itself.[84] The signs of the zodiac are apparently supposed normally to act as intercessors for Israel, but their intercession is effective only as long as Israel is righteous. The *piyyut* thus retains the sense, perhaps implicit in the

---

[81] See Yahalom, "Zodiac in the Early Piyyut," pp. 316–17.

[82] For the best text, see D. Goldschmidt, *Order of Elegies for Tishah Be-Av* (Jerusalem: Mosad HaravKook 1977), pp. 29–30. The translation is once again my own.

[83] From Palms 122:2, "Jerusalem the rebuilt, as a city joined together."

[84] Cf. the *piyyut* for Yom Kippur published by Yahalom ("Zodiac in the Early Piyyut," pp. 319–22), in which the signs of the zodiac are said to rejoice along with all humanity when the high priest exits the holy of holies on the Day of Atonement.

synagogue decoration itself, that the ritual of the synagogue, in this case the communal mourning on the Ninth of Av, mirrors heavenly ritual, but it also strives, like the *qerovah* of Yannai, to read the iconographic motif in light of Israel's historical mythology. Our mourning echoes and continues the mourning of Israel in its destruction, and is in turn echoed by the mourning of the heavenly host, now, like us, reduced to ineffectuality—Gemini appears divided, Cancer wishes to fall to earth, and Pisces averts his eyes. But when we end our neglect of God's law, he will avenge us, and once again cause his light, that is, the signs of the zodiac, to shine upon us.[85]

These poems, and the many others like them, cannot be understood in any simple way as the key to the interpretation of the synagogue decoration. They are occasional pieces, perhaps performed once and forgotten, and thus are elements in the kaleidoscopic, constantly shifting reception of the art. Images that at this moment figure Israel's catastrophic decline and glorious future restoration may, at another moment, figure something else entirely. Taken cumulatively, the *piyyutim* are in some tension with the synagogue decoration. Though some of the *piyyutim*, like those just discussed, retain the idea that earthly ritual mirrors cosmic ritual, they relentlessly incorporate the decoration into a rabbinic-style reading of Pentateuchal narrative and prophetic oracle as prefiguring the great cycle of Israel's past glory, present punishment as recompense for its sins, and future messianic restoration. In this way, they constitute an attempt to subvert any notion of the synagogue service as an adequate substitution for the temple cult or as a reflection of some cosmic worship of God. Those who witness the performance of the synagogue service, Yannai claims, will one day witness the restoration of Israel's glory. Although Israel must continue to proclaim God as its source of light, it now gropes in darkness, and, the anonymous poet claimed, its heavenly intercessors, the zodiacal constellations, are now rendered powerless by Israel's sins. To engage in a perhaps rather vulgar generalization, the *payyetanim* strove to read the synagogue art against the grain, as commemorating not Israel's place in the cosmos but its place in history.

In sum, the late antique remains from Palestine—the wide diffusion of the synagogue, the emergence of a Jewish iconographic language used not only to decorate synagogues (and graves) but also to mark all sorts of small objects, the evidence from archaeology for an increasingly Torah-centered, numinous ritual, and finally the first expressions in the fifth and sixth centuries of anxiety about the use of representation and the contemporaneous emergence of the piyyut—all indicate that the period was characterized by a process of judaiza-

---

[85] This sounds almost like a conscious attempt to stake out a compromise position in the rabbinic debate, ascribed to R. Yohanan and R. Hanina b. Hama, about whether Israel's fate is ruled by the signs of the zodiac; B. Shabbat 156a.

tion. The Jews once again began to construct their symbolic world around the Torah, the (memory of the) temple, and related items, and they began once again to think of themselves as constituting Israel.

Of whatever else their Judaism may have consisted, precisely what effect the symbolic importance of the Torah had on their lives, apart from its occasional public reading, we can scarcely say. The decoration of the synagogues, which is our main evidence outside rabbinic literature and its midrashic and piyyutic offshoots, though obviously "Jewish," is irreducible to theology. It provides some hints, though: the synagogue was a holy place and for some Jews its sanctity may have consisted partly in the fact that it was a kind of microcosm, a reflection of the heavens, so that the rituals performed in the synagogue both reflected and influenced a heavenly ritual. In some synagogues, especially in the sixth century, both the floor decoration and such items as chancel screens served to demarcate zones of special sanctity, culminating in the niche containing the Torah scroll. This tends to conform with the rabbinic idea that the Torah was not simply read but performed, in what the rabbis regarded as a reenactment of the giving of the Torah on Mount Sinai. How widespread the rabbis' interpretation was we have no way of knowing, but this development, together with the emergence of the professional class of *payyetanim*, suggest the increasing importance of the synagogue as a site of elaborate performance, led by a clergy, of a numinous type. The religiosity of the synagogue was very much like that of the church.

But the very emergence of the *piyyut*, and of a discernible iconophobic tendency among some Jews in the sixth century, hints at the appearance of a new tension, or rather the surfacing of an old one. The *payyetanim* whose work is extant relentlessly rabbinized. Their poems were constructed largely out of complex webs of allusions to biblical texts and rabbinic lore; they propounded rabbinic halakhah in rhymes; in the *qerovot*, they transformed the prayer service into an extended paraphrase of and commentary on the weekly Torah reading; concurrently, they strove to read the synagogues' decoration in the light of the Deuteronomist's historical mythology of Israel in its rabbinic version. They tried, in sum, to transform the synagogue from a space that marked Israel's place in the cosmos to one that marked its place in a historical drama.[86]

---

[86] Somehow connected to this may be the inscriptions listing the twenty-four priestly "courses," mainly from the sixth century, and the *piyyutim* based on them. It is worth noting that these inscriptions have so far been found only on separate plaques and not worked into the mosaic pavements, unlike donor inscriptions. For discussion, see L. Levine, "Caesarea's Synagogues and Some Historical Implications," in A. Biran and J. Aviram, eds., *Biblical Archaeology Today, 1990: Proceedings of the Second International Congress on Biblical Archaeology*, (Jerusalem: IES, 1993) 666–78; Levine, *Ancient Synagogue*, pp. 491–500; and cf. Yahalom, *Poetry and Society*, pp. 107–36. Levine concludes that there was a genuine revival of priestly power in late antiquity, in a way that challenged the rabbis, a theme taken up by several participants at a conference on Jewish culture in late antiquity held at the Hebrew University in July 1999. While possible, the evidence seems to me poor.

Payyetanim were of course employed by communities, and their poetry was learned, obscure, allusive, and performed to music. Some community leaders must have approved of their message, but others may have approved mainly of their singing, or may have delighted in their penchant for mystification. The *payyetanim*, and the iconophobia that seems a related phenomenon, are evidence for the beginnings of a process of rabbinization. They serve as powerful reminders that, even in the fourth and fifth centuries, the synagogues, the art with which they were decorated, and the rituals performed in them, not only conveyed meaning but also served as arenas in which meaning was contested.

TEN

THE SYNAGOGUE AND THE IDEOLOGY

OF COMMUNITY

L ATE ANTIQUE JEWS regarded themselves as constituting religious communities and used a special terminology to convey the idea.[1] Inscriptions from Jericho, Bet Shean, Susiyah, Caesarea, Huldah, Husefa-Usfiyyeh, Bet Alfa, Maon, and Hammat Gader mention gifts made to synagogues by the *qahal* (*qadishah*), *benei havurta qadishta*, *benei qarta*, *'iraya* (townspeople?), and the *laos*; the inscription from the En Geddi synagogue discussed in chapter 9 may refer to the townspeople as the *'am* (nation), which corresponds closely to the Greek *laos*.[2] Such terms as *benei qarta*, like their counterparts in Christian and Syrian pagan inscriptions, taken in isolation, inform us mainly of a faint and diffuse rural self-consciousness, according to Fergus Millar not uncommon in the Syrian countryside even in the second and third centuries.[3] This conception, though never directly attested in Palestine in that period, perhaps constitutes another line of ancestry, along with the sectarian community, of the late antique religious community. But words like *qahal*, *'am*, and *laos* are ideologically loaded. Like the word "Israel," also common in the synagogue inscriptions, *qahal* and the others inescapably evoke the biblical people of Israel and thus reflect what might be seen (and what the rabbis, who avoided the words, perhaps saw) as a kind of arrogation by the small settlement of the special religious status, the obligations, and the promises that God granted to and imposed upon the Jews as a whole, according to the Bible.[4]

---

[1] See Baer, "Origins," 6–10.

[2] See Naveh, *On Mosaic*, nos. 69, 46–47, 75–85 (from Susiyah, referring to both the *benei qarta* and *qahala qadisha*), nos. 39, 43, 57, 32–35 (H. Gader: Naveh suggests *'iraya* means the inhabitants of a place called 'Ir; cf. Sokoloff, s.v. *'irayy*; even if it means "townspeople," which is unlikely since *'iraya* is Aramaic in form, but *'ir* means "town" only in Hebrew, the term may be meant to connote not "community" but "permanent residents," as opposed to the visitors responsible for most of the donations. H. Gader was a popular resort frequented by wealthy Jews, as we know from the Talmud and Epiphanius, among others); Lifshitz, *Donateurs*, nos. 64–67, 81.

[3] References to something like "the community" are rare in Palestinian Christian and pagan inscriptions; I have found only the following, from a church at Kafr Makkar, published by Ovadiah, *Mosaic Pavements*, no. 76: "Lord help this village, by the vow of Ioulianos." See also Millar, *Roman Near East*, pp. 250–56.

[4] On these words, see the excellent account by M. Weinfeld in *EJ*, s.v. "Congregation."

The inscriptions found among the remains of synagogues constitute our main evidence for the late antique local religious community. We must be careful not to approach these inscriptions too positivistically. One reason for such restraint is that these little texts must be understood primarily as nuggets of ideology: in their common use of a language drawn equally from the Greco-Roman urban culture of euergetism and the Hebrew Bible's conception of the congregation of Israel, the inscriptions construct a religious world whose relation to embedded social and economic realities is indeterminate. The inscriptions, that is, cannot be used to describe the social structure of rural late antique Palestine; nor is it even clear how much they can tell us about actual social and economic relations within the religious community itself.[5]

Another reason for interpretative restraint is that our evidence is so paltry—about seventy-five usable epigraphical texts. The types of information available to historians of other periods, like the rich documentation found in the Cairo genizah, which has made possible the excellent and detailed studies of the Jewish communities of medieval North Africa by S. D. Goitein, Mark Cohen, and Menahem Ben-Sasson, are not available for antiquity.[6] Such documentation enabled Goitein and his students to produce full accounts not only of how communities functioned, but of the exceptionally complex tripartite relationship between the community as expression of religious ideology, the community as legal, social, and economic corporation, and the cities and towns in which the communities were situated. Nothing comparable is possible for late antiquity.[7]

Notwithstanding all these qualifications, the communal ideology, which most Jewish settlements shared by the end of antiquity, is important in itself because it could influence, in however limited a way, social relations, patterns of expenditure, and mentalities. Thus, though it never eradicated local and

[5] For detailed discussion of the inscriptions, making some points similar to mine, see H. Lapin, "Palestinian Inscriptions and Jewish Ethnicity in Late Antiquity," in E. Meyers, ed., *Galilee through the Centuries: Confluence of Cultures* (Winona Lake, Ind.: Eisenbrauns, 1999), pp. 239–67.

[6] See S. D. Goitein, *A Mediterranean Society: The Jewish Communities of the Arab World as Portrayed in the Documents of the Cairo Geniza*, 6 vols. (Berkeley: University of California Press, 1967–1988), esp. vol. 2; M. R. Cohen, *Jewish Self-Government in Medieval Egypt: The Origins of the Office of Head of the Jews, ca. 1065–1126* (Princeton: Princeton University Press, 1980); M. Ben-Sasson, *The Emergence of the Local Jewish Community in the Muslim World: Qayrawan, 800–1057* (Jerusalem: Magnes, 1996).

[7] Z. Safrai was able to write an entire book on the subject (*The Jewish Community*) by missing the point adumbrated by Salo Baron (*The Jewish Community: Its History and Structure to the American Revolution*, 3 vols. [Philadelphia: JPS, 1942]) and emphasized by Baer that the town and the *qahal* are not identical, and that the Talmud has little to say about the latter. Safrai also reads all rabbinic statements, including prescriptive and idealizing ones, as if they were descriptive, believes them, and combines them to produce an impossible description of the ancient Jewish town.

other differences between Jews, and such differences in fact are an important aspect of the late antique Palestinian remains, it subtly shaped Jewish life, which as a result came everywhere to have a certain sameness.[8] Almost all Jewish settlements built synagogues, thought about themselves in similar terms, perhaps believed they had similar sorts of obligations to the poor (though there is little evidence for this outside rabbinic literature),[9] and eventually came to employ similar sorts of religious functionaries.

Community and Village

Let us begin with an observation and some questions. Any collection of people, even in the simplest societies, is bound (e.g., by familial, tribal, political, ethnic, linguistic, and economic ties) in overlapping, exclusive, and contradictory networks of organization, some of which are more self-consciously constructed than others. In the case of the late antique Jewish communities, we must wonder to what extent an ideology of partial religious self-enclosure was generated or accompanied by, or served to generate, other types of social organization. Granted that communities in rural areas were normally coextensive with villages, were villages coextensive with clans? To what extent did they participate in networks of trade? Did relationships of social dependency, including marriage, cross village lines? (This is an especially important question in light of the possible existence of communal charitable foundations: did these serve to unravel networks of patronage, or were communal charities largely symbolic, with only limited socioeconomic effects?) Were the synagogue patrons named in inscriptions patrons of their villages in a technical sense? Small-town euergetai? Did villages participate in other sorts of networks, for example, centered on the patriarch, before 425, or on rabbis? In sum, precisely how compartmental was the religious community, how constructed, and how far did it succeed in shaping late antique Jewish life?[10]

Some of these questions may be discussed summarily, either because they are unanswerable or because the answers are unproblematic. It is obvious, for instance, that the vast majority of day-to-day contacts occurred within villages. At the same time, in some areas villages might be separated by no more than

---

[8] Contrast L. Levine's emphasis on the diversity of the remains, throughout *The Ancient Synagogue*.

[9] See, e.g., Julian, *Letter to Arsacius, High Priest of Galatia*, apud Sozomen, *Historia Ecclesiastica* 5.16.5ff. = GLAJJ 2.482, written around 362, encouraging the establishment of charitable funds "in every city. . . . For it is disgraceful that, when no Jew ever has to beg, and the impious Galileans (= Christians) support not only their own poor but ours as well, all men see that our people lack support from us."

[10] This paragraph is informed by A. Macfarlane, *Reconstructing Historical Communities* (Cambridge: Cambridge University Press, 1977), pp. 1–25.

an easily traversed wadi or small valley (e.g., Meiron and Horvat Shema, or Khirbet Natur and Khirbet Shura) or might be located only a kilometer or so apart on a plain (e.g., in the Bet Shean Valley). In such cases, which were common in late antiquity, when Palestine is thought to have reached its peak premodern population density, fairly frequent intervillage contact was necessarily normal but could be complicated by other factors.[11] Contacts between two adjacent Jewish villages may have been no more frequent than those between adjacent Jewish and Christian villages, but they may (or may not) have had a different character.

Indeed, anxieties about such contacts may have sometimes helped to generate an ideology of self-enclosure—among both Jews and Christians—as a substitute for its reality (since its reality was impossible) and as a way of regulating those contacts which inevitably occurred. The Jews of En Geddi in the sixth century lived in a sparsely populated, mostly Christian area, which included many monks. The curse inscribed on the synagogue floor hints at some of the ambiguities of the Engeddites' situation, indicating as it does both the frequency and intimacy of contacts with outsiders, specifically called 'amemayah ("the nations," i.e., gentiles), and "the community's" disapproval.

Though villagers might deal mainly with each other, the self-sufficient village exists only in fiction and political propaganda. We know little about the economy of late antique rural Palestine, just enough, in fact, to know something about trading contacts outside the villages. As suggested in an earlier chapter, some of the most important evidence for such contacts is provided by the synagogues themselves, which required the importation of goods, services, and the gold coins to pay for them, into the villages—a paradox, since the synagogue was also the chief monument of the village's religious self-determination. Perhaps, in fact, we should think of the synagogues, and for that matter the churches, as smaller-scale versions of the public structures in high imperial cities, theaters, and temples, which served both as monuments to civic pride, autonomy, and wealth, and also as celebrations of the city's participation in the imperial system. (The other function of the buildings, as memorializations of the generosity/piety of the local elites, will be discussed in detail below.)

The synagogues, and other occasional archaeological finds, may provide evidence both for economic contacts between villages, and between villages and cities, but tell us nothing about what we most need to know—the frequency of such contacts and the social context in which they were embedded. Should we imagine late antique Palestine as constituting a network through

---

[11] See Goodman, *State and Society*, p. 29; such intervillage contacts are well documented for late antique Egypt (see Bagnall, *Egypt in Late Antiquity*, pp. 138–42) and seem to me to be implied, at least in a limited way, in the distribution patterns of the Kefar Hananiah pottery analyzed by Adan-Bayewitz, though this is not how he interpreted the data. See next note.

which goods, services, and coins flowed at a brisk pace, the entirety correspondingly bound together by frequent relationships of friendship, dependency, and family (complicated by the issue of religious difference), in other words, a small but remarkably cosmopolitan society, upon which an ideology of local religious self-enclosure was superimposed almost arbitrarily, perhaps mainly by local elites looking for ways to spend their money and memorialize local loyalties that increasingly lacked material foundation?[12] Or should we rather suppose that religious self-enclosure was more thoroughly embedded in a society that was in any case characterized by *infrequency* of outside contacts, in which coins and "manufactured" goods were available but hard to come by and in which most relationships—social, economic, and familial— were local?

Though this question cannot be answered, it may be worth observing that "late antiquity" lasted three hundred years, in the course of which there were presumably rises and falls in the velocity of trade, both locally and regionally; social and economic practices also varied over time and from place to place.[13] This is not to dismiss the value of generalization, but only to observe that what remained stable in the period, or progressed incrementally, was, as far as we can tell from the inscriptions and patterns of construction, the ideology of the self-enclosed religious community. That is, though this ideology was certainly embedded in some sort of social and material context, it was only loosely so. Similar sorts of synagogues were constructed both by wealthy communities, like that of Meroth in the fifth century, whose treasury contained, by around 500, vast quantities of untouched gold, obviously acquired through fairly extensive trade, and poor ones, like that of Bet Alfa in the sixth century, whose

---

[12] On the theory of the booming rural economy of late antique Syria-Palestine, see above. A quasi-modernizing view of the economy and society of late antique Palestine, like that suggested here, can be extracted from the work of Tchalenko and various followers, and it is influenced by a passage in Libanius' Eleventh Oration. For Jewish Palestine, this is more or less the view of Z. Safrai, *The Economy of Roman Palestine*, as well as of a school of New Testament–oriented archaeologists/social historians, whose views may be found in such collections as D. R. Edwards and C. T. McCullough, *Archaeology and the Galilee: Texts and Contexts in the Graeco-Roman and Byzantine Periods*, South Florida Studies in the History of Judaism 143 (Atlanta: Scholars, 1997). Such views have been bolstered by the rash conclusions that have been drawn (in some but not all cases by the author himself) from D. Adan-Bayewitz's meticulous study of the diffusion of the pottery of Kefar Hananiah: *Common Pottery*. In sum, Adan-Bayewitz's sample of material is too small to be convincingly stratified chronologically, and so its implications about the velocity of trade—a crucial but always overlooked consideration in evaluating the Galilean economy—are weak; it is furthermore uncertain that common pottery can be used unproblematically as a tracer for trade in general; finally, the patterns of diffusion observed by Adan himself disprove his assertion that Sepphoris and Tiberias played a central mediating role in the marketing of the pottery. His findings remain suggestive, but their implications must not be pushed too far.

[13] Cf. the situation in rural northern Syria: Tate, *Les campagnes*, pp. 85–188; Foss, "Near Eastern Countryside," pp. 218–9.

inhabitants had to sell part of their wheat crop to fund the production of a mosaic pavement.[14] This implies that the ideology of community can be profitably approached as primarily a cultural system, no doubt embedded in a loosely constituted social and economic system, and generative in its own right of new types of social relations and patterns of expenditure, which served to lend an air of similarity to all Jewish settlements. But it also implies that the extent to which people defined themselves around the community, the role it played in their lives, varied.

This point is confirmed by the existence of urban communities, in both Palestine and the Diaspora. Though such communities grew up in very different sorts of environments from rural communities, their material manifestations were substantially identical: they too tended to build (usually small) synagogues, decorated in much the same ways as the rural synagogues, and the inscriptions found in these synagogues indicate that they shared an ideology. Though there are differences—for example, Greek was widely used in urban inscriptions, and they yield more evidence for loose hierarchies of communal officials—the similarities are more striking and significant.

Inscriptions in Context

Inscriptions were as essential a feature of the monumental synagogue as its distinctive decoration.[15] Every synagogue with extensive remains has yielded inscriptions, usually more than one. Inscriptions are closely linked to decoration; they are found especially in the most heavily decorated parts of the synagogue—on the façades of the "Galilean" synagogues, worked into the mosaic pavements of the other types—though they have turned up also on columns, chancel screens, thrones, polycandela, and other items of furniture and decoration. The frescoed walls of the Rehov synagogue, like those of Dura Europus, had writing painted on them, and there is no reason to think this was not the case for synagogues whose walls have not survived.

---

[14] Ilan and Damati, *Meroth*; Bet Alfa: Naveh, *On Mosaic*, no. 43.

[15] The most comprehensive study of the synagogue inscriptions is G. Foerster, "Ketovot Mibattei Hakeneset Ha'atiqim Veziqatan Lenusaham shel Berakhah Utefillah," *Cathedra* 19 (1981): 12–39, a gold mine of comparative material and valuable observations, but curiously insensitive to the inscriptions' context and social function, as noted in the brief response by J. Yahalom, in the same volume, pp. 44–46, and Yahalom, "Synagogue Inscriptions in Palestine: A Stylistic Classification," *Immanuel* 10 (1980): 47–56. In brief, Foerster assumes that because the synagogue inscriptions resemble inscriptions found in Hatrean temples (see below) and certain prayers found in later Jewish liturgy, they must have functioned in precisely the same way. Hence the emphasis in my account on context, the importance of which in constituting the meaning of the synagogue inscriptions seems to me to require no special argumentation. For a more nuanced discussion of the relation between the inscriptions and liturgy, see N. Wieder, "The Jericho Inscription and Jewish Liturgy," *Tarbiz* 52 (1983): 557–79; and see Lapin, "Palestinian Inscriptions."

There is a trivial reason for the location of the dedicatory inscriptions: they commemorate donations and so tend to mark the items donated. For the same reason the most expensive items, which were paid for by several donors, mosaic floors for instance tend to have several inscriptions. But the location of the inscriptions has more profound implications, some of which were briefly noted in chapter 9. The mosaic pavements, which is where inscriptions commemorating the generosity of the community as a whole are invariably located, are the symbolic representations of the synagogue's otherness, its special sanctity; among other things, the inscriptions mark the community's, and its leaders', participation in that sanctity, their place in the cosmic order.[16]

Monumental writing is a distinctive practice that is most typical of Greco-Roman culture and was inherited to some extent by its European and Middle Eastern epigones. All public dedicatory inscriptions, on whatever sort of building they are inscribed and however they are phrased, are concerned to memorialize the dedicators and so are, among other things, expressions of a kind of "individualism," whatever precisely that may mean.[17] All mark the inscribers' participation in a loosely constituted but broadly shared set of social and cultural assumptions. It has recently been argued that the explosion of the "epigraphic culture" in the early and high Roman Empire was a response by a more or less individualistic culture to a fear of oblivion intensified by conditions of perceived change and instability, in a society in the throes of expansion. By means of public writing, individuals expressed in a powerful and durable way their desire "to fix (their) place within history, society, and the cosmos" (Woolf 1996, 29).

In a very general way, this argument is convincing, though an attempt to apply it to the rural monumentalization characteristic of late antique Syria, Asia, and Egypt obviously raises problems, which need not detain us here. We may perhaps begin to make some sense of the synagogue inscriptions by paying close attention to some of their distinctive characteristics. There are two complementary and related ways of thinking about the synagogue inscriptions. One is as religious artifacts, parallel to the writing that filled pagan temples and Christian churches, and the other is as a set of social acts, related to the sort of public writing generated by the urban culture of euergetism. In reality, these two aspects of the inscriptions are separable only with difficulty, but there is some heuristic value in attempting to do so. We begin with their religious aspect.

[16] Cf. M. Beard, "Writing and Religion: *Ancient Literacy* and the Function of the Written Word in Roman Religion," in M. Beard et al., eds., *Literacy in the Roman World*, JRA suppl. 3 (1991): 35–58, especially 39–48; and see above on the location of the dedicatory inscription at En Geddi.

[17] See G. Woolf, "Monumental Writing and the Expansion of Roman Society in the Early Empire," *JRS* 86 (1996): 22–39.

The synagogue inscriptions are obsessed with memorialization, more so than is usual in dedicatory inscriptions.[18] Forty-five of the seventy-odd relevant inscriptions begin with the formula "*dakir* (or pl. *dekirin*) *letab*," — "may X be remembered for good," or its Greek, or in one case its Hebrew, equivalent.[19] At first glance, it seems obvious that the nearest parallels to the synagogue inscriptions are those found in temples and churches—a feeling certainly strengthened by the similarity of the dedicatory formulas used in all three types of structure. The *dakir letab* formula is common in dedicatory inscriptions in Syria and its vicinity, though it is rare elsewhere. Linguistically, the most striking parallels to the synagogue inscriptions are votive inscriptions in Aramaic from several temples of the first through third centuries at Hatra, in Mesopotamia, where the *dakir letab* formula is usually qualified by the addition of the words "before the god Y."[20] In some rural Syrian shrines, Greek inscriptions pray that the donors "be remembered" (without the words "for good").[21] Many inscriptions from Palestinian churches read, "O Lord, remember your servant X" or "O Lord, help your servant X." All these dedications could be seen primarily as transactions between the individual and the gods, or as a way for individuals the fix eternally their place in a chaotic and ever changing cosmos, as Mary Beard has argued is the case for pagan votive inscriptions. Surely, the inscribed dedications from Hatra are in this sense, despite their geographical marginality, conventional artifacts of Greco-Roman religion: the dedicant inscribed on a statue or other image his name or the prayer that the god remember him for good. The cella of the shrine, where the dedication is placed, was not an especially public place: laypeople might enter it occasionally, but mainly it was the province of the priests and the gods. No one expected their dedicatory inscriptions to be read; what mattered was the act of naming.

Notwithstanding the similarity in language, the synagogue inscriptions differ from the pagan inscriptions in several important ways. They never ask that the dedicant "be remembered for good" *qodam elaha*, before God, simply that he be remembered for good. While there is no reason to doubt that God is implied, there is also no reason to think that the ambiguity of the common formula is not significant. Here the context of the inscriptions is important, for

---

[18] This is reflected also in rabbinic legislation. According to T. Megillah 3[2]:3 an object donated to a synagogue may not be used for any purpose other than that for which it was donated as long as the donor's name is remembered or, if the object is inscribed, as long as his name is legible (see Lieberman, *Tosefta Kifshutah*, for this interpretation); writing here functions as memory.

[19] Cf. also the inscriptions from Na'aran, where the donors are blessed not with the common wish that God bless their work or that their lot (in the world to come) be among the righteous, but rather with the statement that "their lot is in this (holy) place," that is, that their generosity to the synagogue has secured their immortality (Naveh, *On Mosaic*, nos. 61–66).

[20] See, for example, A. Caquot, "Nouvelles inscriptions araméennes de Hatra," *Syria* 29 (1952): 89–118.

[21] E.g., *IGLS* 2.359

the synagogue inscriptions were public in a way that dedicatory inscriptions in temples were not. Those worked into mosaic pavements, carved onto decorated facades, or scratched into chancel screens and *menorot* were meant to be contemplated no less than the objects on which the writing was made. As the rabbis acknowledged, the synagogue donor expected to be remembered not only by God but by his fellow townspeople. Furthermore, the synagogues were used primarily by the local townspeople in the service of a religious system far more concentrated and centralized than Greco-Roman paganism. The zeal to write one's name was still present but was weaker, its purpose slightly altered. Hence the existence of a small number of "anonymous" dedications (see below).

Indeed, the synagogue inscriptions are in significant respects similar to secular dedicatory and honorary inscriptions from Greco-Roman cities. The voice speaking in the *dakir letab* inscriptions is not that of the donors themselves, as in the corresponding inscriptions in churches and temples, but of the community. (A minority of synagogue inscriptions are in the first person or say simply "N made this".) By having their names written on the synagogue pavements, the donors were not simply eternalizing their place in the cosmic order but in the social order also, or to be more precise, a social order that was itself embedded in a cosmic order and may in fact have been subtly different from the social order prevailing outside the walls of the synagogue. They are marking their place in the holy community of Israel.

The church dedications occupy an intermediate position between their Jewish and pagan counterparts. Like the pagan inscriptions, they commemorate a transaction between the pious benefactor and God, in the form of a prayer that God remember or help him or her as recompense for his or her generosity. Like the Jewish inscriptions, though, they are displayed to the congregation on the mosaic pavement of the nave or the narthex. The congregation is thus expected to "overhear" the donor's prayer and witness his or her generosity, but at a certain distance. An interesting set of exceptions to this generalization are the not uncommon "anonymous" dedications, often phrased roughly as follows: "Gift of the one whose name God knows." Such inscriptions acquire their striking effect precisely from the shared conviction of the congregation that naming is important, that the dedicatory inscriptions are not simply private supplications but are supposed to be read.[22]

---

[22] Pace Beard, 46–47, who assumes that the Christian inscriptions reveal a mentality utterly different from that revealed by the pagan. In any case, at least in Palestine, inscriptions that name donors are overwhelmingly more common than the anonymous type. The anonymous formula appears in two Jewish inscriptions; at Jericho (Naveh, *On Mosaic*, no. 68, in Aramaic), it is part of a long "prayer" on behalf of the *qahal*, and it may serve much the same function in the brief Greek inscription from the "Bet Leontis" in Scythopolis (Roth-Gerson, no. 9: "Offering of those whose names the Lord knows; may He protect them forever"). A partly destroyed mosaic inscription from Hamat Gader may commemorate an anonymous gift, by *hadah itah entoliah* ("a

Inscriptions as Social Acts: Euergetism and Egalitarianism

Like the biblical and rabbinic communities of Israel, the ideology of the late antique Jewish community was characterized by tension between hierarchy and egalitarianism, though in a rather different way. While the Torah and the rabbis granted special status to priests and scribes/scholars, there is little evidence for these groups in the synagogue inscriptions. In the quasi-euergetistic world of the community, it is the handful of named donors who occupied a special position.

There can in fact be no question that the ideology of the community depended heavily on that of the Greco-Roman city, in which the wealthiest citizens were expected to fund public construction, festivals, and games; they, in turn, expected to be honored by a notionally egalitarian citizen body, with the transaction commemorated by public writing. In an important recent study of the inscriptions from Diaspora synagogues, Tessa Rajak has explored the ways in which the Jews transformed euergetism as they adopted it.[23] Some of these transformations seem conscious attempts by Jews living in high imperial cities to distance themselves from some of the characteristic discourse and practice of euergetism, while retaining its essence. For example, while pagan benefactors emphasized that their donations came from their own possessions (*ek ton idion*), Jewish benefactors played this down or even implied that their wealth was a gift of God.[24]

Most of the Palestinian inscriptions, whatever language they were written in, come from a time when the culture of urban pagan euergetism was dying or dead, having given way to the (closely related) culture of Christian charity. The Palestinian inscriptions thus do not reflect the same sort of self-conscious distancing from the discourse of *philotimia*. For example, they quite often note that gifts were made *ek ton idion* (or its Aramaic equivalents).[25] Nevertheless, here, too, the language of *philotimia* has in general yielded to that of religious obligation. In Greek inscriptions, donations are often called *prospho-*

---

certain Law-abiding woman"), if Naveh's restoration and interpretation are correct (*On Mosaic*, no. 34).

[23] "Jews as Benefactors," in B. Isaac and A. Oppenheimer, eds., *Studies on the Jewish Diaspora in the Hellenistic and Roman Periods*, Te'uda XII (Tel Aviv: Ramot, 1996), pp. 17–38.

[24] The common expression at Sardis was, "X gave this *ek ton tes pronoias*" (from the gifts of Providence); see Kraabel, "Pronoia at Sardis," pp. 75–96. A similar locution is used in an inscription from Kokhav Hayarden (Naveh no. 42): "[May . . . be remembered for good] who donated this lintel from the gifts of the Merciful One and from his own property"; for a similar phrase ("[donated] from the things of the god, under Absalmos") carved on a plaque bearing a Mithraic tauroctony, probably from Syria, see A. de Long, "A New Mithraic Relief," *Israel Museum Journal* 16 (1998): 85–90, misinterpreted by de Long.

[25] see Naveh, no. 17, Lifshitz, no. 77a, Naveh, nos. 58, 74, Lifshitz, no. 66. In Palestinian Christian inscriptions, donations are often called *prosphorai* (offerings) or *karpophoriai* (offerings of firstfruits).

rai—roughly the equivalent of *qorbanot* (offerings, or sacrifices) and in Aramaic, *mizwata* (i.e., *mitzvot*). Christians used precisely the same language in their public inscriptions, though we have seen other ways in which the Jews strove to distinguish their language of donation from that of the Christians.

Some of Rajak's other observations are as true of late antique Palestinian as of high imperial Diaspora communities. Most important of these is that in contrast to public buildings in cities, which were usually gifts of a single benefactor, synagogues were almost always built and decorated by several benefactors. (The few exceptions are diasporic and early and will not detain us.) We must wonder why this should have been so.

It is likely that in some cases the multiplicity of donors reflected social and economic realities. In some communities there may simply have been no individual rich enough to fund construction on his or her own.[26] But this cannot always have been the case. I have already indicated that little is known about the social and economic history of late antique Palestine. But it is overwhelmingly likely that some rural communities enjoyed the patronage of an individual grandee. In the first century there had been in Galilee an influential class of great landowners who in some cases controlled villages; this may contradict the archaeological record—no country villas, and only a few large town houses, have yet been discovered in Galilee—but emerges clearly from Josephus's accounts of his own activities in the district.[27] Such quasi-dynastic landowning families, who may not have been terribly rich by the standards of Italy, North Africa, or coastal Asia Minor, are sporadically attested in the Palestinian Talmud (which also knows, and disapproves, of the institution of patronage)[28] and may have continued to exist until the end of antiquity. Like the self-confident and prosperous villages of northern Syria classically discussed in Libanius's oration *de patrociniis*, some Palestinian villages may have been under the protection of influential military officers, government officials, or, indeed,

[26] Cf. high imperial rural Syria: G. Tate, "The Syrian Countryside during the Roman Era," in *Early Roman Empire in the East*, p. 67. But a case is also known of a village belonging to a single owner.

[27] See above; and S. Schwartz, "Josephus in Galilee." For the view, based on archaeology, that there were no very rich people in late antique Galilee, that (what is a very different matter) it was a "largely egalitarian society," see D. Groh, "The Clash between Literary and Archaeological Models of Provincial Palestine," in *Archaeology and the Galilee*, 32 (art. 29–37). But archaeology does not tell the whole story. Goodman, *State and Society* (p. 33) expresses himself more moderately and probably more accurately: "the wealth distinctions in Galilee between classes seem to be much narrower than in other parts of the empire." See next note.

[28] For example, Horayot 3:9, 48c, where the *paganayya* are obviously great country landowners, described in this story as paying court to the patriarch; on patrons, see the remarkable series of homilies in Y. Berakhot 9:1, 12a–b; additional rabbinic material is collected in D. Sperber, *Roman Palestine, 200–400: The Land: Crisis and Change in Agrarian Society as Reflected in Rabbinic Sources* (Ramat-Gan: Bar Ilan University Press, 1978), pp. 119–35. Patronage serves as a pervasive metaphor ("patron" is a common name for God) in the recently published Aramaic *piyyutim* (Sokoloff and Yahalom, *Jewish Palestinian Aramaic Poetry*, p. 361, s.v. *ptryn/ptrwn*).

powerful holy men/rabbis. Until the early fifth century, the patriarchs combined several of these roles, and it would be surprising if they and their entourage did not routinely patronize Palestine Jews, both rural and urban.

Yet there is scarcely a trace of any such people in the synagogue inscriptions. Only at Hamat Tiberias is the gift of a member of the patriarchal entourage commemorated, side by side with those of many other individuals, and of the community collectively. This silence may help confirm my argument in chapter 6 that Jews were gradually excluded from networks of patronage in the course of the fifth and sixth centuries, and most of the synagogue inscriptions may postdate the end of the patriarchate. On the other hand, the inscriptions' failure to mention powerful patronal figures may warn us that among the half dozen or so individuals whose names were commemorated in each synagogue as donors of a few solidi used for the purchase of a column or a panel of a mosaic pavement may be hidden the actual patron or owner of the village; if this is so, his failure to identify himself as such is significant. Rajak was right to emphasize the ideological component of the tendency of the Jewish communities to open the ranks of the named benefactors to even the modestly well-off (some individual contributions were very small),[29] and to commemorate the gifts of the community as a whole. Euergetism was modified by egalitarianism. Conversely, the inscriptions perhaps tell us less than we might have hoped about the socioeconomic life of the villages, and they may even tell us rather little about the actual economic functioning of the communities. Sometimes they may have been far more dependent on individuals than the inscriptions suggest.

Similarly, the Jewish inscriptions imply also the purely local, self-enclosed character of the community. Christian villagers repeatedly acknowledged in the inscriptions in their churches their communities' participation in an ecclesiastical hierarchy, and sometimes also in a political system, by naming bishops and bishops' representatives, by specifying the rank of the local clergy, and by noting gifts from prominent outsiders.[30] In *rural* synagogue inscriptions, by contrast, neither communal officials nor outsiders are mentioned.[31] In part, this distinction between churches and synagogues reflects basic social reali-

---

[29] Monetary gifts are noted in a few cases and range from a substantial five solidi (Hamat Gader, given by a family that included a *comes*, Naveh no. 32) to a very modest gift of one tremissis, by a father and his sons at Eshtemoa (Naveh, no. 74).

[30] The following examples are from the mosaic inscriptions in Palestinian churches published by Avi-Yonah, "Mosaic Pavements in Palestine," QDAP 3 (1934): bishops and chorepiskopoi (nos. 27?, 306?, 336?, 346, 359); an abbot (no. 335a); hegoumenoi (nos. 20, 98); priests (nos. 13, 20, 98, 115, 359, 23 [*hiereus*], 326 [*kahana* in Syriac]; comites (nos. 20, 86, 146, 359); a scholasticus (no. 335a); a primicerius (no. 11); a protoducenarius (no. 306?); a cubicularius (no. 116).

[31] Exceptions: an inscription from Nabratein may mention two local magistrates, if Naveh's interpretation is correct (*On Mosaic*, no. 13); one from Umm el-Amed commemorates the gift of a *hazzan* and his brother (no. 20); another *hazzan*, from Fiq (no. 28); a *parnas*, from Naaran (no. 63). In several places, donors are entitled *Rabbi, kohen*, or *levi*.

ties: there was no Jewish ecclesiastical hierarchy, nor, by the fifth century, many, or any, government officials who had anything to gain by displays of pious generosity to Jewish communities.[32] Furthermore, smaller communities may not have had many formally appointed officials. It may be worth remembering the Talmudic stories discussed previously telling of villagers appointing a single functionary to "fulfil all their (religious) needs." But the implications of such stories should not be generalized. It is overwhelmingly likely that there were archisynagogues, *parnasim*, *gabbaim*, and the like, in the larger villages, some benefactors may have lived elsewhere, and before 425 the patriarch and his men may, as already stated, sometimes have made gifts to Jewish communities. At very least it would have been sensible for them to do so—apart from the fact that a law in the Theodosian Code takes it for granted that one of the last patriarchs commonly helped fund the construction of synagogues (16.8.22, given at Constantinople, 415). Thus, the inscriptions' consistent failure to mention patriarchs, identifiable outsiders, and even local officials may be the result of conscious decision. The villagers thought of their communities as local, self-enclosed, and egalitarian: the only honorifics recorded are the unconstruable title "rabbi" and the hereditary biblically derived designations "kohen" and "levi." The inscriptions thus tell us disappointingly little about how rural communities actually operated, but a great deal about how they thought about themselves.

The Local Community and the Community of Israel

We have already seen that the ideology of self-enclosure may often have been in tension with wider social and economic realities. That it was in tension even with religious realities is obvious enough. After all, by around 500 all Palestinian Jewish settlements *shared* the ideology and all that went with it—the synagogue, the symbolic centrality of the Torah, and so on. Some communities, furthermore, were aware of the tension between their self-conception as loci of religious obligation and meaning, and the biblical view of Israel, inherited by the rabbis, as a single people. On the mosaic pavement of the narthex of their sixth- or early seventh-century synagogue, the Jews of Jericho wrote the following:[33]

> May they be remembered for good, may their memory be for good, all the holy congregation (*qahalah qadishah*), great and small, whom the King of the Universe helped so that they pledged[34] and made [i.e., paid for] the mosaic. May He

[32] Despite the impression created by the law codes that until c. 425 there was a Jewish ecclesiastical hierarchy at whose head stood the patriarch. Some such structure may have existed, but it was certainly loose; see above and contrast Goodman, "Roman State," who supposes that the patriarch was in fact much like a Christian bishop.

[33] Naveh, *On Mosaic*, no. 69.

[34] *'ithazqun*; for the meaning, see Wieder, "Jericho Inscription," pp. 563–64.

who knows their names, and those of their sons and the members of their household, inscribe them in the book of life with all the righteous. (They are) friends
to all Israel. Peace [Amen].

The language of this inscription was derived from a communal prayer that
until recently was known (in Aramaic) only from the prayer books of Kaffa-
Feodosiya in the Crimea, and Cochin in India, both known only in copies
printed in the eighteenth century.[35] Traces of the prayer have now been detected among the fragments of the medieval Palestinian liturgy discovered in
the Cairo genizah, and the Jericho inscription seems to prove beyond a doubt
that the prayer originated in late antique Palestine.[36] How widespread it was
there we cannot tell, though components of the Jericho inscription are paralleled at Hamat Gader, Alma, Dalton, Susiyah, and Chorazin.[37] Of special
interest is the conclusion of the inscription, *haverim lekol Yisrael*, a formula
preserved in the traditional Ashkenazic prayer book, with a slight change, to
haverim kol Yisrael (all Israel are friends), only in the inappropriate-seeming
context of the conclusion of the blessing of the new moon.[38] It seems obvious
that this exclamation is intended to qualify or mitigate the powerful expression
of the religious significance of the local community that it follows; contrary
to what we may sometimes imagine, it seems to say, we are part of the larger
community of Israel.

Two other inscriptions, both in Hebrew and carved by the same artisan on
the lintels of the synagogues of Baram and Almah, probably a few centuries
before the Jericho inscription, seem to convey a similar message: "May there
be peace on this place and on all the places of Israel" (*On Mosaic*, nos. 1, 3).
Nowhere else, though, is this point made so explicitly, and we cannot rule out
the possibility that some communities had a very strong sense of their self-
enclosure and only a weak sense, if any, of belonging to the larger community
of Israel. In other words, they were practically sectarian. Other communities
may have been so secluded in reality that their self-enclosure was almost real;
for them, the community of Israel was purely imaginary. Others still might
have conveyed their sense of belonging to the community of Israel obliquely,
for example, in the expression *shalom 'al Yisrael* (peace on Israel), which
appears in several synagogues, or in ways that have left no material traces.[39]

---

[35] See Foerster, "Ketovot," 23–26.

[36] See Wieder, "Jericho Inscription."

[37] Foerster, "Ketovot," 25.

[38] "May He who performed miracles for our fathers and redeemed them from slavery to freedom redeem us soon and gather our dispersed members from the four corners of the earth. All
Israel are friends, and let us say, Amen." Here the local community is implicitly represented as a
by-product of the exile, an imperfect condition from which we pray to be released, while we
continue to affirm the unity of the people of Israel. The message is different from that of the
Palestinian communal prayer.

[39] But *shalom 'al Yisrael* is uncommon, appearing at Gerasa and Susiyah, and ambiguous. At
Gerasa, the Semitic inscription contains the blessing *shalom 'al kol Yisrael amen amen selah*,

Conclusion

In constructing synagogues and decorating them with a sacred iconography and with monumental writing, the Jews of late antique Palestine were constructing a religious world that bore an oblique and shifting relationship to the social world in which it was embedded. The local religious community was autonomous, self-contained, and egalitarian, although at the same time influenced by old Greco-Roman urban ideas about euergetism and honor. The ideology of the local community not only reflected the disembedding of religion as a category of human experience but, in its turn, also affected the social and economic structure of rural settlements by imposing on them common patterns of expenditure. The Jewish community was in the details of its ideology and function distinctively Jewish. But the Jews, in imagining their villages as partly autonomous loci of religious obligation and meaning, and in acting on this idea by producing monumental religious buildings, were participating in a general late antique process, itself a consequence of christianization.

---

while in the Greek inscription the corresponding blessing reads *erene [sic] te synagoge* (*On Mosaic*, no. 50; Lifshitz, *Donateurs*, no. 78), raising the possibility that Yisrael might sometimes refer primarily to the community.

CONCLUSION

T HE MAIN ARGUMENT of this book has been that attempts to make
sense of the remains of ancient Judaism must consider the effects of
shifting types of imperial domination. The complex, loosely centralized but still basically unitary Jewish society that may be inferred from the
artifacts of the last two hundred years of the Second Temple period was in
part produced by a long history of imperial empowerment of Jewish leaders.
The fragmentation characteristic of the Jewish remains of the high imperial
period imply a profound but partial accommodation to direct Roman rule,
hastened by the disastrous failure of the revolts of 66 and 132. The Jewish
cultural explosion of late antiquity, which can be read from a revival of literary
production and the emergence and diffusion of a distinctively Jewish art and
archaeology, is in complex ways a response to the gradual christianization of
the Roman Empire.

This explanatory scheme has several advantages. It helps integrate the Jews
into the history of the ancient eastern Mediterranean, allowing us to see how
they were simultaneously like and unlike all other subjects. The Jews may
thus be made to serve in some ways as exemplary — even in their difference —
filling in part of a larger picture of the effects of Roman domination, supple-
menting the very different kinds of information available from, for example,
Egypt.

In addition, treating the evidence whole and in the broadest possible context partly solves (nothing can ever fully solve) the problem of infinite regression that I think inescapably affects the monographic approach to ancient
Judaism. That is, in order to begin interpreting some small body of material
(indeed, even to decide what constitutes an appropriate body of material to
study), we must make all sorts of quite specific assumptions about its historical
antecedents, context, and effects. For example, in an earlier book, I tried to
read the works of Josephus in light of the assumption that they testify to a post-
Destruction shift in Jewish politics from priestly to rabbinic or patriarchal
authority. But the conviction that such a shift occurred depended on a particular type of reading of Josephus and of the rabbinic corpus — readings that themselves depended on fairly specific hypotheses about the history of the Jews
both long before and long after the Destruction. Since this sort of regression
is, as I have just observed, infinite, expanding the scope of the investigation
cannot eliminate it. But it can at least make the ground a bit firmer, the
hypothetical structure a bit more solid.

Finally, the approach I have adopted here has the advantage of making
sense not only of the specific pieces of evidence but also of the contours of
the evidence as a whole. In other words, considering the wider political and

social worlds in which the ancient Jews lived can help explain why the evidence is the way it is, why covenant and myth are so inextricably combined in the literature of the Second Temple period, why the archaeology of Jewish Palestine in the second and third centuries seems so similar to that of the eastern Roman Empire in general, while its exiguous literary remains are so different from the products of the "second sophistic," and why, finally, the synagogue and the religious ideology that justified its construction reached their greatest diffusion only under Christian rule.

SELECTED BIBLIOGRAPHY

Adan-Bayewitz, David. *Common Pottery in Roman Galilee: A Study of Local Trade.* Ramat Gan: Bar Ilan University Press, 1993.

Alon, Gedalyahu. *Jews and Judaism in the Classical World.* Jerusalem: Magnes Press, 1977.

———. *The Jews in Their Land in the Talmudic Age.* Cambridge: Harvard University Press, 1989.

Amit, David. "Iconoclasm in Ancient Synagogues in Eretz Israel." *Proceedings of the Eleventh World Congress of Jewish Studies.* Division B. Vol 1. Jerusalem: World Union of Jewish Studies, 1994.

Avi-Yonah, Michael. *Art in Ancient Palestine.* Jerusalem: Magnes Press, 1981.

———. "The Economics of Byzantine Palestine." *IEJ* 8 (1958): 39–51.

———. *The Jews of Palestine: A Political History from the Bar Kokhba War to the Arab Conquest.* Oxford: Blackwell, 1976.

Aviam, Mordechai. "Christian Settlement in Western Galilee in the Byzantine Period." Master's thesis, Hebrew University, 1994.

———. "Yodfat: Uncovering a Jewish City in the Galilee from the Second Temple Period and the Time of the Great Revolt." *Qadmoniot* 118 (1999): 92–101.

Avidov, Avi. "Processes of Marginalisation in the Roman Empire." Ph.D. diss., Cambridge University, 1995.

Baer, Yitzhak. "Israel, the Christian Church, and the Roman Empire." *SH* 7 (1961): 79–149.

———. "The Origins of the Organization of the Jewish Community of the Middle Ages." *Studies in the History of the Jewish People*, 2:60–100. Jerusalem: Israel Historical Society, 1985. Also appeared in *Zim* 15 (190): 1–41.

Bagnall, Roger S. *Egypt in Late Antiquity.* Princeton: Princeton University Press, 1993.

———. *The Administration of the Ptolemaic Possessions outside Egypt.* Leiden: Brill, 1976.

Barag, Dan. "A Coin of Mattathias Antigonos and the Shape of the Shewbread." *Qadmoniot* 105–66 (1994): 43–44.

———. "Hamenorah kesemel meshihi bitequfah haromit hame'uheret ubitequfah habizantit," 59–62. *Proceedings of the Ninth World Congress of Jewish Studies.* B.I. Jerusalem: World Union of Jewish Studies, 1986.

———. "Jewish Coins in Hellenistic and Roman Time." In *A Survey of Numismatic Research, 1985–1990.* Edited by T. Hackens et al. Vol. 1. Brussels: International Society of Professional Numismatists, 1991.

———. "New Evidence on the Foreign Policy of John Hyrcanus I." *INJ* 12 (1992–1993): 1–12.

———. "A Silver Coin of Yohanan the High Priest and the Coinage of Judaea in the Fourth Century B.C.E." *INJ* 9 (1986–1987): 4–21.

Barker, Margaret. *The Older Testament: The Survival of Themes from the Ancient Royal Cult in Sectarian Judaism and Early Christianity.* London: SPCK, 1987.

Baron, Salo. *The Jewish Community: Its History and Structure to the American Revolution.* 3 vols. Philadelphia: Jewish Publication Society, 1942.

Bartlett, John. "From Edomites to Nabataeans: A Study in Continuity." *PEQ* 111 (1979): 53–66.

Baumgarten, Albert I. *The Flourishing of Jewish Sects in the Maccabean Era: An Interpretation*. Leiden: Brill, 1997.

———. "Crisis in the Scrollery: A Dying Consensus." *Judaism* 44 (1995): 399–413.

Baumgarten, Joseph. "On the Nature of the Seductress in 4Q 184." *RQ* 15 (1991): 133–43.

Beard, Mary. "Writing and Religion: *Ancient Literacy* and the Function of the Written Word in Roman Religion." *Literacy in the Roman World*. JRA Suppl. 3 (1991): 35–58.

Beard, Mary, John North, and Simon Price. *Religions of Rome*. 2 vols. Cambridge: Cambridge University Press, 1998.

Beer, Moshe. "On the Havura in Eretz Israel in the Amoraic Period." *Zion* 47 (1982): 178–85.

Benoit, P., J. T. Milik, and R. de Vaux. *Les grottes de Murabba'at*. Discoveries in the Judaean Desert II. Oxford: Clarendon, 1961.

Bickerman, Elias. *Four Strange Books of the Bible*. New York: Schocken, 1967.

———. *God of the Maccabees*. Leiden: Brill, 1979.

———. *The Jews in the Greek Age*. Cambridge: Harvard University Press, 1988.

Bi[c]kerman, Elie. *Institutions des Séleucides*. Paris: Paul Geuthner, 1938.

Blanchetière, F. "Le statut des juifs sous la dynastie constantinienne." In *Crise et redressement dans les provinces européennes de l'empire*, edited by E. Frézouls, 127–41. Strasbourg: AECR, 1983.

Blenkinsopp, Joseph. *The Pentateuch*. New York: Doubleday, 1992.

———. *Prophecy and Canon: A Contribution to the Study of Jewish Origins*. Notre Dame, Ind.: Notre Dame University Press, 1977.

———. "Prophecy and Priesthood in Josephus." *JJS* 25 (1974): 239–62.

———. *Sage, Priest, Prophet*. Louisville: Westminster John Knox Press, 1995.

Blidstein, Gerald. "Nullification of Idolatry." *PAAJR* 41–2 (1973–1974): 1–44.

———. "Rabbinic Legislation on Idolatry: Tractate Abodah Zarah Chapter I." Ph.D. diss., Yeshiva University, 1968.

———. "R. Yohanan, Idolatry, and Public Privilege." *JSJ* 5 (1974): 154–61.

Boccaccini, Gabriele. "Jewish Apocalyptic Tradition: The Contribution of Italian Scholarship." In *Mysteries and Revelations: Apocalyptic Studies since the Uppsala Colloquium*, edited by J. J. Collins and J. H. Charlesworth. Sheffield, U.K.: JSOT Press, 1991.

———. *Beyond the Essene Hypothesis: The Parting of the Ways between Qumran and Enochic Judaism*. Grand Rapids, Mich.: Eerdmans, 1998.

Bohak, Gideon. *Joseph and Aseneth and the Jewish Temple in Heliopolis*. Atlanta: Scholars, 1996.

Bokser, Baruch. "Approaching Sacred Space." *HTR* 78 (1985): 279–99.

———. "Rabbinic Responses to Catastrophe: From Continuity to Discontinuity." *PAAJR* 50 (1983): 37–61.

———. *The Origin of the Seder: The Passover Rite and Early Rabbinic Judaism*. Berkeley: University of California Press, 1986.

———. "Wonder-Working and the Rabbinic Tradition: The Case of Hanina Ben Dosa." *JSJ* 16 (1985): 42–92.

Bourdieu, Pierre, and Loïc J. D. Wacquant. *An Invitation to Reflexive Sociology*. Chicago: University of Chicago Press, 1992.

Bowersock, Glen. "Greek Culture at Petra and Bostra in the Third Century AD." *Ho Hellenismos sten Anatole: Praktika a' Diethnous Arkhaiologikou Synedriou Delphoi 6–9 Noembriou 1986*. Athens: Evropaiko Politistiko Kentro Delphon, 1991, 15–22.

———. *Roman Arabia*. Cambridge: Harvard University Press, 1983.

Bowie, Ewen L. "The Importance of Sophists." *YCS* 27 (1982): 29–60.

Bradbury, Scott. *Severus of Minorca: Letter on the Conversion of the Jews*. Oxford: Clarendon, 1996.

Branham, Joan. "Sacred Space in Ancient Jewish and Early Medieval Christian Architecture." Ph.D. diss., Emory University, 1993.

Brennan, B. "The Conversion of the Jews in Clermont in AD 576." *JThS* 36 (1985): 321–37.

Briant, Pierre. "The Seleucid Kingdom and the Achaemenid Empire." In *Religion and Religious Practice in the Seleucid Kingdom*, edited by P. Bilde et al., 53–60. Aarhus, Den.: Aarhus University Press, 1990.

Brody, Robert. *The Geonim of Babylonia and the Shaping of Medieval Jewish Culture*. New Haven: Yale University Press, 1998.

Broshi, Magen. "The Role of the Temple in the Herodian Economy." *JJS* 38 (1987): 31–37.

———. "Agriculture and Economy in Roman Palestine According to Babatha's Papyri." *Zion* 55 (1990): 269–81.

———. "The Population of Western Palestine in the Roman-Byzantine Period." *BASOR* 236 (1979): 1–10.

Brown, P. R. L. *The World of Late Antiquity*. London: Thames & Hudson, 1971.

Brown, Peter. *Authority and the Sacred: Aspects of the Christianisation of the Roman World*. Cambridge: Cambridge University Press, 1995.

———. *The Cult of the Saints: Its Rise and Function in Latin Christianity*. Chicago: University of Chicago Press, 1982.

———. "The Rise and Function of the Holy Man, 1971–1997." *JECS* 6 (1998): 353–76.

———. "The Rise and Function of the Holy Man in Late Antiquity." *JRS* 61 (1971): 80–101.

Bryson, Norman. *Looking at the Overlooked: Four Essays on Still Life Painting*. Cambridge: Harvard University Press, 1990.

———. *Word and Image: French Painting of the Ancien Régime*. Cambridge: Cambridge University Press, 1981.

Büchler, Adolph. *Studies in Jewish History*. Edited by I. Brodie and J. Rabbinowitz. London: Oxford University Press, 1956.

Butler, H. C. *Syria: Publications of the Princeton University Archaeological Expeditions to Syria in 1904–5 and 1909*. 9 vols. Leiden: Brill, 1907–1949.

Callaway, Philip. *A History of the Qumran Community: An Interpretation*. Sheffield, U.K.: JSOT Press, 1988.

Cameron, Averil. *The Mediterranean World in Late Antiquity, AD 395–600*. London: Routledge, 1993.

Carroll, R. "Twilight of Prophecy or Dawn of Apocalyptic?" *JSOT* 14 (1979): 3–35.

Castritius, Helmut. "The Jews in North Africa at the Time of Augustine of Hippo: Their Social and Legal Position." *Proceedings of the Ninth World Congress of Jewish Studies*, 31–37. B.I. Jerusalem: World Union of Jewish Studies 1986.

Chajes, Hirsch Peretz. "Les juges juifs en Palestine de l'an 70 à l'an 500." *REJ* 39 (1899): 39–52.

Charlesworth, James H., ed. *Old Testament Pseudepigrapha*. 2 vols. Garden City, N.Y.: Doubleday, 1983–1985.

Clerc, Ch. *Les théories relatives au culte des images chez les auteurs grecs du IIme siècle après J.C.* Dissertation Paris, 1915.

Cohen, Jeremy. "Roman Imperial Policy toward the Jews from Constantine until the End of the Palestinian Patriarchate." *Byzantine Studies/études Byzantines* 3 (1976): 1–29.

Cohen, Shaye. "Alexander the Great and Jaddus the High Priest according to Josephus." *AJS Review* 7–8 (1982–1983): 41–68.

———. *The Beginnings of Jewishness: Boundaries, Varieties, Uncertainties.* Berkeley: University of California Press, 1999.

———. "Epigraphical Rabbis." *JQR* 72 (1981–1982): 1–17.

———. *From the Maccabees to the Mishnah.* Philadelphia: Westminster Press, 1987.

———. *Josephus in Galilee and Rome: His Vita and His Development as a Historian.* Leiden: Brill, 1979.

———. "Pagan and Christian Evidence on the Ancient Synagogue." In *The Synagogue in Late Antiquity*, edited by L. Levine, 159–81. Philadelphia: American Schools of Oriental Research, 1987.

———. "The Place of the Rabbi in Jewish Society of the Second Century." In *The Galilee in Late Antiquity*, edited by L. Levine, 157–73. New York: Jewish Theological Seminary, 1992.

———. "Religion, Ethnicity, and 'Hellenism' in the Emergence of Jewish Identity in Maccabean Palestine." In *Religion and Religious Practice in the Seleucid Kingdom*, edited by P. Bilde et al., 204–23. Aarhus, Den.: Aarhus University Press, 1990.

———. "The Significance of Yavneh: Pharisees, Rabbis, and the End of Jewish Sectarianism." *HUCA* 55 (1984): 27–53.

Collins, John J. "Genre, Ideology, and Social Movements in Jewish Apocalypticism." In *Mysteries and Revelations: Apocalyptic Studies since the Uppsala Colloquium*, edited by J. J. Collins and J. H. Charlesworth, 13–23. Sheffield, U.K.: JSOT Press, 1991.

———. *Jewish Wisdom in the Hellenistic Age.* Louisville: Westminster John Knox, 1997.

Cotton, Hannah. "The Guardianship of Jesus Son of Babatha: Roman and Local Law in the Province of Arabia." *JRS* 83 (1993): 94–108.

———. "The Languages of the Documents from the Judaean Desert." *ZPE* 125 (1999): 219–31.

Cotton, Hannah, and Joseph Geiger. *Masada II: The Yigael Yadin Excavations 1963–5, Final Reports: The Greek and Latin Documents.* Jerusalem: Israel Exploration Society, 1989.

Cotton, Hannah, and Ada Yardeni. *Aramaic, Hebrew, and Greek Documentary Texts from Nahal Hever and Other Sites.* Discoveries in the Judaean Desert 27. Oxford: Clarendon, 1997.

Cowley, A. E. *Aramaic Papyri of the Fifth Century B.C.* Oxford: Clarendon, 1923.

Crone, Patricia. "Islam, Judeo-Christianity, and Byzantine Iconoclasm." *Jerusalem Studies in Arabic and Islam* 2 (1980): 59–95.

Dan, Yaron. *The City in Eretz-Israel During the Late Roman and Byzantine Periods.* Jerusalem: Yad Ben Zvi, 1984.

Dandamaev, M., and V. Lukonin. *The Culture and Social Institutions of Iran.* Cambridge: Cambridge University Press, 1989.

Davies, Philip R. *Scribes and Schools: The Canonization of the Hebrew Scriptures.* Louisville: Westminster John Knox, 1998.

———. "The Social World of Apocalyptic Writings." In *The World of Ancient Israel: Social, Anthropological, and Political Perspectives*, edited by R. E. Clements, 251–71. Cambridge: Cambridge University Press, 1989.

de Long, A. "A New Mithraic Relief." *Israel Museum Journal* 16 (1998): 85–90.

di Segni, Lea. "Epigraphic Documentation on Building in the Provinces Palaestina and Arabia, Fourth-Seventh Centuries." In *The Roman and Byzantine Near East* edited by John Humphrey, 2:49–78. JRA Supplement 31. 1999.

———. "The Samaritans in Roman-Byzantine Palestine." In *Religious and Ethnic Communities in Later Roman Palestine*, edited by Hayim Lapin, 51–66. Bethesda: University Press of Maryland, 1998.

Doran, Robert. *Temple Propaganda: The Purpose and Character of 2 Maccabees.* Washington, D.C.: Catholic Biblical Association, 1981.

Dothan, Moshe. *Hammath Tiberias: Early Synagogues and Hellenistic and Roman Remains.* Jerusalem: Israel Exploration Society, 1983.

Dothan, Trude. *The Philistines and Their Material Culture.* New Haven: Yale University Press, 1982.

Dunbabin, Katherine. *The Mosaics of Roman North Africa: Studies in Iconography and Patronage.* Oxford: Clarendon, 1978.

Duncan-Jones, Richard P. *Structure and Scale in the Roman Economy.* Cambridge: Cambridge University Press, 1990.

Dunn, J. D. G. "Judaism in the Land of Israel in the First Century." In *Judaism in Late Antiquity, Part 2: Historical Syntheses*, edited by J. Neusner, 229–61. Leiden: Brill, 1995.

Eck, Werner. "The Bar Kokhba Revolt: The Roman Point of View." *JRS* 89 (1999): 76–89.

Edwards, D. R., and C. T. McCullough. *Archaeology and the Galilee: Texts and Contexts in the Graeco-Roman and Byzantine Periods.* South Florida Studies in the History of Judaism 143. Atlanta: Scholars Press, 1997.

Eisen, Arnold. *Rethinking Modern Judaism: Ritual, Commandment, Community.* Chicago: University of Chicago Press, 1998.

Elayi, Josette. *Pénétration grecque en Phénicie sous l'empire perse.* Nancy, Fr.: Presses Universitaires de Nancy, 1988.

Elbogen, Ismar. *Jewish Liturgy: A Comprehensive History.* Philadelphia: Jewish Publication Society, 1993.

Elizur, Shulamit. "The Congregation in the Synagogue and the Ancient Qedushta." In *Knesset Ezra: Literature and Life in the Synagogue, Studies Presented to Ezra Fleischer*, edited by S. Elizur et al., 171–90. Jerusalem: Yad Ben Zvi, 1994.

Elsner, J. *Art and the Roman Viewer: The Transformation of Art from the Pagan World to Christianity.* Cambridge: Cambridge University Press, 1995.

Endelman, Todd, ed. *Comparing Jewish Societies.* Ann Arbor: University of Michigan Press, 1997.

———. "Pausanias: A Greek Pilgrim in the Roman World." *Past and Present* 135 (1992): 3–29.

Eshel, Hanan. "A Note on the 'Miqvaot' at Sepphoris." In *Archaeology and the Galilee*, edited by D. Edwards and C. McCollough, 131–34. Atlanta: Scholars Press, 1997.

Eshel, Hanan, and Esther Eshel. "Fragments of Two Aramaic Documents Which Were Brought to the Abior Cave during the Bar Kokhba Revolt." *EI* 23 (1992): 276–85.

Even-Shmuel, Y. *Midreshei Ge'ulah: Pirqei Ha-apoqalipsah Hayehudit Mehatimat Hatalmud Habavli Ve'ad Reshit Ha'elef Hashelishi.* Jerusalem: Mossad Bialik, 1953.

Fine, Steven. *This Holy Place: On the Sanctity of the Synagogue during the Greco-Roman Period.* Notre Dame, Ind.: University of Notre Dame Press, 1997.

Fine, Steven, ed. *Sacred Realm: The Emergence of the Synagogue in the Ancient World.* New York: Oxford University Press, 1996.

Finkelstein, Israel. "A Few Notes on Demographic Data from Recent Generations and Ethnoarchaeology." *PEQ* 122 (1990): 45–52.

———. "The Land of Ephraim Survey, 1980–1987: Preliminary Report." *Tel Aviv* 15–16 (1988–1989): 117–83.

Fischer, M. *Marble Studies: Roman Palestine and the Marble Trade.* Xenia, vol. 40. Konstanz: Universitätsverlag Konstanz, 1998.

Fishbane, Michael. *Biblical Interpretation in Ancient Israel.* Oxford: Oxford University Press, 1984.

Fleischer, Ezra. "Lekadmoniot Piyyutei Hatal (Vehageshem): Kerovah Kedam-Yannait Ligevurot Hatal." *Kobez al Yad* 8 (1975): 91–139.

———. *Shirat Hakodesh Ha'ivrit Biyemei Habeynayim.* Jerusalem: Keter, 1975.

Florsheim, Y. "R. Menahem (= Nahum) ben Simai." *Tarbiz* 45 (1976): 151–53.

Foerster, Gideon. "Ketovot Mibattei Hakeneset Ha'atiqim Veziqatan Lenusahim shel Berakhah Utefillah." *Cathedra* 19 (1981): 12–39.

———. "The Zodiac in Ancient Synagogues and Its Iconographic Sources." *EI* 18 (1985): 380–91.

———. "The Zodiac in Ancient Synagogues and Its Place in Jewish Thought and Literature." *EI* 19 (1987): 225–34.

Foerster, Gideon, and Yoram Tsafrir. "Nysa-Scythopolis: A New Inscription and the Title of the City on its Coins." *INJ* 9 (1986–1987): 53–58.

Foss, Clive. "The Near Eastern Countryside in Late Antiquity." *JRA* suppl. 14 (1995): 213–34.

Fraade, Steven. "Interpretive Authority in the Studying Community at Qumran." *JJS* 54 (1993): 46–69.

———. "Rabbinic Views on the Practice of Targum, and Multilingualism in the Jewish Galilee of the Third–Sixth Centuries." In *The Galilee in Late Antiquity*, edited by L. Levine, 253–86. New York: Jewish Theological Seminary, 1992.

Frankfurter, David. *Religion in Roman Egypt: Assimilation and Resistance.* Princeton: Princeton University Press, 1998.

Friedman, Shamma. "Recovering the Historical Ben D'rosai." *Sidra* 14 (1998): 77–92.

Gabba, Emilio. "The Finances of King Herod." In *Greece and Rome in Eretz Israel: Collected Essays*, edited by A. Kasher, U. Rappaport, and G. Fuks, 160–68. Jerusalem: Yad Ben Zvi, 1990.

Gafni, Isaiah. *Land, Center, and Diaspora: Jewish Constructs in Late Antiquity.* Sheffield, U.K.: Sheffield Academic Press, 1997.

Galsterer, H. "Roman Law in the Provinces: Some Problems in Transmission." In *L'Impero romano e le strutture economiche e sociali delle province*, edited by M. Crawford, 13–27. Como: New Press 1986.

Garnsey, Peter. "Religious Toleration in Classical Antiquity." In *Persecution and Toleration*, edited by W. J. Sheils, 1–27. Studies in Church History 21. Oxford: Blackwell, 1984.

———. *Social Status and Legal Privilege in the Roman Empire.* Oxford: Clarendon, 1970.

Garnsey, Peter, and Richard Saller. *The Roman Empire: Economy, Society, and Culture.* Berkeley: University of California Press, 1987.

Gauger, Jörg-Dieter. *Beiträge zur jüdischen Apologetik.* Cologne: P. Hanstein, 1977.

Geertz, Clifford. *Local Knowledge: Further Essays in Interpretive Anthropology.* New York: Basic, 1983.

———.*The Interpretation of Cultures.* New York: Basic, 1973.

Giddens, Anthony. *Central Problems in Social Theory: Action, Structure, and Contradiction in Social Analysis.* Berkeley: University of California Press, 1979.

Ginzburg, Carlo. "La conversione degli ebrei di Minorca (417–418)." *Quaderni Storici* 79 (1992): 277–89.

Goldman, B. *The Sacred Portal: A Primary Symbol in Ancient Judaic Art.* Detroit: Wayne State University Press, 1966.

Goldstein, Jonathan. *II Maccabees.* Garden City, N.Y.: Doubleday, 1984.

Goodblatt, David. *The Monarchic Principle: Studies in Jewish Self-Government in Antiquity.* Tübingen: Mohr, 1994.

Goodenough, Erwin R. *Jewish Symbols in the Greco-Roman Period.* 13 vols. Princeton: Princeton University Press, 1953–1968.

Goodman, Martin. "Babatha's Story." *JRS* 81 (1991): 169–76.

———. *Mission and Conversion: Proselytizing in the Religious History of the Roman Empire.* Oxford: Clarendon, 1994.

———. "Nerva, the *Fiscus Judaicus*, and Jewish Identity." *JRS* 79 (1989): 40–44.

———. *State and Society in Roman Galilee, A.D. 132–212.* Totowa, N.J.: Rowman & Allanheld, 1983.

———. "Texts, Scribes, and Power in Roman Judaea." In *Literacy and Power in the Ancient World*, edited by Alan Bowman and Greg Woolf, 99–108. Cambridge: Cambridge University Press, 1994.

———. "The Roman State and the Jewish Patriarch in the Third Century." In *The Galilee in Late Antiquity*, edited by L. Levine, 127–39. New York: Jewish Theological Seminary, 1992.

———.*The Ruling Class of Judaea: The Origins of the Jewish Revolt against Rome.* Cambridge: Cambridge University Press, 1987.

Gordon, A. E. *Illustrated Introduction to Latin Epigraphy*. Berkeley: University of California, 1983.

Gordon, Richard. "Religion in the Roman Empire: The Civic Compromise and Its Limits." In *Pagan Priests: Religion and Power in the Ancient World*, edited by Mary Beard and John North. Ithaca: Cornell University Press, 1990.

Grabar, Andre. *Christian Iconography: A Study of Its Origins*. Princeton: Princeton University Press, 1968.

Grabbe, Lester L. *Judaism from Cyrus to Hadrian*. 2 vols. Minneapolis: Fortress, 1992.

————. *Priests, Prophets, Diviners, Sages: A Socio-Historical Study of Religious Specialists in Ancient Israel*. Valley Forge, Pa.: Trinity Press International, 1995.

————. "The Social Setting of Early Jewish Apocalypticism." *JSP* 4 (1989): 27–47.

————. "Synagogues in Pre-70 Palestine: A Re-assessment." *JThS* 39 (1988): 401–10.

Graf, David. "Hellenisation and the Decapolis." *Aram* 4 (1992): 1–48.

Greenfield, Jonas, and Michael Sokoloff. "Astrological and Related Omen Texts in Jewish Palestinian Aramaic." *JNES* 48 (1989): 201–14.

Grégoire, H., and M.-A. Kugener. *Marc le diacre: Vie de Porphyre évêque de Gaza*. Paris: Les Belles Lettres, 1930.

Grelot, Pierre. "Sur le papyrus pascal d'Éléphantine." In *Melanges Bibliques et Orientaux en l'Honneur de M. Henri Cazelles*, edited by A. Caquot and M. Delcor, 163–72. Neukirchen-Vluyn: Neukirchener Verlag, 1981.

Gruen, Erich. *Heritage and Hellenism: The Reinvention of Jewish Tradition*. Berkeley: University of California Press, 1998.

Gwyn Griffiths, J. "Egypt and the Rise of the Synagogue." In *Ancient Synagogues: Historical Analysis and Archaeological Discovery*, edited by D. Urman and P. Flesher, 1:3–16. Leiden: Brill, 1995.

Habas [Rubin], Ephrat. "Rabban Gamaliel of Yavneh and His Sons: The Patriarchate before and after the Bar Kokhva Revolt." *JJS* 50 (1999): 21–37.

Habicht, Christian. *2. Makkabäerbuch: Historische und legendarische Erzählungen*. JSHRZ 1.3. Gütersloh: G. Mohn, 1976.

Hachlili, Rachel. *Ancient Jewish Art and Archaeology in the Land of Israel*. Leiden: Brill, 1988.

————. "Changes in Burial Practice in the Late Second Temple Period: The Evidence from Jericho." In *Graves and Burial Practices in Israel in the Ancient Period*, edited by I. Singer, 173–89. Jerusalem: Yad Ben Zvi/IES, 1994.

————. "The Origin of the Synagogue: A Re-assessment." *JSJ* 28 (1997): 34–47.

————. "The Zodiac in Ancient Jewish Art: Representation and Significance." *BASOR* 228 (1979): 61–76.

Hadas-Lebel, Mireille. "Le paganisme à travers les sources rabbiniques." ANRW II, 19, no. 2: 398–485.

Halbertal, Moshe. "Coexisting with the Enemy: Jews and Pagans in the Mishnah." In *Tolerance and Intolerance in Early Judaism and Christianity*, edited by G. Stanton and G. Stroumsa, 159–72. Cambridge: Cambridge University Press 1998.

Halbertal, Moshe, and Avishai Margalit. *Idolatry*. Cambridge: Harvard University Press, 1992.

Hallewy, E. E. "Concerning the Ban on Greek Wisdom." *Tarbiz* 41 (1972): 269–74.

Hamel, Gildas. *Poverty and Charity in Roman Palestine: First Three Centuries C.E.* Berkeley: University of California Press, 1990.

Hanson, Paul D. *The Dawn of Apocalyptic.* Philadelphia: Fortress, 1975.

Harl, Kenneth. *Civic Coins and Civic Politics in the Roman East, AD 180–275.* Berkeley: University of California Press, 1987.

Harries, Jill. *Law and Empire in Late Antiquity.* Cambridge: Cambridge University Press, 1999.

Harris, William V. *Ancient Literacy.* Cambridge: Harvard University Press, 1989.

———. *War and Imperialism in Republican Rome, 327–70 B.C.* Oxford: Clarendon, 1979.

Hayes, Christine E. *Between the Babylonian and Palestinian Talmuds: Accounting for Halakhic Difference in Selected Sugyot from Tractate Avodah Zarah.* New York: Oxford University Press, 1997.

Hayman, A. P. "Monotheism: A Misused Word in Jewish Studies?" *JJS* 42 (1991): 1–15.

Hecker, M. "The Roman Road Legio-Sepphoris." *BJPES* 25 (1961): 175–86.

Heinemann, Isaak. "Wer veranlasste den Glaubenszwang der Makkabäerzeit?" *MGWJ* 82 (1938): 145–72.

Hellholm, David. "Methodological Reflections on the Problem of the Definition of Generic Texts." In *Mysteries and Revelations; Apocalyptic Studies since the Uppsala Colloquium,* edited by J. J. Collins and J. H. Charlesworth, 135–63. Sheffield, U.K.: JSOT Press, 1991.

Hengel, Martin. *Judaism and Hellenism: Studies in Their Encounter in Palestine during the Early Hellenistic Period.* 2 vols. Philadelphia: Fortress, 1974.

———. "Proseuche und Synagoge: Jüdische Gemeinde, Gotteshaus, und Gottesdienst in der Diaspora und in Palästina." In *Tradition und Glaube: Das frühe Christentum in seiner Umwelt, Festgabe für Karl Georg Kuhn zum 65. Geburtstag,* edited by G. Jeremias, H.-W. Kuhn, and H. Stegemann, 157–84. Göttingen: Vandenhoeck & Ruprecht, 1971.

Herman, Gabriel. *Ritualised Friendship and the Greek City.* Cambridge: Cambridge University Press, 1987.

Herr, Moshe David. "The Historical Significance of the Dialogues between Jewish Sages and Roman Dignitaries." *SH* 22 (1971): 123–50.

Hezser, Catherine. *Form, Function, and Historical Significance of the Rabbinic Story in Yerushalmi Neziqin.* Tübingen: Mohr Siebeck, 1993.

———. "Social Fragmentation, Plurality of Opinion, and Nonobservance of Halakhah: Rabbis and Community in Late Roman Palestine." *JSQ* 1 (1993–1994): 234–51.

———. *The Social Structure of the Rabbinic Movement in Roman Palestine.* Tübingen: Mohr Siebeck, 1997.

Himmelfarb, Martha. "A Kingdom of Priests: The Democratization of the Priesthood in the Literature of Second Temple Judaism." *Journal of Jewish Thought and Philosophy* 6 (1997): 89–104.

———. *Ascent to Heaven in Jewish and Christian Apocalypses.* Oxford: Oxford University Press, 1993.

Himmelfarb, Martha. "Elias Bickerman on Judaism and Hellenism." In *The Jewish Past Revisited: Reflections on Modern Jewish Historians*, edited by D. Myers and D. Ruderman, 199–211. New Haven: Yale University Press, 1998.

———. "Judaism and Hellenism in 2 Maccabees." *Poetics Today* 19 (1998): 19–40.

———. "Revelation and Rapture: The Transformation of the Visionary in the Ascent Apocalypses." In *Mysteries and Revelations: Apocalyptic Studies since the Uppsala Colloquium*, edited by J. J. Collins and J. H. Charlesworth, 79–90. Sheffield, U.K.: JSOT Press, 1991.

Hirschfeld, Yizhar. "Changes in Settlement Patterns of the Jewish Rural Populace before and after the Rebellions against Rome." *Cathedra* 80 (1996): 3–18.

———. *The Roman Baths of Hammat Gader: Final Report*. Jerusalem: Israel Exploration Society, 1997.

Holladay, Carl R. *Fragments from Hellenistic Jewish Authors. Vol. 1, Historians*. Chico: Calif. Scholars, 1983.

Holum, Kenneth. "Identity and the Late Antique City: The Case of Caesarea." In *Religious and Ethnic Communities in Later Roman Palestine*, edited by Hayim Lapin, 157–77. Bethesda: University Press of Maryland, 1998.

Hopkins, Keith. "Conquest by Book." In *Literacy in the Roman World*, edited by John Humprey, 133–58. *JRA* suppl. 3 (1991).

Horbury, William, and David Noy. *Jewish Inscriptions of Graeco-Roman Egypt*. Cambridge: Cambridge University Press, 1992.

Horsley, Richard. "Ancient Jewish Banditry and the Revolt against Rome." *CBQ* 43 (1981): 409–32.

———. "Josephus and the Bandits." *JSJ* 10 (1979): 37–63.

Howgego, Christopher. *Ancient History from Coins*. London: Routledge, 1995.

Humphrey, John, ed. "Literacy in the Ancient World." *Journal of Roman Archaeology* suppl. 3 (1991).

Hurtado, L. "What Do We Mean by 'First Century Jewish Monotheism'?" *SBL Seminar Papers* 1993, 348–67.

Ilan, Tal. "Matrona and Rabbi Yose." *JSJ* 25 (1994): 18–51.

———. "Notes and Observations on a Newly Published Divorce Bill from the Judaean Desert." *HTR* 89 (1996): 195–202.

———. "Premarital Cohabitation in Ancient Judaea: The Evidence of the Babatha Archive and the Mishnah (Ketubbot 1.4)". *HTR* 86 (1993): 247–64.

Ilan, Zvi. *Ancient Synagogues in Israel*. Tel Aviv: Ministry of Defense, 1991.

———. "Survey of Ancient Synagogues in Galilee." *EI* 19 (1987): 170–207.

———. "The Synagogue and Bet Midrash of Meroth." In *Ancient Synagogues in Israel: Third through Seventh Centuries CE*, edited by Rachel Hachlili, 21–41. BAR International Series 499. Oxford: BAR, 1989.

Ilan, Zvi, and Immanuel Damati. *Meroth: The Ancient Jewish Village*. Tel Aviv: Society for the Protection of Nature, 1987.

Isaac, Benjamin, and Israel Roll. "Judaea in the Early Years of Hadrian's Reign." *Latomus* 38 (1979): 54–66.

Isaac, Benjamin. "The Babatha Archive: A Review Article." *IEJ* 42 (1992): 62–75.

———. "Jews, Christians, and Others in Palestine: The Evidence from Eusebius." In *Jews in a Graeco-Roman World*, edited by Martin Goodman, 65–74. Oxford: Clarendon, 1998.

————. *The Limits of Empire: The Roman Army in the East.* Rev. ed. Oxford: Clarendon, 1992.

————. *The Near East under Roman Rule.* Leiden: Brill, 1998.

Jacobs, Martin. *Die Institution des Jüdischen Patriarchen.* Tübingen: Mohr, 1995.

Japhet, Sara. "In Search of Ancient Israel: Revisionism at All Costs." In *The Jewish Past Revisited: Reflections on Modern Jewish Historians,* edited by David Myers and David Ruderman, 212–34. New Haven: Yale University Press, 1998.

Jones, A. H. M. *Cities of the Eastern Roman Provinces.* 2d ed. Oxford: Clarendon, 1971.

Juster, Jean. *Les juifs dans l'empire romain.* 2 vols. Paris: Paul Geuthner, 1914.

Kalmin, Richard. "Christians and Heretics in Rabbinic Literature of Late Antiquity." *HTR* 87 (1994): 155–70.

Kasher, Aryeh. *Edom, Arabia, and Israel.* Jerusalem: Yad Ben Zvi, 1988.

————. "Some Suggestions and Comments Concerning Alexander Macedon's Campaign in Palestine." *Beth Mikra* 20 (1975): 187–208.

Kee, Howard Clark. "Early Christianity in the Galilee: Reassessing the Evidence from the Gospels." In *The Galilee in Late Antiquity,* edited by L. Levine, 3–22. New York: Jewish Theological Seminary, 1992.

Keil, J., and A. Wilhelm. *Monumenta Asiae Minoris Antiqua.* Vol. 3. Manchester, U.K.: Manchester University Press, 1931.

Kennedy, Hugh. "From Polis to Madina: Urban Change in Late Antique and Early Islamic Syria." *Past and Present* 106 (1985): 141–83.

Kimelman, Reuven. "The Conflict between the Priestly Oligarchy and the Sages in the Talmudic Period (An Explication of PT Shabbat 12:3, 13c = Horayot 3:5, 48c)." *Zion* 48 (1983): 125–48.

Kindler, Arie. "Donations and Taxes in the Society of the Jewish Villages of Eretz Israel during the Third to Sixth Centuries CE." In *Ancient Synagogues in Israel, Third through Seventh Centuries CE,* edited by Rachel Hachlili, 55–59. BAR International Series 499. Oxford: BAR, 1989.

Kindler, Arie, and Alla Stein. *A Bibliography of the City Coinage of Palestine from the Second Century BC to the Third Century AD.* BAR International Series 374. Oxford: Tempus Reparatum, 1987.

Kitzinger, Ernst. *Israeli Mosaics of the Byzantine Period.* Milan: Collins/UNESCO, 1965.

Klein, Samuel. *Sefer Hayishuv.* Jerusalem: Dvir, 1939.

Kloner, A., D. Regev, and U. Rappaport. "A Burial Cave from the Hellenistic Period." *Atiqot* 21 (1992): 27–50.

Knibb, Michael. *The Ethiopic Book of Enoch.* 2 vols. Oxford: Clarendon, 1978.

Koch, Guntram, and Hellmut Sichtermann. *Römische Sarkophage.* Munich: Beck, 1982.

Kochavi, Moshe, et al. *Judaea, Samaria, and the Golan: Archaeological Survey, 1967–68.* Jerusalem: Keter, 1972.

Kraabel, A. T. "The Diaspora Synagogue: Archaeological and Epigraphic Evidence since Sukenik." *ANRW* 2, no. 19 (Berlin: DeGruyter, 1979): 477–510.

Kraay, Colin. "Jewish Friends and Allies of Rome." *American Numismatic Society Museum Notes* 25 (1980): 53–57.

Kraemer, Clark J., Jr. *Excavations at Nessana. Vol. 3, Non-Literary Papyri*. Princeton: Princeton University Press, 1958.

Kugel, J. "Qohelet and Money." *CBQ* 51 (1989): 32–49.

Kuhnen, H.-P. *Palästina in griechisch-römischer Zeit*. Handbuch der Archäologie, Vorderasien. Vol. 2, no. 2. Munich: Beck, 1990.

Kurke, Leslie. *Coins, Bodies, Games, and Gold: The Politics of Meaning in Archaic Greece*. Princeton: Princeton University Press, 1999.

Kvanvig, H. *The Roots of Apocalyptic: The Mesopotamian Background of the Enoch Figure and the Son of Man*. Neukirchen-Vluyn: Neukirchener Verlag, 1988.

Lane Fox, Robin. *Pagans and Christians*. London: Penguin, 1986.

Langer, Ruth. "Revisiting Early Rabbinic Liturgy: The Recent Contributions of Ezra Fleischer." *Prooftexts* 19 (1999): 179–94.

Lapin, Hayim. *Early Rabbinic Civil Law and the Social History of Roman Galilee: A Study of Mishnah Tractate Bava Mesi'a'*. Atlanta: Scholars Press, 1995.

———. "Palestinian Inscriptions and Jewish Ethnicity in Late Antiquity." In *Galilee through the Centuries: Confluence of Cultures*, edited by Eric Meyers, 239–67. Winona Lake, Ind.: Eisenbrauns, 1999.

———. "Rabbis and Cities in Later Roman Palestine: The Literary Evidence." *JJS* 50 (1999): 187–207.

———. "Rabbis and Public Prayers for Rain in Later Roman Palestine." In *Religion and Politics in the Ancient Near East*, edited by Adele Berlin, 105–29. Potomac: University of Maryland Press, 1996.

———. *Taking Place: Regionalism and History in Northern Palestine in Late Antiquity*. Forthcoming.

Le Moyne, Jean. *Les Sadducéens*. Paris: Gabalda, 1972.

Le Rider, Georges. *Suse sous les Séleucides: Les trouvailles monétaires et l'histoire de la ville*. Mémoires de la mission archéologiques en Iran 38. Paris: Paul Geuthner, 1965.

Lemche, Niels Peter. *Ancient Israel: A New History of Israelite Society*. Sheffield, U.K.: JSOT Press, 1988.

Levine, Lee I. "On the Political Involvement of the Pharisees under Herod and the Procurators." *Cathedra* 8 (1978): 12–28.

———. "The Second Temple Synagogue." In *The Synagogue in Late Antiquity*, edited by L. Levine, 7–31. Philadelphia: American Schools of Oriental Research, 1987.

———. "The Jewish Patriarch in Third Century Palestine." *ANRW* II 19.2. (Berlin: DeGruyter, 1979) 671–74.

———. *Caesarea under Roman Rule*. Leiden: Brill, 1975.

———. "Josephus' Description of the Jerusalem Temple: War, Antiquities, and Other Sources." In *Josephus and the History of the Greco-Roman Period: Essays in Memory of Morton Smith*, edited by Fausto Parente and Joseph Sievers, 234–46. Leiden: Brill, 1994.

———. *Judaism and Hellenism in Antiquity: Conflict or Confluence?* Seattle: University of Washington Press, 1998.

———. *The Ancient Synagogue*. New Haven: Yale University Press, 2000.

———. *The Rabbinic Class of Roman Palestine in Late Antiquity*. Jerusalem: Yad Ben Zvi; New York: Jewish Theological Seminary, 1989.

———. "The Sages and the Synagogue in Late Antiquity: The Evidence of the Galilee." In *The Galilee in Late Antiquity*, edited by L. Levine, 201–22. New York: Jewish Theological Seminary, 1992.

———. "The Status of the Patriarch in the Third and Fourth Century: Sources and Methodology." *JJS* 47 (1996): 1–32.

Levine, Lee I., ed. *Ancient Synagogues Revealed*. Jerusalem: Israel Exploration Society, 1981.

———. "From Community Center to 'Lesser Sanctuary': The Furnishings and Interior of the Ancient Synagogue." *Cathedra* 60 (1991): 36–84.

Lewis, Naftali. "The Babatha Archive: A Response." *IEJ* 44 (1994): 243–46.

———. *The Documents from the Bar Kokhba Period in the Cave of Letters: Greek Papyri*. Jerusalem: Israel Exploration Society, 1989.

Licht, Jacob. "The Attitude to Past Events in the Bible and in Apocalyptic Literature." *Tarbiz* 60 (1990): 1–18.

Lieberman, Saul. *Greek in Jewish Palestine*. New York: Jewish Theological Seminary, 1942.

———. *Hellenism in Jewish Palestine*. New York: Jewish Theological Seminary, 1950.

———. *Studies in Palestinian Talmudic Literature*. Edited by D. Rosenthal. Jerusalem: Magnes Press, 1991.

———. *Texts and Studies*. New York: Ktav, 1974.

———. "The Martyrs of Caesarea." *Annuaire de l'Institut de Philologie et d'Histoire Orientales et Slaves* 7 (1939–1944): 395–445.

Lieu, Judith. "Epiphanius on the Scribes and Pharisees (*Pan.* 15.1–16.4)." *JTS* 39 (1988): 509–24.

Lifshitz, Baruch. "Notes d'épigraphie palestinienne." *RB* 73 (1966): 248–57.

Linder, Amnon. *The Jews in Roman Imperial Legislation*. Detroit: Wayne State University Press, 1987.

Macfarlane, Alan. *Reconstructing Historical Communities*. Cambridge: Cambridge University Press, 1977.

MacMullen, Ramsay. *Paganism in the Roman Empire*. New Haven: Yale University Press, 1981.

———. "The Epigraphic Habit in the Roman Empire." *AJP* 103 (1982): 233–46.

Mann, Jacob. "Sefer Hama'asim Livnei Eretz Yisrael." *Tarbiz* 1, no. 3 (1930): 1–14.

Maoz, Zvi Uri. "When Were the Galilean Synagogues First Built?" *EI* 25 (1996): 416–26.

McKechnie, Paul. "The Career of Joshua Ben Sira." *JThS* 51 (2000): 3–26.

McKenzie, J. S., A. T. Reyes, and A. Schmidt-Colinet. "Faces in the Rock at Petra and Medain Saleh." *PEQ* 130 (1998): 35–50. With an appendix by J. R. Green.

Mélèze Modrzejewski, Joseph. *The Jews of Egypt*. New York: Jewish Publication Society, 1995.

Mendelson, Alan. *Philo's Jewish Identity*. Atlanta: Scholars Press, 1988.

Meshorer, Yaakov. *Ancient Jewish Coinage*. 2 vols. Dix Hills: Amphora, 1982.

———. *City Coins of Eretz Israel and the Decapolis in the Roman Period*. Jerusalem: Israel Museum, 1985.

———. "Sepphoris and Rome." *Greek Numismatics and Archaeology: Essays in Honor of Margaret Thompson*, edited by O. Mørkholm and N. Waggoner, 159–57. Wetteren: Cultura, 1979.

Meshorer, Yaakov, and Shraga Qedar. *The Coinage of Samaria in the Fourth Century B.C.E.* Jerusalem: Numismatic Fine Arts International, 1991.

Meyers, Eric, Ehud Netzer, and Carol Meyers. *Sepphoris.* Winona Lake, Ind.: Eisenbrauns, 1992.

Meyers, Eric, and James F. Strange. *Archaeology, the Rabbis, and Early Christianity.* Nashville: Abingdon, 1981.

Meyers, Eric, et al. *Excavations at Ancient Meiron, Upper Galilee, Israel, 1971–72, 1974–75, 1977.* Cambridge: ASOR, 1981.

Mildenberg, Leo. "Yehud: A Preliminary Study of the Provincial Coinage of Judaea." In *Greek Numismatics and Archaeology: Essays in Honor of Margaret Thompson,* edited by O. Mørkholm and N. Waggoner, 183–96. Wetteren: Cultura, 1979.

Milik, J. T. *The Books of Enoch: Aramaic Fragments of Qumran Cave 4.* Oxford: Clarendon, 1976.

Millar, Fergus. "The Background to the Maccabean Revolution: Reflections on Martin Hengel's 'Judaism and Hellenism.' " *JJS* 29 (1978): 1–21.

———. "Jews of the Greco-Roman Diaspora between Paganism and Christianity." In *Jews among Pagans and Christians in the Roman Empire,* edited by J. Lieu, J. North, and T. Rajak, 97–123. London: Routledge, 1992.

———. *The Emperor in the Roman World.* Ithaca: Cornell University Press, 1977.

———. "The Phoenician Cities: A Case Study in Hellenisation." *PCPS* 209 (1983): 55–71.

———. "The Roman *Coloniae* of the Near East: A Study in Cultural Relations." In *Roman Eastern Policy and Other Studies in Roman History: Proceedings of a Colloquium at Tvärminne, 2–3 October, 1987,* edited by H. Solin and M. Kajava, 7–58. Commentationes Humanarum Litterarum 91. Helsinki, 1990.

———. *The Roman Near East.* Cambridge: Harvard University Press, 1993.

Miller, Stuart. *Studies in the History and Traditions of Sepphoris.* Leiden: Brill, 1984.

Mirsky, Aaron. *Yosse ben Yosse: Poems.* Jerusalem: Mossad Bialik, 1977.

Moehring, Horst. "The Acta Pro Judaeis in the Antiquities of Flavius Josephus." In *Christianity, Judaism, and Other Greco-Roman Cults: Studies for Morton Smith at Sixty,* edited by J. Neusner, vol 3: 124–58. Leiden: Brill, 1975.

Momigliano, Arnaldo. "Flavius Josephus and Alexander's Visit to Jerusalem." *Athenaeum* 57 (1979): 442–48.

Mucznik, S., A. Ovadiah, and C. Gomez de Silva. "The Meroth Mosaic Reconsidered." *JJS* 47 (1996): 286–93.

Musallam, Basim. "The Ordering of Muslim Societies." In *The Cambridge Illustrated History of the Islamic World,* edited by F. Robinson, 164–207. Cambridge: Cambridge University Press, 1996.

Myers, David N. *Re-Inventing the Jewish Past: European Jewish Intellectuals and the Zionist Return to History.* New York: Oxford University Press, 1995.

Naeh, Shlomo. "Sidrei Qeriat Ha-Torah Be-eretz Yisrael: Iyyun Mehudash." *Tarbiz* 67 (1998): 167–87.

Nagy, R. M., et al., eds. *Sepphoris in Galilee: Crosscurrents of Culture.* Winona Lake, Ind.: Eisenbrauns, 1996.

Najman, Hindy. "Interpretation as Primordial Writing: Jubilees and Its Authority-Conferring Strategies." *JSJ* 30 (1999): 379–410.

Naveh, Joseph. "A Nabatean Incantation Text." *IEJ* 29 (1979): 111–19.

———. "On Jewish Books of Magic Recipes in Antiquity." In *The Jews in the Hellenistic-Roman World: Studies in Memory of Menahem Stern*, edited by I. Gafni, A. Oppenheimer and D. Schwartz, 453–65. Jerusalem: Merkaz Shazar, 1996.

———. *On Mosaic and Stone.* Jerusalem: Sifriyat Maariv, 1978.

———. *On Sherd and Papyrus.* Jerusalem: Magnes, 1992.

Naveh, Joseph, and Jonas Greenfield. "Hebrew and Aramaic in the Persian Period." In *Cambridge History of Judaism.* Vol. 1, *The Persian Period*, edited by W. D. Davies and Louis Finkelstein. Cambridge: Cambridge University Press, 1984.

Naveh, Joseph, and Shaul Shaked. *Amulets and Magic Bowls: Aramaic Incantations of Late Antiquity.* Jerusalem: Magnes, 1985.

———. *Magic Spells and Formulae: Aramaic Incantations of Late Antiquity.* Jerusalem: Magnes, 1993.

Ne'eman, Y. *Sepphoris in the Second Temple, Mishnah, and Talmud Periods.* Ph.D. diss., Hebrew University, 1993.

Netzer, Ehud. "The Synagogues in Gischala and Khirbet Shema: A New Look." *EI* 25 (1996): 450–54.

Neusner, Jacob. "Comparing Judaisms." *History of Religions* 18 (1978): 177–91.

———. *Judaism: The Evidence of the Mishnah.* Chicago: University of Chicago Press, 1981.

———. *Judaism in Society: The Evidence of the Yerushalmi.* Chicago: University of Chicago Press, 1983.

———. *The Systemic Analysis of Judaism.* Atlanta: Scholars Press, 1988.

Nitzan, Bilhah. *Qumran Prayer and Religious Poetry.* Leiden: Brill, 1994.

Nock, Arthur Darby. *Essays on Religion and the Ancient World.* Edited by Zeph Stewart. 2 vols. Oxford: Clarendon, 1972.

Noethlichs, Karl-Leo. *Das Judentum unter der römischen Staat: Minderheitenpolitik im antiken Rom.* Darmstadt: Wissenschaftliche Buchgesellschaft, 1996.

North, John. "The Development of Religious Pluralism." In *The Jews among Pagans and Christians in the Roman Empire*, edited by J. Lieu, J. North, and T. Rajak, 174–93. London: Routledge, 1992.

Noy, David. *Jewish Inscriptions of Western Europe.* Vol. 1, *Western Europe outside Rome.* Cambridge: Cambridge University Press, 1993.

Olyan, Saul. *A Thousand Thousands Served Him: Exegesis and the Naming of Angels in Ancient Judaism.* Tübingen: Mohr Siebeck, 1993.

Oppenheim, A. Leo. *Ancient Mesopotamia: Portrait of a Dead Civilization.* Chicago: University of Chicago Press, 1977.

Oren, E., and U. Rappaport. "The Necropolis of Maresha-Beth Guvrin." *IEJ* 34 (1984): 114–53.

Ovadiah, Asher, and Ruth Ovadiah. *Hellenistic, Roman, and Early Byzantine Mosaic Pavements in Israel.* Rome: L'Erma di Brettschneider, 1987.

Parkes, James. *The Conflict of the Church and the Synagogue: A Study in the Origins of Antisemitism* London: The Soncino Press, 1934. Reprint. New York: Hermon, 1974.

Parkin, Timothy. *Demography and Roman Society.* Baltimore: Johns Hopkins University Press, 1992.

Porten, Bezalel. "Aramaic Parchments and Papyri: A New Look." *BA* 42 (1979): 74–104.

Porten, Bezalel. *Archives from Elephantine: The Life of an Ancient Military Colony.* Berkeley: University of California Press, 1968.

Pucci Ben-Zeev, Miriam. "Caesar and Jewish Law." *RB* 102 (1995): 28–37.

————. *Jewish Rights in the Roman World: The Greek and Roman Documents Quoted by Josephus Flavius.* Tübingen: Mohr Siebeck, 1998.

Qimron, Elisha, and John Strugnell. *Qumran Cave 4, V: Miqsat Ma'ase ha-Torah.* Discoveries in the Judaean Desert 10. Oxford: Clarendon, 1994.

Raban, Avner, and Kenneth Holum. *Caesarea Maritima: A Retrospective after Two Millennia.* Leiden: Brill, 1996.

Rabello, M. A. "The Legal Condition of the Jews in the Roman Empire." *ANRW* 2, no. 13 (1980): 662–762.

Rabinovitz, Zvi Meir. *Halakha and Aggada in the Liturgical Poetry of Yannai: The Sources, Language, and Period of the Payyetan.* Tel Aviv: Alexander Kohut Foundation, 1965.

————. *The Liturgical Poems of Rabbi Yannai.* 2 vols. Jerusalem: Mossad Bialik, 1985–1987.

Rahmani, L. Y. "A Bilingual Ossuary Inscription from Khirbet Zif." *IEJ* 22 (1972): 113–16.

————. "Five Lead Coffins from Israel." *IEJ* 42 (1992): 81–102.

Rajak, T. "Jews as Benefactors." In *Studies on the Jewish Diaspora in the Hellenistic and Roman Periods.* Te'uda XII, edited by B. Isaac and A. Oppenheimer, 17–38. Tel Aviv: Ramot, 1996.

————. "The Hellenization of the Hasmoneans." In *Jewish Assimilation, Acculturation, and Accommodation,* edited by M. Mor, 1–13. Lanham, Md. University Press of America, 1992.

————. "The Rabbinic Dead and the Diaspora Dead at Beth Shearim." In *The Talmud Yerushalmi and Graeco-Roman Culture,* edited by Peter Schäfer, 349–66. Tübingen: Mohr Siebeck, 1998.

————. "Was There a Roman Charter for the Jews?" *JRS* 74 (1984): 109.

Rajak, Tessa, and David Noy. "Archisynagogoi: Office, Title, and Social Status in the Greco-Jewish Synagogue." *JRS* 83 (1993): 75–93.

Rappaport, Uriel. "Les Iduméens en Egypte." *Revue de Philologie* 43 (1969): 73–82.

Reed, J. L. "Galileans, 'Israelite Village Communities,' and the Sayings Gospel Q." In *Galilee through the Centuries: Confluence of Cultures,* edited by Eric Meyers, 87–108. Winona Lake: Eisenbrauns, 1998.

Reif, Stefan C. *Judaism and Hebrew Prayer.* Cambridge: Cambridge University Press, 1993.

Reynolds, Joyce, and Robert Tannenbaum. *Jews and Godfearers at Aphrodisias.* Cambridge Philological Society Supplementary, vol. 12. Cambridge: Cambridge Philological Society, 1987.

Richardson, Peter. *Herod: King of the Jews and Friend of the Romans.* Columbia: University of South Carolina Press, 1996.

Rives, James B. *Religion and Authority in Roman Carthage from Augustus to Constantine.* Oxford: Clarendon, 1995.

————. "The Decree of Decius and the Religion of Empire." *JRS* 89 (1999): 135–54.

Rosenberger, M. *The Rosenberger Israel Collection.* 3 vols. Jerusalem: N. p., 1972–77.

Rosenthal, David. "Mishnah Abodah Zarah: A Critical Edition with Introduction." Ph.D. diss., Hebrew University, 1980.

Rosenthal, R. "Late Roman and Byzantine Bone Carvings from Palestine." *IEJ* 26 (1976): 96–103.

Roth-Gerson, Leah. *Greek Inscriptions from the Synagogues in Eretz-Israel.* Jerusalem: Yad Ben Zvi, 1987.

Rowland, Christopher. "The Parting of the Ways: The Evidence of Jewish and Christian Apocalyptic and Mystical Material." In *Jews and Christians: Parting of the Ways, AD 70 to 134*, edited by J. D. G. Dunn, 213–37. WUNT 66. Tübingen: Mohr Siebeck, 1991.

Rubin, Nissan. *The End of Life: Rites of Burial and Mourning in the Talmud and Midrash.* Tel Aviv: Hakibbutz Hame'uhad, 1997.

Rubin, Zeev. "Christianity in Byzantine Palestine: Missionary Activity and Religious Coercion." *The Jerusalem Cathedra* 3 (1983): 97–113.

———. "Joseph the *Comes* and the Attempts to Convert Galilee to Christianity in the Fourth Century C.E." *Cathedra* 26 (1982): 105–16.

———. "Porphyrius of Gaza and the Conflict between Christianity and Paganism in Southern Palestine." In *Sharing the Sacred: Religious Contacts and Conflicts in the Holy Land*, edited by A. Kofsky and G. Stroumsa, 31–66. Jerusalem: Yad Ben Zvi, 1998.

Ruggini, Lelia. "Ebrei e Orientali nell'Italia Settentrionale." *Studia et documenta historiae et juris* 25 (1959): 186–308.

Rutgers, Leonard Victor. *The Hidden Heritage of Diaspora Judaism.* Leuven: Peeters, 1998.

———. "Incense Shovels at Sepphoris?" In *Galilee through the Centuries: Confluence of Cultures*, edited by Eric Meyers, 177–98. Winona Lake, Ind.: Eisenbrauns, 1999.

———. "Some Reflections on the Archaeological Finds from the Domestic Quarter on the Acropolis of Sepphoris." In *Religious and Ethnic Communities in Later Roman Palestine*, edited by Hayim Lapin, 179–95. Bethesda: University Press of Maryland, 1998.

Sacchi, Paolo. *Jewish Apocalyptic and Its History.* Sheffield, U.K.: Sheffield Academic Press, 1990.

Safrai, Zeev. "Godel Ha-ukhlusiya Be-eretz Yisrael Bi-tequfah Ha-Romit-Bizantit." In *Hikrei Eretz: Studies in the History of the Land of Israel Dedicated to Prof. Yehuda Feliks*, edited by Yvonne Friedman, Zeev Safrai, and Joshua Schwartz, 277–305. Ramat Gan: Bar Ilan University Press, 1997.

———.*The Jewish Community in the Talmudic Period.* Jerusalem: Merkaz Shazar, 1995.

Saldarini, Anthony. *Pharisees, Scribes, and Sadducees in Palestinian Jewish Society: A Sociological Approach.* Wilmington: Michael Glazier, 1988.

Sanders, E. P. *Jewish Law from Jesus to the Mishnah.* Philadelphia: Trinity Press International, 1990.

———. *Judaism, Practice and Belief: 63 BCE–66 CE.* Philadelphia: Trinity Press International, 1992.

Sartre, Maurice. *Bostra: Des origines à l'Islam.* Paris: Paul Geuthner, 1985.

Schäfer, Peter. *Der Bar Kochba-Aufstand.* Tübingen: Mohr Siebeck, 1981.

Schäfer, Peter. *The History of the Jews in Antiquity.* Luxembourg: Harwood Academic Publishers, 1995.

———. *Rivalität zwischen Engeln und Menschen.* Studia Judaica 8. Berlin: De Gruyter, 1975.

Schams, Christine. *Jewish Scribes in the Second Temple Period.* Sheffield, U.K.: Sheffield Academic Press, 1998.

Schiffman, Lawrence. "Was There a Galilean Halakhah?" In *The Galilee in Late Antiquity,* edited by L. Levine, 143–56. New York: Jewish Theological Seminary, 1992.

Schirmann, Hayim. "Hebrew Liturgical Poetry and Christian Hymnology." *JQR* 44 (1953): 123–61.

———. "Yannai Ha-payyetan: Shirato Ve-hashqafat Olamo." *Keshet* 23 (1964): 45–66.

Scholem, Gershom. *The Messianic Idea in Judaism: And Other Essays in Jewish Spirituality.* New York: Schocken, 1971.

Schorsch, Ismar. *From Text to Context: The Turn to History in Modern Judaism.* Hanover: Brandeis University Press, 1994.

Schwabe, Moshe. "Letoldot Teveryah: Mehqar Epigrafi." In *Sefer Yohanan Lewy,* edited by Moshe Schwabe and Yehoshua Gutmann, 200–251. Jerusalem: Magnes, 1949.

Schwartz, Daniel. "MMT, Josephus, and the Pharisees." In *Reading 4QMMT: New Perspectives on Qumran Law and History,* edited by Moshe Bernstein and John Kampen, 67–80. Atlanta: Scholars 1996.

———. *Studies in the Jewish Background of Christianity.* Tübingen: Mohr Siebeck, 1992.

Schwartz, Joshua. "Hayei Yom-Yom Beteveryah Bitequfat Hamishnah Vehatalmud." *Teveryah: MeYisudah ad Hakivush Hamuslemi: Meqorot, Sikumim, Parashiyot Nivharot Vehomer-Ezer,* edited by Y. Hirschfeld, 103–10. Jerusalem: Yad Ben Zvi, 1988.

———. *Jewish Settlement in Southern Judaea from the Bar Kokhba Revolt to the Muslim Conquest.* Jerusalem: Magnes, 1986.

———. *Lod (Lydda), Israel: From Its Origins through the Byzantine Period.* BAR International Series 571. Oxford: Tempus Reparatum, 1991.

Schwartz, Joshua, and Joseph Spanier. "On Mattathias and the Desert of Samaria." *RB* 98 (1991): 252–71.

Schwartz, Seth. "Gamaliel in Aphrodite's Bath: Palestinian Judaism and Urban Culture in the Third and Fourth Centuries." In *The Talmud Yerushalmi and Graeco-Roman Culture,* edited by Peter Schäfer, 203–17. Tübingen: Mohr Siebeck, 1998.

———. "The Hellenization of Jerusalem and Shechem." In *Jews in a Graeco-Roman World,* edited by M. Goodman, 37–45. Oxford: Clarendon, 1998.

———. "Israel and the Nations Roundabout." *JJS* 42 (1991): 23.

———. "John Hyrcanus I's Destruction of the Gerizim Temple and Judaean-Samaritan Relations." *Jewish History* 7 (1993): 9–25.

———. *Josephus and Judaean Politics.* Leiden: Brill, 1990.

———. "Josephus in Galilee: Rural Patronage and Social Breakdown." In *Josephus and the History of the Greco-Roman Period: Essays in Memory of Morton Smith,* edited by Fausto Parente and Joseph Sievers, 290–306. Leiden: Brill, 1994.

———. "Language, Power, and Identity in Ancient Palestine." *Past and Present* 148 (1995): 3–47.

———. "A Note on the Social Type and Political Ideology of the Hasmonean Family." *JBL* 112 (1993): 305–9.

———. "On the Autonomy of Judaea in the Fourth and Third Centuries B.C.E." *JJS* 45 (1994): 159–61.

———. "The Patriarchs and the Diaspora." *JJS* 50 (1999): 208–22.

Segal, Alan. *The Other Judaisms of Late Antiquity.* Atlanta: Scholars, 1987.

Seow, C. L. *Ecclesiastes.* Anchor Bible 18C. New York: Doubleday, 1997.

Shaw, Brent D. "Bandits in the Roman Empire." *Past and Present* 105 (1984): 3–52.

———. "Tyrants, Bandits, and Kings: Personal Power in Josephus." *JJS* 44 (1993): 176–204.

Sherwin-White, Susan, and Amelie Kuhrt. *From Samarkhand to Sardis: A New Approach to the Seleucid Empire.* London: Duckworth, 1993.

Sievers, Joseph. *The Hasmoneans and Their Supporters from Mattathias to the Death of John Hyrcanus I.* Atlanta: Scholars, 1990.

Simon, Marcel. "Les sectes juives chez les Pères." In *Studia Patristica I,* edited by K. Aland and F. L. Cross, 526–39. Texte und Untersuchungen zur Geschichte der Altchristlichen Literatur 63. Berlin: Akademie Verlag 1957.

Smallwood, E. Mary. *The Jews under Roman Rule.* Leiden: Brill, 1981.

Smith, Jonathan Z. *Map Is Not Territory.* Leiden: Brill, 1978.

Smith, Morton. "Goodenough's Jewish Symbols in Retrospect." *JBL* 86 (1967): 53–68.

———. "Helios in Palestine." *EI* 16 (1982): 199–214.

———. *Palestinian Parties and Politics That Shaped the Old Testament.* New York: Columbia University Press, 1971.

———. "Rome and the Maccabean Conversions." In *Donum Gentilicium: New Testament Studies in Honour of David Daube,* edited by Ernst Bammel, 1–7. Oxford: Clarendon, 1978.

———. *Studies in the Cult of Yahweh.* Edited by Shaye Cohen. 2 vols. Leiden: Brill, 1996.

Sokoloff, Michael. *Dictionary of Jewish Palestinian Aramaic of the Byzantine Period.* Jerusalem: Bar Ilan University Press, 1992.

Sokoloff, Michael, and Joseph Yahalom. *Jewish Palestinian Aramaic Poetry from Late Antiquity.* Jerusalem: Israel Academy of Sciences and Humanities, 1999.

Speidel, M. Alexander. "Roman Army Pay Scales." *JRS* 82 (1992): 87–106.

Sperber, Daniel. *A Dictionary of Greek and Latin Legal Terms in Rabbinic Literature.* Jerusalem: Bar Ilan University Press, 1984.

———. *Roman Palestine, 200–400: The Land: Crisis and Change in Agrarian Society as Reflected in Rabbinic Sources.* Ramat-Gan: Bar Ilan University Press, 1978.

Spiegelberg, Wilhelm. *Die sogennante demotische Chronik des Pap. 215 der Bibliothèque Nationale zu Paris.* Leipzig: J. C. Hinrichs, 1915.

Steiner, Richard. "Incomplete Circumcision in Egypt and Edom: Jeremiah 9.24–25 in the Light of Josephus and Jonckheere." *JBL* 118 (1999): 497–505.

Stemberger, Günter. *Jewish Contemporaries of Jesus: Pharisees, Sadducees, and Essenes.* Minneapolis: Fortress, 1995.

———. "Zwangstaufen von Juden im 4. bis 7. Jahrhundert: Mythos oder Wirklichkeit?" In *Judentum—Ausblicke und Einsichten: Festgabe für Kurt Schubert zum Siebzigsten Geburtstag,* edited by C. Thoma, G. Stemberger, and J. Maier, 81–114. Frankfurt Main: Peter Lang, 1993.

Sterling, G. E. " 'Thus Are Israel': Jewish Self-Definition in Alexandria." *Studia Philonica Annual* 7 (1995): 1–18.

Stern, Ephraim. *Material Culture of the Land of the Bible in the Persian Period, 538–332 B.C.* Warminster: Aris & Phillips, 1982.

Stern, Menahem. "The Politics of Herod and Jewish Society towards the End of the Second Commonwealth," *Tarbiz* 35 (1966): 235–53.

Stern, Yissachar [Sacha]. "Images in Jewish Law in the Period of the Mishnah and the Talmud." *Zion* 61 (1996): 397–419.

Stone, Michael. "Reactions to Destructions of the Second Temple." *JSJ* 12 (1981): 195–204.

———. *Selected Studies in Pseudepigrapha and Apocrypha.* Leiden: Brill, 1991.

Strack, Hermann, and Günter Stemberger. *Introduction to the Talmud and the Midrash.* Minneapolis: Fortress, 1992.

Strobel, K. "Jüdisches Patriarchat, Rabbinentum, und Priesterdynastie von Emesa: Historische Phänomene innerhalb des Imperium Romanum der Kaiserzeit." *Ktema* 14 (1989): 39–77.

Stroumsa, Guy. "Religious Contacts in Byzantine Palestine." *Numen* 36 (1989): 16–42.

Sussmann, Jacob. "A Halakhic Inscription from the Beth-Shean Valley." *Tarbiz* 43 (1973–1974): 88–158.

———. "The History of Halakhah and the Dead Sea Scrolls: Preliminary Observations on Miqsat Ma'ase HaTorah (4Q MMT)." *Tarbiz* 59 (1989): 11–76.

———. "Ve-shuv Li-yerushalmi Neziqin." In *Mehqerei Talmud: Talmudic Studies*, edited by Y. Sussmann and D. Rosenthal, 2:55–133. Jerusalem: Magnes, 1990.

Swain, Simon. *Hellenism and Empire: Language, Classicism, and Power in the Greek World, AD 50–250.* Oxford: Clarendon, 1995.

Syme, Ronald. *Emperors and Biography.* Oxford: Clarendon, 1971.

Talgam, R., and Z. Weiss. "The Dionysus Cycle in the Sepphoris Mosaic." *Qadmoniot* 83–84 (1988): 93–99.

Tate, G. *Les campagnes de la Syrie du Nord I.* Institut français d'archéologie du proche-orient, Bibliothèque archéologique et historique 133. Paris: Paul Geuthner, 1992.

Taylor, J. E., and P. R. Davies. "The So-Called Therapeutae of De Vita Contemplativa: Identity and Character." *HThR* 91 (1998): 3–24.

Tchalenko, Georges. *Villages antiques de la Syrie du nord.* 3 vols. Paris: Paul Geuthner, 1953–1958.

Tcherikover, Victor. *Hellenistic Civilization and the Jews.* Philadelphia: Jewish Publication Society, 1959.

———. "Palestine under the Ptolemies." *Mizraim* 4–5 (1937): 9–90.

Tcherikover, Victor, Alexander Fuks, and Menahem Stern. *Corpus Papyrorum Judaicarum.* 3 vols. Cambridge: Harvard University Press, 1957.

Thompson [Crawford], Dorothy. "The Idumaeans of Memphis and Ptolemaic Politeumata." *Atti del XVII congresso internazionale di papirologia*, Naples: Centro Internazionale per Lo Studio dei Papiri Ercolanesi, 1984, 1069–75.

Tsaferis, Vasilios. "A Roman Bath at Rama." *Atiqot* [English series] 14 (1980): 66–75.

Tsafrir, Yoram. *The Land of Israel from the Destruction of the Second Temple to the Muslim Conquest.* Vol. 2. Jerusalem: Yad Ben-Zvi, 1984.

———. "The Synagogue at Meroth, the Synagogue at Capernaum, and the Dating of the Galilean Synagogues: A Reconsideration." *EI* 20 (1989): 337–44.

Tsafrir, Yoram, ed. *Ancient Churches Revealed*. Jerusalem: Israel Exploration Society, 1993.

Tsafrir, Yoram, Lea DiSegni, and Judith Green. *Tabula Imperii Romani: Iudaea-Palaestina*. Jerusalem: Israel Academy of Sciences and Humanities, 1994.

Urbach, Ephraim E. "The Rabbinical Laws on Idolatry in the Second and Third Centuries in the Light of Archaeological and Historical Facts." *IEJ* 9 (1959): 149–65, 229–45.

van der Horst, Pieter. "Was the Synagogue a Place of Sabbath Worship before 70 CE?" In *Jews, Christians, and Polytheists in the Ancient Synagogue: Cultural Interaction during the Greco-Roman Period*, edited by S. Fine, 18–43. London: Routledge, 1999.

VanderKam, James. *Enoch and the Growth of an Apocalyptic Tradition*. Washington, D.C.: Catholic Biblical Association, 1984.

Veyne, Paul. *Bread and Circuses*. New York: Penguin, 1990.

———. *Did the Greeks Believe Their Myths? An Essay in the Constitutive Imagination*. Chicago: University of Chicago Press, 1988.

Wallace-Hadrill, Andrew. *Houses and Society at Pompeii and Herculaneum*. Princeton: Princeton University Press, 1994.

Wallace-Hadrill, Andrew, ed. *Patronage in Ancient Society*. London: Routledge, 1989.

Wasserstein, A. "A Marriage Contract from the Province of Arabia Nova: Notes on Papyrus Yadin 18." *JQR* 80 (1989): 115.

———. "Rabban Gamliel and Proclus the Philosopher." *Zion* 45 (1980): 257–67.

Waszink, J. H., and J. C. M. van Winden, eds. *Tertullian's De Idololatria: Critical Text, Translation, and Commentary*. Leiden: Brill, 1987.

Weber, Max. *Economy and Society: An Outline of Interpretive Sociology*. Berkeley: University of California Press, 1978.

Weiss, Herold. "Philo on the Sabbath." *Studia Philonica Annual* 3 (1991): 83–105.

Weiss, Zeev. "Social Aspects of Burial in Beth Shearim." In *The Galilee in Late Antiquity*, edited by L. Levine, 357–71. New York: Jewish Theological Seminary, 1992.

Weiss, Zeev, and Ehud Netzer. *Promise and Redemption: The Synagogue Mosaic of Sepphoris*. Jerusalem: Israel Museum, 1996.

———. *Zippori*. Jerusalem: Israel Exploration Society, 1994.

Weitzman, Steven. "From Feasts into Mourning: The Violence of Early Jewish Festivals." *Journal of Religion* 79 (1999): 545–65.

Wenning, Robert. *Die Nabatäer: Denkmäler und Geschichte*. Göttingen: Vandenhoeck-Ruprecht, 1987.

Westerholm, S. "Torah, Nomos, and Law." In *Law in Religious Communities in the Roman Period: The Debate over Torah and Nomos in Post-Biblical Judaism and Early Christianity*, edited by P. Richardson and S. Westerholm, 45–56. Waterloo: Canadian Corporation for Studies in Religion, 1991.

Wharton, A. J. *Refiguring the Post Classical City: Dura Europos, Jerash, Jerusalem, and Ravenna*. Cambridge: Cambridge University Press, 1995.

White, D. "The Eschatological Connection between Lead and Ropes in a Roman Imperial Period Coffin in Philadelphia." *IEJ* 49 (1999): 66–91.

White, L. Michael. "Synagogue and Society in Imperial Ostia: Archaeological and Epigraphical Evidence." *HTR* 90 (1997): 23–53.

―――. "The Delos Synagogue Revisited: Recent Fieldwork in the Graeco-Roman Diaspora." *HTR* 80 (1987): 133–60.

Whittow, Mark. "Ruling the Late Roman and Early Byzantine City: A Continuous History." *Past and Present* 129 (1990): 3–29.

Whybray, N. "The Social World of the Wisdom Writers." In *The World of Ancient Israel: Social, Anthropological, and Political Perspectives*. Edited by R. E. Clements. Cambridge: Cambridge University Press, 1989.

Wieder, Naftali. "The Jericho Inscription and Jewish Liturgy." *Tarbiz* 52 (1983): 557–79.

Wilken, Robert. *John Chrysostom and the Jews: Rhetoric and Reality in the Late Fourth Century*. Berkeley: University of California Press, 1983.

Will, E. *Histoire politique du monde hellénistique*. Nancy: Presses Universitaires de Nancy, 1979.

―――. "Poleis hellénistiques: Deux notes." *échos du monde classique/Classical Views* 15 (1988): 329–51.

Williams, Margaret. "Domitian, the Jews, and the 'Judaizers': A Simple Matter of Cupiditas and Maiestas?" *Historia* 39 (1990): 196–211.

―――. "The Jews in Early Byzantine Venusia: The Family of Faustinus I, the Father." *JJS* 50 (1999): 38–52.

Wolff, H. J. "Römisches Provinzialrecht in der Provinz Arabia." ANRW II.13, 763–806. Berlin: DeGruyter, 1978.

―――. "Le droit provincial dans la province romaine d'Arabie." *RIDA* 23 (1976): 271–90.

Woolf, Greg. *Becoming Roman: The Origins of Provincial Civilization in Gaul*. Cambridge: Cambridge University Press, 1998.

―――. "Monumental Writing and the Expansion of Roman Society in the Early Empire." *JRS* 86 (1996): 22–39.

―――. "The Roman Urbanization of the East." In *The Early Roman Empire in the East*, edited by Susan Alcock, 1–14. Oxford: Oxbow, 1997.

Yahalom, Joseph. *Liturgical Poems of R. Simon bar Megas*. Jerusalem: Israel Academy of Sciences and Humanities, 1984.

―――. *Poetic Language in the Early Piyyut*. Jerusalem: Magnes, 1985.

―――. *Poetry and Society in Jewish Galilee of Late Antiquity*. Tel Aviv: Ha-kibbutz Ha-me'uhad, 1999.

―――. "Synagogue Inscriptions in Palestine: A Stylistic Classification." *Immanuel* 10 (1980): 47–56.

―――. "The Zodiac in the Early Piyyut in Eretz-Israel." *Mehqerei Yerushalayim Besifrut Ivrit* 9 (1986): 313–22.

Yaron, Reuven. "The Murabba'at Documents." *JJS* 11 (1960): 157–71.

Yuval, Israel. "Yitzhak Baer and the Search for Authentic Judaism." In *The Jewish Past Revisited: Reflections on Modern Jewish Historians*, edited by David Myers and David Ruderman, 77–87. New Haven: Yale University Press, 1998.

Zahavy, Tzvee. *Studies in Jewish Prayer*. Lanham, Md.: University Press of America, 1990.

Zeyadeh, A. "Urban Transformation in the Decapolis." *Aram* 4 (1992): 101–15.

Zlotnick, Dov. "Proklos ben PLSLWS." In *Saul Lieberman Memorial Volume*, edited by Shamma Friedman, 49–52. New York: Jewish Theological Seminary, 1993.

Zori, N. "The House of Kyrios Leontis at Beth Shean." *IEJ* 16 (1966): 123–34.

Zuckerman, Constantin. "Hellenistic *Politeumata* and the Jews: A Reconsideration." *SCI* 8–9 (1985–1988): 171–85.

INDEX